THEATRE PLAYS

TREVOR GRIFFITHS

Theatre Plays One

The Wages of Thin
Sam, Sam
Occupations
Apricots
Thermidor
The Party
Comedians
The Cherry Orchard

SPOKESMAN

First published in 2007 by Spokesman
Russell House, Bulwell Lane
Nottingham
NG6 0BT
Phone 0115 970 8318. Fax 0115 942 0433
e-mail elfeuro@compuserve.com
www.spokesmanbooks.com

ISBN: 0 85124 720 2
ISBN-13: 978 085124 720 5
A CIP catalogue is available from the British Library

Printed by the Russell Press Ltd (phone 0115 978 4505).

For Gill

*Whose contribution has been immense
and whose commitment total*

Trevor Griffiths was born and educated in Manchester, and has been writing for theatre, television and cinema since the late 1960s.

The first volume of his collected theatre plays covers the period 1969 to 1980.

Volume two contains the plays written between 1981 and 2001.

His extensive work for the screen includes three major television series – *Bill Brand*, *Sons and Lovers*, and *The Last Place on Earth*; numerous single plays including *All Good Men* and *Through the Night*, and the television films *Country* and *Food for Ravens*. Many of his stage plays have also been produced on television.

For his film *Reds*, written with Warren Beatty, he received the Writers Guild of America Best Screenplay award and an Oscar nomination. Other films have included *Country*, directed by Richard Eyre, and *Fatherland*, directed by Ken Loach.

From the 1980s onwards he has also directed his own work both in theatre and on film. *Food for Ravens*, which he wrote and directed for BBC Wales, won both a Royal Television Society award and a Welsh BAFTA.

In 1982 Trevor Griffiths was given the BAFTA Writers Award.

CONTENTS

THE WAGES OF THIN

One about 30. Smallish, rather dapper, balding.

Two mid-thirties. Tall, fattening.

Thin 40. Nondescript, unremarkable. Purely a marble. His voice is educated but unprivileged.

Taped Voice of man about 26. Effeminate, lisping, upper class.

One and **Two** speak in recognizable working-class accents for most of the play, assuming their normal establishment voices only when Thin has left.

The Wages of Thin was first performed at the Stables Theatre Club, Manchester, on 13th, 14th and 15th November 1969 with the following cast:

One Richard Wilson

Two Richard Howard

Thin William Simons

Director Roger Tucker

The Wages of Thin

A public convenience, stage right, a cubicle, door closed. Centre, three urinal stones, handsomely mounted. Left, a door into a storeroom. The urinals hiss suddenly (they do this throughout the play).

One *and* **Two** *enter, from the storeroom. They whistle Brahms' Double Concerto (second movement opening), reflectively. Two walks to the cubicle door, kneels, peeps through a knothole, stands, nods at One. They take up positions at each side of the stones.*

Thin *enters. He carries a briefcase. He is neat, nondescript. He pees in the centre stone. One and Two watch him, candid rather than furtive. He finishes, zips up, steps down, moves towards his briefcase.*

ONE: (*Quite softly*) So you came back after all.

THIN: I beg your pardon. Are you addressing … ?

ONE: So you came back. We've been waiting, you know.

THIN: I'm sorry, I don't think I understand. I've …

ONE: Yes, we know. Alfred Rimbaud THIN. Born April 1930, Park Royal Nursing Home, Woking. Height 5' 8". No marital status, no other disfiguring features, brown hair, grey eyes. Size 8 shoes, $7\frac{5}{8}$ hats, 16 collars. Do you want any more?

THIN: Look, is this some sort of joke? Eh? Is it the boys from the office having a little jape, then, is it? I can quite understand their wanting to, I suppose. I'm not the most popular area manager, I know …

ONE: (*Gently*) Why did you come back, Thin? Oh why do you all come back?

THIN: (*Very uneasy now*) I don't understand. I come here every day, in my lunch hour. There's nothing very mystifying in that. A human need, no more.

ONE: (*Ignoring him*) You do your worst, your ugly, nasty sickening worst, and. back, back, BACK you come to look at it, to smell the foetid crapulous horror of it.

THIN: Look here, I think you've said quite enough. Now if your friend wouldn't mind … stepping out of my way, I'll be …

ONE: My credentials. Read them, READ THEM. (*He doesn't of course*). One's the name, Detective Inspector ONE. We're on to you, THIN. Your particular game is up. UP laddie.

THIN: For god's sake, would you please …

ONE: Shut up. Show him, Two.

TWO: Sir.

Two crosses floor, drops penny in slot, creaks door melodramatically open.

THIN: Oh God.

A body lolls floppily on lavatory seat, trousers round ankles.

Is he?

ONE: You know as well as I do, Thin. He'll never pull a chain again. We've waited all morning for you to come back, you know. We've got a great deal to ask you.

THIN: My god, you don't really think I had anything to do with this, do you? I'm a respectable member …

ONE: Yes? I'll be interested, to hear about that in due course. You won't do anything silly, will you? That man against the door is thoroughly savage. Nothing would please him better than to snap your femurs for you.

THIN: I … I want to ring my solicitor. At once. It's my right, you know.

ONE: We know your rights, laddie. (*Softly*) But we don't have a phone.

THIN: Then you can't hold me. (*Moves for the briefcase, to go*)

Two makes for the briefcase. Thin tries to sprint for the steps. One shouts 'watch him'. Two catches Thin. They scuffle. Two hits Thin heavily, methodically.

ONE: That's enough, Two. Christ, what're you trying to do, turn him into powder?

Thin lies flattened across the urinal step. One and Two swiftly bring out a table and chairs from the storeroom. Thin groans, coming round. One and Two slip into the Brahms again.

TWO: (*Breaking off*) Here he is. Shall I get him something to drink?

THIN: Oh, my head. God, my head, my head.

ONE: Get him something to drink.

TWO: (*To One*) Coffee or tea? (*No answer*) Coffee or tea? (*No answer*) Coffee or tea? (*Thin groans. No answer. He resumes his whistling, very badly*)

ONE: Coffee, I think. I think he'd like coffee. Coffee will clear his head, restore his senses, soothe his nerves, prick his taste buds into prickly life. Coffee, I think.

TWO: I'll have to nip out for some. We haven't got any coffee.

Silence. Thin groans. Silence.

ONE: Tea, then.

TWO: I'll get him some tea, then, shall I?

ONE: (*Philosophically*)Yes indeed. Yes indeed.

Two goes off, whistling his piece, very well. Thin groans, gasps, groans.

THIN: What? Who? Oh god, it's you.

ONE: You resisted arrest. You resisted the law. A clear sign of guilt in any court in the land. Get up, please.

THIN: Please, would you just lay your charge and allow me to ring my solicitor. I say nothing until he gets here.

ONE: Very sensible. Get up. You sound as if you've been through all this before.

THIN: (*Getting groggily up*) I've said all I'm going to say. I want my solicitor.

ONE: Have him you shall, laddie. Have him you shall. Empty your pockets.

THIN: Oh don't be ridiculous.

ONE: (*Thrusting him violently face down across the table*) EMPTY YOUR POCKETS. You are *not* within your rights to refuse to empty your pockets.

THIN: This is quite pointless. (*One begins to throw things on to table*)

ONE: One pocket handkerchief, one keyring, one leather cigarette lighter, one black comb, one notebook, two letters in envelopes – opened – four shillings and one, two, three pence – one wallet. Contents of wallet – two, four, six, eight, thirteen pounds, one RAC card, one driver's licence – expired – one car insurance certificate, one packet of superior condoms – condoms? (*incredulous*) – well, well, well – and two, three obscene photographs.

Rattling of cups on tray.

TWO: The tea.

ONE: Ah yes. Tea. You'll have some tea with us, Thin, won't you.

THIN: (*Subdued*) No, if you don't mind. I don't drink tea, thanks all the same. You wouldn't have coffee by any chance, would you?

ONE: We wouldn't. We don't much approve of coffee here. (*To Two*) Put it down there and get your notebook. I want a complete inventory of this man's personal effects and a verbatim record of everything he says from now on. (*To Thin*) Your driving licence has expired, laddie.

THIN: Yes I know. I've been meaning –

ONE: To do something about it? Yes, yes, the predictable response. It's an offence, you know.

THIN: (*Angry*) Oh for God's sake ...

ONE: Stop that! I can't imagine a man like you doing very much for God's sake. Dirty pictures, contraceptives. Writhing filth about your person, in a wallet next to your heart. I don't think God wants to know, laddie, so don't go calling him. You've got your purgatorio yet, before you get through to him again.

THIN: I want to phone my solicitor. Brian Yates, Hampstead 23 ...

ONE: What are these figures doing in the photographs? Would you care to describe their actions for the record or shall I?

THIN: I refuse to answer any more questions until I have seen my solicitor. Now ...

ONE: I see. Then I shall have to describe them myself. Are you ready, Two? (*Inventory voice*) Contents of obscene photographs. On the first: two unclothed figures, one male, one possibly female, cavort lewdly upon a large double bed. On the second: the same pair of unclothed persons lasciviously embrace. On the third: the – ah yes – *female* in the previous two pictures disports herself in disgraceful fashion in full view of the beholder. The index finger of her right hand points unambiguously to an unmentionable portion of her unclothed person beneath which the words 'Wish you were here' are printed in a bold white italic. (*To Thin*) Would you say those were accurate descriptions of the contents of these … art works? Mmm? Mmm?

TWO: (*Tentatively*) If I could say a word, sir …

ONE: (*Sharply*) I would prefer to be interrupted, if I must be, when I am not actually speaking, Two. It's considerably less …

TWO: I'm sorry, sir, it was just that …

ONE: You've done it again. Vous m'avez interrompu, homme mauvais, méchant, stupide!

TWO: (*Very quietly*) And you me, sir.

Long silence

ONE: Your word is what, Two?

TWO: Cavort, sir.

ONE: Cavort?

TWO: Cavort, sir. I quote (*reads deliberately, court voice*) 'On the first: two unclothed figures, one male, one possibly female, cavort lewdly upon a large double bed'.

ONE: You have some objection to the word?

TWO: Not objection, sir. It is hardly my place to object. However, with your permission I should like to make some … observations … on its use in this particular context.

ONE: I see. Permission refused.

TWO: Very good, sir.

ONE: Damn it, it's a perfectly ordinary word used in a perfectly ordinary context. On what possible grounds can there be objections? …

TWO: (*Peeved*) Observations.

ONE: Don't … interrupt!

Silence

What about you, Mister Thin? If you've any *observations* to make on my description of the activities of the unclothed persons in the first of the three obscene pictures extracted from your wallet, you are obliged to make them now. (*Pause*) Well?

THIN: (*Wearily*) I don't really see that it matters.

ONE: Get that down, Two. Suspect endorses my use of 'cavort' in the particular context.

THIN: I didn't say that. I said it didn't much matter.

ONE: (*Soft, silky*) Look laddie, don't come the flash with me. We're not here to conduct a seminar in frigging semantics you know. We can do without the Wittgenstein, thank you very much.

THIN: I'm not starting anything.

ONE: (*Loudly*) You're bloody right, you're not, you scrofulous little lecher, you wormy man, you sly gusset-sucker.

THIN: (*Loudly*) This is ridiculous. I protest. (*Dead silence. Shaken by the silence*) I … protest. (*Silence. An attempt at normality*) There are certain things I would like to know.

ONE: Well, well. At last, a purpose in common. Though I don't think I'd confine the things I want to know merely to the 'certain'. There are certain 'uncertain' things I would break both your femurs to find out. And shall, if I must.

THIN: (*Attempting calm*) Look, just, please, tell me this. First, why you imagine I could have had anything to do with the death of that man …

ONE: Ah, that man.

THIN: And, and, why you insist on behaving in this … ludicrous, this ludicrous fashion; beating me over the head, conducting this bizarre and pointless interrogation, threatening further violence, subjecting me to humiliations and taunts that your position as police officers ought to prompt you to protect me from, not inflict.

ONE: (*Softly*) Go on.

THIN: And, and, what on earth are we doing in this dirty little … Why aren't we, well, why aren't we in a police station?

ONE: (*Disgusted*) Would you just listen to him? Would you? You've got a mind festering with stereotypes, area manager. Heavy with comfortable clichés. Sodden with the instantly recognised, the immediately familiar. Life's not a bit like that, Thin. Not a bit tidy. Not a bit predictable. (*Pause*) Not neat. Tell him about your gran, Two.

TWO: (*Flatly in the dark*) My gran.

ONE: Your gran. Tell him.

TWO: My gran. (*Gathering his invention*) All right. Lovely woman, my gran. My gran lived in the same street for forty-nine years. Paradise Terrace, Camden. By common consent the cheeriest, liveliest, hardest working, most generous and popular person in the neighbourhood. Loving of others to a fault, my gran. A gypsy's dream, a tradesman's delight.

ONE: And the milkman?

TWO: (*Quickly*) Yes, I'm coming to the milkman. One morning ... she goes to, erm, she goes to put out the, erm, the milkbottles at the backdoor. That's right. So, she opens the backdoor and whoosh in comes the *milkman* (*Triumphant glance at One*) – been delivering her milk for twenty years or more – throws her on the kitchen floor, ups with her kilt, rapes her. No by your leave, rapes her, then slices her throat open with the first breadknife to come to hand. Blood all over the place. (*Pause*)

ONE: Is that all?

TWO: (*Peeved*) It proved enough for my gran.

ONE: What about the trial?

TWO: Oh well yeah, there *was* a trial. Milkman pleads diminished responsibility, dunne, – says his wife hadn't allowed him the conjugals for over fifteen years, just couldn't stand it any longer. So he raped my gran and slit her throat. Got H.M.P. They threw away the key.

THIN: Well, of course I'm sorry. A terrible case. But I don't really see how it applies here. I mean.

ONE: Why this ... convenience? I'll tell you. Because we were ordered to. Ordered. In this business it doesn't pay to question those who hand out the orders. The less we all expect the less we'll be disappointed. Why do we suspect you of killing that man? I think you'll discover that soon enough, laddie. We've had you two under surveillance for quite some time now. Don't interrupt me. You can't ask questions and not listen to the answers. As to why we beat you over the head, you seem to be forgetting that you were resisting arrest. You had to be dissuaded from so doing. Your head offered, Two accepted. You ought to be thankful it wasn't your femurs.

THIN: I want my solicitor. I have a right to call him.

ONE: When did you stop sleeping with your mother?

Long silence

THIN: I'm not, what do you mean, I'm *not* going to stand for that kind of talk, I don't care, look here, what in God's name do you think, do you think I'm some sort of, look ... are you suggesting I'm a ... I'm some kind of a ...

ONE: (*Pleasantly*) Pervert. Precisely. In your case it's on the way to murder, which is my sole reason for drawing attention to it. When did you?

THIN: This is outrageous! Outrageous and disgusting!

ONE: I do agree. I'm sure Two could concur. But we have really rather too much evidence for you to be going on in this way. (*To Two*) I should be personally obliged if you would stop whistling and set up the tape recorder. (*Two produces a Phillips Cassette from the table drawer, fiddles with it*). (*To Thin*) Straight from the horse's mouth, as you might say. Suppose you were to give us a simple statement now. Nothing ornate, no embellishments, no Jacobean literary flourishes. Just the plain, unadorned truth. (*Rustles paper*) Something along the lines of this simple statement I happen to have here about my person. (*Clears throat*) 'I, Alfred Rimbaud Thin, being of sound mind and body, do hereby confess to the murder of Hilary Fester, alias Peter the Pusher, alias Freddie the Fix, alias Kenny the Kink, alias the PVC Kid, and do further agree to append below my reasons for so doing. Signed ...' Nothing exceptionable in that now is there? Neat, unflorid, unobtrusive, unambiguous prose of the sort no-one need be ashamed to put his name to. Now what do you say? Eh?

THIN: (*Frightened*) You can go to hell!(*Pause*)

ONE: (*Softly*) We can all do that, laddie. Ah, the tape recorder. Thank you, Two. If you'd be so good as to place it upon the table – just there, that's it, thank you. And. the tapes, ah yes, thank you very much. (*Inserting first cassette*) Just ... so. Good. There we are. Now then, Mr Thin. Since you are not prepared to co-operate, it seems we must present the evidence to hand, however sordid and degrading an experience it proves for all of us. For myself, I tell you frankly, I look forward to this with an enormous absence of relish. However, your obdurateness leaves one no choice.

TWO: Quite.

ONE: The thing becomes inescapable.

TWO: Unavoidable.

ONE: Inescapable.

TWO: Unevadable. Uneludable. Unrepudiatable.

ONE: The tape.

TWO: Inescapable. (*Switches on tape. Silence for a moment. Opening bars of 3rd movement of Brahms' Double Concerto orchestral version, very loud.*)

ONE: (*Shouting above the music*) Oh no, no, no, no. No. (*Two switches off tape*) What *is* wrong with you? Um? Insouciance? Étourderie? Eh?

TWO: Neither would appear to fit the bill, I venture to say. Insouciance is, let's face it, over-feminine ...

ONE: (*Patiently but with menace*) Change the tape.

TWO: Étourderie is close, I suppose. But there's an absence of ...

ONE: Shut up! Shut up and change the tape, you ... you ergoteur!

TWO: (*Marvelling*) Ergoteur! Beautiful! At once, sir. (*He whistles the Brahms joyously and well, produces another cassette, inserts it*) Quite ready now, sir. I'll switch on, with your permission, Inspector.

ONE: Sempiternally grateful.

Click. Hum. Silence. Hum again.

TAPE: *(Effeminate public school voice, a slight lisp) (Reading)* I, Hilary Fester, being of sound mind and limb, do make the following deposition freely and under no sort of duress whatsoever.

A fairly long silence. Some dull muttering. The sound of a deep, gruesome blow, a brief scream, a slight choking blubber.

ONE: *(Reflectively)* A modicum of editing wouldn't go amiss there, Two.

TWO: As you say, sir, perhaps a modicum.

TAPE: *(Recovering breath; reading)* My association with Alfred Rimbaud Thin began some three years ago, on the evening of Christmas Eve as I recall it. I had been anxious to answer two advertisements – *cris de coeur* I would prefer to call them – in the Quay Street Public Lavatories, Manchester. One of them had been a most heartwringing plea, I remember 'Wanted, suitably servile footservant for masterly but frustrated sadist. Suggest date for meeting.' Fancying myself to be capable of rendering some small service in this field, I had attempted to meet the man in question, but either my qualifications or my handwriting were not to his liking, for he kept none of the appointments I suggested, though I kept them all. At no small inconvenience to myself, I might add. Mr Thin's was the other *cri*, as it turned out. 'I want to talk to someone – anyone – about sleeping with my mother', it read quite simply. Nothing glossy or overdone about it. Just a plain, unvarnished cry from the heart that instantly found a place in mine.

One clicks tape off.

ONE: Do you want to hear any more of this offensive peroration, Mr Thin?

THIN: *(Sick, stunned, frightened)* I want to talk to my solicitor.

ONE: About sleeping with your mother, perhaps? Nothing like using the equipment on the premises, is there, laddie?

THIN: *(Breaking)* Look, for Christ's sake, what do you want? What do you want?

Pause

ONE: Let's hear some more.

THIN: I didn't kill him!

Silence

(Very quietly) I haven't seen him in … in two years or more.

ONE: You said you didn't know him.

THIN: He called – calls? – himself Elsie. Elsie Leaper.

ONE: *(To Two)* Elsie Leaper. Got that, Two?

TWO: *(Writing)* Elsie … Leaper. I have indeed, sir.

ONE: *(Kindly)* Tell us. Tell us everything. Alfred. Why don't you, eh? Clear the air.

TWO: Get it off your chest.

ONE: Make a clean breast.

TWO: Publish and be damned.

ONE: What do you say?

THIN: (*Tightly*) I've nothing to say. I want my solicitor present.

ONE: (*Sighing*) You force my hand.

TWO: Leave no alternative.

ONE: (*Angering*) More of this defilement, this contamination, this.

TWO: Defoedation?

ONE: This fetor, this decay, this.

TWO: Putrescence?

ONE: Slop, recriment,

TWO: Sprue, feculence, draff.

ONE: Spawn, offal, garbage.

TWO: Pus, matter, suppuration.

ONE: Dung, sewage, muck.

TWO: Coprolite.

ONE: This ... shit, this ... this.

TWO: Tape?

ONE: If you please.

Click. Voice immediately.

TAPE: We met. In the Palace Bar, full of Christmas cheer stale with people. We stayed most of the evening, talking casually about this and that. I didn't mention his mother at that stage. There are ... proprieties to be observed whatever the circumstances. (*A fit of coughing, brief but furious*) Do you mind if I have a cigarette? (*Sound of Two whistling in the tape background. Match being struck, man inhaling deeply*) Thanks. Thanks very much. We, er, then we went back to my place. My car. I touched his knee once or twice changing gear. Tweaked his lower thigh. Pays to find out early what's required. You know. Anyway, there wasn't much of a response. He'd gone very quiet since we left the bar. Sort of depressed. So. We arrived at my flat and I drove into the forecourt, pitch black, a bit of snow down, cold, bloody cold as I remember. I switched the lights off and said 'Well, here we are' and he just sat there, breathing and snuffling, saying nothing, just snuffling away as though he'd caught cold. So. I said 'I think we ought to get ourselves upstairs, darling' or something like that, something perfectly normal and friendly, the sort of thing anyone might say, and what happens? He weeps. Breaks into tears. A deluge, sobbing and choking, sobbing and ...

THIN: (*Weeping.*) Turn it off. Please. Please. Please. Please. Please. Please. Plea ... Sesese.

ONE: Thank you, Two.

Two clicks tape off.

THIN: I can't, can't listen to any more. It's. Horrible.

ONE: Then you shan't, laddie. Nor shall you, I might have said. Use your own words, take your time, in your own way.

TWO: You're too easy. Too easy.

ONE: (*Same voice, but a sliver of menace there*) I don't think so, Two. In any case. It isn't really your pigeon, is it? Why don't you go and wash the tea things?

Thin sobs, weeps on. Two whistles uncertainly. A longish pause.

THIN: I. Feel a trifle sick. Do you think I might have a glass of water.

ONE: A glass of water for Mr Thin.

TWO: It will have to be a mug. (*No answer*) It will have to be a mug. (*No answer*) Or a cup. We have a cup as well.

THIN: Please get me some water.

Exit Two sharply.

ONE: (*Brusquely*) You told our friend Hilary Fester all about yourself, then. About your impotence. About your murky obsession with pornography and obscenity. About your tussles with your true homosexual self. Most of all, about sleeping with mummy. The first time, when you were 15.

THIN: 14.

ONE: 14? Mmm. Then the other times, when daddy was away. Off to mummy's bed. Warm, loving mummy, always ready to kiss you better, always happy to snuggle your head between those soft, safe breasts.

THIN: Please. Let me have some water.

ONE: Water you shall have. Water is at this moment virtually inevitable. Unfortunately you have not yet done with the fire.

TWO: (*Returning sharply*) The water. I put it in the mug. The cup was more elegant, the mug more capacious. Taste succumbed to utility. I put it in the mug.

THIN: (*Drinking*) Thank you. Thank you.

ONE: Let me get it straight, since all of this will need to be presented coherently in another place at another time. You claim you haven't seen our friend Freddie for over two years.

THIN: At least two years.

ONE: At least two years? I See. I see. What do you think of life abroad, Mr Thin?

THIN: Abroad?

ONE: Abroad. Life abroad.

THIN: Well, I can't say I've had all that much experience of it. I've …

ONE: You've travelled in the principal cities of at least eleven European countries during the last twelve years, Mr Thin.

THIN: Yes, yes I have. Look, how?

ONE: If you could confine yourself to *answering*, Mr Thin. You have a divagatory tendency to match questions with questions which is causing this tedious and distasteful interview to be protracted beyond its natural limit. You are fairly well acquainted with European foreign capitals, are you not?

THIN: Yes, I am, if you call ten-day visits living in hotel rooms and doing business all day being well acquainted.

TWO: Fairly.

THIN: I beg your pardon.

TWO: Fairly well acquainted was the experiential state my colleague asked you to comment on in so far as it was reasonable to apply it to yourself.

THIN: I … I know a fair bit about a fair number of European cities. Yes.

ONE: Good. We progress. What were you doing in these places?

THIN: Business. Exports mainly.

ONE: You worked all the time is what you are suggesting we should believe.

THIN: More or less, I've always been considered pretty conscientious in my work.

ONE: I don't doubt it. Not for one minute. Two, you have some names for us I think?

TWO: Indeed I have. I have them here in my notebook. Shall I read them aloud?

ONE: If you would.

TWO: One, Heinz Krull. Two, Janos Vorkas. Three, Michel Gaparin. Four, Gunther Halle. Five, Miep Wallstein. Six, Anders Anderson. Seven, Vladmir O'Grady. Eight, Bertolini Krappenhausen.

Long silence

ONE: I take it you would not deny knowing these persons.

THIN: No, I would not.

ONE: What, business associates? How would you describe your relations with them?

THIN: I don't know. I. They were. They were people I met and. Grew friendly with.

ONE: Grew friendly with. Yes indeed. It would certainly seem so. I think you have some brief biographies for us, Two?

TWO: (*Clearing throat, importantly*) Heinz Krull, age 34, born Munich. Manages 18 female and 12 male prostitutes in Berlin. Served 4 years Städe Prisson, 1959-1963, for his part in the death of Bette Schültz, who was found naked, bound, flogged and rather massively deflowered in one of his apartments and died later in hospital. Happily married, three children. Likes Richard Strauss and football matches.

ONE: Vorkas?

TWO: Janos Vorkas. Born Budapest 1919. Joined Hungarian Fascist League of Youth 1934. Fought for Falangists in Spanish Civil War 1937-38. Joined crack S.S. Division during Second World War. Fled to Vienna in 1945. Prominent Blackmarketeer in immediate post-war era. Recently been running guns to white mercenaries in Africa. A voracious homosexual and transvestite. Favourite pastimes: reading selected works of literature and dressing up to go out.

ONE: We have more, of course. Gaparin, Halle, Miep Wallstein. A celebrated list. And you grew friendly with all of them, you say. You must have an unflinching capacity for friendship, laddie. How did you find them, these friends of yours?

THIN: I didn't kill that man.

ONE: Which man did you kill, Mr Thin?

THIN: I've killed no one. I've never killed, never.

ONE: We'll get there. Don't worry. We've got all the time. Tell me about Europe.

THIN: What do you want to know? I can't see …

ONE: (*Gradually angering*) You're not asked to. A great deal of public money went into my training, a great deal of energy and effort and skill. I've been trained to see, to find out, to make the unseen seen. Or at least seeable. Don't be so bloody arrogant. Why should *you* see, you scurvy little amateur. You'll see in God's good time and not before.

TWO: Perhaps some more water would help.

ONE: (*Solicitous*) Do you want some more water?

THIN: No. No thank you. I … have some left still.

ONE: Drink it up. Go on, drink it up. I'll fetch you some more. Go on, there's plenty more where that came from.

TWO: Plenty.

THIN: (*Drinking*) Thank you.

ONE: There. You just relax; take it easy. Take your coat off, loosen your tie, smoke a cigarette.

THIN: Thank you. Very much. (*Strikes match*) It's very good of you.

ONE: Not at all. Think nothing of it. You sit there and have your cigarette. I'll fetch your water. (*Leaves, whistling violin*)

Pause. Two whistles cello softly. Thin smokes.

TWO: (*Reflectively*) He's basically a good man, is One, you know. A highly developed moral sensibility and a massive impatience with the sham and the mendacious. But a good man all the same. In other circumstances I feel sure you'd grow to like him.

THIN: Yes?

TWO: Oh yes. You've a great deal in common really, under the skin.

THIN: (*Feeling the ground*) Look, is there any chance of my being allowed to make a phone call? I'd ... er ...I'd be prepared to pay ... er ... for the call.

TWO: You're *entitled* to make a phone call. Payment is therefore out of the question. But all in due course. You are inclined to hurry things, Alfred.

THIN: (*Weary, sick*) God! So this is British justice!

TWO: (*Admonishing*) Ah, ah, ah. You mustn't judge a whole system from a solitary experience. See it in the round, see the whole thing ...

THIN: (*Wildly*) Why, why, why are you doing this to me? What have I done to deserve it? I haven't done anything. I'm innocent. (*Breaking*) I'm innocent. I'm inn... inn... inn... ocent.

TWO: Of course you are, Alfred. And that's the worst sort of guilt. You really mustn't expect to be put into the picture, you know. We have a job to do, you have another. You can't expect us to do yours for you. The clearer things are, the harder our job, the easier yours. Don't you agree? You're probably a very nice fellow, Alfred. I've quite got to like you in the short time we've been acquainted. But we're not on the same side at all and it's silly to pretend different. If you really want to help yourself you ought to try to try to make things clearer, answer the questions put, be graphic, pellucid, luminous. The clearer you are, the more difficult you make things for us; the fewer pieces you leave for us to slot in, the harder it is to change the picture we're building. There, I shouldn't have told you that. For God's sake don't tell One, he'd fracture my femurs if he knew.

THIN: But *what*? What is it you want to know?

TWO: Oh come on, you can't expect me to turn all the cards face up.

THIN: I don't see it.

TWO: Don't try. There's plenty more to come. (*Goes to urinal, begins to pee*) I've a caseful of tapes in there. One way or another, you'll see soon enough. You've led a funny life, you know. Hhoo. Very odd. Don't scratch hard, I've always said. Don't know what you'll find underneath. Met an Irish nun once, a medical mother from Drogheda. Now there's a place for a woman of pure love to come from. And pure the love was, for all God's creatures irrespective. Most of her time she spent in Nigeria. No greater sacrifice has life than that. Not for her anyway. She hated blacks. *Hated*. Oh she didn't say as much, but every time she spoke about them the hate spurted across her eyes and down her pure loving face. She it was who first said it. 'You don't have to scratch hard' she said, about blacks, 'you don't have to scratch hard to get down to the bottom.' (*Zips up, returns*)

Pause. Two whistles cello abstractedly.

ONE: (*Returning, at the door*) Good. Your water, Mr Thin.

THIN: Thank you. I.

ONE: Good. Now, let's get on. I've no doubt you've been more than impressed by our thoroughness in this case. Fact is we've got all the corroborative evidence we need to make it stick. But for reasons of our own we'd prefer you to make a simple statement admitting your guilt ...

THIN: I'm innocent. How many more times. I'm innocent, innocent.

ONE: (Continuing) ... and bring this nasty business to an end. You are *childish*, Mr Thin. Don't confuse childishness with innocence. What have we established so far, Two?

TWO: A great deal, sir. Mr Thin admits incest, homosexual relations, and involvement – as yet undetailed – with assorted sex criminals on the continent.

THIN: That's my *private* life. It has nothing to do with it.

ONE: It ought to. I tell you, if it doesn't, it ought to. Think of Hume and Heath.

TWO: Think of Sidney Fox, Charles Floyd.

ONE: Think of Max Güfler.

TWO: Pornography, transvestism, homosexuality, fetishism, prostitution, murder.

ONE: Conjugations of the same verb.

TWO: Paradigm; lust.

ONE: Indeed. Indeed.

Pause. They whistle their parts reflectively. They end together on a dying note. Long pause.

Did anything nice ever happen to you, Thin? Anything nice and normal, everyday? (*Thin starts to protest*) No, you know what I mean. Something I could put into an official biography. Do you like your job, for instance?

THIN: Yes I do. I love my work.

ONE: That's nice. And do it well, I daresay.

THIN: *I* think so. I've had no complaints.

ONE: Nice. No complaints. (*Pause*) We get complaints all the time. It's in the nature of the work. (*Pause*) Still. (*Pause. Softly*) Why do they send you to Europe?

THIN: Exports. We're a very progressive firm, anxious to expand our markets abroad. You've got to be …

ONE: No, why *you*? Why do they send *you*, Thin? What's wrong with Buckle?

THIN: Mr Buckle?

ONE: That's right. I thought Buckle was your Export Manager. Specially appointed for the job. Why don't they send *him* to Europe, then?

THIN: Mr Buckle runs the London office and handles the American market. I take the rest.

ONE: Who looks after your area while you're away?

THIN: My assistant manager. It's perfectly normal. I don't see what you're making such a song about. I'm abroad about once a year for less than a fortnight …

ONE: But why *you*, Thin? Why doesn't Buckle's office handle Europe?

THIN: Look, I do what I'm told. If my firm wants me to handle contacts in Europe, that's what I do. I speak French, Italian and German pretty well. A bit of Russian. And I'm good at my job.

ONE: I think you have some figures for us, Two?

TWO: Many. (*Clears throat, the usual importance*) Bagg and Flit Co. Ltd., makers of photographic equipment. Annual turnover last year: £982,714. Value of exports to America: £2,464. Value of exports to members of EEC: £1,012. Value of exports to EFTA countries: £832. Value of exports to other European countries: £816. Total value of all exports: £5,124. Exports as a percentage of total turnover: approximately one half of one per cent.

ONE: Not exactly setting the world alight are we, Mr Thin?

THIN: This is a highly competitive field … In any case, I don't know whether your figures …

ONE: Trust them, Mr Thin. We have nothing to gain by cooking the books. Nonetheless a peculiar state of affairs. (*Beckoning Two, who holds the notebook up for inspection*) I wonder, was it Mr Bagg or Mr Flit who decided that they should pay Buckle $4\frac{1}{2}$ thousand a year, his assistant $2\frac{1}{2}$, their secretaries another 15 hundred, plus overheads – let's say a thousand for convenience – that's $4\frac{1}{2}$, 7, 8, $9\frac{1}{2}$ thousand to sell less than $2\frac{1}{2}$ thousand quidsworth of equipment to America. On top of that, was it Bagg or Flit – or even both perhaps – who decided to withdraw an area manager from the home market at God knows what cost to travel to Europe yearly to sell about two dozen loaded cameras there for similar amounts of peanuts. Puzzling, Two?

TWO: Bewildering, as you say.

ONE: An enigma

TWO: Baffling.

ONE: Perplexing.

THIN: I just don't see …

ONE: Nor we. But I can see you have an explanation. Please.

THIN: I don't see that an explanation is really called for. In any case, I'm not on the board, so I'm not privy to decisions made in the boardroom …

TWO: Rudolph Hess is reported to have said at Nuremburg: 'I had nothing to say but *jawohl*'.

ONE: (*Pause*) Is he now? Well, well, well. That's very interesting, Two. Might I ask where you discovered this pearl of great price?

TWO: I really couldn't say. Just one of those things that sticks in the mind. (*Pause*) It seemed … apposite.

ONE: Apposite, if a trifle obscure. Mmm. (*Pause*) Nothing adds up, does it, Mr Thin? You're a sinister man with sickening habits, vicious nasty friends and a suspicious occupation. One tenth of what we know about you would make hardened criminals vomit their intestines up, but we still don't know everything, do we? What other stenches can you make? Why don't you tell us, eh? Turn *our* stomachs with your purulence. Make us keck and splurt like exploding ulcers with it. What is it, you wormy toe-rag? What is that we don't know? Help us to see it. Make it all of a piece before we pack you off. Oh, we're packing you off, we know enough to do that. But it's not enough to know enough. Make it add up, the whole festering pile. Your mother, Fester, Krull, Vorkas, Halle, Wallstein and the rest, Bagg and Flit. Put it all together. You owe us that.

THIN: (*Very quiet*) I owe you nothing.

ONE: (*Queer's voice*) O you do, faggot.

TWO: (*Queer's voice*) O you do, queenie.

ONE: (*Queer's voice*) Mummy's boy.

TWO: (*Queer's voice*) Anybody's boy.

ONE: (*Queer's voice*) Wag your queer tail, Alfie.

TWO: (*Queer's voice*) Naughty boy.

ONE: (*Queer's voice*) Come on, you camp little back-to-front.

TWO: (*Queer's voice*) Butchie, butchie, butchie.

ONE: (*Queer's voice*) Butchie, butchie, butchie.

ONE/TWO: Come on butchie, butchie, butchie. Come on butchie, butchie, butchie. Come on butchie, butchie, butchie.

In the middle of this last onslaught, Thin starts a long scream which ends in …

THIN: Shut up! God damn you, who do you think you ARE! It's my private life! That's the way I AM! What makes you so special? Do you think sleeping with women makes you special? (*Pause. More controlled*) Perhaps it does. All I know is, listening to you two makes me feel ashamed to be a member of the same species. What do you know about anything? What do you know about … love? Loving? What do you know about walking down Karl Marx Allee at five in the morning with the man you love, breathing *fresh* air and watching the hares leaping the tram tracks? What do you know about dancing with your loved one at Van's in Brussels or Gimpel's in Antwerp? What do you know or care about being free to hold hands or kiss in public? Do you have any idea what it's like to scratch out your heart on a lavatory door? Do you know what it's like to spend half your life making love to strangers? How would you know? You're special, aren't you? You belong to the club, don't you? Oh God, you fill me with revulsion, you and your normality. Brutal, callous, unfeeling, uncaring penises looking for shelter in the nearest woman to the applause of the world.

Silence. Thin sobs softly. Silence. One and Two simply do not respond, remain feelingless throughout, as though not making any sense at all out of Thin's words.

THIN: That's all. That's everything. You get no more. I didn't kill anyone. I couldn't. I couldn't kill a fly to save my life.

Long pause.

ONE: (*To Two*) Do you smell something?

TWO: (*Sniffing, a bit comically*) Mmm. There *is* a smell.

ONE: What does it smell like? To you?

TWO: (*Hopefully*). Nectarines? (*One shakes head. Two sniffs again, more purposefully*) Turmeric? (*Headshake*) Mansion polish? (*Headshake*) Armpit? (*Faster now*) Middle finger. Old Poultice. Shag. Rabbit. Eau de Cologne. Eau de Hamburg. Eau de Con. Odorono. Shark sperm. Toothpaste. Dubbin. Bürenwurst. (*Slowing down*) Green bananas? Wet rubber? Tar? (*Long pause*) Venison pâté? (*Headshake*) Pigeon feathers? (*Headshake*) I give up. What is it?

ONE: I don't know. (Sniffs) I really don't know.

They both turn to Thin, who lies half slumped on the table.

ONE: It's not material. The door behind you leads to the street, Mr Thin. Take it.

THIN: (*Slowly*) You mean … I can go.

ONE: I mean that exactly.

THIN: I'm not … you don't … I mean …

ONE: (*Deadpan*) You are free to leave. Please pick up your belongings from the table on your way out. And check they're in order before you leave the premises. We don't want complaints afterwards. Of course you're perfectly free to lodge any complaints you may care to, once you've left. But I think it's fair to warn you that they would probably fail to make much headway and would certainly make things most unpleasant for yourself. Don't think too badly of us. It's a difficult job and we sometimes have to undertake investigations that are in the normal run of things pretty repellent, but there you are. You can't defend democracy with kid gloves. The door's behind you, Mr Thin. Goodbye.

THIN: (*Still incredulous*) You're not charging me, then?

ONE: What for? An expired driver's licence? We're a little busy for that sort of thing, Mr Thin. But I should certainly renew it if I were you.

THIN: The murder …

ONE: The murder? Good God, no. It never really seemed likely that you'd done that. I mean it was always pretty obvious you couldn't … well … kill a fly to save your life. Still, we had to be sure, didn't we?

THIN: Yes, but, I mean, what makes you sure now?

ONE: Call it judgement, Mr Thin. That's what I was trained to pass, judgement. That's what I've done. Please go now. Show Mr Thin out will you, Two. Goodbye, Mr Thin. And good luck.

THIN: (*Bewildered*) Goodbye. Thank you. Goodbye.

TWO: This way, sir. Mind the steps now.

Silence. One whistles the final bars of the Concerto abstractedly. He then opens a small door in the wall and takes out a telephone, dials a number very slowly, pausing between each turn of the dial. When the number rings out, he sighs deeply several times. An indistinct voice answers. When One speaks it is in a totally changed voice heavy with upper-class vowels and inflexions.

ONE: Hello, Hello, sir. One. (*Pause*) Yes, sir. No, sir. No, sir, I don't think so. Two's gone down with him. No, sir, I'll have Three come round to pick up the body. It'll be back in the mortuary within the hour, sir. (*Pause*) Certainly, sir, I'll write it all up just as soon … (*Pause while voice goes on at other end*) … you shall have it first thing tomorrow, sir. (*Pause. One laughs*) Yes, indeed, very tricky. And very difficult to say offhand. I think we might have found something. Perhaps we could use him abroad. I wouldn't really like to commit myself at this stage. (*Pause*) Very good, sir. Mm..mm. Quite so, sir. Yes, indeed, first thing tomorrow. Thank you, sir. Goodbye.

Puts phone down. Deep weary sigh. Lights cigarette. Two enters. His voice, too, has altered utterly.

TWO: (Wearily) Chri-i-i-st! I don't want another of those for a while! What a mess.

ONE: Here, have a weed.

Two takes and lights a cigarette.

TWO: (*Drawing deeply*) Thanks. Mmm, I needed that.

ONE: I hate these bloody weirdies. (*Crosses to cupboard, opens door, takes off trench coat. Hangs it up. Now he wears evening dress, immaculate, with white tie.*) Still, there might be something there for us.

TWO: Let's hope so. I'd hate to have done that little lot for nothing.

ONE: (*Reflectively*) Yes. (*Pause*) You really did rather well, you know.

TWO: Thank you.

ONE: Your gran was delicious. I'd love to have met her.

TWO: So would I.

They laugh. Two whistles Brahms, stops, grins, moves over to cupboard, removes trench coat, reveals evening dress, black tie.

I liked your sense of authority.

ONE: Did you? Thought you might. (*Looking around*) OK. Let's get the hell. Give the place a wipe before you go, will you, Peter. (*Laughs gently*) Can't be too careful. And ... and see the caretaker's taken care of.

TWO: Will do. See you at the Club?

ONE: (*In thought*) What? Oh yes, surely. It'll probably be later on though. I've this little lot to write up first.

TWO: Ring in?

ONE: Yes. While you were out with ...

TWO: Ahunh. Right. About ten-ish, then.

ONE: Fine. I'll buy you a drink. Perhaps you'll tell me some more about that gran of yours.

They both laugh. Two begins to wipe up. One produces a bag for the props etc. They leave.

END

SAM, SAM

Sam Shatlock, about 27

Sam Shatlock, about 26

Mrs Shatlock, their mother, late 50s

Sandra, Sam 1's wife

Patricia, Sam 2's wife

Winston, her father

Naomi, her mother

Mr Shatlock, Sams' father

Counter Clerk

Krysta, au pair at Sam and Patricia's

*Note: The brothers Sam are played by the same actor. Since the play
describes, in part, the Pyrrhic victory of environment over genes, it is
important to sustain this fiction steadily throughout, and especially (however
confusing to an audience) the shared use of the single name Sam.*

.

Sam, Sam was first performed at The Open Space on 9 February 1972, with the following cast:

Sam1   Nikolas Simmonds

Naomi   Vanda Godsell

Mrs Shatlock   Shelagh Fraser

Mr Shatlock   Charles Lamb

Sam2   Nikolas Simmonds

Sandra   Catharine Kessler

Clerk   Anthony Milner

Patricia   Tamara Hinchco

Winston   Tom Macaulay

Krysta   Ann Henning

Directed by   Charles Marowitz

Designed by   John Napier

Lighting by   Caren Liebman

Sam, Sam

ACT ONE

Black. **Sam** *seated, in spot. About 27, from Stockport. He holds a large bowl in his lap, drips the contents from a ladle, engrossed. Finally he looks out.*

SAM: How do you like me up to now? (*Pause*) Never mind, we're not short of time. (*Pause*) It's icing. For me cake. Me birthday. Twenty-six. I've had a cake for me birthday every year for the past twenty-four years to my certain memory. Iced. (*Tastes it with finger*) I bloody hate icing. I shall have to tell her. P'raps I should just flush it down t'lav and say nowt about it.

MRS SHATLOCK: (*off*) Where's my icing?

SANDRA: (*off*) Who?

MRS SHATLOCK: (*off*) Icing.

SANDRA: (*off*) What icing?

MRS SHATLOCK: (*off*) For his cake. (*Calls*) Sam.

SANDRA: (*off*) Oh.

Door bangs. Sam on his feet quickly.

SAM: Shit, she's here. (*Looks round, moves towards audience*) Here, cop hold of that. (*Hands it over*) Help yourself.

Mrs Shatlock *in. Sam turns to face her.*

MRS SHATLOCK: You seen my icing?

SAM: Icing? What icing?

MRS SHATLOCK: Icing. For your cake.

SAM: No. (*Hand to face*)

MRS SHATLOCK: Here. (*Takes hand, licks finger*) You're lying, aren't you. You're a bad bugger, Sam Shatlock.

SAM: I haven't eaten your rotten icing. Wharra you talking about?

MRS SHATLOCK: (*advancing*) Come on. Let's have. Where is it?

SAM: I haven't had it, honest. Whaddaya take me for? Bloody icing.

She pushes him aside, sees the bowl.

MRS SHATLOCK: Here. That's my bloody icing. (*To person holding it*) Cheeky sod. (*Advancing on Sam*) You know your trouble, don't you? Your eyes are bigger than your belly. That's your trouble. (*She begins to leave, turns, looks straight at dispossessed member of audience*) And you're no better, either.

She leaves. Sam shuffles back into spot.

SAM: Bloody humiliating, innit? (*Now she's gone*) Go on, piss off, you old boot. (*Pause*) That's all they're fit for, humiliating you in front of you. (*Sits down, begins easing shoe off*) I'm sorry about that. She's er, me mam, she's all right really when you get to know her. She's had a HARD LIFE, as they say. (*Already becoming absorbed in his feet through the giant spud in his sock*) Anyway, I'm er, I'm sorry. A quite unnecessary embarrassment for you. (*He removes sock completely, begins rhythmic rubbing of webs*) Gorr. Eeeh. Uuuh. Bloody athlete's foot. Drives you mad in the hot weather. It's a fungus, you know. TINEA PEDIS, that's its proper name. I've got some ointment for it, from the doctor. Burrit dunt seem to do owt for it. It's a fungus, growing on you. Uuuu. (*He holds a piece of white flesh up*) Just look at that. That's dead, that. That's completely dead. Sucked dry by the fungus.

He takes his other shoe and sock off, begins to scrub vigorously at the veins of his left foot.

SAM: Uuuu. Thing is, it spreads. It's a complete mystery to me how it does it, burrit does. Look at that. (*He holds up a piece of white flesh*) Dead as me gran is that. It must travel up your leg, over t'top and down the other one. Aye, it's a bloody mystery. (*Pause*) What day is it? Friday, Friday. Bath night. I'll have a bath.

Lights on. There's a small bathroom stage left, with a door leading on to a cramped landing, on which Sam now stands. **Sandra**, *Sam's wife, is in the bath. She's blonde and pretty and small. She is reading a magazine. Sam rattles the door, discovers it locked. Offers a pained expression to the audience.*

SAM: Hey.

Silence. Sandra reads on. He rattles the door.

Hey, you, pinhead.

Sandra ignores him.

(*To audience*) Innit marvellous. Bloody wives. Who'd have 'em! They're like athlete's foot are wives, a mysterious spreading FUNGUS.

He kneels down, peers through the keyhole.

SAM: Hey. Fungus. Open t'bloody door.

SANDRA: (*not shifting the magazine*) Piss off.

SAM: (*still peering*) Mmm, that's lovely, that is. Piss off. The culmination of ten years' full-time education in two well-chosen words. PISS. OFF.

SANDRA: (*still reading*) And stop ogling, you dirty sod.

SAM: (*repeating as part of the 'culmination'*) AND. STOP. OGLING. YOU. DIRTY. SOD. S'got a rare beauty, that phrase. A lot of culture there.

He stands up and rattles the door violently.

Right, come on. I've had enough of this. Open the bloody door. Come on, I wanna pee. (*Getting petulant*) And it's me bathnight. I always have a bath on Friday, you know that. (*Silence*) Sandra. Open the door. I wanna pee.

SANDRA: Pee in t'sink, I'm busy.

Sam turns away, walks forward to chair.

SAM: Bugger it, I'll go without.

The lights go out behind him. He sits down and begins to put on his socks and shoes.

> She's a cow, her, you know. A right bloody cow. She sits in that bloody bath for hours reading her comics.

He stands up to fasten his shoes.

> I don't suppose she's so bad really. She's had a HARD LIFE too. Eee, bloody hell. I really do want a pee now. Hell fire.

He walks into the blackness of the stage, there's the sound of clanking pots.

> God almighty, it's full of bleeding pots.

Pots clank on, being moved from sink to draining board. Finally a cold water tap begins to splash, then stops. Sam reappears, fastening his flies.

> Innit funny, you start thinking about it and next thing you know you want to. 'Cept wi' sex. That's other way round. You start off wantin' to and you end up thinking about it. Hey, that's bloody good you know. That's what you call a maxim. Mmmm, I like that, I do. (*He relishes it in silence for a moment*) I'm quick. Have you noticed? (*He sits on his stool*) I was down the labour week before last, job'd just finished on them new council offices, and there's this little Hitler chap behind t'counter. Watch him, they said, he's a right little bastard, he'll rub your nose in it.

*Sam remains seated. Lights snap on to reveal the **Clerk** behind the counter. He is small, neat, bespectacled; his hair parts severely down the middle of his head. He exudes bureaucratic coldness. On his counter a large sign decleares him to be Mr Birkett.*

CLERK: I run an efficient counter. There's many can't say that much. I don't want any truck with layabouts. I don't want any messing about with people who've lost their papers. If you've no papers, you don't exist, right? Right. That's my maxim for living. I've read as much Pinter as the next man. Name?

SAM: (*still sitting facing audience*) Sam Shatlock.

CLERK: Spell it.

SAM: S. A. M. Sam. It's short for …

CLERK: Right, right, right. I haven't got time to waste indulging your pathetic, undeveloped, infantile sense of humour. Spell Shatlock.

SAM: Oh. Oh I see. S. (*He waits*) H. (*Again*) A. (*Again*).

CLERK: (*looking up slowly*) Oh. A genuine comedian.

SAM: I haven't finished. T.

CLERK: L. O. C. K.

SAM: Eh. You got that from somewhere.

CLERK: All right Shatlock, what's … (*your line*).

SAM: Call me Sam.

CLERK: I'd sooner call you … Shatlock, if it's all the same.

SAM: Well, it's not as friendly, is it? Shatlock. Sounds like a curse or someat. Still, it's up to you, BIRKETT. (*He spits this.*)

CLERK: Look, Shatlock, if you're serious about signing on at this labour exchange, you'd be wise to put Mr in front of that name.

SAM: (*to audience*) This is where the quick bit comes in. (*He stands up, walks over to the counter slowly, leans confidentially close to the Clerk*) Look, Birkett, if you don't get cracking on them forms I'm gonna ram 'em up your arse.

Lights out over counter. Sam returns to his seat.

SAM: Oscar Wilde? I've shit 'em. That's what you call LOW CUNNING. Just one weapon in the incredible armoury of the downtrodden in their endless battle against tyranny and oppression. Act stupid. If that dunt work, stick one on 'em. That dunt work, rearrange the following words into a well-known phrase or saying. OFF, PISS. and scarper.

The sound of a chain being pulled, flushing, a cistern filling, water draining from a bath. A door slams sharply.

She's out. (*Consults his watch*) Christ, she's improving. Under the hour. Right. (*He stands up*) I'll have me bath. (*Begins to take his tie off*) I met her in a bathroom. Well, it wasn't a bathroom actually, it was a WC. At a party. I walked straight in and there she was, stuck round this feller. Gorr, you should'r seen her. Lovely it was. So, I waited outside for her, took her home, HAD MY WAY WITH HER up against their privet hedge, knees trembling like new mortar. Six weeks later I get the good news – Shatlock's hit the jackpot – and I'm engaged to be married. (*Takes shirt and vest off*) Still don't know if it's really mine or someone else's. Dunt much matter now, does it? It's my bloody post office savings book he feeds off, whoever made the first deposit.

Sam moves towards the landing as the lights come on. The bathroom scene as before. This time, his mother sits on the lavatory, reading a paper. Sam rattles the door, which is locked. His look is incredibly pained.

I thought you were out.

MAM: She is. It's me.

SAM: I'm waiting for a bath.

MAM: Well you'll have to wait, won't you. I'm on the lavatory.

SAM: I thought you might be. Well, gerra bloody move on.

MAM: Don't be so cheeky. I shall be as long as it takes. You can't hurry nature.

Sam kneels down and looks through the keyhole.

SAM: You can't hurry *Racing Form* you mean, Come *on*, gerra move on.

MAM: (*venomous*) You're a bad bugger, Sam Shatlock. Peeping at your mother in the bathroom. I don't know where you get it from. It's not from your poor father, God rest his soul. He never peeped through bathroom keyholes. He was a gentleman, one of nature's own.

SAM: He was a drunk.

MAM: May God strike you where you stand for that wicked lie.

SAM: He was a drunk, you raddled old mug. Just like you, only worse. He had a bigger bladder, that's all. If you'd had a bigger bladder you'd've been as big a drunk. Every bloody night, out at the boozer, back home pissed as crocodiles. Don't tell me about my old dad. Best thing God ever did when he carted him off.

MAM: I'll not sit here listening to that good man's name being dirtied like that. I'll not. (*She sits on.*)

SAM: Well bloody well move then.

MAM: (*tight of lip*) I won't. I won't budge.

Lights out. Sam comes back resignedly.

SAM: God, I'm up to here with this lot. It's like a madhouse. She'll stink that bloody place out and I've still got to have me bath. (*Sits down*) I read somewhere that kids won't do their business sometimes to spite their parents. A psychologist, it was. In *Reveille*. He dint say out about parents refusing to do it to spite their kids, though. Not his fault, I suppose, never having met that old bag sitting on t'throne in there. (*Slips his shirt back on*) Jesus, it's a bit nippy. (*He scratches his nose, looks around the audience.*) Right. I'll have to think of the number I first thought of, double it, take away my age, go directly to jail, avoid passing Go and fail to collect £200. And I could just as easily have had two public conveniences on the Old Kent Road, if it hadn't been for her. By the way, is there a Mr J. Smith in the audience? Mr J. Smith? (*He looks around carefully.*) Mr J. Smith? No Mr J. Smith? Bloody amazing. Commonest name in the English language. Three and a half million J. Smiths in England alone, according to *Reveille*. Not a bloody one here. We had one last night. Nice chap. Very ordinary. No edge. Skin all over his face. Lovely teeth, a lovely pair of teeth. Come all the way from Brighton, he had. Mr J. Smith. Brought the wife with him too. Little fat chap, walked with a lisp. They made a very nice couple. I asked 'em to come behind afterwards but they said they had to be back before lights out. Still. (*Ad lib here if there is one. 'I thought there might be. We had one last night too.'*)

He shouts over his shoulder.

Have you finished?

No answer. He gets up, walks towards the landing. Lights snap on. The bathroom's empty. He pushes the door open, looks round it. walks in.

I'm in. (*Offers his own lip-version of a fanfare*) I'm bloody IN. S'only second time this month I've managed it. Puhurr, oh puhurr. (*He wafts the air around hopefully*) I swear that mother of mine saves it up till Friday night. Gorr, dear me. (*He opens the window*) God, it's not on, int this. I can see her walking around all week all cramped up holding on to it till Friday. Then Friday, one great big dollop five minutes before I have me bath. There's a lot to be said for separate, you know. Know what I mean? Bathroom, bath, sink, all that sort of stuff, that's one room. Then another with just a lav. For me mam. Actually, she should have one to herself. In a different house.

He takes off his shirt, folds it with great care, and throws it deliberately in a heap across the room. His socks and shoes follow.

Our kid's got separate. Me brother. Our kid. He, he went to college, our kid. You know, university. Got his GCEs and that. Very clever, he was always very clever. Anyway, they've got a separate lav. He's married. A right cow. You've seen mine, you should see his. Christ, it costs a dollar to speak to her. Not from round here. She's not like us. Her dad's a bank manager. Burk. (*He moves to turn the water on, catches sight of the bath.*) Oh Jesus, look at that. The dirty bugger. (*He rushes on to the landing*) YOU DIRTY BUGGER. CAN'T YOU CLEAN THE BLINDING BATH AFTER YOU'VE USED IT?

MAM'S VOICE: You what?

SAM: Not you, you faggot, HER.

He turns, stalks back in, slams the door, begins to slosh water round the bath.

They're like bloody pigs some people. (*To audience directly*) If there's any pigs here tonight, I don't mean you personally. (*He finishes cleaning the bath, puts the plug in*) She's a right scrubber. I tell you if she lived in Smethwick, the coloureds'd complain.

He sits on the lavatory, picks up the Racing Form, *flicks through it desultorily as the bath fills. Sandra appears on the landing, knocks on the door.*

SAM: It's open.

Sandra comes in. She's dressed in white cotton knickers, black bra and blue fluffy slippers. She has a towel round her hair.

SANDRA: Did you want me?

SAM: I can't remember when I last wanted you.

SANDRA: I thought you were shouting.

SAM: No, it weren't me. Musta bin another feller.

SANDRA: Oh. (*She stands and watches him cleaning the bath*) What you doing?

SAM: I'm writing a novel. What d'you think I'm doing, you dizzy lump? I'm CLEANING THE BATH. It's part of me Friday night ritual. Sometimes I have to use a Black and Decker drill to get the shit off it. Depends what sort of a week you've had.

SANDRA: (*ignoring him*) Where's your cigs?

SAM: Eh?

SANDRA: Your cigs. Where's your cigs?

SAM: Me cigs? Why?

SANDRA: I amt got any. I want one.

Sam turns water off, fiddles in his pockets, pulls out a ten packet of Woodbines, hands her one. She takes the packet, hands him one. They light up and sit on the bath edge, facing the audience.

SANDRA: There's nowt on t'box.

SAM: (*abstracted suddenly*) Mmm.

SANDRA: D'you fancy t'pictures? (*Pause*) I wonder what's on. What's *on* at t'Cosmo? Eh? (*Pause. Sam smokes on, not really listening*) Still it's ter much bother. Gerrin ready. Asking her to mind the baby. (*Pause*) Anyroad, when's your kid going to have her? She's his mother as well as yours, you know. She's gerring on my nerves, I'll tell you. She's, well she's dirty. You don't see it half the time. You're never in. And she's your mother and you don't notice things when it's your mother. (*Pause*) I can't stand her underclothes. God, what a mess she makes. I wouldn't be a bit surprised if she's inconsequent in a few year's time, the way she's going on. (*Pause. She looks at Sam, who stares vacantly before him*) Fat lot you care, you selfish sod. Bet y'aren't even listening.

SAM: Fancy a pint. Think I'll go down the Miners for a pint.

SANDRA: I can see your brother's wife cleaning her knickers. She'd have a fit.

SAM: I wonder whether Jim'll be in. Owes me a dollar, that bugger.

SANDRA: Dunt even wash her own, dunt that bugger. Has a WOMAN IN to do it all for her.

SAM: He could be at that. Dart team's no match this week.

SANDRA: Wouldn't know a pile of washing from a glass of Tizer wouldn't that one.

SAM: (*directly to audience*) You can clear off for a bit if you like. See what we're up to, can you? Both of us talking away, neither of us listening, makes the point very nicely, no communication, you know the stuff. Load of shit really. I mean look at us, three feet apart. I ask you, how could I fail? Especially with her. Got a voice like an early warning system. Fact is, though, there's no point in listening, she NEVER SAYS ANYTHING NEW. Know what I mean? (*Sandra smokes on, not listening*) Fancy her calling anyone dirty! Her! She qualifies for an agricultural subsidy just on what she's growing in her ears. As

for washing knickers, she hasn't washed a pair of her own knickers since she
started having periods. No point, she says, just get dirty again next month.
(*Looks at her, mock loving*) She's a LOVELY PERSON, aren't you, chuck?

SANDRA: (*moving towards the door*) Stinks in here.

SAM: Where you going then?

SANDRA: Downstairs. Think I'll watch tele.

SAM: Oh. Do you fancy?

SANDRA: What?

SAM: Oh, you know.

SANDRA: No. What?

SAM: Bit of. Urm. Bit of. Urm.

SANDRA: Bit of urm? Don't think so. Think I'd sooner watch tele.

SAM: Come on. Let's have a bit.

SANDRA: Let's have a bit? What *can* you mean? Let's have a bit? What've I got
that you could possibly want a *bit* of?

SAM: Come here and I'll show you.

SANDRA: No. you've got to tell me.

SAM: COME ON.

SANDRA: Why don't you say what you want.

SAM: (*very loud, sharp*) I WANT A BIT OF CUNT.

SANDRA: Charming. A bit of cunt. You make it sound just like the grocer's.
(*Assuming Sam's voice, rather comically*) Yes, Mrs Hardcastle, I'll take a bit of
cunt. No, four ounces'll do, it's just for me. Wrap it if you will, love. It'll keep
it fresh till I get it home. Thank you very much. Good day, Mrs Hardcastle.

SAM: Look, you, don't get bloody funny, I'm telling you.

SANDRA: Why, what you gonna do? Stick one on me? Eh? You big oaf? Just cos I
won't let you get your miserable little end away. (*She starts to walk out*) You
make me SICK. (*She goes out, slamming the door. Sam rushes across the
room, throws the door open, shouts at her receding footsteps.*)

SAM: Them Woodies, you cow. Let's have 'em. Come on, I saw you pocket 'em.
Let's have 'em back.

SANDRA: (*distanced*) Go and fuck yourself!

*He stands on the landing for a moment longer, searches for a meaningful riposte,
thinks he has it, discovers he hasn't, turns away defeated. He turns on the bath
water, removes his trousers, gets some toilet paper, wets it and begins scrubbing
the bath. He throws the wet paper down the lavatory, renews it. He gradually
becomes aware that the water is cold and lunges for the door.*

SAM: (*shouting*) You lousy rotten cow! Y'aven't even put the immersion on. (*He pauses a moment, his cup running over*) I'll break your bloody neck for you yet. (*A child begins to cry, low at first, then quickly louder and more insistent*) And you've gone and woke him up now you ...

He turns back to the bathroom, switches the tap off, picks up his clothes, dumps them on his chair. Lights out on bathroom. He begins dressing again.

Beginning to feel like a club stripper. (*Laughs*) Eh, I bet I'd be alright too, sexy devil like me. (*Bump and grind music up quickly. He does an excellent if jokey version of a routine, involving the audience as much as he can*) Wasn't that fantastic? All right, all right, simmer down, there's nowt for you up here. I'm going steady. (*Begins to dress again, taking his time. Confidential, mock-serious*) I went steady once. Two years. No, nearly two years. I finished it just before the Christmas. (*Reflective*) Yeah. She was ... big. I think that's the word for her. Big. A footballer. S'right. Played right half for Heaton Moor Ladies. She had these huge ... knees. (*Slight reflective giggle*) I don't know how she ran. I mean, all of her was ... big. You know. When she moved, she went in about four different directions. I met her in Woolies. Hammock department. Buying a bra. Used to wear corsets as well. S'right. I remember first time I felt her arse, it was like stroking bottom of a rowing boat. I bet you're beginning to think what an 'orrible life he leads, aren't you? I bet you're saying 'Christ, the poor benighted blaighter, livin' in all that lot. What chance has he ever had!' Well, actually, it's got nowt to do wi' chance. Nothing whatsoever. You see (*dressed now, he rests one foot on the chair, leans on braced thigh in Will Rogers fashion*), there's two sorts of person. There's them as have it up here (*taps head*) And there's them as have it down here (*points to crotch*) Our Sam, he's got his up there (*taps head*). Bags of it. You lot, yours'll be up there, if you've gorrit anywhere. (*Points to crotch*) Mine's down there. S'what makes me so cocky. Irresistibly cocky, you might say. (*Savours the phrase, says it over a few times, the sense diminishing as the sounds roll together*) Actually, it sounds more like a bloody infection. Irresistibili cocci. (*Solicitous tones of a doctor delivering the bad news*) We did everything we could Mrs Shatlock, but we were too late to save him, poor devil. The irresistibili cocci had penetrated his lower groin. Too late for surgery, too far gone for drugs. But I think you should know he died like a man, Mrs Shatlock. (*Drops his voice*) One thing. Before he died, he asked me to make sure you received (*holds out both hands in clasped position*) the contents of this jar. Ah, there's love for you. I see you've recognised them already. Yes, they're his genitals. He wanted you to have something useful to remember him by. Take them, keep them always. Change the salt solution every three days and they should last for ever.

He stands up straight, rams hands into pockets, shivers.

Our kid'll probably leave his brains pickled in a jar when he's gone. You should meet our kid, he's all right. Nowt like me. We still have a pint now and then, but, well, he's living a DIFFERENT SORT OF LIFE now, isn't he? Big house, car, phone, downstairs lavatory, cleaning woman. No more pubbing it Sunday dinnertime, no more Sat'day afternoon football. Ah, I hear you say, that's what's wrong with the poor chap, he's consumed with jealousy of his successful brother! Is that what you're saying? It is, isn't it? COBBLERS. (*With some passion*) Bloody cobblers! He's welcome. I mean that. Welcome. I'm happy with me own, here, where I belong. I wanna know where I am. I wanna know the rules. This is my world. (*His mother appears on the landing.*)

MAM: Sam.

SAM: (*turning*) Yeah, what you want?

MAM: I been thinking.

SAM: Don't. How many times have I got to tell you? You weren't made for it.

MAM: I been thinking about what you said about Dad, God rest his soul.

SAM: Why, what did I say?

MAM: You said he was a drunk.

SAM: Did I?

MAM: You said he came home drunk every night.

SAM: I did?

MAM: I admit he liked a drink now and then.

SAM: Yeah.

MAM: So did I.

SAM: Mmm.

MAM: S'not the same as being drunk, though. You shouldn't say things like that about the dead, Sam. They hurt.

SAM: They can't hurt the dead, mam.

MAM: No, but I'm not dead yet, and they hurt me.

SAM: Gorra fag, ma?

She hands him a Player's No 6 filter. He tears the filter off and lights the cigarette.

SAM: Sit down, mam.

She sits down on the chair. Sam sits on the floor near her feet.

MAM: He was good to me, your dad. And you two lads. We never went short for nothing while he was in work. You always had food in your bellies and coke on the fire and a shirt on your back.

SAM: Aye, it was a good shirt, that.

MAM: D'you remember that rabbit he bought you both?

SAM: Aye. T'chap in Tib Street swore it were a four and sixpenny English White and our kid looked it up in t'book and found it were a two and sixpenny Dutch.

MAM: Generous to a fault, your dad was.

SAM: Bloody thing were stiff as a board next morning. Died of the Dutch pox, I shouldn't wonder.

MAM: He'd go without himself before he'd see his lads short.

SAM: I really appreciated that tanner spends. Some weeks it'd take me a good twenty or thirty seconds to spend it all.

MAM: (*standing up*) I know you both loved him as much as I did. That's why it hurts me when you talk as though you didn't. (*Moving towards landing area*) I think I'll have an early night. There's nowt on downstairs.

SAM: Shall I nip out for a stout for you?

MAM: Don't bother, love. I've one in my bedroom. (*Turning*) Y'always were a good 'un, our Sam. Always ready to help anyone. Too good-hearted, if anything. (*Shakes head philosophically*) Good night.

SAM: (*not turning round*) Aye, goodnight, ma. Sleep tight.

She exits. Lights down over landing. Sam pulls himself up on to the stool.

It's tragic. There's no other word for it. Bloody tragic. She has no idea … she has no idea … she has no conception … not an inkling … of what her life has been. God blimey. How old is she, 56, no 57. Fifty-seven years of age, that woman, and NOTHING has penetrated. Doesn't matter what happens to her, it all finally gets turned into that … Ugghh! Listen, no kidding now, she's lived a life of UNRELIEVED DRUDGERY since the day she popped out. Right? Look, I *mean* drudgery – Christ, I can hear that word rolling around inside your heads like wind, I can see the images forming in the danker reaches. (*Hampstead-intense voice*) God, do you think I don't know what *drudgery* is? Huuh? Three weeks last summer we were without the Bendix, last Christmas the au pair went down with glandular fever just when David's parents had decided to spend a fortnight with us, and then Tarquin gets this infected tooth. Don't talk to me about drudgery, darling, I invented the term! (*Normal voice*) No? Not really you? All right then, let's try someat else, shall we? How about this?

Lights up stage right. A small, dismal kitchen. Mother sits sobbing at table, head in hands. **Father,** *short, squat, ferocious, in dirty work clothes, stares moodily at the wall, hands in pockets. As Sam bursts abruptly in. Mother looks up to reveal a huge, almost comic black eye. (Despite which the scene must be played very straight.) Sam looks at eye, at Father, back at eye.*

SAM: You coward, you daren't do that when I was in.

FATHER: (*swinging round, very mad*) Dossn't I? Dossn't I? Ha'e much more o' thy chelp, my young jockey, and I'll rattle my fist about thee. Ay, an' I sholl that, dost see.

SAM: (*quiet and intense*) Will yer? It'd be the last time, though.

(They stoop, looking as though they'll fight.)

MOTHER: (*hard voice*) Stop it, both of you. We've had enough for one night. And you, that's your son you're threatening.

FATHER: You nasty little bitch. He's like yourself; you've put him up to your own tricks and nasty ways – you've learned him in it, you 'ave.

She stares at him coldly, refusing to answer. He glares back for a moment. Then pulls his boots off, flings them under the table, and stalks out.

SAM: Why didn't you let me have a go at him? I could easily have beaten him.

MOTHER: A nice thing – your own father.

SAM: *Father*! Call *him my* father!

MOTHER: Well, he is, and so

SAM: But why don't you let me settle him? I could do, easily.

MOTHER: The idea! It hasn't come to *that* yet.

SAM: No, it's come to worse. Look at yourself. *Why* didn't you let me give it him?

MOTHER: Because I couldn't bear it, so never think of it.

Lights down quite slowly, as they stare at each other. Sam returns to his stool.

SAM: How's that then? That a bit better? That a bit closer to your authentic working class drudgery, is it? 'Course it is. Come on, own up, that's the real thing, innit? Eh? Who was it said Lawrence was more authentic than life itself? That were Lawrence that – 'Sons and Lovers', actually. Come on, who was it? Hands up if you know. Anyone know – 'Lawrence is more authentic than life itself?' No, nobody? All right, I'll tell you. It was our kid. S'right. Last weekend. Well, that was last time I heard him say it. It's not a saying he's ever been really sparing on. You know? Anyway, drudgery. Have I made me point? (*Grins*) About three hours ago, looking at you lot. Well, me mam, what I said was, me mam's got no idea what's been going on around her all these years. Or as our kid'd say (*Good voice, Bravura*) 'She hasn't gone from one particular to one general since the day she was born'. She just hasn't had time to look. Drudging. (*Grins, inconsequentially*) If there's owt cheers me up, it's thought that she's last of a dying breed. No bossman's gonna catch that bloody cow of a wife of mine with her drawers down. (*Pause*) Let me put that another way. She's got her head screwed on, she knows what's what. Know what I mean? All that tele, for a start. What did that fat chap call it, died of cancer, you know the one. Anyway, a window on the world he called it. It's good that, I like that. Window on the world. Just draw the curtains back and there it all is, happening, the whole wonderful, startling, exciting, baffling, human universe. List 'em : Coronation Street, Double Your Money, Take Your Pick, University Challenge! (That's an education in itself.) It's a Knockout. The Black and White Minstrel Show. Val Doonican. Grandstand. International Golf. Meeting Point. I could go on, but I've made the point. All human life is there, in the deathless words of the Sunday Syphilis (one wipe and you've got it for life).

He turns his back for a moment, turns back, chair in hand, sits down, a look of deep concentration on his face. He pulls an imaginary glove over his right hand, thrusts it into an imaginary cloth bag, draws out an imaginary small wooden ball, twiddles it in his fingers to steady it, then hands it to his right, moves right to become the man receiving it, takes it, studies it, calls

SAM: Number 7.

Moves right again, to become the man scanning the ledger, finger stopping at 7.

(*Clearing throat*) Stockport County.

(He goes back through the routine, until he arrives at the third man's post again. So it's)

Number 3.

Inter-Milan. Stockport County versus Inter-Milan.

(Back again. This time he calls)

All the fours.

(Fast, no gap)

Thirty-eight.

(He shoots up very fast from his chair)

House! (*Grin*) Aye. There's no end of rich, satisfying, life-enhancing things to do for anyone with a mind to do 'em. Just reflect for a moment upon the discriminations afforded the human sensibility by the very act of bingo. It's not far from an art form, int bingo. Not just something to do of an evening for t'ladies. And ... crib. Down the *saloon* bar, for the young ... bucks. By Christ, it's nearly t'new fucking renaissance.

*He takes up the stance of an Elizabethan courtier, short cloak clasped at edges, walks towards kitchen table, where his mate sits drinking a pint and riffling a pack of cards. Hum of pub chatter. There's a crib board, and beer mats on the table. Sam holds his glass until **Jim** addresses him.*

JIM: (*looking up*) Hya, Sam.

Sam breaks.

SAM: Hi. What you having?

JIM: (*gesturing to pot*) I'm all right. Ged's up. Give him a shout.

SAM: No. I'll get me own. Can't stand any fucking rounds this week.

He walks off, returns a second later with a pint.

SAM: (*sitting*) Cheers.

JIM: (*lifting pint, drinking*) Aye. (*Pause*) Eh, we fucking hammered 'em last week, didn't we.

SAM: We did that.

JIM: Fucking pissed 'em.

SAM: Aye.

JIM: (*mildly*) Bloody does me good, that. Rubbing their faces in it. They say I'm prejudiced against 'em, at work. It's not true. It's not true at all. I don't mind who fucking beats 'em. (*Grinning*) Wharrabout Georgie then?

SAM: (*laughing*) Dirty bugger.

JIM: Our Dave says he's got balls in his head.

They laugh.

SAM: I wouldn't mind stroking a through ball to his latest, once in a while. You know, laying one off.

JIM: Hehe. Aye. You know what they say. Position's everything.

They laugh again, subside.

SAM: (*finally*) Nine tenths of the law.

JIM: What?

SAM: Nowt.

They pause. Drink their beer. Fall silent, trapped in a tiny run of thoughts inside their heads. Finally

JIM: Fancy a … (*gesturing to pack*).

SAM: Aye, go on. Up down and up?

JIM: Right. Put some …

Sam takes matches out, puts two markers in each starting hole. While Jim shuffles, cuts, deals.

JIM: Dollar?

SAM: Fuck off. I aint fucking got a dollar.

JIM: (*winning cut, dealing*) What's up, she keeping you short?

SAM: What you talking about? I'm out of fucking work. There's a fucking million of us, haven't you heard. I heard about it on t'news. Others I mean. I knew about me.

They close off, studying the cards, throw away two each into the box.

JIM: Bob?

SAM: Bob. You cunt.

JIM: Give us a cut then.

Sam cuts deep. Jim turns top card over, they study again.

SAM: Seven with a seven.

JIM: Er. Fucking hell. Eight.

SAM: Nine for two. (*Scores two.*)

JIM: Ten for six. Hehe. (*Scores six.*)

SAM: Fourteen. Don't say you've got the other fucker.

Jim *shakes head, they pick up cards.*

SAM: I've got … fifteen two.

Jim checks, nods. Sam puts two up.

JIM: Same pair. Wanted a face card there. (*Picks up box*) Mmmmm, I've … er … fifteen two, fifteen four, three's seven.

SAM: Jammy twat.

Sam picks up cards, shuffles, deals. The game takes care of itself from now on. They make calls and score as and when.

JIM: Took her to t'pictures, Tuesday.

SAM: Aye.

JIM: Cosmo.

SAM: (*cards*) No.

Jim plays last card, scores.

SAM: Owt on?

JIM: No. Heap of crap. Love Story.

SAM: Was it?

JIM: No, that were t'title.

SAM: Oh. (*Pause*) S'it about?

JIM: It's a skriker. Tart's picture.

SAM: I'll have to send mine then.

Silence. Busy with cards and beer.

SAM: (*unexpectedly*) What are you thinking about?

JIM: What?

SAM: What are you thinking about, at this moment?

JIM: How do you mean?

SAM: Do you … ever think about … the future?

JIM: How do you mean?

SAM: About yourself, and t'wife. And t'lads.

JIM: (*reluctantly*) Aye. (*Pause*) How do you mean?

SAM: Dunt matter.

Silence.

JIM: Who's box?

SAM: I dunno. Yours.

JIM: Give us a cut.

They look at each other for quite a while. Finally, Sam cuts the deck. Fade slowly. Sam out to centre, with chair.

SAM: Eh. It's gerrin a bit serious this, innit? I shall have to watch that. Don't want to start sounding bitter. I mean, it's not as if we didn't have everything we could possibly want, is it? Like me dad said when he passed on: 'It's all yours, Sam, yours and your Mam's, to do with as you see fit.'

Lights up. Dad lying on a settee in the corner of the living room.

DAD: (*weak*) Do you hear me, lad?

SAM: (*abstractedly, picking feet*) What?

DAD: I said do you hear me?

SAM: D'you say someat?

DAD: I said it's all yours, Sam, yours and your mam's.

SAM: To do with as we see fit?

DAD: That's right, son. Give us a fag, will you.

SAM: Don't be daft dad. You're dying of lung cancer.

DAD: Give us a bloody fag, you stingy bugger.

SAM: (*getting cigarette out*) Christ, you don't half play on it you know. Here. (*Lights and gives it him*) It's not as if you're ever gonna be in a position to give it me back, is it?

DAD: You've plenty comin', when I'm away.

SAM: Oh aye.

DAD: (*taking box feebly from under bed*) It's all yours, yours and your mam's, when I'm gone.

SAM: To do with as we see fit?

DAD: That's right.

SAM: Show us what you got then, dad.

Dad begins coughing horribly, disappears for a while under the covers, which throb and writhe above him. Sam gets up, goes over.

SAM: Here, come on, let's have that fag. I told you not to have it, you know.

He takes the cigarette, dimps it carefully on the floor, restores the end to his packet; finally his Father recovers, very drained.

You'd better get your head down, hadn't you?

DAD: (*feebly*) I want you to know what's going to be yours when I've gone.

SAM: Aye, all right then. You tell us. Here, I'll help you up a bit. (*He props him up somehow against the settee arm*) Right, let's have it. I can't wait to hear my good fortune.

DAD: (*absorbed, feeble, halting*) There's me watch. Thirty-five years' service with the same firm, that were for. All me working life, bloody near. (*He holds it up*) Thirty-five years. Says it ont' back somewhere. Can you see where it says it our Sam?

SAM: (*not looking*) 'To Ernest Shatlock, in recognition of thirty-five loyal and dedicated years' service as chemical process worker in the firm, this small token of our gratitude.'

DAD: Them's good words, lad.

SAM: Oh aye, dad. Good words.

DAD: Eee, I feel right queer.

SAM: I'm not surprised, dad.

DAD: No, I mean now. Everything's gone … everything's … gone.

SAM: Wharelse've you got in there dad?

DAD: (*faint*) Eh?

SAM: In your box.

DAD: Oh. There's … there's me bowls cup … me bowls cup … and the cuff links … and fourteen, fourteen pounds in notes … and …

SAM: Go on, dad.

Sam's mother comes in. She sniffs.

MOTHER: Have you been smoking in here our Sam?

SAM: No. It was him.

MOTHER: Don't be daft. You know he can't smoke since they … And what in God's name's he doing sat up like that? (*She crosses to the settee, goes to set the old man down, gives a little involuntary shriek as she touches him*) Oh my God, what's wrong with him!

SAM: (*very flat, not looking*) I think you'll find he's dead, mam. It's one of the few things you seem to be able to depend on in a terminal illness. (*Gets up, very solemn, walks out of set as lights dim*) He didn't even finish telling his legacy. Didn't get to t'rent book for the palace.

Gesturing around him.

Pause. Finally, very cold, deliberate.

I, er, I sat down, after we'd, er, after we'd put him below, I sat down and worked out how much he'd earned during that thirty-five years he worked for that scabby bunch of hounds. Do you know how much? Thirty-Five-Years. Do you know how much? About twelve thousand quid. What do you think of that,

eh? Twelve thousand fucking quid. My old man. The perfect industrial man.
What the masters of the industrial revolution dreamt of, worked for all their
lives. What Stalin slaughtered his kulaks to achieve. Me dad. The perfect
mechanical man, the human workslave. You could set your clock by him,
second finger as well. Working shifts all his working life for the same scabby
bunch of hounds, cleaning out giant acid vats the size of this theatre and feeding
moving hoppers with sulphur on a shovel the size of a railway truck. Never late.
Never late once. On mornings he used to wake himself at twenty past five, brew
tea in the mug, cut a slice of bread and marge and catch first bus to the plant. I
can see him sloping off down the street, army pack over his shoulder, the four
jam butties for his lunch snug inside, the old grey trilby stuck on his head like
an organic growth. But it was only appearance, there was nothing *really* organic
about me dad, just clockwork that needed oiling every mealtime so that it could
keep going: No temperament. No personality. Just a great ... gap ... dressed up
like a human. No preferences that mattered, no fads even, no passions, no
weaknesses, save the booze. Trot trot click he went all his bloody miserable
exploited life and I fill up with snot and tears and shame and anger whenever I
remember the way he was. (*Pause*) He couldn't even manage an ironic ending,
dying of something human like VD or wanker's cramp. No, he has to get lung
cancer from breathing shit for thirty-five years. Five stone of skin and Bleb,
ulcer and stench, refusing to scream like the good machine he was.

(Pause. He walks to a wardrobe, begins to put on an immaculate dress suit.)

Fortunately, it's ALL GOING TO BE DIFFERENT IN THE FUTURE. No
more exploitation. No more grinding the faces of the workers in the shite. It's
called HISTORICAL INEVITABILITY. All we've got to do is stand around
and wait. Suppose that's what inevitability means, when you look at it. Trouble
is, sounds a bit like terminal illness, put like that. Still. (*Straightening shirt
cuffs, facing front*) Do you like this? Smart, innit? S'not mine. Don't suppose
you thought it was. S'our kid's. s'our Sam's. He keeps it here. Dunt want the
cleaning woman to see it or someat. I don't mind having it here. We don't have
a cleaning woman. I can't think she'd be bothered if we did. Anyhow, it's our
Sam says everything's gonna be different in the future. He's a socialist. Votes
Labour and all that. They've got a plan for us all. It's all gonna be all right. So
there we are. (*Thinks*) I don't honestly know what all right'd be, really. What
it'd be like, if it was all right. OK. I'll see you.

*Walks downstage. Lights up on living room. Sandra sits watching tele. Mother
reads a propped Sporting Chronicle at the table, drinks a milk stout from the
bottle. Sam stands stock still for a moment. They don't see him. He pirouettes
nicely, arms high and wide. They ignore him. He walks over the furniture,
unobserved, to the player, puts a record on, switches volume very loud, strides
across table, picks up bread knife, begins to conduct the intensely loud music.
(Choral Movement: Beethoven's 9th.) They ignore him. Finally he turns to the
audience. Lights down.*

SAM: All right, then. You all know this one. Let's hear it big and clear. With me now.

As he says this, a hanging flat appears with the words up.

'O Freunde, nicht diese Töne!

Sondern lasst uns angenehmere

anstimmen und freudenvollere.'

CURTAIN

ACT TWO

A mainly bare stage. At the rear, raised and across it, a large back projection of the Labour Party National Executive, (any year will do). Beneath their platform, a speaker's podium, equipped with flashing red light to indicate time limit on ongoing speeches. Crude TV arc lights flood the front of the stage; there is the hum and bustle of party conference in session. Throughout the scene the thinly realised reality of the location is sustained, save for the occasional but crucial moments of hesitation or reflection on Sam 2's part, during which the stage is black and he is presented in a single spot.

Sam 2 *appears – Levi cords, calf-high brown boots, long hair, Ben Sherman shirt – and carries a clipboard to the podium. He moves hesitantly, as though baffled by the lights, the occasion. Arrived, he nods briefly to the back projection, turns to face the audience. Noises down a little. When he speaks, his words are received standard English, well and pleasantly vowelled; only the consonants faintly suggest Northern working class beginnings.*

SAM 2: Sam Shatlock, delegate, East Stockport Labour Party. Comrades, it was not my intention to speak in this … crucial debate here today. I have no mandate from my branch and will vote, when the time comes, with my conscience. I'm on my feet and talking because I'm convinced that the case *isn't being put*. It simply *isn't, being, put,* comrades. (*He checks his watch*) What *are* the issues at work in this debate? Let me tell you. Money, that's one. Can we afford *better* schools, with more and better trained teachers, auxiliary staff, teaching and learning aids, true community relations, with the school at the centre of the neighbourhood? That's the first issue: can we, do we want to, *afford* all this? And the second is: have we the guts and the vision to dismantle much of what we have already in order to construct this new thing, this new organism? Are we prepared to scrap our grammar schools, those great examination factories stamping out O-level Man in his thousands every year? Or our secondary moderns, those splendid monuments to the courage and vision of 1944, our brave new borstals of the future? That's the second issue. (*Looking at watch*) Hang on, hang on.

Lights out. Sam 2 in spot. Voice moves closer to Sam 1's, though the distance is not entirely spanned.

I could put the courage and vision bit first, for the laughs, then push in the loot piece after. (*Makes notes on clipboard*) Yes, makes more sense that.

WIFE'S *voice off:* Sammy, (*He carries on writing*) SAMMY!

SAM 2: (*shout, very sharp*) Yes.

WIFE: (*convinced, pleased with the conviction*) It was steak au poivre. With leaf spinach. And you had celery hearts.

SAM 2: Right. I'm working.

WIFE: (*drily*) It just suddenly came back to me on the loo.

SAM 2: (*curt*) Yeah, OK, fine. (*He waits a minute. She has gone silent. He scratches a note or two more on the clipboard*) Right. Let's see how we go from there. (*Lights up: conference hall again*) The issue nobody has yet raised – neither here, in Parliament nor in Transport House – is a desperately plain one. What for? For whom? All this education, all this training? Whose interests do we think it serves, or should serve? We say 'more education' or 'less education' or 'better education' but we none of us examine the term itself. (*Looks at watch. Change of key*) I'm a teacher. A humble teacher. You know, overpaid, underworked, overholidayed, yes, you've got it. Anyway, I reckon I know something you don't. And it's this. *Education* is at the base of this capitalist society of ours, and if you want to change the one you'll bloody well *have* to change the other. (*Stops. Scratches head. Spot on him, rest black*) Mmm, Do we risk a bloody well there? ... and if you want to change one you'll, can't say jolly well. Better leave it. If you want to change one you're *going* to have to change the other. That's fine. (*Notes it down on board*).

Lights up: Conference hall.

SAM 2: My kids don't *want* to be capitalists, they don't *want* to be part of the capitalist system. But *education makes* them parts, we see to that. We run it on behalf of the capitalist society, and here we are today, discussing ways and means of making it more efficient and effective, (*Looks at watch. Red light on podium begins to flash on and off*) Bollocks. Right. Foot down. The lesson, comrades, is unmistakable. We need a structure of education that is positively socialist. We need socialist economics, socialist history, socialist philosophy in the curricula. And we need to make true soviets of our schools. There must be full participation in decision-taking. Student councils must form the base of the school power structure. (*Turning to back projection platform*) I know, comrades, time is short. A moment more, I beg you. (*Turning*) In short, is it too fanciful to fashion as our slogan for tomorrow: 'Every school a red base'? (*A child begins to cry upstairs*) I say it isn't. (Wife's *voice:* 'Sammy') I say ... it isn't. ('Sammy') Not when as of now (*baby crying. 'Sammy' from* Wife) every school is a blue bastion. I beg to move. (*Gathers papers, moves from podium.*)

Lights up, back projection down. The living room of a fine early Victorian house is revealed, with tasteful and expensive Scandinavian furnishings and superb, large portraits of Marx, Lenin, Trotsky, Mao and Guevara on the walls, forming a sort of design motif. Sam 2 strides to the open door towards the middle of the wall. His wife still calls his name, the child still cries. He stops in the doorway.

SAM 2: Will you stop shouting Sammy in that fucking defective's voice of yours?

WIFE: Have you finished?

SAM 2: Yes, I've finished.

WIFE: Thank Christ. I thought you were going to a Party Conference, not a bloody Nuremburg Rally.

SAM 2: Can you just shut up. You idle bag.

WIFE: A singular pleasure.

Sam turns to the audience. Tumultuous applause (on tape) from conference. He waves and disappears through the doorway.

CURTAIN

ACT THREE

Sam 2's living room. Sunday afternoon. Late summer light. There's a Jimmy Hendrix LP on the expensive Hi-Fi, though the room is empty. Sam 2 comes in in his underpants and boots. He has clearly just come from his bed. He ambles over to the player, rejects the Hendrix, puts Bartok's 6th String Quartet on, walks away as the first few bars beat out, turns and rejects that too. Switches off. Walks to armchair, picks up Observer, *folds himself into chair; throws* Observer *away, picks up* Sunday Times, *covers his head with it; simply squats there. After a moment or so* **Patricia***, his wife, comes down the stairs, seen through the widish living-room door, and enters the room. She wears only panties. She's busy looking for something on and around the furniture. She is lovely, in a cold, desirable, unattainable way. Her blonde hair is long, muzzed. Despite its length, it fails – as in life – to cover her good cream breasts.*

She goes to Sam's chair, lifts the paper in two disdainful fingers, stares impassively at the impassive Sam.

PATRICIA: My bra.

SAM: What about it?

PATRICIA: I can't find it.

SAM: Oh.

PATRICIA: Where is it?

SAM: How should. I know? I'm not wearing it.

She replaces the paper with some distaste.

PATRICIA: Of course not. Not you. Not on a Sunday anyway. Too much pathetic proletarian *guilt* about you for that. (*She looks around the room*) Still, you could be hiding it till Monday.

SAM: (*from under paper*) Piano.

PATRICIA: What?

SAM: (*removing paper*) Oh Christ, look at you. Get something on before your
daddy arrives. He'll only want a handful if he sees you like that.

PATRICIA: (*ignoring him*) What?

SAM: It's on the piano.

PATRICIA: The piano? (*Turning towards the white, baby piano in the corner of the
room, then back to Sam. They look at each other in silence for a moment. Then
Sam slowly smiles. She smiles back*) Oh yes.

*She walks over to the piano, opens the stool and takes out her bra, scrutinizes the
fastening, then puts it deftly on. Sam watches steadily. She dips again, pulls out a
brief skirt, steps into it, zips it up at the side; dips once more for the sweater,
turns it right side out, shrugs into it; and finally for the headband, to trap her
hair.*

PATRICIA: You always end up in the bedroom. No matter where you start from.

SAM: That's pathetic proletarian guilt too.

PATRICIA: Isn't it just. Do you want a drink?

SAM: If I'd only had your advantages.

PATRICIA: (*flopping down in the low settee*) I'll have a Campari and lemon.

SAM: … think what a whore I could've been.

A short silence. She runs her palms down her inner thighs.

PATRICIA: How long do you plan being away at this thing of yours?

Sam gets up and strides to the drinks cabinet. Pours drinks neatly, practised.

SAM: (*handing hers to her*) And lemon. Three days. I'll be back Thursday. Make a
note of it. On your arse if necessary. That way one of you can be counted on to
remember it.

PATRICIA: (*cool*) My god, but you're childish.

SAM: My god but I am.

*He stands over her for a moment. She sips her drink, ignoring him. He goes back
to his chair, flops noisily down.*

SAM: (*mock reflective*) He probably wouldn't be able to read it anyway. Not with
the light out. (*He begins to laugh, amused.*)

Patricia just stares at him. A gesture will give him the point. He subsides. Silence.

SAM: What time can we expect the Munsters this week?

PATRICIA: (*evenly*) About five.

SAM: I thought daddy was abroad.

PATRICIA: He was. He came back last night.

SAM: Oh good. I'm so glad. Sunday afternoons just wouldn't be the same without a heart-to-heart with Daddy Munster over tea and cakes. (*Pause*) Do you think he's got a bit of end over there?

PATRICIA: What?

SAM: He's never in the country these days. Where is it, Geneva? I bet he has. I bet he's dipping his furious wick in some discreet *pension* from morning till night. With a, let me see, with a stiff lady clerk from a Swiss clearing house. God, what a truly horrible thought.

PATRICIA: It's yours. What else would it be?

SAM: I bet he's a coitus interruptus man, too. *There's* bragadoccio! And he wipes her stiff belly off with frayed fivers and soiled bills of credit. A necessary prodigality, by God. Yes.

PATRICIA: (*holding glass out*) I'll have another. Soda. No lemon.

He gets up, takes her glass to the cupboard.

PATRICIA: What are you going to do?

SAM: I don't know.

PATRICIA: Will you apply?

SAM: I don't know. That's what 'I don't know' means.

PATRICIA: Isn't it what you want?

SAM: (*handing her the drink*) I don't know.

He goes over to the bookshelves, rummages for something.

PATRICIA: Gerald says you'd be crazy not to. He says you'd get the nomination.

SAM: (*matter-of-fact*) What the bloody hell does *he* know? As president of the Junior Chamber of Commerce he's not exactly at the throbbing heart of the Labour Party organisation in this town, is he?

PATRICIA: He *knows*. He knows the agent, for a start. And he had lunch with the Trades Council executive last week. Words passed.

SAM: Christ, I bet they did. Where's the Lenin?

PATRICIA: What?

SAM: (*insultingly patient*) A large, grey-backed book, published by the Moscow Foreign Publishing House, seductively titled 'Lenin: Selected Works'. Vol. I is missing from the shelf.

PATRICIA: It's by the bed.

SAM: By whose bed?

PATRICIA: Mine.

SAM: What for? Look, how many times have I told you about cutting your toenails on my books ...

PATRICIA: I'm reading it.

SAM: (*blankly*) You're reading it.

PATRICIA: Yes.

SAM: Oh. (*He scuffs his nose with his fingers, searches the shelves briefly, goes back to his chair*) Why?

PATRICIA: I don't know. I wanted to see what all the fuss was about.

SAM: Oh. (*Pause*) What fuss?

PATRICIA: Papers, TV, you. So.

SAM: And do you?

PATRICIA: Not really.

SAM: Oh,

PATRICIA: I haven't finished it yet.

SAM: No.

Long silence. She drinks her drink. He gets up and pours himself a scotch, puts water to it, turns to face her.

SAM: What do you talk about with this one?

PATRICIA: Which one? What?

SAM: The one who likes it with the lights out.

PATRICIA: Do shut up.

SAM: Well, you must talk about *something*. What do you talk about? (*She gives him a rasing glance, then turns her back to him, looks out into the auditorium*) Do you talk about, erm, me for instance? About my little bedtime quirks and all that? Mmm?

PATRICIA: This might come as something of a shock, but the times you've been the subject of my conversation when I'm in bed with someone would fall considerably short of two. Why don't you for Christ's sake put something *on*.

SAM: What for?

PATRICIA: Because you look bloody stupid.

SAM: Go on. Really. (*Gets up to pour himself another drink*) I thought I looked rather fetching. Still, I don't suppose your mother would approve. All this ... codpiece flopping during tea. Do you think she still takes a bit? Eh?

PATRICIA: Oh God.

SAM: No, do you? Last-Friday-in-the-month style of thing? I wouldn't be surprised. Probably has the days marked off in her Letts Table Diary for the whole year. I knew a bird once, had a code for indicating degrees of sexual progress made by the fellers she went out with. One star for tits over, two stars for tits under, three stars for a hand between the legs, four for a finger inside the elastic. [Fantastic.] I went with her for nearly six months. She used to call me Patrick Moore, in the diary. I can't think why she went to all the trouble. Suppose it switched her on, later. Surveying the galaxies.

PATRICIA: What was her name?

SAM: (*rapt*) Who?

PATRICIA: The girl. With the stars.

SAM: (*glib*) Letitia. Letitia Porrington-Smythe.

PATRICIA: (*seeing*) I see.

SAM: She married a breadman from Oldham. I wonder how he's doing?

PATRICIA: Have you finished?

SAM: Why *don't* you talk about me?

PATRICIA: (*looking at watch*) Clothes.

SAM: No, tell me. I'm interested.

PATRICIA: Why should I? Clothes.

SAM: Does he know you're married?

PATRICIA: I don't know. Yes. Does it matter?

SAM: No. I don't know. What does he think?

PATRICIA: Are you going to get dressed?

SAM: No. Yes. In a minute. What does he do?

PATRICIA: What?

SAM: Oh I remember. Insurance, isn't it? Well, that's nice and ... steady, I suppose. And it probably makes a nice change from working.

PATRICIA: Sam.

SAM: (*absorbed*) Yes?

PATRICIA: Put some clothes on.

SAM: Where's Krysta?

PATRICIA: Pictures. With Margit. It's Sunday.

SAM: (*inspecting a frayed edge on the crotch of his Y-fronts*) Yes. I noticed. All those bloody bells. Poor kids don't know where they are, rushing out into the streets for ice cream all day, and it's only the Vicar of Bray having a quick pull before the next service. (*Going straight on*) He doesn't sound very real to me.

PATRICIA: Who?

SAM: HIM.

PATRICIA: (*watch again*) Look, it's almost half past four. My parents are due at five and I'd be grateful if you'd have the decency to dress before they get here. Just, please, get it quite clear in your head, now: we have an agreement. It can't be broken unilaterally. Just, please, leave it alone.

Long silence. They look at each other. Finally Sam gets up, ambles over to the drinks cupboard, deposits his glass and walks to the door. There, he turns to look at Patricia.

SAM: OK. Lover. You really love a contract, though, don't you?

He goes out. We see him climb the stairs. Patricia sits there, tight-lipped, wrought, a moment longer; drains her glass; gets up and walks slowly towards the door. The doorbell rings softly, once.

PATRICIA: (*calling*) All right, I've got it. Please get a move on.

Checking watch, frowning. She looks round room, picks up the used glasses and a dirty ashtray, moves quickly off towards kitchen, recrosses the open door on her way to the front door. Sound of muffled voices. She returns with Mrs Shatlock.

MRS SHATLOCK: (*clearly worried in Patricia's presence*) It's not right dropping in like this, and I'm not stopping. I just really only wanted a word with our Sammy. If that's all right.

PATRICIA: Of course, Mrs Shatlock. Please sit down. Sam's upstairs … shaving.

SAM: (*from upstairs*) Who was it then?

PATRICIA: (*in doorway, curt*) It's your mother.

SAM: Right. I'm on my way. (*Voice moving towards Sam 1's*) Hello ma.

PATRICIA: (*to Mrs Shatlock*) Please make yourself comfortable. You'll have to excuse me. I've got to make a spot of tea for my parents. They'll be here at five. (*Mrs Shatlock half rises with an 'Ooh, I didn't realise …', but she's waved down*) No, no, please, Sam'll be right down.

Mrs Shatlock resumes her seat, her back more or less to the door. Patricia turns to leave, meets Sam in the doorway. She points to her watch meaningfully. Sam brushes past her, she takes his arm, makes the same gesture, leaves. Sam maddens visibly.

SAM: Hello, ma,

MRS SHATLOCK: Hello, Sammy, how are you, love?

SAM: I'm fine, mam. How're you? Let's have a look at you. (*He surveys her at arm's length*) Looking a bit pinched, my dear. Can't see you landing much at the Palais looking like that.

MRS SHATLOCK: Give over. My landing days are long past.

SAM: What! Never. Bouncing Belle Shatlock, the Queen of Stockport Lido, retiring! Unthinkable.

MRS SHATLOCK: Look, don't mess about. Her people'll be here in a minute and ...

SAM: So what? Don't you worry yourself about that toffee-nosed crowd of crabs, ma. Right? You bet it's bloody well right.

PATRICIA: (*from kitchen*) Sam!

SAM: (*ignoring her*) Are you all right, ma? Are you short? (*Going for back pocket.*)

PATRICIA: (*louder*) Sam!

MRS SHATLOCK: No, love. It's not money. I've enough for what I want, God knows.

PATRICIA: (*louder*) Sam!

MRS SHATLOCK: Hadn't you better answer her?

SAM: She's all right. What was it then, love?

MRS SHATLOCK: Well, it's our Sam. You know he's out of work again. Nine weeks this time and no sign of him getting another job. Well, he's ... things aren't right. With her and him, I mean. I wondered if you could do something ... *for* him. Have a talk to him. Set him right. He'll listen to you.

PATRICIA: (*in doorway*) Could you come in the kitchen a moment? Excuse us Mrs Shatlock. (*She leaves as abruptly as she arrived.*)

SAM: Just hang on a minute, mam. I won't be a minute. You stay here. I'll be right back.

He leaves quickly. A huge shouting match explodes in the kitchen. It grows fiercer. The baby wakens upstairs, begins its own fevered wauling. Mrs Shatlock, plainly overcome by it all, moves hesitantly into the hallway, looks once at the kitchen, and moves off towards the front door. She bangs it to. The din cuts sharply on the door slam and Sam appears in the living room doorway.

SAM: Mam? Mam? (*He walks to the stairs*) Mam? Are you up there? (*Looks in direction of front door, then pulls long leather coat from cupboard under stairs and puts it on*) You bloody pig! You'll eat shit for this, you fucking bourgeois! (*He belts out. Door slams.*)

Only the baby yowls now, and he's calming. Finally, Patricia appears at the foot of the stairs.

PATRICIA: All right, darling. All riiiiight. Mummy's here, my love, my sweetheart, my lovely. That's all right, that's all right. Mummy make you nice bottle soon. Yeeeeeees. There now. There now. That's right. That's right. Yeeeeeees.
The yowling becomes mewling, the mewling turns to snuffles, then silence.

Patricia stands in the doorway, leans against one jamb. She is strained, tense; her hair is faintly muzzed, mouth very tight. She closes her eyes, rests her head and cheek against the wood. Her hands are clenched inside the pockets of the short apron she's put on to prepare the tea. After a moment, she crosses to the drink cabinet and pours herself a long gin, takes a quick rinsing mouthful and dumps the glass down. The bell rings sharply once. Patricia doesn't move, her bent back is towards us, her hands on the cabinet in front of her. The bell rings again, again sharply. Slowly she revives, straightens, runs a hand through her hair, perfunctorily inspects the room, moves out to the front door. The bell rings twice: bring, bring. The baby begins to cry again. Patricia shouts 'Christ' very loudly. Sound of front door opening. Voices. She reappears in the living room doorway with her parents. **Winston**, *her father, is a kept and handsome 54. He'll probably stay attractive, at least until his first coronary, when inactivity and worry will begin to pile the flesh up or drag it down. His voice is full, rich, pleasant and very assured: it's a voice that expects to be listened to. It knows little about contradiction.* **Naomi**, *though about his age, is a 54 year old woman, and therefore remarkable only for her achievement in holding anything together that might thinly pass for beauty. She's thin, grey, angular, rather bright, beautifully dressed. She has never cared for her only child and has now begun to evince a mild but far from kindly contempt for her husband. Her characteristic speaking mode is detached, faintly ironic, as though a bright commentator were offering descriptions of a social scene he knew much about and cared nothing for.*

The baby cries on.

WINSTON: How's my grandson? You leave him to me, pet. Let the hand of experience rock the cradle.

PATRICIA: He's a total sod, if you want to know. No, I'd better do it. You'd probably frighten him to death.

WINSTON: Nonsense. I'm his grandpappy. I'll see to him.

NAOMI: Don't be ridiculous, Winston. (*To Patricia*) That was your husband we saw rushing from the house, wasn't it, darling?

PATRICIA: Yes. He … rushes from the house from time to time, Naomi. It doesn't usually add up to very much.

NAOMI: (*sitting down*) As long as he … rushes back from time to time. I don't suppose it does. Could someone pour me a drink?

WINSTON: (*moving to cabinet*) He seemed in one hell of a hurry, pet. Drink?

PATRICIA: (*shaking head*) I'll be down directly, when I've settled him. (*She leaves.*)

WINSTON: (*calling*) Don't you worry, sweetheart. We're perfectly able to look after ourselves,

Patricia passes up the stairs. Winston pours the drinks, hands Naomi one, who ignores him in taking it, sits down on the settee roughly opposite her chair. A long

vacancy appears. Somehow all the tedium of their fagged out relationship is contained in this mindless silence. Each sits for a long moment as though alone. One almost expects some private act from one of them: a fart, perhaps, or the scrutiny of an upper set. We hear faint sounds of Patricia hushing her baby, and the chink of ice in their glasses. Finally.

WINSTON: *He* won't last long.

NAOMI: Mmm.

WINSTON: Guttersnipe. That's what he was when she brought him home, that's what he is now. A pig. (*Naomi yawns*) You're very quiet.

NAOMI: Am I? Would you like me to say something?

WINSTON: If she'd only listened to me, just once in her stupid spoiled little life.

NAOMI: What was your man's name?

WINSTON: What?

NAOMI: With the boat. The man with the boat.

WINSTON: Oh. Dealey. Why do you ask?

NAOMI: How do you spell it?

WINSTON: I don't know. D.E.A.L.E.Y. I suppose. Something like that.

NAOMI: Wasn't there someone at Harewood named Dealey?

WINSTON: I don't recall anyone. No, not at all.

NAOMI: What about the one with the guns?

WINSTON: Pratt, you mean.

NAOMI: Was it?

WINSTON: Pratt. Edwin Pratt.

NAOMI: Oh.

Silence. He gets up, collects her glass, walks to cabinet, fills it and his own up again, returns hers, sits down.

NAOMI: Buy the boat anyway.

She takes a long drink and begins to browse through the Observer *on the floor by her chair.*

WINSTON: Young Monkton says the seat's ...

NAOMI: Who?

WINSTON: Teddy Monkton's boy, Gerald, you ...

NAOMI: (*still reading*) Oh yes. What does he say?

WINSTON: God in heaven, woman, can't you bloodywell listen, I'm trying to TALK to you.

Naomi puts down the paper very deliberately (but not too slowly, not hamming the movement) and sits looking at her husband. The silence wells up between them again. Winston is slightly discomfited by his loss of control.

NAOMI: *(finally)* Gerald says?

WINSTON: It doesn't matter, *(She listens on. Winston chews his lower lip)* He says this fellow *(waving arm in loose direction of hall)* could have the nomination for the Central seat any time he wanted.

NAOMI: *(after a pause)* Does he?

WINSTON: Does he what? Who?

NAOMI: Does Gerald say that?

She stares at him. He looks away. She looks at him blankly for another moment, then picks up the paper and begins reading it again.

WINSTON: Don't you care?

NAOMI: No.

WINSTON: She's your *daughter*, for Christ's sake.

NAOMI: She's *his* wife.

WINSTON: Precisely.

NAOMI: *(stopping reading)* What?

WINSTON: Precisely the reason you should care.

NAOMI: On the contrary, it's precisely the reason one shouldn't. She has a perfect right to take this thrusting young idealist to her bosom. She has no right at all to sympathy when he turns out, as predicted, to be a squalid proletarian romantic with a poor temper and no nerve.

WINSTON: She has *my* sympathy.

NAOMI: Rubbish. She has an admixture of fading lust, rank jealousy and battered *amour propre* from you. And she needs that like she needs cancer of the cervix.

WINSTON: *(bitter)* Thank you very much. So the grubby sod can trample all over her for all you care?

The front door slams loudly. Sam 2 appears in the doorway, face hard and set. Winston swings in his chair, a trained greeting smile on his face.

WINSTON: Hello, Sam. *(Pause. Sam looks at them)* We're a ... We're a little early.

Sam stays a moment longer, then whirls out, undoing and removing his coat on the way, in the direction of the kitchen. A few bangs and crashes.

WINSTON: My God, I don't see why I have to sit here and suffer this. The ignorant boor, he's nothing else. Insufferable, ignorant, jumped-up ...

Sam is in the doorway again. Winston suppresses his ending. They look at each other dully, from behind an animosity that has been assiduously banked-up for just such a Sunday afternoon. Though she hasn't acknowledged Sam's entrance with a look, Naomi recognises the jewelled heat of the situation and mechanically moves to damp it down.

NAOMI: (*reading on, glass stretched high but elegantly above her head*) Would it be too much to ask one of you to pour me a drink? (*Looking up*) Hello, Sam. Pour me a drink, there's a pet.

WINSTON: (*getting up, sharply*) Here, I'll do it. (*Proceeds to cabinet.*)

NAOMI: Thank you, darling. Well, Sam, and how are you? You're looking pale again, poor dear.

SAM: (*sitting in his chair, the one Winston has just vacated*) (*Very broad*) I'm fine, Naomi. How's yourself, chuck? You're looking as fit as ever. (*Winston hands her her drink, sits down on the Chesterfield with his own*) They can say what they like, these doctors, the preservative powers of alcohol are truly remarkable.

There's a long silence. Naomi looks at Winston, who drinks steadily from his glass, eyes lowered, then back at Sam, who lolls in the chair opposite, one booted leg high and wide across its arm, crotch thrust forward like a provocation.

NAOMI: (*laughing, unforced, unhurried*) That's really rather funny, Sam. There's something finally endearing about your particular brand of puerility.

SAM: I know what you mean. How would we put it, then? What about, yes, this is it: farouche but not rebarbative. How's that sound?

NAOMI: Sounds fine, Sam. Does it have a meaning too?

SAM: Farouche: wild, like an animal. Rebarbative: ugly, unattractive, repellent. Me?

NAOMI: Oh yes. Very much you, I'd say.

SAM: Aye. (*Long deep breath*) How's things, then, lass? Bought t'schooner yet?

NAOMI: (*cold smile still there*) No. Not yet.

SAM: Oh, you should buy t'schooner. No family should be without one. (*Pause*) You'd look nice. In the skipper's hat.

Silence. Winston drinks. Naomi drinks.

SAM: (*matter of fact*) We were wondering, Patricia and I, that is, whether you still … took a bit, Naomi?

A hissy silence.

WINSTON: Oh for God's sake …

SAM: I think your husband wants to speak.

WINSTON: (*getting up*) I think I've had quite enough of this. (*Sam grins theatrically at Naomi, who smiles back*) Look, if you've something to say, why don't you spit it out.

SAM: Spit it out! SPIT IT OUT! (*He jumps to attention, salutes sharply, bangs his feet together like a trainee infantryman*) 23168912 Pte Shatlock S., Sir. Request permission to spit it out, sir.

Patricia appears in the doorway.

PATRICIA: (*cold*) I thought games were Wednesday afternoons.

SAM: (*still erect, at attention; theatrically, from side of mouth*) Why don't you do the world a favour and put your head in the oven. (*Squaddie's voice again*) Have I your permission to spit it out, sir?

WINSTON: (*red, bullish*) Come to it, you ... Come on, say it.

SAM: (*Squaddie*) Prefer to spit it out, sir, all the same to you, sir.

WINSTON: (*dropping*) Do what you like.

SAM: Thank you sir. (*He steps smartly back with a one, two, one-two, picks up his glass, fills his mouth, ratatats forward to within two feet of Winston and splats the contents of his mouth into his face. Winston blinks ferociously*) Thank you very much, sir. I enjoyed that quite a lot. (*He salutes, about turns, marches back to his chair, flops down into it.*)

WINSTON: (*finally*) Naomi. (*She gets up slowly, gently drunk by now.*)

PATRICIA: Daddy.

WINSTON: Never mind it, sweetheart. (*Begins to wipe face with handkerchief*) If this weren't your house and he your husband, things might be very different. We shan't come here again. And I don't ever want to see him again in mine.

PATRICIA: Daddy, please, don't, it isn't worth it. (*Sam begins to laugh, the tension hissing out of him. Louder and louder*) SHUT UP, YOU PIG. SHUT UP, YOU ROTTEN STINKING PIG. SHUT UP SHUT UP SHUT UP SHUT UP SHUT UP SHUT UP SHUT UP SHUT UP. You spat on my father, damn you.

SAM: (*recovered, very cold*) AND YOU SHAT ON MY MOTHER. May your ovaries melt into your bowels for it. (*Pause.*)

NAOMI: (*To Pat, dry*) Thank you for a lovely time, darling. There's something ... profoundly civilised about Sunday afternoons at the Shatlocks'. (*She goes out.*)

WINSTON: (*terse*) I'll call you. Just ... you know you've only got to ring and I'm at the door.

Patricia nods dumbly. Winston looks fiercely at Sam, who's retired to his loll in the chair, and leaves. Patricia goes with him. Chat in the hall. Sam gets up, scratches his nose, goes over to the cabinet, pours two large scotches, waters

*them, puts ice in one, sips from the other, eyes closed, facing out. Front door
closes. Patricia comes back into the room. She is very quiet, very coiled,
exquisitely clenched. Without turning, Sam holds out the iced glass to her. She
takes it without sound and sits down on a long mat stool downstage left. Very
gradually we can discern that she's crying; or rather, a steady pulse of tears
pushes down from her eyes, involuntary leakage or seepage. At any rate, it's
soundless: Sam, upstage, is not aware of it throughout his next speech.*

SAM: (*Mississippi drawl*) Dear Father, This is my last letter to you. I went into
battle this evening as courier for General Hetlo. I have been struck by a piece
of shell and my right shoulder is horribly mangled and I know death is
inevitable. I am very weak but I write to you because I know you would be
delighted to read a word from your dying son. I know death is near, that I will
die far from home and friends of my early youth but I have friends here too
who are true to me. My friend Fairfax will write you at my request and give
you the particulars of my death. My grave will be marked so that you may visit
it if you desire to do so but is optionary with you whether you let my remains
rest here or in Mississippi. I would like to rest in the graveyard with my dear
mother and brothers but it's a matter of minor importance. Let us all try to
reunite in heaven. I pray my God to forgive my sins and I feel that his
promises are true that he will forgive me and save me. Give my love to all my
friends. My strength fails me. My horse and my equipments will be left for
you. Again a long farewell to you. May we meet in heaven. Your dying son, J.
R. Montgomery, alias Sam Shatlock.

He pours himself another long drink.

Funny what you remember. Had to learn that sod for an imposition. Lower
Fifth. (*Drinking deeply*) Bet it cheered his old man up no end. I mean, it's not
every day you learn you've been left a horse and 'equipments'. (*Another deep
drink, draining glass*) Perhaps it isn't so funny. Perhaps calendar wisdom's the
only wisdom there is. (*Pours another drink, begins to walk about along the far
wall*) 'The hand that rocks the cradle is the hand that rules the world.' Dedah!
What a beaut. What a timeless deathless beaut. Erm. 'The multitude is always
in the wrong.' The Earl of Roscommon. Erm. 'But what is woman – only one
of nature's agreeable blunders.' My god, the wisdom of the ages. (*No
perceptible shift in tone or key*) I never knew your daddy didn't like me. Now
there's a turn-up for the books. Old Winston. Thought we got on pretty well,
on the whole. Never can tell, with humans, if you'll extend the meaning of that
vastly overstretched word to include your parents. (*Pours another drink*) Anyway. One all.

*He's moved over to the chair, flops down on the floor and leans against it. He
would now have a quarter-profile view of Patricia, save that he is doing his best
not to put her up into frame. A long silence. Patricia sits very still; stonefaced; no
longer crying. Sam begins to polish his eyesockets with the heels of his hands, as
very old men do in trying to clear rheum. We become aware of a rather mannered
sniffing and snuffling; it sounds like someone establishing the fact that he's*

crying.

PATRICIA: I really think I hate you. (*She gets up, crosses the room and stands over him*) You. (*She kicks him hard on the thigh*) You. I said I hate you. (*He takes his hands down and looks up at her. She crouches down and hits him across the face, left hand. right hand, a dozen or more times, The blows are hard: blood lurches front his upper lip and nose. He takes it all unflinchingly*) I said I hate you. You … guttersnipe. (*She kneels athward his thighs, takes head in hands, kisses his blooded lips with frightening vehemence. Slowly she forces him on to his back, where he is partially hidden by his chair*) You . . . nobody. Dirty little nobody. Snoteating alsoran. You should have stayed with your own kind, Mr Shatlock. Down *there*. Where you belong. (*She rides him like a dead crocodile. He is completely flat and inert. She backs down his legs. undoes his broad leather belt and front zip and slides full length up him again. They begin a frenzied session. Their lovemaking is hyenal. Patricia retains the upper perch throughout.*) What's your name?

SAM: Shatlock.

PATRICIA: Shatlock what?

SAM: Shatlock, madam.

PATRICIA: That's better. Mustn't forget our station must we, Shatlock?

SAM: No. Madam.

PATRICIA: No. And where do you come from, Shatlock?

SAM: Water Lane, madam. Number Three, Water Lane, East Stockport.

PATRICIA: What kind of district is that, Shatlock?

SAM: Poor, Ma'am. Very poor.

PATRICIA: And dirty.

SAM: And dirty, ma'am.

PATRICIA: Is that why you smell, Shatlock?

SAM: Yes, ma'am.

PATRICIA: You should take a bath, Shatlock. You positively stink.

SAM: Yes, ma'am.

PATRICIA: Give yourself a good scrubbing. (*No response*) Understood?

SAM: Yes'm.

PATRICIA: And come and show me when you've finished.

SAM: Yes'm.

PATRICIA: I want to see you … gleam.

SAM: Yes'm.

PATRICIA: Understood?

SAM: Yes'm.

PATRICIA: We'll clean you up yet, won't we, Shatlock?

SAM: Yes'm.

PATRICIA: Make you … presentable.

SAM: (*close*) Mmm. Mmm.

PATRICIA: Make you *fit*.

SAM: Mmm. Mmm.

The phone rings. Patricia sits upright a moment, then begins to go to answer it. Sam makes to draw her back but she pushes his hands away and crosses to the phone, restoring her dress and muzzed hair on the way.

PATRICIA: (*to phone*) Yes. Oh hello. No. Look, hang on, I'll talk to you upstairs. No it's all right, I haven't forgotten. Yes. In a moment.

She lays the phone down and goes out without looking. Sam sits up slowly, gets to his knees, does up his pants and belt, rises finally and crosses to the phone. After a second's deliberation he picks it up and listens for a while, the earpiece several inches from his ear. Very faintly we pick up the conversing voices.

SAM: (*into phone*) Excuse me, this is Samuel Shatlock, Patricia's husband. I've no doubt you've heard about me. Yes. I thought so. I've heard a fair bit about you, too. Not too good, I'm afraid. Not too good at all. In fact, from the descriptions offered, I'd say you were a right burk. But there you are. It's all right, love, I shan't be a minute. Oh, tch tch tch. (*Takes phone from ear, pokes finger in theatrically*) Never did have much patience, our Patricia. (*We see her hurtling downstairs through the living room entrance*) Anyway, what I wanted to say was … (*She rushes into the room and tries to take the phone away from him*) Hang on a second, there seems to be a little trouble this end. (*Quite deliberately, he takes hold of the scruff of Patricia's front hair in clenched fist and holds her painfully off at arm's length while he conducts the phone call with the other*) That's better. What I was going to say was: Why don't you just hang that thing of yours up and retire? At all events, keep it out of my wife. Understood? Right.

He slams the phone down and releases Patricia. She swings a wild arm at him which he counters with his left. His right smashes into her face with force enough to topple her over the Chesterfield, where she lies dazed and sobbing.

SAM: As the lady said, games on Wednesday afternoons. (*He picks up his drink, freshens it at the cabinet, drains the glass, pours another*) You just never know what's playing and what's real, that's your trouble.

PATRICIA: (*dully*) We had an agreement. You broke it.

SAM: (*very loud*) Fuck the agreement! You can't *have* an agreement. It isn't on. Surely you can *see* that.

PATRICIA: No.

SAM: YES.

PATRICIA: No. NO.

SAM: I love you, Pat.

PATRICIA: What difference does that make?

SAM: I love you, Pat.

Extend at this point, to take the relationship back to its essential patterned undisturbed hopeless aridity. They must be seen to have weathered the crisis, to have reached the harbour of their agreement. He must return to smarting complaisance, she to gelid indifference.

PATRICIA: (*checking her flushed face in mirror*) Oh well, what do you know. Three pathetic miserable BOURGEOIS ... words and he thinks the whole hideous puzzle falls into place. Don't worry, you can put the pills away, turn the gas taps off, you can step down from the parapet. I LOVE YOU. That's great. That's so ... infantile, it's nearly magnificent.

SAM: (*softly*) All right.

PATRICIA: Do you know what you just said?

SAM: (*sharper*) ALL RIGHT.

PATRICIA: It's not all right. It's far from all right. But this is the way we are. And we've got to make the best of it. So the sooner you grow a few scabs the better: you can't go on bleeding away for the rest of your life.

SAM: (*shouting*) Will you just, look, just SHUT UP, will you. (*Calming*) The agreement stands. OK? Fine. We'll be ... rational about it. You to yours and me to mine. And never the twain shall meet. OK? Right. Leave it.

Silence again. She looks round the room for something, doesn't see it, examines her face again. He stands by the large gunmetal multiple (gold and red magnetic discs) on the wall over the record player.

PATRICIA: (*finally*) Have you seen my comb?

SAM: (*turning*) Your comb? No.

PATRICIA: I must've left it upstairs. (*She stands up*) Are you going to ring daddy?

SAM: What for?

PATRICIA: Better do it before you go off to Scarborough or wherever it is you're going. He'll only fret.

SAM: Poor Daddy.

PATRICIA: (*gently*) Do it now.

Sam doesn't answer. He moves a disc on the multiple, replaces it. Patricia goes out into the hall, takes an attractive fur out of the cupboard and puts it on. She stands in the doorway.

PATRICIA: Tell Krysta his bottles are in the fridge for the morning.

SAM: (*laying his hand on her arm*) Don't go.

PATRICIA: There's cold meat in the larder. Get yourself something.

SAM: Please.

PATRICIA: Let go.

SAM: Please.

She refuses to look. He releases her. She goes into the hall and leaves by the front door. Sam stands sipping his drink, listening. Sound of a powerful car drawing out in reverse down drive, then away. It's quite dark now in the room. Sam puts on a single tall standard lamp by his chair, sits down in the chair, crosslegged, very straight and sombre, staring ahead at nothing. After a moment he gets up, crosses to the phone, dials a number, waits.

SAM: Allo. Allo. Is det der Abattoir zum Stockport. (*Waits*) Iss not abattoir? Of det you er sure. Naturlich, naturlich. Danke, danke sehr.

He clicks his heels, puts phone down smartly, stands a second longer, picks it up again, waits, then hums opening bars of 'Deutschland Uber Alles' into mouthpiece, looks shocked at the response from the other end, replaces the receiver, returns to his chair.

SAM: 'We shall not enter into the kingdom of socialism in white gloves on a polished floor.' Trotsky, December 1917. Right, Lev Davidovitch. Put that in your calendars sometime.

Krysta, *the pretty young au pair, has come in from the back and now stands in the doorway.*

KRYSTA: Mr Shatlock?

SAM: Hello. Krysta.

KRYSTA: Are you well, Mr Shatlock?

SAM: I'm well. How are you, Krysta?

KRYSTA: I'm pretty well, thank you. Mr Shatlock.

SAM: Have a drink. Sit down. There, that's right. I'll get you a drink. What'd you like?

KRYSTA: Nothing really. I'm not drinking many things.

SAM: (*at cabinet*) Well, just drink one thing, with me. A nightcap.

KRYSTA: What kind of drink is it, nightcap?

SAM: It's very nice. It's one of the nicest drinks you could ever drink. It's like a rather powerful cocoa. (*He pours her a large scotch and splashes ginger ale into it*) There, put that inside you. (*Crosses to chair, picks own glass up*) Cheers, love.

KRYSTA: Cheerslove.

She splutters a little as it goes down.

SAM: How d'you like it? I told you it was good.

KRYSTA: It tastes like whisky.

SAM: Ah. Well. That's the secret of nightcap. It rather does tend to taste like whisky.

KRYSTA: I think you are joking me, Mr Shatlock.

SAM: Cross my heart and hope to die, Krysta.

KRYSTA: Is Mrs Shatlock here?

SAM: She's out. Bottle's in the fridge for the ever-open door upstairs.

KRYSTA: Will she this evening come home again?

SAM: I think not, Krysta. Just you and me, I'm afraid.

KRYSTA: (*putting drink down*) I'm tired. I must to bed.

SAM: Did you ever meet my brother, Krysta?

KRYSTA: No, Mr Shatlock.

SAM: You should. He's a nice chap. You'd like him. (*Pause*) Do you know what I mean?

KRYSTA: No.

SAM: (*losing thread, still quite drunk*) Another thing. He's happy, somehow. Satisfied. Know what I mean?

KRYSTA: (*standing*) I must to bed.

SAM: Course, *he's* the *loser*. That's the joke. Life's full of them. Losers.

KRYSTA: (*crossing to the door*) Goodnight, Mr Shatlock.

SAM: Krysta.

KRYSTA: Yes, Mr Shatlock.

SAM: Krysta.

KRYSTA: No, Mr Shatlock.

SAM: (*pause*) Goodnight.

KRYSTA: Goodnight.

Sam sits dead still for a moment, then jerks quickly up, crosses to the phone, dials a number, waits. Finally...

SAM: Hello. Hello, it's Sam here. (*Quickly*) Hello. Thought you'd been cut off. What? (*Tones of incredulity*) Abattoir? No, of course not. Some nut, I shouldn't wonder. Well, I wanted a word with Winston, if he's there. Oh, I see. About eleven. Fine, OK, right, I'll ring just after eleven. Fine, OK. Thanks, Naomi.

Yes. Yes. OK. Goodnight.

He smacks the receiver down on to its cradle, thrusts hands into pockets, tenses body, reaches up on to tiptoe, breathes loud through nose. After a moment he starts to uncoil, and begins a slow walk round the room. He picks up objects – a piece of blue Swedish glass, a delicious bright brass timepiece, a grey pot – inspects each one desultorily and puts it back in its place. He tampers with the large multiple on the wall by the record player – black gunmetal base, large gold and red magnetic circles. Finally he restores the original pattern. He ducks down to the record cabinet, surfaces with a record, puts it on, returns to centre of the stage, stands upright facing out and glass in hand as the player clicks and spluts the arm on to the table. We hear the Brighouse and Raistrick Brass Band playing Lloyd (or Sladeburn). Sam does a sort of salute with his glass. And drinks. Lights down.

END

OCCUPATIONS

Occupations, my first full-length play for the stage, was researched and written in 1969 and received its first production at the Stables Theatre in Manchester in the following year. Though the story of the play is bedded in a lost moment of European socialist history – the occupation of the factories in Northern Italy in 1920 – there are clear resonances with strategically similar struggles in Europe and Britain at the time of its writing. In spite of a fine, clear and impassioned chamber production by Gordon McDougall in Manchester and a powerful restatement of the piece by the RSC a year later under the direction of Buzz Goodbody, reviewers were, as is commonly the case with my work, predictably divided

In Defence of *Occupations*

Shortly after completing its successful run at The Place, London, Occupations *was featured in a two-page article by Tom Nairn in 7 Days (3 November 1971). Trevor Griffiths responded to this article with the following letter disagreeing with Tom Nairn's critical approach to theatre and answering his major criticisms of the play.*

It's important to respond to historical plays as art-works, not as selected documentary accumulations containing historico-political speculations evaluable largely in terms of a 'known', historical and political reality. And we must learn to look for 'historicity' more as Lukacs finds it in the histories of Shakespeare. As for example when Lukacs says: 'Shakespeare states every conflict, even those of English history with which he is most familiar, in terms of typical-human opposites; and these are historical only in so far as Shakespeare fully and directly assimilates into each individual type the most characteristic and central features of a social crisis.' Nairn's it's-either-historically-'accurate'-or-it's-purely-and-only-'symbolic' is just too crude and unfruitful a measure of the value of a play (or, indeed, of anything else).

Since he has established the parameters of the discussion firmly inside that approach, however, I have no option but to do likewise. He makes four major points, of varying weight and accuracy.

First, the 'historical' character of Gramsci is wrong; moreover, the characterization in *Occupations* is romantic, even sentimental. Second, the 'symbolic' meanings of Kabak, the Comintern representative, are deeply ahistorical; the Comintern in late 1920 was never like this, though it may well have pursued foolish or even damaging policies. Third, the play's naturalistic form tended to undermine, even devalue, the promise of its content and themes. Fourth, the play is pessimistic, and therefore not revolutionary.

I'll respond to the last three points briefly, leaving the central question of the true 'historical' personality and character of Gramsci till last. Some conflation of 'different epochs of Communist history' does admittedly occur in the characterization of Kabak. For example, the Sovnarkom decree (and the seventy-two cleared concession items) that forms the basis of the final exchange with the Fiat boss was actually passed in November, some *five weeks after* the scene took place in the play's time scheme; though it's worth pointing out that the decree simply served to crystallize a whole strand of Soviet foreign policy that had been nursed (quite correctly in my view) since the summer of 1918.

After the autumn of 1920, however, with the failure of the Italian Revolution, the emphasis on the defence of Soviet national interests toughened, as the retreat from a policy hostile in principle to all capitalist government (while the prospect of proletarian revolution remained alive) got under way. As far as I can see, the play simply states that emphasis as a pragmatic, unavoidable fact.

Perhaps the weight of compressed meaning upon Kabak in that final scene with Valletta is just too great (a 'formal' weakness; by no means the only one): his need to play a role *vis-à-vis* Valletta (brandy, jokes, cigars, portfolios, *business)* obscures the representative values of his actions by inviting a cynical and pessimistic response. But the *intention* is quite other; and it's an intention still substantially realizable in the text.

That Nairn should see that scene as conflating Stalinist adventures in Spain with sixties' deals for Fiat factories on the Volga is as much, one suspects, the result of his own grasp of the period as of the play's structural weaknesses.

As to whether the play is pessimistic and whether, if it is, it is therefore necessarily non-revolutionary, I would support Gramsci's assertion that 'It is a revolutionary duty to tell the truth', even where there is little comfort to be had from it. *Occupations* was written as a sort of Jacobinical response to the failure of the '68 revolution in France. *What it asserts* is that courage and optimism do not, of themselves, ensure the success of revolutions, unless they are harnessed, disciplined, tightly organized; in a word, *led.*

And what it *asks* – because it's a play that, characteristically, asks rather than asserts – is whether the courage and optimism aren't in some way necessarily damaged, distorted, in that disciplining process. (And that's a 'meaning' for Kabak that Nairn barely smells, he's so often away from the play's muscle, skin and sinew.)

But Gramsci; where to begin?

Nairn: 'In reality … all accounts agree … Gramsci was a hard, even a harsh, figure in most public situations.' Well, in the play, his second speech to the workers would rate as pretty harsh, I think; and in his first scene with Kabak, he's cold, suspicious, and unyielding for a long time, until Kabak's identity is finally established beyond doubt; certainly 'hard', one would have said.

But 'in reality', Gramsci was rarely ever *only* that. Nino Danielli: 'Good, almost sweet, with that large intelligent face on that greatly deformed body, quick to smile and every word full of thought, Gramsci was charming from the beginning …' Nino Bruno: 'He was a very cheerful fellow, laughing and joking all the time.' Carlo Bocardo: 'Gramsci let us talk … (he) never lost patience with us, he never acted like a theoretical know-all; he set great store by other people's opinions and was a good listener.' Nairn suggests that Gramsci's letter to Giulia, in which he refers to himself as 'cross-grained' and 'spiteful' – one who made 'everything a matter of pure intellect and mathematical calculation' – is a good guide to the sort of person Gramsci was in September 1920 (when the occupations occurred).

If Nairn had read or remembered more of the letter than is printed in the English version of Fiori's *Life of Gramsci,* however, he would have known that the description refers to a *much* earlier period, to those 'sewers of my past' when he lived like a 'bear in a cave.' The 'bear in a cave' period, Fiori points out, ended around 1915. That he wasn't referring to 1920 when he spoke of his over-emphasis on 'pure intellect and mathematical calculation' is further suggested by his letter to Togliatti (27 March 1924) in which he argues: 'We must seek to rebuild an atmosphere like that of 1919/1920 … At that time, no project was undertaken unless first tested by reality and until we had sounded out in many ways the opinions of the workers. Consequently our projects always had an immediate and broad success and appeared as the interpretation of a widely felt need, never as the cold application of an intellectual scheme.'

'In reality', Gramsci moved, throughout his life, from states of deep depression to states of warm and generous sympathy. The image of Gramsci as consistently 'hard, even harsh' is founded in Lisa's and Lay's descriptions of him in prison in the thirties when Gramsci developed (understandably) personality problems not dissociable from physical suffering (TB, arteriosclerosis, angina, etc.); and, in its way, it's this myth that's damagingly romantic, sustaining, as it does, the notion that rebarbative personality is a necessary (or at any rate useful) prerequisite of serious revolutionary activity.

As to the 'sinewy intolerance inseparable from Gramsci's particular form of greatness', the evidence in refutation is so extensive as to require another article in itself to present. Gramsci's long dialogue with the anarchists, his sustained 'openness' towards non-communists and Catholic workers and intellectuals; his appointment of Gobetti, a liberal, as *Ordine Nuovo's* theatre critic; his continued fight against Piedmontese working-class anti-clericalism all serve as evidence to the contrary. And even in prison, as Lay points out, Gramsci's costive testiness did not mean that he 'could not tolerate disagreement with his ideas. Athos Lisa was not in agreement with Gramsci's thesis ... nevertheless, Gramsci esteemed and valued him.'

Gramsci's two factory speeches are a *device* for projecting two very different sets of theses developed by him in *Ordine Nuovo* essays at the time. Tasca and Degott are right: Gramsci was no great orator; nor are these speeches great oratory; nor are they delivered by a man who imagines he's a great orator. In the first one, he's constantly plagued by interruptions; in the second, he speaks to almost total, unsympathetic silence. But they *are* clear and concise accounts of some of his thinking at the time. And Gramsci did – incontrovertibly – address large gatherings of workers in the factories. Spriano notes that he spoke to a big meeting at Garrone Fiat on *'Domenica Rossa'* (I have him at Fiat Centro – another 'documentary inaccuracy'); Terraccini told me that Gramsci addressed workers' meetings, large and small, pretty well every day, sometimes three or four times a day.

There's no doubt that the workers responded very favourably to him (Terraccini spent a long time detailing the workers' response to Gramsci); little doubt, too, that since 1916, when he made his first public speeches, he had made considerable strides in overcoming his basic diffidence and reserve. Degott's view that Gramsci's appearance affected audiences unfavourably is not borne out by anything Terraccini had to say on Gramsci. According to him, the Turin workers 'loved him' (*'Molto, molto, molto'),* they loved his untidiness, his raffish dress, his floppy hat – which they threw into the river, once, for a joke, then rescued – his jokes and fables. (Terraccini told me this against himself: *he* was not well liked by the workers, who detested his 'bourgeois correctness' of dress and manner.) Celeste Negarville refers to 'Gramsci's singular talent for talking with working people'.

Finally, though it would take too long to detail Gramsci's growing preoccupation with the relationship between public and private forms of experience, there is no doubt that 'love' was a basic reference for much of his social thought. He it is (not me) who asserts: 'One cannot divide oneself into fragments and make only one part function; life is a whole, and each activity is strengthened by all the others; love strengthens the whole of one's existence … it creates a new equilibrium, a greater intensity of all other feelings and sentiments.' Mucking about with love and Revolution?

All this notwithstanding, I'm truly grateful to your paper for printing such a long, detailed, and responsible piece. Of all the notices I've read, it's the one most likely to help me make the next play a better one. Is there any higher praise than that, from a writer?

Occupations was first performed at The Stables Theatre Club, Manchester, on 28th October 1970, with the following cast:

Polya   Clare Welch

Kabak   Richard Wilson

Libertini   Paul Williamson

Angelica   Katherine Barker

Gramsci   Richard Kane

D'Avanzo   John Flanagan

Terrini   William Simons

Valletta   John Horsley

Directed by   Gordon McDougall

Occupations was first performed in London by the Royal Shakespeare Company at The Place, on 13 October 1971, with the following cast:

Polya   Heather Canning

Kabak   Patrick Stewart

Libertini   Philip Locke

Angelica   Estelle Kohler

Gramsci   Ben Kingsley

D'Avanzo   John York

Terrini   Clement McCallin

Valletta   Sebastian Shaw

Directed by   Buzz Goodbody

Occupations

ACT ONE

SCENE ONE

The stage is in total darkness. We hear, faintly at first, growing gradually louder and more insistent, a sung version of 'The Internationale'. A projected image slowly emerges: the famous Ты *('You – have you enrolled as a volunteer yet?' D. S. Moor, Russia, 1920). It's held, red and challenging, for several moments. Cut suddenly, as a fast spot reveals* **Polya** *bending over the bed to inject the writhing* **Angelica**. *Angelica shudders, quietens. Polya cools her brow with a cloth. Music down. Excited hubbub of conference. Take out spot a second after the* **Voice** *begins. Replace with El Lissitzky's 1920 abstract, 'With the Red Wedge Divide the Whites'.*

VOICE: Comrade delegates to the Second Congress of the Third International; Lenin's promise is being fulfilled before your eyes. Denikin's treacherous hordes in the south have been quelled. Now it is the turn of Marshal Pilsudski and his reactionary Polish divisions to feel the bite of our revolutionary anger. Comrade Trotsky sends apologies for his absence – he is taking a short holiday in Poland, in the company of Generals Tukhachevsky and Buddenny and a few thousand comrades of the Red Army. *(Pause.)* Comrade delegates, Europe is little more than dry couch-grass and kindling, waiting for a spark. *(Fade up 'Internationale' here.)* Waiting for *you*, comrades.

Singing louder, more strident. The abstract fades. As it does, 'The Internationale' shifts from march-time to slow waltz, the male choir to small twenties dance band. Fade up on hotel room, the play's single set. Take music out. Hotel Fiorina: good, solid, tasteful, bourgeois. The set represents these values without fully realizing them through committedly naturalistic design. (We have already used a wall for projection, and we'll use it again.) It's mainly furniture anyway: a solid bed and bed table, a divan, a table and three chairs, a couple of armchairs, a carpet, an upright phone. Two doors lead to adjoining rooms and the hotel landing respectively.

Angelica lies in bed. She wears a long and superb nightdress and négligé. She sleeps: lies wholly motionless.

Knock at door. Quiet, firm. Short silence. **Kabak** *in. He stands in the doorway, a bag in each hand, for some moments, reading the room. He is big, very physical, with full beard and black hair. Dressed as he is in impeccable bourgeois style, there is something not quite right about him, as though the form were somehow at war with the content. He closes the door, puts down the bags, walks quietly to the bed, stares impassively at the sleeping face. Finally he picks up a used ampoule from a kidney bowl on the bedside table, smells it, lays it down, wipes his hand on the overlay. His face gives no sort of clue to state of mind or to any discovery he may have made.*

He returns to his case, is bending to open it when Polya comes in, some sewing in her hands. She is young, sturdy, attractive in a heavy, peasant way. She gives a stifled yelp at his presence. He presses his palms downward on the noise, inclining his head towards the bed.

POLYA: I'm sorry sir ... Your letter said tomorrow ...

KABAK: *(crossing to the table with a work case)* I didn't want to waken ... *(He's stuck for a word: he can't say 'Madam' or 'Your mistress', yet 'Angelica' isn't right either.)* ... the Countess. If you insist on calling me 'sir' I shall insist on calling you Pelagia.

POLYA: I'm sorry.

KABAK: Except when I need you to. And when I do, I'll tell you. And don't keep saying you're sorry.

POLYA: I'd forgotten, that's all.

Kabak has opened the smaller of the two bags and removed some files and a black leather notebook. Polya stands uncertainly near the door. Kabak looks for an address and phone number in the notebook.

(advancing) I'll take your bag through ...

KABAK: *(working on)* Leave it.

Silence.

POLYA: I could make you some tea ...

KABAK: *(absorbed)* No thank you. I had a late lunch at the station.

POLYA: *(bursting it out)* The mistress ...

KABAK: In a moment, Polya. Let me finish this first.

Polya subsides grudgingly. There's a sharp outburst from the phone. Kabak crosses the room and picks it up, the black notebook open in his hand.

Yes. *(Slight pause.)* Perfectly satisfactory, thank you. Yes, everything ... Thank you, yes. *(quickly)* One thing. I'm expecting a visitor some time today. Send him up as soon as he arrives, will you. Gramsci. Yes, there is. *(checking notebook)* I want you to ring the Cavaliere D'Avanzo, that's right, at 271. 271. Do it now, I'll wait. *(Pause. He stands very still as he waits.)* Hello, this is Kabak. Yes, this evening. Hotel Fiorina. Room 2, first floor. Tonight would be very convenient. Good. *(He replaces the phone, turns to face Polya.)* What is it, Polya?

POLYA: It started last March. In Vienna. You'd left for Berlin ...

KABAK: April.

POLYA: April. I don't know, I don't know when it was. She started losing ... blood. And, she didn't eat anything hardly. And, she wouldn't see a doctor, of course. Then the pain.

KABAK: The blood came from where?

POLYA: It's a woman's … thing. It's … private.

KABAK: And?

POLYA: *(stumbling)* She's going … she's going … she's going to die.

KABAK: Did *he* say that?

She nods, looks down at her sewing. Kabak stands up, paces the carpet a moment.

Did he say when?

There's a gentle knock at the door.

(fierce, but contained) Damn. Damn. Damn. Damn.

A *second knock.*

You answer it, Polya.

Polya rises to go, drying her eyes.

And Polya.

Polya turns.

Sir?

Polya nods and goes to the door to admit **Libertini**, *the hotelier, a fine, delicate, artistic-looking man of fifty or so, with wavy silver hair and a smart moustache.*

LIBERTINI: *(expansive, pleasantly deferential)* May I come in, Mr Kabak? Thank you. I'm sorry I wasn't here to welcome you when you arrived. Turin is a city at war with itself, as I'm sure you realize, and there is much for a simple hotelier to do, if he is to survive the holocaust.

KABAK: Please, Mr …

LIBERTINI: Libertini. *(advancing well into the* room) Now then, is everything to your liking, Mr Kabak? You have only to say, you know. We're honoured that you and your … wife, the Countess, should grace us with your presence.

KABAK: Everything is perfect, thank you.

LIBERTINI: Sure? *(Waits theatrically for rejoinder that clearly isn't coming.)* Well then. I shan't take up any more of your valuable time. *(He dwells.)*

KABAK: Is there … something else?

LIBERTINI: Well. I was actually wondering how long you intended … staying. The suite, I mean. Your letter from Vienna was somewhat … unspecific.

KABAK: I'll let you know.

Silence. Kabak looks at him for a moment. He might be staring at a grease stain on a wall.

LIBERTINI: Mr Kabak, these are difficult times. The whole of Italy is but a push and a slip away from disaster. A man must pick his way with care … I, er, I understand you're expecting a visitor, a Signor Gramsci ... *(Kabak says nothing.)* If I could give a stranger to our city some advice ... This is not a good man. Indeed there are those who consider him the principal cause of our troubles here in Turin.

KABAK: Mr Libertini *(very patient)* What is it you are trying to say?

LIBERTINI: *(carefully)* Simply, Mr Kabak, if it became known to the authorities that revolutionary leaders were frequenting my hotel, I think it would be a close thing which I lost first, my clientele or my licence.

KABAK: *(silent for a moment, then)* Aah. *(He crosses to his leather case, takes out a hand-sized satchel.)* Mr ... Libertini. I have been in business, one way or another, since I was a boy. And I believe there is no more satisfying and inspiring a way of making a living. So *we* must accept its ... distasteful aspects. There was a time when the world was calm and ordered, when men knew their class, their place, their limits. We now live in less comfortable times. Yet business cannot watch and wait: it has to be working. And if, in its course, I have to shake hands with anarchists and communists and revolutionary subversives of this sort or that, allow me to make my choice and do it.

LIBERTINI: But of course, Mr Kabak. I had no intention of ...

KABAK: *(ignoring him)* I have two things. First: a note, stamped with the Prefect Taddei's own stamp and signed by the Cavaliere D'Avanzo, Commissioner of Public Safety, authorizing me to move freely in pursuit of my work in Turin. *(He shows him the note.)* And ... gold. *(Long pause. He takes out a small wallet, hands it to Libertini.)* Thank you for sparing me your time, Mr ... Libertini. I think we can say a bargain has been struck? *(He takes Libertini's elbow and moves him to the door.)*

LIBERTINI: Yes, indeed, Mr Kabak. *(pocketing the wallet at once)* There's actually no need. No need at all. I simply wanted ...

KABAK: Thank you. And good evening.

Libertini stiffens slightly, converts the gesture into a short formal bow, leaves. Kabak closes the door behind him. It's growing dark now, and Kabak walks round the room switching on the two standing lights but leaving the one by the bed – so that the bed area recedes visually. There is barely a clue as to his mental state, but there is a tenseness, a coiledness about his movements.

KABAK: No need at all! When did you last hear that?

POLYA: I don't know. Vienna? Munich? *(Pause.)* Don't you have ... any fear?

KABAK: Fear? *(Pause.)* No. *(Pause.)* Of what?

POLYA: Prison. Death.

KABAK: I've been in prison. *(scratching his chest reflectively)* And death's a state of mind. A communist is always on leave from death. That little ... eunuch has been dead for years.

He turns involuntarily towards the bed and stares at Angelica. Polya stands up, gathers her sewing, and prepares to go.

POLYA: Will you want food? *(Kabak doesn't answer.)* Let me know if you want food.

KABAK: How long … has she been having cocaine?

POLYA: *(stopping, turning)* On and off, two or three months, I suppose.

KABAK: And it *is* cocaine?

POLYA: That's what they say.

KABAK: How long does it keep her … like this?

POLYA: It depends. Sometimes a day, sometimes less than an hour. It's not dependable.

KABAK: Does she … do it herself?

POLYA: I do it. But she knows how.

KABAK: Thank you.

POLYA: Is that all?

KABAK: Thank you, yes.

POLYA: Ring if you want me. Madame won't hear it now.

KABAK: Good night.

POLYA: Good night, sir. *(She stops, turns.)* Sorry.

KABAK: *(gently)* Good night.

She leaves, by the connecting door. Kabak stands looking at Angelica for a moment longer then uproots a bottle of vodka from his case and takes a long, rather violent pull from it, before fishing out a pair of knee-boots and an old, high-necked smock. He wanders round the room, removing jacket, waistcoat and shirt, pulling hard on the bottle from time to time; clicks off one light, another; carries a chair from the table to the bed and sits down facing Angelica, his face very close to hers. After a moment he clicks on the light by her bed. The bed area is now pooled, the rest virtually extinguished. He pulls again at the bottle, then drops his head on to his chest. Angelica half-wakes, enough anyway to recognize his presence, though the drug continues to separate perception and feeling, and to draw upon realities from different points in her person. She strokes his hair very gently.

ANGELICA: You came.

KABAK: *(lifting his head)* Hello, my love.

ANGELICA: You said you'd come and you came.

KABAK: Shh. You'll tire yourself.

ANGELICA: I couldn't believe it when your letter came. It's been so long.

KABAK: Five months.

ANGELICA: Five months. Five deaths. And I so wanted to be well for your arrival.

KABAK: Now, now. We'll talk in the morning. Sleep.

ANGELICA: Christo.

KABAK: Mmm.

ANGELICA: Say something.

KABAK: Yes, I do.

ANGELICA: That's good. That's good. Christo.

KABAK: Shh.

ANGELICA: I can't ... love you ... tonight.

KABAK: I know.

ANGELICA: It's ... the time of the month.

KABAK: Angelica ...

ANGELICA: Soon. *(taking his hand)* Soon.

KABAK: Yes.

ANGELICA: And you'll take me to the summer estate.

KABAK: Of course.

ANGELICA: This time you will. You really will.

KABAK: I really will.

ANGELICA: To be free of St Petersburg for a while. It can be quite stifling, even to one who loves it as I do. Tell me how it was.

KABAK: *(pause)* Not ... greatly changed.

ANGELICA: *(faintly)* Tell me. Please.

KABAK: *(playing by ear throughout)* The Tsar was in residence in the early spring. A ball every night for a month. Nights filled with the jangle of sleighs and the snuffling of horses. And then the greenness of leaf and grass over the city. The river *moving* again. *(He checks she's asleep, continues his narrative without a shift of tone or inflexion.)* And the revolution *moving* again. Soviets. An ecstasy of willed achievement. The Whites brought to their knees. The class enemy brought down like quail. The iron brain of Comrade Lenin hammering out the future.

Angelica screams briefly, troubled in her sleep. Kabak continues gently.

No place for you, my love. No place at all.

He leans forward and kisses her forehead. She moans but sleeps on. Kabak stands, looks at the bottle but does not drink, and switches out the light.

SCENE TWO

Lights up. Kabak sits in a chair staring at the landing door. He wears the full Bulgar dress – trousers, high boots, high-necked smock, a thick leather belt clasped round the waist. The bottle and two glasses are on the table by his right hand. Silence for sometime. A quiet knock.

KABAK: Come in.

The door opens and **Gramsci** *enters. He is of dwarf-like stature, though not a dwarf, seriously hunchbacked – his spine was broken as a very young boy – with a heavy head, broad brow, thin lips, big lively eyes behind rimless glasses. His black hair is thick and bushy, his skin swarthy. He's 28. In spite of his deformity, he moves with grace, almost supplely. His hands are particularly fine: thin and elegant. His dress is careless, untidy, a little raffish, full of stains and patches: he could almost be a painter preoccupied with some important canvas. When he smokes – which is virtually continuously – he often leaves the cigarette between his lips the whole time, so that his coat and trousers receive the dropping ash. He carries a dark, wide-brimmed, very scruffy, soft felt hat in both hands.*

GRAMSCI: Kabak?

KABAK: Gramsci. Come in, comrade. I'm honoured you came so soon. Will you have a drink? I have only vodka here at the moment, but I could easily … send out for something else if you'd prefer it.

GRAMSCI: *(interrupting)* Thank you, no. I don't drink. *(He has advanced into the room; he takes out a box of cigarettes, lights one abstractedly, stands staring at the Countess's bed.)* It has less far to go in me than in most, the doctors tell me. *(He stares on.)*

KABAK: We could move into another room, if you'd rather.

GRAMSCI: *(turning)* No, no. I hadn't expected …

KABAK: Perhaps I should explain …

GRAMSCI: Not at all. Please.

A small silence. Kabak moves to the table, takes up the second glass.

KABAK: We won't disturb her.

GRAMSCI: Good.

KABAK: *(a little uneasy)* Won't you sit down? *(He gestures to the table.)*

GRAMSCI: Thank you, yes.

He takes a chair, back to the bed, eases himself on to it, very tired. He lights another cigarette, looks carefully round the room, does nothing about Kabak's unease.

KABAK: Perhaps I could begin by explaining my presence here.

GRAMSCI: *(a slight pause)* To be frank, I'd be happier if you would begin by furnishing some proof of identity. Forgive my caution, but the city is ringed with troops and every third hotel waiter is a police informer. I'm intrigued to know how you managed to penetrate the cordon.

KABAK: Of course. *(crossing to briefcase on floor by table)* My name is Christo Kabak. Executive Member of the Communist Party of Bulgaria. Here, take this. *(Hands, him wallet from briefcase.)* Representative of the Executive Council of the Communist International in Moscow. Please read it. It's all there.

GRAMSCI: *(glancing briefly at the opened wallet)* I've no doubt. At least the picture's a likeness. *(a dry grin)* Regrettably I have no Russian.

KABAK: *(at last)* All right, it could be a forgery.

GRAMSCI: Civility did not permit. But the forging of papers of accreditation has grown into a major Italian industry. I've no doubt its workers will soon be demanding union recognition.

KABAK: Well, then?

GRAMSCI: Well, then. *(Pause.)* You came by train.

KABAK: This morning.

GRAMSCI: From Moscow?

KABAK: No, from Rome.

GRAMSCI: From Rome?

KABAK: I had business there.

Pause.

GRAMSCI: Business. You are in fact travelling as a businessman. You arrived at Porta Nuova dressed as a bourgeois, not er – *(Waving hand at Kabak's dress.)*

KABAK: Yours is a bourgeois country, comrade.

GRAMSCI: *(smiling) Touché.* But we're working on it.

KABAK: I saw Chiarini in Rome. He sends his regards.

GRAMSCI: Does he?

KABAK: *(reaching for wallet again)* And this letter.

GRAMSCI: *(taking it)* Ah, Italian. Of a kind. *(Reads. Finally)* So you're Il Cuculo.

KABAK: I believe so, yes.

GRAMSCI: *(holding out hand)* Welcome to Turin, comrade.

Kabak crosses the room, draws Gramsci to his feet, kisses and hugs him unrestrainedly.

KABAK: Thank you, thank you. It's an honour to be with you.

GRAMSCI: The honour is ours, Comrade Kabak. The factories will welcome your arrival with open arms.

KABAK: Well, perhaps we should talk about that. I'm … my visit is not exactly … planned. What do I mean? It's not … official. I have no particular brief to conduct here in Turin … at least as far as you and the movement are concerned.

GRAMSCI: *(pausing)* I see. That's an exaggeration. I don't see.

KABAK: My mission in Italy is both delicate and … secret. I'm afraid I'm unable to say what it is. Except that I have to see a number of people. *(Pause.)* In Rome three days ago, nearing the end of my mission, I heard from Chiarini of the possibility of confrontation between employers and workers in the north. It … seemed right that I should come here and see for myself. That's all.

GRAMSCI: You have no messages, nothing?

KABAK: Nothing.

GRAMSCI: And? *(Gesturing towards the bed.)*

KABAK: From Vienna, two days ago, I think. She is, in a manner of speaking, my wife.

Gramsci gets up, walks about a little, goes back to the table, takes out a cigarette, lights it from the stub in his mouth.

GRAMSCI: How long will you stay?

KABAK: As long as I think I might be useful.

GRAMSCI: You think?

KABAK: That's right.

GRAMSCI: But you won't address the factories.

KABAK: I don't know. Perhaps I'll be more useful doing other things.

GRAMSCI: Like?

KABAK: I have gold. I have … influence in the Prefect's office.

GRAMSCI: D'Avanzo?

KABAK: D'Avanzo.

GRAMSCI: We call him 'the snake'. One day somebody will take a stick to him.

KABAK: And ... I have some experience … of revolution.

GRAMSCI: Of course, comrade. I had not meant to …

KABAK: Of course not. Please. (A *short silence. Kabak sits opposite Gramsci.)* I'd be deeply grateful if you would agree to give me the necessary background. I

have seen the troop encampments outside the city. I have heard something
about the work-to-rule. And I understand from tomorrow's *Avanti* that workers
have taken over factories in Milan. Beyond that, very little.

GRAMSCI: *(drawing deep breath)* It's hard to know where to begin. Whatever
account I give will inevitably include elements you understand as well as much
you don't. If you fall asleep, I'll know I've failed to get the balance right.

KABAK: Tell me how we've arrived here.

GRAMSCI: *(grinning)* You mustn't ask for the whole of Italian history. But ... our
situation is probably not greatly different from Germany's or France's or
Austria's. That's to say, we suffered massively from a ruinous war. That's to
say, the people suffered. The capitalist simply grew fatter. Prices soar, wages
plummet. Inflation bites like a mad bitch, and Pirelli declares a profit of seven
million lire – seven million lire – in 1917. And while thousands die of
starvation and misery, our capitalist masters are working the rackets. In 1918
we discover a dozen top firms exporting silk by-products to Switzerland,
whence they are re-exported to Germany – where else? – and used for
munitions. And when Italian soldiers capture German trucks, whose tyres do
you imagine they find on them? Pirelli. Only the best. The Socialist Party of
Italy opposed the war completely, of course. But we weren't immune to the
suffering it created among the mass of our people.

KABAK: But the Socialist Party of Italy was the first party to affiliate
unequivocally to the Communist International.

GRAMSCI: It depends what you mean by unequivocally. In Italy, there is always a
considerable distance between form and content. We subscribe to the Third
International and do nothing to further its aims. Perhaps we require another word.

KABAK: And now?

GRAMSCI: Since the war ended, the Party and the unions have sat on the
revolutionary ardour of the organized workers and peasants. I'm sure it's a
familiar story. We have pressed for reforms, not transformations. We have
struck for better wages, better conditions; but we have led from the rear.

KABAK: I heard Turin was different.

GRAMSCI: From whom?

POLYA: Lenin.

Pause.

GRAMSCI: You flatter us. Turin is very special. Turin is the industrial city *par
excellence*. The proletarian city *par excellence*. The Turinese working class is
compact, disciplined, mature, wise, different perhaps from any other in Europe.

KABAK: And you lead them.

GRAMSCI: *(laughing)* No, no. My God, no. I am an intellectual who works alongside them. They have leaders enough from within. Parodi, Boero, Forticchiari. Big men.

KABAK: Go on. About Turin.

GRAMSCI: Turin is the vanguard of the Italian revolution. But there is still much work of education, of preparation. We have suffered more than our share of defeats. We are still learning Lenin's lessons: a slow and painful process.

KABAK: Do you have time?

GRAMSCI: I don't know. We must make time.

Pause.

KABAK: Are you so sure it isn't now?

GRAMSCI: No. But I'm not sure it *is*, either. In each factory we have planted together a single seed of revolution: the factory councils. Free from Party direction; free from trade union interference. Not merely here in Turin, but throughout Italy. But they must sprout *together,* or there is no harvest. Merely a series of frail stems waiting for the scythe.

KABAK: *Could* it be now? After Milan.

GRAMSCI: Objectively, I fear not. The Party under Serrati offers no genuine revolutionary leadership. The unions are content to press wage claims. *(Pause.)* Olivetti is Secretary of Confindustria, the Employers' Federation. Do you know what he said last month, here in Turin? 'The future belongs to the organized classes.' What about that? In Italy, only the Marxist fails to recognize that as a self-evident truth.

KABAK: What happened last April?

GRAMSCI: *(surprised a little)* Last April? The strike, you mean.

KABAK: Chiarini said something about it, before I left Rome. Not a lot. But he said it was important.

GRAMSCI: He was right. *(Pause.)* In April we were forced into a crippling strike in Turin, in defence of the factory councils. We held out for *eleven days:* imagine that, a general strike for eleven days. Half a million workers. Peasants in surrounding areas even provided us with food and money. After five days we asked the Party and the General Confederation of Labour to extend the strike; to make it national. Serrati, our national leader, answered personally: 'We are not bound to accept battle every time that the enemy provokes it. Apparently the leaders of the Turin movement think differently. Let them not try to burden the broad shoulders of the Party directorate with the responsibility for a defeat that does not touch it at all.' With socialists like that, who needs a bourgeoisie? For the first time in our history, a proletariat undertook a struggle for the control of production, rather than for economic advantage. And they have their heads spat upon by their leaders, who themselves understand history about as profoundly as chickens understand soup. In Sardinia, we tell a fable of a

badger pursued by a hunter. Badger learns that the hunter is sick and will die
unless he can secure a physic concocted from Badger's testicles. So, in order to
survive, Badger chews them off himself. And swallows them. And survives. In
a manner of speaking. I won't labour the point.

KABAK: But the employers *are* going to take you on? After Milan.

GRAMSCI: That's right.

KABAK: To smash your strength in the factories?

GRAMSCI: Yes.

KABAK: So what will you do?

GRAMSCI: We will fight.

KABAK: *(softly)* How?

GRAMSCI: The union has ordered factory occupations if there are lock-outs.

KABAK: And after?

GRAMSCI: We will run the factories. We'll rename them 'soviets' and continue
   production ourselves. That's what the factory councils are for, in the long run.

KABAK: And then?

GRAMSCI: I don't know. We shall have to see.

KABAK: You sound doubtful.

GRAMSCI: There are only two possible outcomes to the present situation.
   Revolution. Or the most horrendous reaction. No other possibility exists. If we
   fail, perhaps we fail utterly.

KABAK: *(searching the wallet)* Perhaps there *was* one message. Here. *(opening
   folded foolscap sheets)* I had it from Chiarini in Rome. *(reading)* To the Central
   Committee and all members of the Italian Socialist Party. To the Revolutionary
   Proletariat of Italy. *(reading hurriedly down the page, to himself)* Here. *(now he
   is translating)* 'The Executive Committee of the Third International knows that
   there are circumstances in which it is more advantageous for the proletariat to
   wait, until its own forces are stronger and those of the bourgeoisie weaker. But
   it should not be forgotten that every hour's respite will be used by the
   bourgeoisie in their turn to rally their forces, to form a bourgeois white guard.'
   And ... listen ... to this *(scanning page, turning it)* This is it. 'It is clear ...
   quite clear ... that nowhere in the world is the victory of the proletariat possible
   without suffering and deprivation for the workers. If the revolution does not
   come quickly in other countries, the Italian proletariat will have to travel the
   same hard and painful road as the Russian proletariat. The Italian working class
   shows astonishing unanimity – it is as one *for* the revolution. The Italian
   bourgeoisie cannot count on their regular troops, who will at the decisive
   moment go over to the rebels, and the greater part of the peasantry are *for* the
   revolution. It is now up to the Italian workers' party'.

GRAMSCI: Chiarini?

KABAK: More. 'We repeat that we are opposed to artificially provoked putsches, we are opposed to actions that have not been thought out in advance. Equally, we are opposed to the proletarian party turning itself into a fire brigade, which puts out the flame of the revolution, when that flame is breaking through every crevice in capitalist society. *(placing deliberate emphasis on next three sentences)* In Italy there are at hand all the most important conditions for a genuinely popular, great proletarian revolution. This must be understood. This must be the starting point. This is the contention of the Third International. The Italian comrades must themselves determine the next steps. The decisive struggle is approaching. Italy will be Soviet.' Signed. G. Zinoviev, President; N. Bukharin and N. Lenin, Members, Executive Committee of the Communist International. Moscow. August 27th, 1920.

Silence.

It seems Comrade Lenin has already heard the story of the badger with no balls.

GRAMSCI: It's a very old story.

Telephone rings.

KABAK: Excuse me. *(lifts receiver)* Thank you. Ask him to wait. *(phone down)* D'Avanzo.

GRAMSCI: *(rising)* I'll go.

KABAK: No, please. Let him wait.

GRAMSCI: No, I must. Talking tires me shamefully. *(Fiddles for pocket watch, inspects the time closely, brow furrowed.)* Tomorrow I might be helping to run Fiat Centre Plant. Tonight I should sleep. Good night.

KABAK: You'll ... keep me informed.

Gramsci turns at the door, looks steadily at Kabak.

GRAMSCI: Of course. Comrade. *(smiling)* So long as you promise me the same. You know you can get me through the Chamber of Labour. And I know you're here. *(Turns to leave. Turns back, hand on open door.)* Watch out for D'Avanzo. He's most dangerous when he rattles.

Gramsci leaves. Kabak stretches, aware of his own fatigue. He shrugs out of his tunic and stands for a moment, fingering a deep scar across his chest. Finally he takes a bathrobe from his bag and slips it on. At the table he drains the bottle of vodka, crosses to phone, picks it up.

KABAK: Would you send the Cavaliere up now, please. Thank you.

Kabak replaces phone, crosses to bed, stares down at Angelica, who stirs fitfully. **D'Avanzo** *knocks and enters. Kabak turns quickly to face him.*

D'AVANZO: Mr Kabak? I'm awfully sorry, I didn't ...

KABAK: Please. Do come in. It's good of you to call at such an hour. Won't you have a seat? *(gesturing to armchair)* Let me get you a drink.

D'AVANZO: *(sitting down)* Thank you. Anything will do. *(Mops neck with handkerchief.)* Did you ever know such a summer? Do you wonder the world's at sixes and sevens, in heat like this.

KABAK: *(handing half-filled glass)* Vodka. Be careful. It's very deceptive.

D'AVANZO: Thank you. Like most things Russian, I fancy. *(Looks around room.)* I couldn't help noticing you'd already been busy. *(looking finally at Kabak, who stares back impassively)* The dwarf. I saw him leaving. He's a dangerous man, that one. Pity. A brilliant brain.

KABAK: *(holding glass up) Salute!*

D'AVANZO: *Salute!*

They drink.

Mmm. That's good. That's very good.

They stare at each other in silence. Finally.

Well, Mr Kabak, could we get down to business. I take it you received your authorization permits in Rome.

KABAK: I did, yes.

D'AVANZO: And you had no difficulty with the troops outside the city.

KABAK: None at all.

D'AVANZO: Excellent. *(Pause.)* Did ... Chiarini mention ... the price?

Kabak nods briefly.

That's good. I find I haggle rather poorly. My dignity is a serious obstacle.

KABAK: *(ironically)* I can imagine.

D'AVANZO: *(still mildly, unoffended)* You must not think dignity is the unique preserve of the poor or the professional revolutionary, Mr Kabak.

KABAK: *(drily)* I'll try not to. What else can you do for me?

D'AVANZO: You have only to ask. If it is within my power I will do it. For a price.

KABAK: Good. I take it you have no especial objection to being paid in gold, Cavaliere?

D'AVANZO: *(very seriously)* None at all, Mr Kabak.

Kabak gets up and paces the room. Turns.

KABAK: How long before they catch you?

D'AVANZO: Catch me? At what?

KABAK: This. Corruption. Treason.

D'AVANZO: My dear Kabak, this is Italy. I doubt if there's a civil servant in the country who isn't taking something home each week for services rendered. I just happen to have given more time and thought to the matter than most of my colleagues. That's why I'm here now.

KABAK: Go on.

D'AVANZO: Italy will have its revolution. In an uncertain world, that is one certainty I am prepared to stake my future life and prosperity on. Despite which, most of my state functionary colleagues continue to support the bourgeois cause, with a kind of lemming blindness that would be quite touching if it weren't so appallingly pathetic. Since the end of the war I have made it abundantly clear, in a thousand practical ways, that I will be available for duty *the morning after* the revolution takes place. *(Pause. Drinks.)* I'm not a revolutionary, Mr Kabak. I'm a realist. You will have need of us the morning after.

KABAK: And the Prefect?

D'AVANZO: Taddei? Pure as snow. Impeccable, innocent, honest, loyal, boring. Show him a brothel and he'd think it was a shrine to the Virgin Mary. He's no problem.

KABAK: *(decisive)* All right. Answer me this. Could the factory occupations in Milan trigger off a revolution throughout the country? And if so, which person or group is likely to direct it?

D'AVANZO: *(holding glass out)* Could I have another?

KABAK: *(taking glass, filling it)* Certainly.

D'AVANZO: Thank you. It's funny, I thought you'd have heard from Gramsci.

KABAK: Heard what?

D'AVANZO: The owners have declared lock-outs in almost every major town in Italy. Here in Piedmont alone, apart from Turin, over a dozen large towns are affected. Alessándria, Asti, Novara, Vercelli, Acqui, Arquata Scrivia, Novi Ligure, Casale, Tortona, Callarate. In Lombardy, besides Milan, of course, there's Bergamo, Cremona, Crema, Pavia, Legnano, Como, Lecco, Varese, Brescia. In Veneto there's Verona, Udine, Padua, Venezia, Treviso, Castelfranco Veneto, Battaglia. Do you want more? There's plenty yet. In Emilia: Bologna, Modena, Ferrara, Reggio, Piacenza. In Tuscany: Firenze, Pisa, Siena, Pontedera, Piombino, Portoferráio, Livorno, Arezzo, Pistoia, Grosseto, San Giovanni Valdarno, Castelfiorentino, Lucca. In Marche: Ancona. In Umbria: Terni and Perugia. In Campania: Napoli, San Giovanni, Castellammare, Torre Annunciata. In Sicily: Palermo. *(Pause.)* I imagined he'd have told you.

Long silence.

KABAK: *(very quietly)* Go on.

D'AVANZO: Two things. Turin will occupy the factories tomorrow morning. Within two days there will not be an engineering factory in Italy that is not in the hands of the workers.

KABAK: And?

Long pause.

D'AVANZO: The government has at present no intention of using troops to eject the workers and repossess the factories on behalf of the owners. Our illustrious prime minister is keen to appear impartial in the matter. Besides which, he has a pathetically inadequate military force; and he can't be at all certain that what he does have won't defect to the side of the workers if matters get out of hand. *(Long pause.)* Does that answer your question?

KABAK: Not quite. You suggest that the objective conditions for revolution might well exist. But revolutions must be led. The question still is: by whom?

D'AVANZO: I'm not a politician, Mr Kabak, I'm a poor state bureaucrat trying to survive in rather difficult times. If I were a gambling man, I should put my money on the Socialist Party Directorate being unable any longer to damp down the revolutionary ardour of the glorious Italian proletariat. Serrati will be a revolutionary hero in spite of himself, I shouldn't wonder.

KABAK: What about Gramsci?

D'AVANZO: Strong enough in Turin, I understand, but without a power base nationally. I doubt it, quite honestly. For one thing, he's uncommonly modest, for one so arrogant in other ways. Personally diffident, if you know what I mean.

Kabak goes to the table, begins scribbling rapidly on a piece of paper. Finished, he folds it and hands it to D'Avanzo, who opens it and looks at it with furrowed brow.

KABAK: *(while he now takes small wallets from case)* It won't make too much sense to you unless you read Russian. I want you to send it to Moscow – I've put the address in Italian at the bottom, can you see it? Here. *(handing two hand-sized pouches over)* You'll find twice the sum you agreed with Chiarini. And there is more.

D'AVANZO: *(taking the pouches)* This could prove extremely dangerous, Mr Kabak.

KABAK: *(hard but quiet)* But you'll do it none the less.

D'AVANZO: *(getting up)* I shall do my best.

KABAK: And your best will be good enough. That telegram must reach Moscow by the end of the week.

D'AVANZO: I shall do everything in my power to see that it does.

KABAK: *(tossing another small pouch at him)* Do that. Good night, Cavaliere.

D'AVANZO: *(stiffening formally)* Good night, Mr Kabak.

D'Avanzo leaves. Kabak drains his glass slowly, sways just a little with fatigue and the effects of the alcohol, finally walks to the bell and rings it, quite loudly. He stands by the table until Polya arrives, struggling into her dressing gown.

POLYA: *(tired)* Yes.

KABAK: *(taking bathrobe off, again scratching scar)* Have you got any goose grease?

POLYA: Any what?

KABAK: Goose grease. Goose grease.

POLYA: Goose grease? Where would I get goose grease from? What would I be doing with goose grease anyway?

KABAK: *(sharply)* All right. You haven't got any goose grease.

POLYA: *(a bit sullen)* What is it for?

KABAK: I'm stiffening up. Here and here. *(pointing to bullet wound across pectorals and another in shoulder. Grinning)* I suppose it means it's going to rain.

She still stares on.

I wanted you to rub it on me. Massage. Never mind. Go to bed.

POLYA: There's some oil.

KABAK: What kind of oil?

POLYA: Oil. Olive oil, I think.

KABAK: Would that do?

POLYA: I don't know. Can't imagine it being any worse than goose grease.

KABAK: All right. Fetch it.

She goes. He takes his boots and socks off, stands naked save for trousers. He sits down in the chair facing out and rests head on arms on the table. Polya returns with the bottle.

POLYA: It's olive oil. You'll smell like a waiter when I've finished.

KABAK: All right. Just rub it in.

She starts the massage.

POLYA: *(examining the scar on his shoulder)* Uushh! Just look at that. That's really ugly. Uushh! Was it a bullet?

KABAK: Two bullets. Can you see, lower down? *(She traces down with her finger.)* That's it. *(Showing her.)* Came out under the arm here.

POLYA: I can't imagine why you do it.

KABAK: I don't suppose you can. Any more than I can understand why you consent to being a personal maid all your life.

POLYA: *(laughing)* Well, nobody's shot at me yet.

KABAK: You have your scars, Polya. *(Leans back, so that she can begin to massage the front of his neck and down across his pectorals. He's now looking up at her.)*

POLYA: Just look at that. I don't know how you survived, I don't really.

KABAK: Because I wanted to, Polya. Needed to.

POLYA: Well, an inch to the left and all the wanting in the world wouldn't have saved you. *(She rubs on, gradually becoming aware of his steady stare.)*

KABAK: *(finally, low voice)* Polya.

Polya ignores him, continues the massage.

Polya.

POLYA: What?

KABAK: Polya.

POLYA: Please, just, please let me just … do this and go back to bed.

KABAK: *(stretching arms up and back to clasp her upper arms)* Polya, Polya.

POLYA: *(she freezes)* Please don't. Please. Please don't.

Kabak gets up quickly, tries to take Polya in his arms. She resists, but very unsurely, aware of her position as servant.

Please don't. Please. Please don't, sir.

KABAK: Polya, listen. Polya. Polya, listen.

He quietens her with the palm of a hand. She is in some disarray. Her eyes glare above the hand.

Listen. I don't want to force anything upon you. I … I want to sleep with you. I'm lonely. I want to love somebody. I want … to love somebody. That's all. *(He removes his hand gently. She still stares at him like a small, frightened night animal.)* That's all. That's all.

POLYA: *(shaking her head)* No. No I couldn't. I couldn't. No I couldn't. I love my mistress and I couldn't do that to her. No. I couldn't.

KABAK: Then don't. It's all right. *(Pause.)* Look, she's going to die. Right? It doesn't matter what you do, she's going to die. *Think* what that means to you. Hunh? Just think of that. Go on.

POLYA: I couldn't. I couldn't. I don't care. She trusts me and I love her.

They stare at each other for a long moment. Then.

ANGELICA: *(not moving, but clearly awake))* Polya.

POLYA: *(startled)* Madame?

ANGELICA: Do it.

POLYA: Madame?

ANGELICA: Do it, Polya. Do what Mr Kabak asks.

Silence again. Kabak has frozen, his back to the bed. Slowly Polya begins to unbutton her dressing gown, takes it off, unbuttons her nightdress, removes it. She stands naked before Kabak, her eyes cast down, her body slightly crouched. He looks at her very carefully, then picks up his bag and leaves through the adjoining door. Polya stands staring ahead of her at the bed. Angelica makes no move.

SCENE THREE

Stage completely black. Bring up factory sounds, machinery. Men's voices, in meeting. Fade up, centre, and take out again, the following: pictures of workers defending factory gates; preparing food; tramway strike; railway strike at Mantua; communist group at Lancia (Turin) during occupations; Red Guards on factory roof, armed with rifles, pistols, machine guns (all available through Centro Gobetti, 6 Via Fabbro, Turin). As this last image appears, the men begin singing 'Bandiera Rossa', the mood jubilant yet disciplined. The image remains throughout the 'factory meeting' that follows, but is taken out for the Gramsci-Kabak exchanges.

Gramsci walks hesitantly forward as the singing ends. There is cheering, whistling, jocularity as the crowd catches sight of him. (The interjections from the men may be done on tape, or by actors in the auditorium.) As Gramsci reaches a sort of lectern at the front, the side walls of the auditorium are gradually lit to reveal blow-up photographs of this actual meeting (available at Centro Gobetti). The theatre is now the factory; the audience, the workers.

GRAMSCI: Comrades. *(Noise begins to die down gradually.)* Comrade workers, representatives of the factory councils of Fiat Centre, Fiat Diatto, Fiat Brevetti, Scat, Acciaien Fiat, Lancia, Itala, Lingotto Fiat, Industrie Metallurgiche, representatives of the Turin Chamber of Labour and of the Turin section of the Socialist Party of Italy. Perhaps I should begin by thanking the owners for the use of the hall.

Laughter.

I mean it, comrades. I mean you. You are the owners now. And you must never forget it. Sunday, September 5th, 1920. Red Sunday. Our first. And we choose to celebrate it ... by working, first of all; and then, by discussing, sensibly, seriously, above all honestly, what we have done and what is left to do. That's as it should be. You are right to feel happy. You are right to feel exhilarated.

But it would be a sort of treason, comrades, to let that euphoria blind us to the gravity of our position or to the enormity of the task that confronts us.

VOICE: Cheer up, Nino, it might never happen.

Laughter.

GRAMSCI: *(drily)* Precisely, comrade. It might never happen. It's that that makes me sad.

VOICE: It will, Nino, it will.

Great cheer.

GRAMSCI: *(as they subside)* What we have done. We asked for better wages and conditions. They said it wasn't possible. We applied a work-to-rule. They applied a lockout. We occupied. The industrial strength of Turin, of all Italy, is in the hands of the Italian working class. Production continues. Despite difficulties of materials supply, transportation, capital, markets for finished products, and the defection of technical support, we continue to produce. Our first great lesson, comrades: we are learning how to become producers, active, vital, controlling, instead of mere consumers, passive, inert, controlled. You will have heard of peasant uprisings, in Sicily, in Lucania, in support of our cause. Peasants supporting workers, just think of that, comrades! It could almost be Russia!

Laughter, cheers. Somebody begins singing 'The Internationale,' others join in.

The state, meanwhile, stands by. The Old Fox hasn't even bothered to come back off his summer holiday. He's still at Bardonecchio, sunning himself.

Laughter.

The army stands by. We wait. Italy waits. Europe waits.

Somebody sings 'Why are we waiting'; others join in, amid laughter and cheers.

Meanwhile, we make a few discoveries. In the director's safe at Fiat Centre, for example, mountains of anti-Russian propaganda, a blacklist of militant workers, and details of an espionage service against the labour movement that would make the work of the carabinieri seem gentle horseplay between young lads of the same village. On the blacklist, every factory council member, almost without exception. Though the exceptions are interesting. As well as others: in particular, Matteo Dotta and Domenico Arduina, who died at the hands of the fascists in this year's May Day parade. At last, at last we can get a clear and undistorted picture of our employers, not as individuals, not as people with particular skills and functions, not as loose arrangements of reciprocal needs and interests, but nakedly, as a class, organized against us, an army in a war, capable of any heroism or treachery in the defence of their motherland. And we can see, too, that this motherland is not Italy, that fat-headed, sore-arsed sow: the motherland is Capital, sleek, dark-eyed, bright, warm, passionate Capital. Who wouldn't defend her, the young, delicious whore! Well, perhaps one or two of us.

Laughter.

VOICE: She's got the pox anyway, Nino.

Laughter.

GRAMSCI: Well, that's what we've done. We've taken power into our own hands. And we have shown that workers' control is a reality. The question that now concretely confronts us is the question Lenin posed many years ago: simply, what is to be done? Between *here* and *there,* the whole of our history trembles. Our leaders are in little doubt. Even now, Buozzi and D'Arragona are in a huddle with the employers, 'seeking solutions'. But in this new situation, where remote trade union leaders no longer direct, where the moral position of the worker assumes a different form and value, it is *you,* comrades, who will decide. And if I say, honestly and clearly, what *I* think should happen, I do so in the knowledge that you will listen – *(twinkling)* with no more respect than I deserve of you – and then make up your own minds, on the evidence confronting you. *(Pause.)* There are many possible lines of march. But make no mistake, comrades: if you want revolution, you must take it for yourselves. It will not be handed to you, on a plate. *(consulting watch)* I have spoken too long already.

A *few shouts of 'Aye', quickly followed by a thunder of Noes.*

They may be right, comrades. Intellectuals always imagine words win wars. And they don't. Let me finish with three slogans, the simple signposts of *my* line of march. One: create urban soviets. Two: prepare for insurrection. Three: forge links with the peasants. If we are to win, we must break out of the factories, wage war on the state as well as the employer. If we are to win, we must arm ourselves for a prolonged *offensive.* Merely defending the factories against attack is not, in itself, an insurrectional act. And if we are to win, we must eat, and that means we must involve the peasants in our struggle.

Cheering, applause.

One last word. You are my comrades, in the deepest sense that history allows for that word. You are the best disciplined, most mature working class in Europe, in the world. Soon you will be invited, by your enemies, I'm afraid to say, to put up or shut up. No other city proletariat will have the experience or the deep courage to act as insurrectional vanguard. All I want to say is: decide for yourselves. It is no cowardice to say no, if by saying it you survive to fight more fruitfully another day. It is no heroism to say yes, to be mown down by overwhelming force of opposing arms, while your party and your unions stand by with folded arms and watch you destroyed. Find your courage where it is. Beware rhetoric! Even mine!

He steps down. Cheering. Applause. Singing 'Bandiera Rossa', deep and melodic. Fade to black.

Stage in complete darkness. Kabak snaps on light on table. Gramsci walks into the light, throws his hat on to the table and sits down in the chair opposite Kabak. A cigarette hangs from his lips. He is tired but wide awake. Kabak has been drinking but isn't drunk.

GRAMSCI: Did Palmi ring?

KABAK: Nobody rang.

GRAMSCI: He said he'd ring as soon as the meetings broke up.

KABAK: Relax. It's barely nine. In any case, you know what will happen. Togliatti will tell you nothing you don't know already. D'Arragona will urge moderation. Bordiga will urge intransigence. Everyone else will urge a compromise. When reformist leaders talk to capitalist employers, what else can happen?

Silence. Gramsci lights another cigarette from the stub of his current one. Kabak tops up.

GRAMSCI: Any word from Moscow?

Kabak shakes his head. Another silence.

You place extraordinary faith in D'Avanzo.

KABAK: Faith? *(a short bark of a laugh)* I place faith, extraordinary or otherwise, in nobody. Believe me, Nino. It is not a question of faith. It's just the nature of the occupation I'm embarked on. Help I must have. Whether I win it or buy it isn't important. But I cannot choose whether I have it or not.

GRAMSCI: Perhaps it's Moscow.

KABAK: *(finally)* Perhaps it is.

Pause.

GRAMSCI: Have you spoken to D'Avanzo?

KABAK: Just the once. Seven, eight days ago. Just after I met …

GRAMSCI: Yes, I remember.

KABAK: Not a word since. Not a peep. He might be just a little out of his depth, the way things have blown up.

GRAMSCI: Your gold could keep him afloat for a while.

KABAK: *(gravely)* My gold will take him to the bottom.

The phone rings shrilly. Kabak unhooks it.

Yes. Just a moment. For you.

Kabak hands receiver to Gramsci.

GRAMSCI: Hello. Hello, Palmi. *(silence as he listens)* Go on. *(silence again)* D'Arragona did? Ahunh. And what did you say? Yes, surely, surely. Look, Palmi, I'm with our friend. Can I ring you back? Just a moment. *(Fishes pencil and pad from pocket.)* Go ahead. 792. Got it. Thanks, Palmi. Half an hour at the most. All right. *(He hangs up).* The meeting continues. Recessed for an hour.

KABAK: And?

Pause.

GRAMSCI: The Directors of the General Confederation of Labour want to know whether the Turin section will be prepared to lead an insurrection.

Silence. Kabak pours another drink, takes a long swig.

KABAK: What hangs on the answer?

GRAMSCI: Perhaps nothing. Perhaps everything. They don't say. They don't commit themselves at this stage to any course of action. They simply want to know if we are prepared to present them with one more possibility, before they make up their minds.

KABAK: *(mildly, as though remarking on the weather)* Then you say yes.

GRAMSCI: *(quietly)* No. We say no.

KABAK: *(low)* You cannot say no. If there is no insurrection, there is no revolution.

GRAMSCI: And if we lead the insurrection and there is still no revolution, there is no longer a working class in Turin.

KABAK: Jesus God, man, this is warfare you're talking about. Of course there are dangers. Somebody, sometime, must be moved up to the front. Surely you can see it!

GRAMSCI: But is it now? And is it us?

KABAK: *(searching for words and patience)* Look … Holy Christ … look, erm, isn't it this way? The Party and the unions, like the state and the employers, want peace. Revolution is not on the agenda. The Party and the unions are currently meeting in Milan to see how negotiations with the employers might be reopened. That's right isn't it? All right. Now, only one thing stands in their way. The working class of Italy. *They* don't want peace. Perhaps they don't know yet what they do want. But as yet it isn't peace. The Confederation knows it. The Party knows it. You know it. The workers are forcing their national leaders into increasingly more radical postures. At length, those miserable men are forced to consider the possibility of an insurrectionary thrust. Not surprisingly, they look in your direction. Now, Nino … if you say no, they have called you out, make no mistake, comrade, they have called you out and from now on in we'll have only rhetoric to fall back on, because the real action will be OVER. You'd better be oh so clear about that, comrade, because that's the way it will be. Now I'm telling you. *(He is angry, trembling a little. He takes a drink, rather hastily, spills a bit on his shirt front, begins dragging at it with the palms of his hands.)*

GRAMSCI: *(very quiet)* Have you finished?

KABAK: *(not looking, still wiping his front)* I've finished.

GRAMSCI: It's possible you're right ...

KABAK: *(interrupting; fierce)* I am right.

GRAMSCI: It's just possible we're both right. That's to say, both wrong as well. Neither yes nor no, I mean. From where we are, there is no answer to make that will advance the cause of a communist revolution.

KABAK: Metaphysics, Nino. They don't become you.

GRAMSCI: You know what happened last April. We led the Italian proletariat, the Party and the unions in a general strike. Unfortunately, though not by accident, they did not follow. So we were isolated, our supply lines cut, our carefully nurtured alliance with the Piedmont peasants smashed. We crawled back to work on our hands and knees. The compact between capital and labour couldn't have been more complete. Bosses, union and Party leaders conspired to fill our mouths with soil. Now, the same people are inviting us to put ourselves at total risk, in all-out confrontation, without any commitment on their own part to support us.

KABAK: It is a risk you must take. It's September now.

GRAMSCI: We have risked too much already. I will not allow that class to be wiped out. I could not survive it.

KABAK: No sentimentalisms, please. You must not confuse revolutionary duty with bourgeois conscience.

GRAMSCI: Nor shall I, comrade.

KABAK: You cannot say you love your working class too much to put them at risk, and then imagine you're saying something profoundly revolutionary.

GRAMSCI: That isn't what I'm saying. I am saying that they are too important to the world revolutionary movement to squander on a dubious adventure that could well have been concocted precisely to produce their annihilation.

KABAK: And you ... could not survive it? Do you mean ... you love them?

GRAMSCI: Yes I do. That's exactly what I mean.

KABAK: I see.

GRAMSCI: What?

KABAK: You cannot *love* an army, comrade. An army is a machine. This one makes revolutions. If it breaks down, you get another one. Love has nothing to do with it.

Gramsci is overwhelmed by this. He gets up, walks away from the table, comes back to it, lights another cigarette.

GRAMSCI: *(finally)* Oh, comrade. Oh, comrade. Listen. *(very quiet, very gentle)* There is nothing more relevant than love. There is nothing in the world more relevant than love. When I was a child – inside this … body – I imagined I could never be loved. For many years, the thought that I could be loved seemed an absolute, almost fatal, impossibility. So perhaps I came to the masses with the same mechanical view of them, and my own relation to them, as you have just propounded. Use them. Tool them up. Keep them greased. Discard them when they wear out. But then I thought, how can a man bind himself to the masses, if he has never loved anyone himself, not even his mother or his father. I thought, how can a man love a collectivity, when he has not profoundly loved single human creatures. And it was then I began to see masses as people and it was only then that I began to love them, in their particular, detailed, local, individual character. You would be wrong to see this … love … as the product of petit-bourgeois idealism. It is the correct, the only true dialectical relationship between leaders and led, vanguard and masses, that can ensure the political health of the new order the revolution seeks to create. Treat masses as expendable, as fodder, *during* the revolution, you will always treat them thus. *(Pause.)* I'll tell you this, Comrade Kabak, if you see masses that way, there can be no revolution worth the blood it spills. *(Long silence. Gramsci picks up the phone.)* Yes. Milan. 792. Thank you.

He holds the receiver in his hand, fishes for a cigarette and lights it with the other.

KABAK: You are wrong, Comrade Gramsci.

GRAMSCI: I think not, Comrade Kabak. *(to phone)* Hello. Hello, Palmi. Yes. *(Long pause. He listens gravely for some moments.)* No, say what we agreed. 'We in Turin cannot assume the responsibility of an armed struggle without assurance that the rest of Italy would also fight, without assurance that the Confederation and the Party, in their usual way, would not let all the military forces of the state concentrate on Turin as in April.' Do you have it? Good. That's fine, Palmi. Good luck comrade. *(Puts phone down.)*

KABAK: *(finally)* So?

GRAMSCI: *(very tired now)* I don't know. Palmi says he smells a deal. D'Arragona and the Party are pressing for a referendum.

KABAK: Of whom?

GRAMSCI: The General Confederation of Labour.

KABAK: On what issues?

GRAMSCI: Basically, to stay here or move to there.

KABAK: *(bitter)* This isn't a revolution, it's a bloody Italian farce. Jesus God, revolution by referendum. You could almost laugh. *(Takes another drink.)* Well, comrades, what do you think, eh? Shall we have a revolution, or shall we just play silly buggers for a bit and see what happens? Now it's up to you, so take your time, don't hurry it now.

There is a high shriek from the bed, a babble of words. Kabak strides swiftly over, clicks on the bed light. He begins to swab Angelica's face with a wet cloth from the bed table.

ANGELICA: It's here. Underneath. Under the skin. It's not a part of me. It's foreign. I can feel it moving. Underneath. In the hands. In the legs.

KABAK: Hey, hey, hey, hey, hey, hey, hey, hey. *(He mops her brow with the cloth.)*

ANGELICA: Russia *is* in Europe. You'll have to tell them. They don't appear to know. Underneath. Not a part. But *there* all the same.

KABAK: Yes love. Now sleep. Come on. Sleep. *(He soothes her.)*

ANGELICA: I saw a soldier. He was crawling in the snow and ... he had something ... in his hand. And ... when the carriage ... got closer ... I saw it was his ... boot. As we passed him, he raised the boot in the air. And I saw it still had ... his foot in it. We ... drove on ... and ... I didn't look back.

KABAK: Sh, sh, sh. Hey, hey, hey. You must sleep, love. Try to sleep. Try to sleep.

ANGELICA: Yes. Yes. *(Drowsing.)*

KABAK: There ... now. There ... now.

ANGELICA: *(eyes closed; very rational voice)* Why do you do it, Christo?

KABAK: Do what, love?

ANGELICA: Why do you kill? And maim?

KABAK: Please. Sleep.

ANGELICA: Tell me.

KABAK: It would take too long.

ANGELICA: Longer ... than there is, you mean.

KABAK: Yes. For both of us.

ANGELICA: Say it, Christo.

KABAK: Yes, I do.

ANGELICA: *(low, fierce)* Say it.

KABAK: I love you. I love you.

ANGELICA: Why is it always so hard?

KABAK: It isn't. It's just ... so pointless.

She sleeps suddenly, the cocaine reasserting. Kabak stands up, waits a moment longer, clicks off the light, returns to the table.

GRAMSCI: I think I should leave you.

KABAK: *(a lot of emotion just held under)* She's dying. She has a cancer in her womb. A lonely fruit for a womb. We occupied the family estate in Kiev. 1918. Her husband fled, she ... remained. We've been ... *(He stops suddenly, turns his back on Gramsci, swivelling in the chair.)*

GRAMSCI: Is there anything you need?

Kabak doesn't answer. He sits staring into the darkness. Gramsci rises.

I'll say good night. *(Pause.)* Comrade.

He leaves. Kabak turns to the light. He weeps quietly and hopelessly. Finally he clicks off the light.

ACT TWO

SCENE ONE

Project factory slides. 'Bandiera Rossa', now muted, over. At the end, very unexpectedly, the distant thud of marching boots, and a slide of fascist guards holding Roman daggers aloft (Moro, Milan). This holds the stage, unexplained, for half a minute, then fades. Lights up on hotel bedroom. Night. Kabak is at the telephone. The bed is empty.

KABAK: *(who's been holding)* I see. Do you know where he is? Yes, I know he's a busy man but ... yes, I know that too. Milan? With Taddei? But you're not sure. Ahunh. Well, thank you. *(Depresses receiver rest several times.)* Hello. Hello. *(Pause.)* Yes, do you happen to know the Prefect Taddei's number? That's right, the Prefect. All right, I'll wait.

He takes out a large black revolver from the table drawer, breaks it, takes aim at the connecting door through which Polya arrives suddenly, carrying the sleeping Angelica in her arms. She stops in the doorway. Kabak lowers the revolver slowly, replaces it in the drawer.

POLYA: Is it safe?

KABAK: *(to phone)* Good. Try it please. Now. I'll wait.

Polya carries the Countess to the bed, places her in it, covers her solicitously. She does it with stolid power, not unlike a peasant carrying a calf.

POLYA: She's clean.

KABAK: But dying.

POLYA: She'll die clean.

KABAK: Good.

POLYA: It's not bad.

They look at each other hard. Finally Polya breaks the gaze and leaves.

KABAK: *(to phone)* Hello. Good evening. I wonder if you could tell me whether the Cavaliere D'Avanzo is there at the moment. *(Listens briefly.)* Yes. My name is Kabak. I'm here on business and ... there is a matter I have to settle with the Cavaliere. Thank you.

He holds receiver away again, holding. He looks casually at the bed. Angelica lies stone white in it. She could be dead already. Polya comes back in.

POLYA: I've made coffee. Do you want some?

Kabak nods. Polya withdraws.

KABAK: *(to phone)* Yes. *(listens)* I see. Perhaps in Milan? Well, thank you anyway. No, no message. Goodbye.

Kabak puts phone down, stands, stretches, walks round room, looks out of window. Polya carries tray in, places it on the table, pours coffee.

POLYA: Sugar?

KABAK: No.

POLYA: *(turning)* Anything else?

KABAK: Polya. Stay a minute.

She stands, impassive.

Sit down. Please.

Polya sits stonily on one of the hard chairs by the table. Kabak moves from the window towards the centre of the room.

(uncertain) I'm ... not very sure ... how long I'll be able to remain in Italy.

Polya stares ahead, totally unresponsive.

I've lost contact with Moscow. The man who was to have helped me appears to be more interested in helping himself. And my comrade in Rome has gone to ground. In any case, it looks as though things're through here ... *(Silence. Polya doesn't reply.)* There is the question ... of the Countess. *(Another silence.)* I can't take her with me.

POLYA: *(very quiet and tight)* Can't you?

KABAK: You know I can't. I never did ... not even when she was ... well.

POLYA: That was when she was well.

KABAK: *(very patient)* Polya, listen to me. Your mistress will die. In a week. In a month. She will die.

POLYA: And you should be with her.

KABAK: Perhaps. But I can't stay here. And she should die in a bed, not a couchette between nowhere and nowhere.

POLYA: It would not be nowhere if you were there. *(Silence.)* What do you want me to do?

KABAK: Just stay. Be with her.

POLYA: You insult me to imagine I would de otherwise.

Knocking at door.

KABAK: I'm sorry, thank you.

Polya crosses to the door, opens it. Libertini enters, carrying a small package. Polya closes the door.

POLYA: Will that be all, sir?

KABAK: Thank you, yes.

Polya leaves by the connecting door.

LIBERTINI: *(curious, looking round)* Good evening, Mr Kabak. A fine evening. I think things are at last looking up for us all, in Turin.

KABAK: I'm glad you think so, Mr Libertini.

They look at each other for a moment. Libertini remembers the package.

LIBERTINI: Ah, This package arrived by special messenger from Berlin. From … I happened to notice the sender's name here … a Signor Chiarini.

KABAK: *(taking it)* Thank you. It's good of you to bring it yourself.

LIBERTINI: Not at all. A pleasure.

Silence again.

KABAK: Was there something else?

LIBERTINI: No. No, no. I … er … I simply wanted to know how you were faring in our city. I seem to have seen very little of you, since you came.

KABAK: I'm faring very well. Thank you.

LIBERTINI: Well. I won't disturb you any further then.

KABAK: Thank you.

LIBERTINI: I take it he's a … business associate of some sort.

KABAK: What?

LIBERTINI: *(pointing to the package in Kabak's hand)* Chiarini. I take it he's a business …

KABAK: Yes.

LIBERTINI: It really is amazing, you know. All this conflict and turmoil and destruction, and anarchy, and yet somehow, we manage. We manage to keep the wheels oiled, the pumps primed. Somehow we manage. We will not be stopped, will we, Mr Kabak?

KABAK: *(a tired irony somewhere)* We will not, Mr Libertini.

LIBERTINI: At the office of the Prefect only yesterday, *(Kabak looks at him sharply, momentarily startled. Libertini rambles on, seemingly unaware.)* waiting for my licence to be renewed, they were laying 5 to 1 on a full return to work by the end of the month. I suppose you had heard that the results of the referendum are due very soon.

KABAK: Yes, I had.

LIBERTINI: I think we have a victory on our hands, Mr Kabak.

KABAK: Very likely. *(Long pause. Neutral, final)* Well.

LIBERTINI: *(fiddling in waistcoat pocket)* Ah. While I remember. There is the matter of the ... telephone. *(Finds paper; takes it out; studies it.)* I'm not sure how you would care ... to pay. I have had a list of ... outgoing calls drawn up by reception. Would you care to check it? It's simply ...

Kabak stretches a slow hand for it, looks hard at Libertini as he takes the paper back, finally looks down at it, studies it for a long time. Libertini stands very still, tense; a tiny exultancy is working to get out, but his control is supreme.

KABAK: *(finally)* Yes. You appear to have it all there. Would you prefer I paid you now?

LIBERTINI: As you wish, Mr Kabak. Entirely as you wish.

Kabak takes out a wallet, riffles 1000-lire notes, looks at Libertini, who smiles rather sweetly at him.

KABAK: I imagine ... ten thousand lire might cover it?

LIBERTINI: Amply, Mr Kabak.

Kabak hands him the notes. Libertini smiles, counts them, places them gravely in his own wallet, holds out his hand once more. Kabak hesitates.

The list, Mr Kabak.

It registers. Kabak hands it to him.

I shall need it for the accounts. Well, that's ... er ... that's very good. I've enjoyed our little chat. I always find foreign businessmen ... curiously invigorating. You will let me know if there's anything more I can do for you.

KABAK: There is one thing.

Libertini turns back.

It's possible I shall be called away rather suddenly in the next few days.

LIBERTINI: Ah. I'm sorry to hear it.

KABAK: However, I should like to rent the rooms for, say, another month. Long enough for ... my wife to recover her health.

LIBERTINI: Delighted to accommodate you.

KABAK: *(smiling)* Yes. *(He draws his wallet out.)* Ten thousand lire, how does that sound?

LIBERTINI: It sounds excellent, Mr Kabak.

KABAK: *(handing him the money)* Good. Thank you very much.

LIBERTINI: Thank you very much. *(Pause.)* Will you be returning to Bulgaria?

KABAK: Does it matter?

LIBERTINI: *(quickly)* No, no. I simply wondered …

Libertini begins to move towards the door. Kabak begins to tear open the package, read its contents, his back now half-turned, his body tensing as he reads. As Libertini opens the door, he discloses **Terrini** *framed in the doorway. Terrini makes a small silencing beckon to Libertini, who offers a small and rather scruffy smile in return, bows, looks once at Kabak, and leaves. Terrini stands unannounced for a moment longer; reads the room; looks hard at Kabak's back; then knocks, very deliberately, on the jamb.*

KABAK: *(sharply)* Come in. *(He turns towards door, seeing Terrini in already.)*

Terrini is tall, slightly stooped, about 40, hardfaced, sombre, tough. Though he is a commendatore, his dress is sober, unflamboyant. In some ways, he is the physical and moral counterpart of Kabak: the state's professional guardian of the status quo.

TERRINI: Mr … Kabak?

KABAK: That's right.

TERRINI: Terrini. Commendatore.

KABAK: I'm sorry, I don't think …

TERRINI: From the office of Prefect Taddei.

KABAK: I see. Won't you come in?

TERRINI: Thank you.

KABAK: Have a chair.

TERRINI: Thank you. *(Sits in armchair.)*

KABAK: Can I get you a drink?

TERRINI: Thank you, no.

Silence. Kabak looks at Terrini, who looks back with composure.

KABAK: What can I do for you, Commendatore?

TERRINI: Your presence in Turin this past three weeks hasn't gone entirely unnoticed, Mr Kabak.

KABAK: I'm flattered. I can't imagine why the Prefect's office should be interested in an obscure Bulgarian businessman.

TERRINI: Can't you? Come now, Mr Kabak. Of all your possible deficiencies, I shouldn't have thought imagination was among them. Can't you really?

KABAK: I'm supposed to have done something? Infringed a business code, perhaps? Even so, it's hardly a matter for the Prefect to concern himself with.

TERRINI: Not ... business, Mr Kabak. Not, at least, the sort of business you are ostensibly here to pursue.

KABAK: Look, Commendatore. I'm perfectly prepared to play mouse to your cat for as long as it amuses you. But if you could devise some speedier means of arriving at your substantive point, I'm sure we'd both appreciate the time you saved.

TERRINI: Brevity has never been our strong suit, Mr Kabak. To an Italian, arrival is anti-climax. The only excitement is the journey itself. *(Feeling inside coat for wallet, opening it, taking out folded piece of paper)* However. Since you appear to be in something of a hurry. Here.

Hands Kabak paper, which he reads.

Yours I think. Your telegram. Russian *and* code. It kept us busy, I can tell you. *(Pause.)* D'Avanzo really isn't to be trusted.

Kabak stands up quickly.

Oh, I don't mean to say he betrayed you. Not that he wouldn't have, mind, if he'd seen more gold in it for himself. No, it's simply that we've had the Cavaliere under scrutiny for some time now. His every move has been monitored since the beginning of the year. Quite an impressive dossier it makes too. You should read it sometime.

KABAK: Perhaps I'll get the chance to, one day.

TERRINI: I really do doubt that Mr Kabak. I really do. We ... er ... didn't arrest him because ... well, frankly, he was more use to us where he was. Attracting all the sordid deals and all your sort of ... business ... into one small, manageable cesspool. Couldn't have worked better.

KABAK: So what do you want of me?

TERRINI: Well, it did occur to me you might quit Turin rather soon. Say, tomorrow morning? There's a good train for Berlin leaves at 10.15. I'd consider it a personal favour to me if you'd agree to be on it.

KABAK: And if I refuse?

TERRINI: You won't refuse. You've nothing to keep you here now. The ... revolution is over. Or didn't you know. The workers are about to ratify the national agreement. And that particular book is closed for ever, I fancy.

KABAK: I wouldn't count on it, Commendatore.

TERRINI: I'm afraid I have to, Mr Kabak. My life will be spent in the service of the Republic. And this Republic will not sanction a communist revolution. You're not playing games with children, Mr Kabak.

KABAK: Am I allowed to send a telegram? I shall need ... instructions.

TERRINI: Leave it be. Comrade Lenin has enough problems. Just take the train.

KABAK: I have no choice.

TERRINI: Precisely. What an enviable state.

KABAK: My wife is sick. She can't be moved.

TERRINI: The Countess can stay. She won't ...embarrass us.

KABAK: *(finally)* All right then.

TERRINI: Splendid, splendid. I knew you'd see it. *(standing)* Oh, in case you oversleep, I have arranged for a couple of my aides to be in attendance to ... run you down to Porta Nuova.

KABAK: You're too kind.

TERRINI: Not at all. It's the least we could do. *(Pause.)* The power is coming back, Mr Kabak. It's a good feeling, after all that ... anarchy. The man Gramsci. I understand he's planning to address factory meetings tonight, when the final results of the referendum are through. Have a word with him, there's a good fellow. Make him see reason. Turin can't go it alone. It makes no sense to remain in occupation when the rest of the country has pulled out.

KABAK: Gramsci doesn't need my advice, Commendatore.

TERRINI: Well, perhaps not. *(Moving to door)* I'll take my leave of you, Mr Kabak.

Kabak stands unmoving in the middle of the room. Terrini gives an ironic bow.

I'm sure we shall not meet again.

Terrini leaves. Kabak walks nervously about, then rings bell for Polya. After a moment she arrives, begins clearing up crockery.

KABAK: It's tomorrow.

POLYA: What's tomorow?

KABAK: I leave tomorrow.

Long silence. Finally Polya begins to stack coffee things on tray.

I'll leave you gold. The room will be yours for another month. That should ... I'll need my bag packing tonight.

POLYA: *(loudly)* It's not ...

KABAK: (fierce) Shut up. I'm not concerned with your stupid peasant loyalties and your ... sentimentalisms. Do what I say. Is that clear? Just ... do what I say. *(calming)* I'll leave you an address poste restante. If you need me ... you can contact me there. All right? All right.

Polya walks out, eyes lowered, face set. Kabak picks up phone, bumps rest up and down impatiently.

(eventually) Yes. 442. That's right. *(Waits, still tense.)* Hello. Chamber of Labour? Yes, is Comrade Gramsci there, please? Where? I see. Do you know ...? No, it doesn't matter. Thank you. Oh, just a minute. Yes. Have we had the results of the referendum yet? Ahunh. Could you tell me what they ...? *(listening)* Ahunh. Ahunh. Thank you very much indeed. Thank you comrade. And you. *(Puts phone down. He paces a moment, rubbing palms together, then returns to the phone.)* Can you find me the number of Signor Valletta? Valletta. That's it. Of Fiat, that's right. No. I'll wait.

Lights out.

SCENE TWO

Total darkness on set. The factory-meeting slides slowly reappear (cf page 95). This time there is no music, no gaiety, no excitement. Men's voices are muted, anxious. A spot on front of stage, into which Gramsci walks, carrying papers in his hands. His floppy hat is on his head. He is deeply tired, apparently beaten. But his eyes are still fierce, uncontained, behind the rimless spectacles. A small cheering and drumming set up, as he appears; but they quickly subside. And still there is no singing. He takes up the position, stage left, he had in the first factory scene.

GRAMSCI: Comrades.

Noise dies quickly.

I have to announce the results of the national referendum of all workers in occupation of the factories. For acceptance of the agreement negotiated by the union with the employers: 127,904. Against the agreement: 44,531.

Some slight cheering, tailing swiftly off.

Abstentions: approximately 210,000. You cheer too soon, friends. We will see what there is to cheer about. *(Pause.)* The agreement this vote has ratified is as follows: ONE, an increase of 4 lire a day across the board throughout the industry, equivalent to an average 10 per cent wage increase; TWO, half of one per cent increase on overtime rates; THREE, six paid holidays a year for all workers in the industry; FOUR, payment to be agreed by negotiation for all production undertaken and completed during the occupation; FIVE, no victimization of militants, and particularly those who took leading roles on the factory councils; SIX, under pressure from government, the employers have agreed to implement a policy of workers' control ...

Big burst of cheering.

... in principle, comrades. IN PRINCIPLE. No details have been worked out. No minimum conditions imposed by our union leaders. This big empty clause simply offers 'workers' control' at some unspecified date in the future. *(Long pause.)* That is what you have voted for today, comrades. That's the 'package' they offered and you accepted. Now, think back to that first wonderful heady Red Sunday, and of what we talked and hoped for, and ask yourselves again what it is we have to cheer about. *(Pause.)* All right. Perhaps our optimism was unwarranted. Perhaps we should have been able to predict all along the precise way in which our leaders would betray us with this massive act of class collaboration. For that is what it has been, comrades. And perhaps we should have prepared ourselves in advance for that most perfect tool of such collaborative acts: I mean, of course, the referendum. What an exquisitely democratic, deeply counter-revolutionary form the referendum is! For what is its main, its essential function? To strengthen the shapeless mass of the population and to crush the vanguards that lead those masses and give them political consciousness. So that even here, in Turin, the vanguard's vanguard, it has worked.

Shouts of 'no'.

Oh yes, comrades. The figures are unequivocal. *(Consulting papers.)* For the agreement: 18,740. Against: 16,909. Abstentions. 1,024. *(Pause.)* Even here, comrades. *(Pause.)* Well, we will see. Perhaps your determination to be the last to go back will help. But it is perspective, not pride, that we are in need of now. *(Pause.)* It might be that the working class can chalk up a great leap forward. Certainly as a mass, shaped and disciplined in the factories by its direct representatives, it has shown itself vibrantly capable of running its own affairs. And that, *as a fact*, may have consequences of incalculable social importance. Only half a century ago – a single tock of time in the long history of class struggle – that same class was still, in Marx's phrase, a sack of potatoes, a ... generic unknown, a ... shapeless gathering of individuals, without ideas, without will, above all without perspective. It was, if you like, comrades, a blind boil on the arse of capitalism: annoying, but hardly fatal. *(Pause.)* Today, it appears to be the entrepreneurial class that has become a sack of potatoes, an aggregation of the useless and the idiot, powerless, nerveless, will-less. *(Pause.)* If we find this; if we find that this action, these occupations, have advanced the proletariat as a ruling class; if we find, too, that this new political situation is a spring driving irresistibly towards the conquest of power –

Cheering has begun earlier in this speech, but sporadically, a sort of nervous punctuation to Gramsci's political syntax: now it begins to reach for a full period, more certain of itself, happier with the drift of the rhetoric. Gramsci waits in silence till it subsides.

WHAT THEN? *(Long pause. Gathering passion, bitter vehemence)* Why doesn't it happen? Why has no genuine attempt been made to reach our goal?

We must find answers, comrades, or these questions will outstare us for ever. *(Long pause.)* All right. Let us look at the 'tactics' pursued by our 'leaders', culminating in today's referendum. The 'leadership' of our movement boasts that it bases itself in the 'masses'. What does that mean? It means, comrades, that it asks the 'masses' for prior permission to act; and it 'consults' those 'masses' when and how *it* chooses. *(Hardening. Very emphatic)* Learn this, comrades, and teach it to your children. A revolutionary movement cannot be led in this way. A revolutionary movement can only be led by a revolutionary vanguard, with no commitment to prior consultation, with no apparatus of representative assemblies. *(Pause. Then very big)* Revolution is like war: it must be scrupulously prepared by a working-class general staff, as a national war is prepared by the army's general staff. *(Long pause. Some coughing, mumbling, muttering)* Comrades, Comrade Trotsky said, between the revolutions of '17: 'We shall not enter into the kingdom of socialism with white gloves on a polished floor.' Comrades, Comrade Trotsky was right. For Italy as for Russia. Today, the proletarian vanguard stands rocked, disillusioned, threatened with fragmentation, dispersal, even rout. Why? Because we have consistently failed to face up to the major problem of revolutionary movements; I mean, the problem of political organization. Examine our base, inside the General Confederation of Labour, inside the individual unions, inside the Socialist Party of Italy. What do you find? Nothing worth crossing the street for. *That's* the real situation, comrades. And it won't be oaths and reproaches that change it, it will be tenacious, patient and ruthless preparation. In this way, we will make it possible for a revolutionary general staff to emerge, capable of carrying out wide-scale collective action with intelligence and with daring. *(Long pause. Gathering himself for the final assault)* Today, we have the referendum. It must not be made the occasion for despair and dissolution. Rather we must see it as an urgent lesson from history; as a call for tighter, even more disciplined action. The liberation of our class is not a part-time hobby, and it isn't the work of small minds and feeble imaginations. When disillusion prospers like malaria in a southern swamp, when a cause has been recklessly squandered by those to whom it should never have been entrusted, only he who can keep his heart strong and his will bright as steel can be regarded as a fighter for the working class; can be called a revolutionary. *Evviva* Lenin! *Evviva la rivoluzione!*

The men take up the slogans, which boom like tribal chants. Gramsci's light fades slowly.

SCENE THREE

Lights up. Kabak, in suit, white shirt, tie, sits by the table staring at the landing door. Polya in, with brandy and cigars. She places them at the table. A quiet knock at the door. Polya crosses to open it. Kabak stands. In the doorway, **Valletta**, *personal assistant to Giovanni Agnelli, Chairman and Managing Director of Fiat. Valletta is about 60, a very fine example of old-style, courteous, bourgeois gentleman; civilized; very cultured; gentle.*

KABAK: Please do come in, Signor Valletta. It's very good of you to agree to see me like this at such short notice.

VALLETTA: *(moving into room)* Not at all, Mr Kabak. No trouble at all. Business never is.

Polya closes door, leaves.

KABAK: Have a seat, won't you.

VALLETTA: *(taking an armchair)* Thank you.

KABAK: Some brandy, perhaps.

VALLETTA: Well, perhaps just a little.

KABAK: Good. Good. *(He begins to pour.)* You've worked for Fiat a long time, I take it.

VALLETTA: Since it became Fiat. This is my twenty-second year with the company. Sometimes I think you don't work for Fiat, you live for it. What is important is that I am able to speak for Fiat. *(Pause.)* That's to say, as Chief Executive Assistant to Giovanni Agnelli, founder and Chairman of the company. I have his personal authority to present your … propositions to the board for their scrutiny.

Kabak opens the table drawer and removes a slim case, from which he draws a file. He hands the file to Valletta.

KABAK: My portfolio. There's a summary of proposals on the first page.

Valletta opens the file, flicks through it, quickly, then settles to read the summary. Kabak prepares two cigars, hands Valletta a glass.

VALLETTA: Ah. Thank you.

And a cigar.

Thank you. *(Lights it deftly.)* Mmm. Mmm.

KABAK: *(the toast)* To business.

VALLETTA: To business.

They drink. Valletta settles into the file. Kabak resumes his seat opposite, sits very still, glass in hand. There is a long silence while Valletta reads.

(Finally) I take it you have … credentials.

Kabak begins to get up.

No, no I would … have to see them, I mean, before we parted.

KABAK: Of course.

VALLETTA: *(purposefully)* I think I can say we would be interested.

KABAK: Good.

VALLETTA: Naturally, I should need to read the portfolio more fully.

KABAK: Naturally.

VALLETTA: Perhaps you would be good enough to fill in some of the background now.

KABAK: By all means. *(Pause.)* More brandy?

VALLETTA: Just a little.

Kabak stands to take Valletta's glass. Pours, speaking as he does.

KABAK: It has taken our government some time to make up its mind on concessions to foreign capitalists. Our major problem is simply to prime the industrial pump. We have, as you no doubt know, vast natural resources. Timber in the north – 2,000 miles of it, from the Yablonovi Mountains in the east to the Finn of Karelia in the west. In Siberia there's tin, iron, coal, copper. And a whole range of non-ferrous metals. In the south and east, enormous agricultural concessions, *(Hands Valletta his glass; resumes seat; homes in now.)* And of course, we have oil; particularly in Kamchakta. You'll see that forms the basis of a separate protocol in the portfolio. *(Pause.)* There are those inside the Soviet government who would argue – still, I fear – that the granting of concessions in return for capital, or capital equipment, credit and services, is the kiss of death to revolutionary socialism. Comrades who have never understood the first thing about capital or its uses have imagined we can, in some magical 'communist' way, run a state and a society without it. Fortunately, they look to have been defeated. Our central economic planning authority has recently issued a major decree broadly supporting a concession policy. You will find, as an appendix to the portfolio, a list of seventy-two items already cleared. *(Pause.)* Is there anything further I can tell you, Signor Valletta?

VALLETTA: Well, you might indicate, however tentatively at this stage, what it is your government would require of Fiat, in return for ... concessions.

KABAK: Certainly. First, capital.

VALLETTA: Difficult. We are ourselves currently negotiating a massive capital loan from America.

KABAK: But not impossible, I fancy. Particularly if you can reinvest at a higher rate than the interest on the original loan.

VALLETTA: *(smiling)* As you say, not impossible. You'll make a good capitalist, Mr Kabak.

KABAK: *(laughing)* I've been trained to regard that phrase as a necessary contradiction in terms, Signor Valletta. But I thank you for the compliment.

VALLETTA: What else?

KABAK: Equipment. Plant. Marine and stationary. Cars. Lorries. Tractors. Locomotive boilers. Machine tools. Maintenance and repair. Three-quarters of your product, in fact. *(smiling)* You can keep your aeroplanes for the time being.

Longish pause.

VALLETTA: What would happen if we wanted, say, for example, to set up a Fiat enterprise in Russia?

KABAK: You'll find it clearly taken care of in the portfolio. The decree sets it all out, I think: remuneration, exporting rights, agreed proportions to host state. It's all there.

VALLETTA: What about duration?

KABAK: Long enough to ensure an adequate return on investment. In addition, a cast-iron guarantee against nationalization or confiscation.

VALLETTA: There would have to be. *(Pause.)* And labour?

KABAK: Available under the conditions prescribed in the Soviet labour code.

VALLETTA: That's a code I'm not exactly ... familiar with. Could you ...?

KABAK: You have nothing to fear from it, Signor Valletta. It's all in the portfolio, of course, but after the events of the last few months in Italy, I fancy you would find labour relations in our country a distinctly welcome change.

Silence for a fair bit.

VALLETTA: *(eventually)* Good. I'm glad I met you, Mr Kabak. May I take the file with me?

KABAK: By all means. *(Phone rings.)* Will you excuse me for a moment. Please help yourself to brandy.

Kabak answers the phone, Valletta pours himself a small drink, sits down again, browses through the file.

(into phone) I said I wasn't to be disturbed. *(Pause.)* I see. No, tell him ... ask him to wait. That's right, wait. No, down there. Thank you. *(Puts phone down.)* I'm sorry about that. Somebody has arrived to see me.

VALLETTA: *(rising)* Well, since we appear to have done our business ...

KABAK: *(signalling him down)* Please, Signor Valletta ... I would be offended if you left. Please.

Valletta subsides, smiling.

Thank you. *(Kabak pours himself another drink.)* In any case, you haven't seen my credentials. *(He opens the drawer, removes an envelope, takes a small book like a passport from it, which he hands to Valletta.)* I think you'll find it all in order.

VALLETTA: *(studying it)* I'm sure I shall, Mr Kabak. I'm sure I shall. Yes, that seems perfectly proper. *(handing it back)* Thank you very much.

KABAK: Thank you, sir. *(raising his glass)* Your health, Signor Valletta.

They drink.

VALLETTA: Thank you. I'd like to propose another toast, but I fear you'd find it in dubious taste.

KABAK: Please.

VALLETTA: My toast is: business as usual.

A beat.

KABAK: *(raising his glass)* Why not? Business as usual.

They drink. Kabak sits down again.

VALLETTA: Why did you leave it so long?

KABAK: I don't ...

VALLETTA: Before seeing me, I mean. I heard of your arrival almost a month ago.

KABAK: I see. I ... there were other pressing matters I had to deal with.

VALLETTA: Yes.

KABAK: Personal. You understand.

VALLETTA: Of course. It did just occur to me you might have been awaiting the outcome.

KABAK: I wouldn't say that. The outcome never really seemed in much doubt, I regret to say.

VALLETTA: I must confess, I would have enjoyed a little of your sang-froid at the time.

KABAK: I prefer to call it ... professionalism, Signor Valletta.

VALLETTA: Call it what you will. We were trembling in our boots, I can tell you.

KABAK: I know. Unfortunately, so were we. At least, our leaders were.

Silence.

VALLETTA: I have read some Marx, you know.

KABAK: Really.

VALLETTA: At university. Here, in Turin. He makes a lot of sense.

KABAK: We think so.

VALLETTA: But there *is* a flaw.

KABAK: Ah.

VALLETTA: There is. He underestimates us. The bourgeois. He underestimates our passion. He underestimates our intelligence and our discipline. Above all he underestimates our ability to adapt. *(Pause.)* Today, I was putting the final touches to our plans for a new social welfare programme. You'd have been impressed, Kabak. We're establishing a new Central Training School. It will offer free training to all apprentices between 14 and 18 who gain admission. We're establishing a health organization, to care for the health not only of employees, but of employees' families too. It will begin as a mutual benefit society, but I can see a day when our workers will receive, free of charge, every kind of medical, dispensing and hospital treatment; when Fiat will provide sick pay; even grants in aid to cover funeral expenses. We'll provide convalescent homes; recreational facilities; sanatoria in the hills; holiday camps for workers' children. I can see a day when Fiat workers will live in Fiat houses; when every Fiat worker will live Fiat, when every Fiat worker will be Fiat.

KABAK: *(finally)* And God said, *'Fiat Lux'*; and there was Fiat.

VALLETTA: My vision amuses you.

KABAK: No. Not amuses. *(Pause.)* Not … amuses.

Long pause.

VALLETTA: We will adapt, Mr Kabak. We will become the comrades of the future. *(He gets up, places his glass on the table, stubs his cigar.)*

KABAK: Once again, thank you for coming.

VALLETTA: Not at all. My pleasure.

KABAK: I can be contacted through Chiarini in Rome. I look forward to your decision.

VALLETTA: I'll do what I can.

(He's at the door.)

KABAK: Signor Valletta.

Valletta turns. Kabak crosses to a small cupboard, takes from it a small wallet.

I'd like you to take this, as a personal gift from my government. As an earnest of our sincerity and good intentions.

VALLETTA: What is it?

KABAK: Gold.

VALLETTA: No. I mean, what is it for?

KABAK: I told you. It's a gift.

VALLETTA: *(smiling bleakly)* I've already said I'll do what I can. Good night, Mr Kabak.

He leaves. Kabak places the wallet on the table, drains his glass, pours another drink, crosses to the phone, picks it up.

KABAK: Hello. Yes, send him up now, please.

He replaces the receiver, crosses to the table, takes the revolver out of his jacket pocket and places it in the table drawer. A knock at the door.

   Yes.

Gramsci enters. He is drawn, tired, very slow in his movements.

   Gramsci. Come in. I'm sorry you had to wait. I had someone to see me.

GRAMSCI: *(remaining in doorway)* I saw him leaving. Vittorio Valletta.

KABAK: That's right. Come in, rest your feet.

GRAMSCI: *(standing firm)* I can't stay. I've work to do. *(Pause.)* I heard you were leaving.

KABAK: That's right. Tomorrow. The Prefect's booked my ticket. One-way to Berlin.

GRAMSCI: I see. I wondered if there was … anything … *(He gestures towards the bed.)*

KABAK: No, comrade. That's … taken care of.

GRAMSCI: Right. That's … all right, then.

KABAK: Ahunh.

GRAMSCI: Did you hear about D'Avanzo?

KABAK: No.

GRAMSCI: Shot. They dragged him out of the canal this evening.

KABAK: An occupational hazard. Perhaps he had simply outlived his usefulness.

Long silence.

GRAMSCI: I'll say goodbye then.

KABAK: Oh, while I remember. Chiarini sent me details of a letter from Moscow to the Italian workers. Did you see a copy?

Gramsci shakes his head.

   It's here somewhere. *(fumbling in overcoat across chair-back)* Here it … is. It's in Russian, so I'll have to translate … Let's see now. *(rushing opening)* 'From the Executive Council of the Communist International to the Italian Proletariat, 22nd September, 1920. Comrades, strike after strike, rising after rising, are breaking out in Italy. Matters have gone as far as the mass seizure of factories, houses, etc. by the workers. The labour movement in Italy is faced by decisive …

He looks at Gramsci, who leans against the door jamb, eyes closed.

I don't suppose it says anything you didn't already know.

GRAMSCI: *(struggling to stay awake)* Please ... go on.

KABAK: *(skimming)* It's all ... fairly familiar, really. Seizure of factories and workshops to continue ... scope of the movement to be extended and generalized ... the whole of Italy to be covered with workers', peasants', soldiers' and sailors' councils ... Begin at once to arm ... prepare for genuine insurrection ... drive out reformist leaders ... mobilize all the genuinely revolutionary forces of the country. *(Pause. Very deliberately)* Et cetera. Et cetera. Et cetera. Signed. Lenin. Bukharin. Zinoviev.

GRAMSCI: A nice irony. Right but late.

KABAK: Yes. I thought you should ... know.

GRAMSCI: Yes.

Pause.

KABAK: What will you do?

GRAMSCI: *(toneless)* Build. Prepare for the backlash. There'll be fascists at every street corner from now on. First I have to go to Sardinia. My sister is dying.

KABAK: I'm sorry.

GRAMSCI: Hundreds die every year. Emma just happens to be my sister. It's a kind of malaria. You don't actually have to dig the ditches to have a chance of contracting it. And it's not always fatal. Just another of capitalism's little lotteries. *(He straightens.)* But we'll win, comrade. Go well. *(He starts to leave.)*

KABAK: *(softly)* You still love them too much, comrade.

Gramsci turns, looks at Kabak for a long time, leaves without answer. Kabak drains his glass, sits in a chair, tries to sleep.

SCENE FOUR

Daylight. A brilliant day. Kabak is dead asleep, sprawled like a drunk, legs thrust right forward. Angelica is awake, upright in the bed, two pillows stiffly propping her. She is drained. Her face is garish with rouge and lipstick, which she is still applying. Polya enters through the connecting door, a small kidney bowl in her hands. She stops when she sees Angelica.

ANGELICA: Not now, Polya. Later. I'm feeling much better.

POLYA: *(looking at the sleeping Kabak)* I'm not sure you should be sitting up like that, Madame. Remember what the doctor said about ...

ANGELICA: *(snapping compact firmly to)* Thank you, Polya. That will be all.

Kabak stirs. Stretches. Polya looks at him again, unsure. Finally.

POLYA: *(turning)* Very well, Madame.

She leaves. Kabak stretches, yawns, stretches, stands – clothes in disarray – back more or less to the bed, stretches again, begins to button shirt and do up cravat. He sorts a watch out from his waistcoat, checks time, returns it. In the middle of this he turns and sees Angelica.

ANGELICA: Good morning.

KABAK: Good ... morning. Should you be ...

ANGELICA: Don't, please. You're worse than Polya. I'm feeling better. How do I look?

KABAK: *(recovering; crossing the room to the bed)* Radiant.

He kisses her forehead. She holds him by shoulder and neck, kisses him full on the lips with surprising strength and passion. Kabak is kissed; his lack of response is almost palpable.

ANGELICA: You don't have to lie, you know. It hasn't affected my eyes yet. *(Indicating compact.)*

KABAK: And it hasn't affected mine. Radiant.

Pause.

ANGELICA: Thank you.

KABAK: *(bowing slightly; ironic)* Not at all. My pleasure, ma'am. *(He gets up, moves towards the chair he slept in, slips his coat from the chair-back, puts it on. He begins smoothing his hair with flat palms.)*

ANGELICA: You're beautiful. Do you know that?

KABAK: It's not important.

ANGELICA: Christo.

KABAK: Mmm.

ANGELICA: You know what I'd like?

KABAK: *(looking for boots)* What's that, love?

ANGELICA: Winter in Carlsbad.

Kabak stops fractionally, back to her, then continues the search.

KABAK: I can't find my boots.

ANGELICA: We could go to Darmstadtbaden. There's still a staff there of sorts. I think I could grow well again, there. Christo,

KABAK: *(ringing bell)* Yes, love, I've got to have boots.

ANGELICA: Christo.

Polya comes in.

KABAK: Have you seen my boots?

POLYA: Yes. I had them cleaned.

Kabak looks hard at Polya.

KABAK: Did you? *(Pause.)* Would you mind … bringing them then.

Polya looks at Angelica, back at Kabak.

POLYA: Certainly. *(She leaves.)*

ANGELICA: Christo.

Phone rings. Kabak answers it.

KABAK: Yes. That's right. Oh. *(Pause.)* Tell them I'll be down in five minutes. *(Pause.)* I know what time the train leaves. Tell them five minutes. *(Bangs phone down.)*

ANGELICA: Christo. Who is it? What train?

Polya comes in. She carries the boots on one arm, Kabak's grips in the other hand. She stands about a yard inside the door. Kabak and Angelica look at her in silence.

ANGELICA: *(finally)* Put them down, Polya.

Polya puts them down; leaves. Kabak crosses the room, picks them up, places the grip near the landing door, takes the boots to an armchair, sits to put them on.

Christo.

Kabak concentrates on his boots.

(struggling to quit the bed) Christo?

Kabak gets up, stamps his boots snug.

KABAK: I haven't much time, so listen carefully. I have been ordered to quit Turin. They have sent men to escort me to the station.

ANGELICA: *(not listening; yowling rather)* Oh why? Christo? Oh why? Oh why?

KABAK: *(fierce)* Listen. I have … Listen will you … I have made arrangements …

ANGELICA: Why? Why? Why?

KABAK: *(shouting)* I couldn't. How could I? You're dying.

ANGELICA: *(standing; very still)* Do you think I don't know that?

Long silence.

KABAK: *(finally)* I've made arrangements with the hotel. When you're … you can join me in Berlin. I've left an address with Polya.

ANGELICA: I don't want to die on my own.

KABAK: Polya will be ...

ANGELICA: I don't mean that. Oh God. I don't mean that.

KABAK: I must go. *(He approaches her.)*

ANGELICA: No, No.

Kabak stops. Looks at Angelica.

KABAK: Love. I must.

ANGELICA: *(turning her back; small and quiet)* No.

Kabak waits a moment longer, then turns, picks up the grip at the door. Leaves. Angelica finally sits on the bed, head on hand, back to audience. She sobs. At length she opens the drawer, takes out syringes and capsules, prepares one, draws up her nightdress, plunges needle into thigh. She then repeats the process. For a moment she sits upright, very stiff, then rings the bell for Polya and lowers herself slowly into the bed. Polya comes in quickly.

POLYA: *(crossing room)* Are you all right?

ANGELICA: Yes. Draw the curtains, will you.

POLYA: *(complying, solicitous)* Try and sleep. There's nothing a good sleep won't put right.

ANGELICA: Thank you. Now. Go downstairs and see whether you can get me a morning paper.

POLYA: I can ring down.

ANGELICA: *(sharp; eyes closed)* Go. Please.

Polya goes finally. Angelica is very still for a moment longer then surrenders to a voluptuous spasm, and another, and another. She screams slightly, on the upthrust. It is a little orgasmal: intense, powerful, almost an ecstasy. Words tumble from her, shredded from her life.

The Tsar was in residence in the early spring a ball every night for a month Fabergé swore he'd never seen such costumes such diamonds such ...

She screams once, sharp, anguished, then holds her breath. The scream cues an image on the wall behind her: the corpse of Nicholas II. Cut the image as she speaks again.

(shouting) Bolsheviks Bolsheviks Bolsheviks bread riots strikes bread peace land they were there underneath here now here ...

She screams again, cueing a second image: Lenin embalmed in the catafalque. The image is cut on her next word.

All things will bend all things the iron brain of Lenin hammering the future will will will what will stop them stop them who ...

She screams again: Tato's 'March on Rome.' She screams again: Mussolini embracing Hitler. She screams again: Stalin in profile stares across a black gap at Hitler, who stares back. She screams again: the gap is filled with an image of Molotov and von Ribbentrop signing non-aggression pact. She screams again: cut to black.

APPENDIX

The version of *Occupations* printed here differs, in parts substantially, from the text first published in 1973. Such improvements as I've managed to make I owe to several key productions of the play: in particular, to the first production at The Stables Theatre; to Buzz Goodbody's at the RSC; and to a new and remarkable presentation of the play in 1980 by the Dutch socialist theatre group, Sater.

What appears here represents a decade's intermittent but intensive effort to arrive at a definitive text of the play. And yet, notwithstanding, I publish the original final scene in this appendix, impenitently unwilling to consign it wholly to the deliberations of scholars.

* * *

Polya goes finally. Angelica is very still for a moment longer, then surrenders to a voluptuous spasm, and another, and another. She screams slightly, on the upthrust. It is a little orgasmal: intense, powerful, almost an ecstasy. She is shouting now. Gradually her words begin to make a little sense.

ANGELICA: ... My estate. My estate. Darmstadtbaden. A good winter. Hear the snow hiss past the carriage. Steady, Mikhail. Coax him. Raska won't submit to bullying. You should know that. *(Pause.)* Another winter. '15. '16. Grigor looked so handsome in his uniform. Was Denikin there? Grigor came from Turkey, I remember. Did Denikin come? Perhaps he didn't. *(Pause.)* But who wasn't there! Tsar Nicholas. Her. The Friend. Tchernikov. Pterepnin. All the princes. Bankers. Heads of the Commissariat, industrialists, ballerinas of the Tsar and the Grand Dukes, prelates, ladies in waiting, deputies, generals, lawyers, mandarins, innumerable nephews and nieces. *(Pause.)* Fabergé swore he'd never seen such costumes, such diamonds, such settings ... *(Pause.)* Not a word about the war. Not a word. *(She screams with pain.)* Or those ... Bolsheviks. *(Pause.)* Was that the last winter? *(She sits up stiffly, hugs her stomach.)* But they were there all right. They were there. Bread. Riots. Strikes. They were there. Here now. You can't see them, but they're here now. Underneath. Under the skin. *(Stretching hands)* There. Underneath. Erupting there. There. And here. *(clutching stomach)* Oh God. Oh Blessed Theodosia, save me from these ... foreign bodies. Save me from these ... intruders. Protect me, Blessed Theodosia, patron saint of lost causes, protect my estate in Kiev, protect my lands in Darmstadtbaden . They moved her bones, Christo. Did you know? Grigor took them, very solemnly, from the shrine at Kiev, and led the honour guard to Moscow, where the blessed bones were solemnly laid in the Basilica. Nicholas said the bones should stay in Kiev. The Germans would not dare touch them, he argued; and if they did, so much the worse for the Germans ... A raspberry-coloured shirt he wore. In the Pripet Marshes. Canoeing. Shooting crows. Walking. Where the Dnieper meets the Beresina. Was it breeding, I wonder, that ... calmness? Or simply poverty of the spirit? A weakness of the will? You used to call him something, Christo. What was it?

She is racked by a huge spasm. From this point her fit becomes apocalyptic.

Grigor saw it. The last winter. They were there, under the skin, waiting to ... consume us. Waiting to consume Europe. Our Europe. What ... appetite they displayed! And we are powerless. Our skin needs them perhaps. We must share the same pelt. Even Theodosia. By the sea. Even Theodosia they took. They erupted from under the skin of Theodosia; they confiscated even that. And they will. They will. What did Christo say? All things will bend to Lenin's iron will. They will. They will. Nicholas. Her. The Friend. Grand Dukes, bankers, ballerinas. They've all had their last winter. Everywhere. They will. Will. Will. Will. What will stop them? Will anything stop them?

She slides gently to the floor. Lies very still. Fade slowly to black. We hear the sound of jackboots, very clear, close. On the screen, Tato's 'March on Rome.' After a while, it is replaced by Fascismo *(an anti-Fascist poster, c. 1921). This in turn is replaced by the picture of Mussolini's bodyguard (Moro, Milan). A fourth slide – Mussolini embracing Hitler – replaces this. Its place is taken by a picture of Stalin. Then a slow mix to Molotov and von Ribbentrop signing the German–Russian non-aggression pact. This fades to black. In its place, the factory-roof slide from page 95. The theatre walls are lit. We are in the factory again. Factory noises. A hooter sounds. Silence.*

END

APRICOTS

I wrote *Apricots* on a train from Leeds to London in the Spring of 1971. It was first performed on 28th June 1971 at the Basement Theatre, Greek Street, with Peter Sproule as Sam and Tamara Hinchco as Anna. It was directed by Robert Walker.

Apricots

Nearly night. The day has been hot; sticky. Now it's cooler, but the air retains a kind of heavy warmth. A garden at the side of a house. Light falls from the house on to the stone strip of patio. There is a kid's swing, an Indian tea-chest painted flat white, a small blocky table, a round-backed chair. On the table, ashtray, cheroots, matches, several bottles of red wine. **Sam** *lies face down on the stone, as if asleep. A half-full glass of wine stands in the crook of his right hand. A door bangs inside. A baby yowls briefly; is shushed to sleep. Sam registers nothing.*

Anna *in. She is smallish, dark, mid-thirties, fattening gently, still attractive. She looks round tiredly, sees Sam, fails to react. Lights a cigarette at the table. Sits on the round-back, legs pushed wearily forward.*

SAM: *(finally, not stirring)* All down?

ANNA: Ahunh.

SAM: *(eyes still closed)* That's good.

Silence.

SAM: Did you see them?

ANNA: I saw you.

SAM: Big.

ANNA: All right.

SAM: I never saw areolae that brown.

ANNA: All right.

Pause.

SAM: Do you think he minds?

ANNA: Why don't you get up?

SAM: Do you? *(Sitting up.)* Do you think he minds?

ANNA: I don't know. Tell me.

SAM: *(decisive, then unsure)* I'm ... not sure. He never looked at them once. I watched him. All night he never gave them a glance.

ANNA: Well. *You* can hardly be said to have ... neglected her.

SAM: He probably does mind.

ANNA: Mmm.

Sam stands, drinks, puts glass on table, lights cheroot, fills glass, carries it to the swing, sits carefully down on the narrow strip of wood.

SAM: What's he like?

ANNA: What?

SAM: Pete. What's he like?

ANNA: What's he like what?

SAM: All right.

ANNA: Oh come on, don't be so ...

Pause

SAM: You *know* what I mean. Every sodding time we have to go through this boring
ritual of rendering down the euphemism. *(Pause; very deliberate.)* Does. He.
Fuck. Well?

ANNA: Yes. Very.

SAM: Ah. Good.

ANNA: Is it?

SAM: Yes, I would think so.

Pause. Anna fiddles with a bottle, examines a glass.

SAM: I remember you. I remember you when you smelt cleaner than leaves. I
remember you when you had clean, firm unpractised breasts. So new. So
balanced. And callow daubs of fat on your arse. And your belly was like a
dancer's, full of zest, contained. Fucking you then was like running a finger over
a green apple. I remember you when your cunt smelt of apricots. *(Pause)* He
hated it.

ANNA: No. He loved it.

SAM: Really?

ANNA: Yes.

SAM: Did he tell you?

ANNA: He loves watching you watching her. He likes your eyes on her breasts. It
saves him having you.

SAM: Did he say that?

ANNA: You'll break that swing.

Sam stops swinging, reaches down for his drink.

ANNA: Apricots ?

SAM: What ?

ANNA: *(spreading legs slightly)* Apricots?

SAM: Oh. *(Pause)* Yes.

ANNA: Come here.

Sam stays

ANNA: Come here. Come.

Sam stands slowly, slowly walks over, stands in front of her.

ANNA: Now?

Sam kneels in front of her, pushes his head up her skirt until his lips meet her crotch. He stays for perhaps thirty seconds. Emerges.

ANNA: Mmm? *(He doesn't answer.)* What's the word?

SAM: I don't know.

ANNA: I like you best of all on your knees.

Sam gets up, crosses to the tea chest, sits on it with his back to Anna.

ANNA: Aww. Poor Sam. Poor Sammy. Poor Sammy had his bottom smacked for being a naughty boy. Sammy shouldn't invent nasty lies about Mummy, should he, now! Never mind, soon be better. There, there. There, there, there.

SAM: Fuck off, will you!

Anna laughs. Lights cut very fast.

Lights up fast. It's a little darker. Some late redness is creeping in.

Sam and Anna, still fully dressed, fuck. Anna kneels on all fours, her forearms resting on the tea chest. Sam kneels behind her, his lower belly scooping out the arc around her buttocks.

Sam makes several long, slow, reflective thrusts. Anna stolidly rests.

SAM: Who else?

ANNA: *(pause)* I should think … Margaret.

SAM: Yes?

ANNA: Margaret would.

SAM: How?

ANNA: She'd have you kiss her.

SAM: *(quickening)* Yes.

ANNA: Tongue her.

SAM: Yes.

ANNA: Push your tongue.

SAM: Yes.

ANNA: Inside her.

SAM: Yes.

ANNA: Past the lips.

SAM: Yes. Yes.

ANNA: Past the beard. Past the juice.

SAM: Mmmm.

ANNA: Deep. Deep. Deep.

SAM: Tongue in. (*He pushes his tongue out*)

ANNA: Would you like that?

SAM: Mmmm.

ANNA: Would you?

SAM: Yes.

Pause. They gentle down again.

SAM: I don't know that I would.

ANNA: What?

SAM: Margaret. Like it.

ANNA: Oh?

SAM: She's very thin.

ANNA: So.

SAM: And ... knowing.

ANNA: Oh? I've always thought she's rather a stupid woman. Ah.

SAM: *(quickly)* What?

ANNA: That's nice. You touched my womb, I think.

SAM: I didn't say she was clever. I said she was knowing.

ANNA: So what does that mean?

SAM: Nothing ever happened to Margaret for the first time. That's what I mean.

ANNA: Mmmm

Pause. They fuck on a little.

SAM: You couldn't surprise her with a stoat inside your pants: 'Oh, not stoat again, darling.' Anyway, she's too thin. Are you nearly there?

ANNA: No,

Pause.,

ANNA: Are you?

SAM: No.

ANNA: My arms are hurting.

Sam withdraws, gets up slowly, crosses to the swing, sits down. Anna remains on all fours.

ANNA: I didn't say that. I said my arms were hurting.

SAM: Same thing.

Anna gets up, smooths herself, picks up a glass, tastes the wine.

ANNA: Tea?

SAM: Are you making?

ANNA: Ahunh.

SAM: All right.

She leaves. Sam waits for a moment, then gets up, crosses to the tea chest from behind which he removes a cassette recorder with mic attached. Clicks it off. Kneels, as before. Winds back. Sets it on chest in front of him. Clicks for replay.

SAM: *(tape)* Who else?

ANNA: *(tape)* I should think … Margaret.

SAM: *(tape)* Yes.

Sam's hand on prick. Begins to masturbate, still on his knees, rocking gently, rhythmically.

ANNA: (tape) Margaret would.

SAM: *(tape)* How?

ANNA: *(tape)* She'd have you kiss her.

SAM: *(tape)* Yes.

SAM: Yes.

ANNA: *(tape)* Tongue her.

SAM: *(tape)* Yes.

SAM: Yes.

ANNA: *(tape)* Push your tongue.

SAM: *(tape)* Yes.

SAM: Yes.

ANNA: *(tape)* Inside her.

SAM: *(tape)* Yes.

SAM: Yes.

ANNA: *(tape)* Past the lips

SAM: *(tape)* Yes. Yes.

SAM: Yes. Yes.

ANNA: *(tape)* Past the beard. Past the juice.

SAM: *(tape)* Mmmm.

SAM: *(on the way)* Mmmm.

ANNA: *(tape)* Deep. Deep. Deep.

SAM: *(tape)* Tongue in.

Sam pushes tongue out.

ANNA: *(tape)* Would you like that?

Anna returns with the tray. She is behind Sam; stands and watches in silence.

SAM: *(tape)* Mmmm,

SAM: *(closer)* Mmmmmm.

ANNA: *(tape)* Would you?

SAM: *(tape)* Yes.

SAM: *(there)* Yeeeeeees.

He arches backwards, shooting. Holds it for half a minute. Slowly comes to; straightens. Opens eyes. Clicks recorder off. Slowly stands. Turns. Sees Anna. They look at each other steadily for a long while.

ANNA: (*moving forward, placing tray on table*) That was nice.

Lights out very fast.

Lights up very fast. Anna sits at the table, smoking, drinking tea from a mug. Sam is standing by the swing. Even darker; cooler too.

SAM: *(emphatically)* Holy.

ANNA: Rubbish.

SAM: Holy.

ANNA: How? Just tell me how.

SAM: I don't know. It just was. Sacramental.

ANNA: Ah.

SAM: Ah what?

ANNA: Communion? Or confession?

SAM: What?

ANNA: Drink your tea.

Pause. He waits, looking at her.

You said sacramental. I *asked* if you were referring to the sacrament of holy communion or the sacrament of confession.

Pause.

ANNA: Well?

SAM: Neither.

ANNA: Mmm. Extreme Unction perhaps?

SAM: All right.

ANNA: Well, what did you mean?

SAM: *(slowly)* I meant ... that once ... it used to be ... graceful. Full of grace.

ANNA: Christ.

Silence.

ANNA: And now it isn't.

SAM: That's right. Look, forget it, will you. It isn't that important.

ANNA: I think you're right.

SAM: You would.

ANNA: What's that supposed to mean?

SAM: Nothing.

ANNA: Drink your tea.

Silence. Anna lights another cigarette. Sam shivers.

SAM: It's getting cold.

She doesn't answer

   Aren't you cold?

Silence.

   Do you want to go in?

ANNA: You forget ... natural grace. *(Pause)* Nineteen. I remember dressing that morning. I remember choosing my underwear. Apricot knickers; apple green slip and bra. I remember frothing my pubic hair with talcum powder. I remember dabbing my nipples with cologne. And I remember thinking I wonder what his ... thing's like. I wonder if it's big, fat, small, thin, light, dark, sallow, hot, cool, red, white. I remember thinking: I wonder what his stuff is like. I've never seen it before. Does it smell? What does it smell like? Is it ... sticky? Is it hot? Suppose he asks me to ... kiss him. Take him in my mouth. Suppose he ... draws himself down the bed and begins to kiss me. Mine. What will I do? What will it be like? *(Pause)* And then I put on my pink pinafore dress and flat shoes and left to meet you at the station. *(Pause)* And later, that night, in York, you said: 'It's never been like this before.' And 'I've never experienced such joy before.' And I lay there and thought: 'But what does it look like?', because you undressed in the dark. 'And what does it taste and feel like?' because you kept it inside your rubber until it was all over, and 'Perhaps he doesn't like cologne and talcum powder,' because not once did your lips move down me. I was, to you, a face and a hole. That's all. I don't think I've ever known such absolute fear in anyone. And now you have the … nerve to call it holy.

Long silence.

SAM: Sometimes you frighten me.

Silence.

SAM: Do you want to go in?

ANNA: No.

SAM: What do you want?

ANNA: I want you to fuck me.

SAM: No.

ANNA: Yes.

SAM: No. I can't.

ANNA: Yes. You can. You will. I want you to fuck me hard and strong and long. I want you to make my cunt sing with it. Scream with it. I want you to get in there, all of you, I want the whole in there, prick and balls and body and mind and senses and conscience and remorse and hope. Everything. I want it *all in there.*

SAM: No. I can't.

ANNA: Yes. You can.

SAM: I can't. I can't.

ANNA: You won't. You mean.

SAM: I can't.

ANNA: No. You won't.

Long silence. Sam walks to the table, picks up his cigars and matches.

SAM: Let's go in.

ANNA: You go.

SAM: Bring the things?

ANNA: Mmm.

SAM: All right. Goodnight.

(He bends to kiss her. She doesn't respond. He pecks her cheek. Leaves.)

Anna sits very still for several moments longer, then puts her right hand between her legs and begins to rub. After a moment she stops takes her hand to her face, smells the fingers. Stands. Lights out.

END

THERMIDOR

Thermidor was first performed, in a double bill with *Apricots*, on 25 August 1971 at the Festival Fringe, Cranston Street, Edinburgh by the 7:84 Theatre Company, with Peter Sproule as Yukhov and Tamara Hinchco as Anya. It was directed by Robert Walker.

Thermidor

The time is late summer 1937: the place, NKVD Headquarters, Moscow.

A desk, cluttered with papers, files, trays, a phone, blotter, pens, ink-wells, intercom, newspapers, a flask, a cup, a tin of biscuits. At it **Yukhov** *reading from a pair of files, his body flicking gently from side to side in his bucket swivel chair. After a moment, not taking eyes from the paper, he feels for his cup and takes a small swig of coffee. By the side of the desk, a filing cabinet; a couple of deal tables and chairs line the room walls. A meagre, very cheap carpet on the floor. Somewhere – on the wall, preferably – a large photograph of Stalin and a map of the USSR, next to a street map of Moscow with small red and blue markers in it. The phone rings once. He picks it up immediately, says 'yes' followed by 'yes', puts it down, returns to the files. A knock at the door. He calls 'come in,' still reading.* **Anya** *enters. She blinks in the brightness of this room, focuses finally on the desk.*

ANYA: Comrade Yukhov?

YUKHOV: Come in. Bring that chair and sit down,

She looks for the chair he means, carries it toward the desk, sits on it with a solid show of confidence. Yukhov reads on a moment longer, slams files shut, takes them to filing cabinet, replaces them, returns to chair.

YUKHOV: *(looking at sheet of paper)* Anya … Pakhanova.

ANYA: That's right.

YUKHOV: Thirty-seven, Kotka Street, Moscow.

ANYA: That's right.

He writes something down on the sheet, puts pen down, faces her squarely.

YUKHOV: You've been called here to answer a few questions. Just a preliminary investigation.

ANYA: I see. *(Pause)* May I smoke?

She fumbles cigarettes out.

YUKHOV: If you wish. It would help greatly if you would answer clearly and without frills. My time is paid for by the working people of this country and must be strictly accounted for. Intellectual … digressions will not be welcomed.

She offers cigarette.

No.

ANYA: Very well. I have no wish to waste your time or the people's money.

YUKHOV: *(taking up pen again)* You were expelled from the party two months ago.

ANYA: Yes.

YUKHOV: Would you care to say why?

ANYA: Don't you know?

YUKHOV: Just ... answer the question.

ANYA: *(pausing, gathering)* I was accused of insufficient vigilance in the matter of Anatoly Kostiuk.

YUKHOV: To which you replied?

ANYA: I replied that I had known Kostiuk no better than two dozen other comrades knew him, on the District Committee, and that at no time had I so much as dreamt he was in the pay of imperialist agents.

YUKHOV: You were found guilty of the charge, nevertheless.

ANYA: Yes, I was.

YUKHOV: And given a chance to disarm?

ANYA: Yes.

YUKHOV: Which you refused.

ANYA: Yes. If you wish to put it that way.

Pause. Yukhov takes off his glasses; deliberately.

YUKHOV: How would you wish to put it?

ANYA: I find it a far greater crime to my party and to my country to ask its forgiveness for trangressions I *haven't* committed. For in that way, I am asking the party to believe a lie.

YUKHOV: Would you not agree that, objectively, anyone who refuses to disarm when called upon by the party to do so gravitates towards the position of its enemies?

ANYA: *(same slight, weary heat)* It depends what you mean by disarm.

YUKHOV: Not what *I* mean, comrade. Few things could be of smaller significance than what *I* mean by this or that.

ANYA: Well, what *is meant* by 'disarm.'

YUKHOV: No, no. No, no, no. *(Lights a cigarette, blows smoke, waves it around with his free hand.)* You do not make a matter *objective* by placing it in the impersonal form. *(Pauses)* You mean, what the party means.

Silence. She looks down, discomfited.

YUKHOV: Don't you.

ANYA: Yes, of course.

YUKHOV: So, objectively, anyone who refuses to disarm when called upon by the party to do so gravitates towards the position of its enemies.

ANYA: Yes.

YUKHOV: You agree.

ANYA: Yes. Except, in my case, I do not believe I ... gravitated.

YUKHOV: And tolerance towards anti-party elements leads objectively to disloyalty.

Silence.

YUKHOV: You agree?

ANYA: I'm not sure what you mean ... what the party means by 'tolerance'.

Yukhov writes something on a sheet in front of him.

YUKHOV: *(finally)* I see. *(Very light)* How did you come here today?

ANYA: By bus to Ilinka. Then I walked.

YUKHOV: When did you last use a government car?

ANYA: A government car? I don't remember. Round about the time my husband died, I think.

YUKHOV: When was that?

ANYA: Last year. April.

Yukhov gets up, goes to the filing cabinet, takes out two files from different drawers, looks at them a moment, brings them back to the table, sits down, begins to study them.

ANYA: Why ?

YUKHOV: Mm.

ANYA: Why do you ask? About the cars?

Yukhov stares at her impassively, goes back to the files. Finally, finger on a sheet in the middle of one file.

YUKHOV: From the record of your interrogation by Comrade Poskrebyshev at Moscow City Party Headquarters. *(Quoting)* Comrade Poskrebyshev: How did you get here? Pakhanova: By car. Comrade Poskrebyshev: Whose car? Pakhanova: A Regional Committee car was sent to fetch me. Comrade Poskrebyshev: Oh? At whose instruction? Pakhanova: I do not know. There has always been a car at our disposal. *(He reads on in silence. Closes the file.)* That was in July of that same year. *(Questioning look)*

ANYA: Yes, I'm sorry, I'd forgotten. A car was sent for me on that occasion.

YUKHOV: But you have no idea by whom.

ANYA: No, I haven't. I imagined it was sent by Poskrebyshev himself, to make sure I was present for the ... interrogation.

YUKHOV: You can't think of anyone else who might have sent it?

ANYA: No. Of course, we had friends at Black Square. But they were not people who would dispose of state favours for social reasons. And we weren't people who would ever have wanted them to.

Pause.

YUKHOV: It must have been nice, having a car at your disposal.

ANYA: Comrade Yukhov, my husband and I spent ten, twelve hours a day, every day, week in, week out, on party business. We did not use the cars for our own convenience or pleasure.

YUKHOV: There may be thousands who devote their whole life to the party, Comrade, and never so much as set foot in a government car. *(Pause)* The chit authorizing your use of the car on that particular day was signed by Leped. Did you know him?

ANYA: Very slightly. We were in the League of Youth together, Moscow Three Division.

Yukhov waits. Anya has finished.

YUKHOV: Yes?

ANYA: That's all.

YUKHOV: I see. That is the extent of your … association with 'Comrade' Leped.

ANYA: Yes. More or less.

YUKHOV: You weren't ever … particularly friendly.

ANYA: No. No, I don't think so.

YUKHOV: So it came as, what, a surprise, no surprise, to learn that he was a Trotskyist plotting against state and party.

ANYA: I can't honestly remember, I don't think I ever really thought about it. He wasn't anybody we'd had any dealings with.

YUKHOV: Of course. Kostiuk said the same thing. *(Pause)* Leped's confession did, nevertheless, lead to the arrest of some forty-two other fellow-travellers. Kostiuk among them.

ANYA: But he could not truthfully have named me! I never knew the man, I had absolutely nothing to do with him.

Pause.

YUKHOV: *(biting)* So you say.

Long silence.

YUKHOV: *(turning a couple of pages in the file)* You joined the party when?

ANYA: Nineteen nineteen. February. My twenty-first birthday.

YUKHOV: Where, here?

ANYA: Yes.

YUKHOV: And your parents?

ANYA: My father was a teacher. Mother was an actress.

YUKHOV: Ah yes. She was with Meyerhold, isn't that right?

ANYA: *(wearily)* Yes. For a time. Before his ideas became … anti-Bolshevik.

Long silence.

YUKHOV: You worked at the Pedagogical Institute.

ANYA: Yes.

YUKHOV: Teaching history.

ANYA: Yes. Mainly nineteenth century.

YUKHOV: And now?

ANYA: *(strong, very straight)* I clean offices.

Pause.

YUKHOV: *(unmoved)* You edited a university theoretical journal.

ANYA: Co-edited.

YUKHOV: Co-edited. *(Turns a page in the file. Studies it)* With Piatagorsky.

She nods assent. He begins unscrewing the cap on his flask and pouring himself some coffee during this speech. He draws on the file a great deal for what he says, and is often doing little more than quoting chunks of a report filed there. He is in no sense master of the ideas the report handles.

YUKHOV: In 1928, an article was published under the title 'Notes of an Economist', written by N. I. Bukharin, who even then had demonstrated for all to see his total contempt for inner-party discipline, besides evincing ineradicable Rightist tendencies. In that article – *(flicking a page in the file)* – he argued that the all-out drive for industrialisation of our country, coupled with a ferocious squeeze on the rich peasant class, was the road to economic, social and political disaster. In spite of the binding decisions to the contrary taken at the 15th Party Congress and in the Plenum of the Central Committee, of which he was, at that time, a member. *(He closes the file, looks straight at her.)*

ANYA: Yes, I remember the article.

YUKHOV: Go on.

ANYA: It was considered an authoritative piece of polemic on the vital question of the rate at which industrialisation should be organised. Four articles stating the Central Committee and Politburo view were published in the same year. *(Pause)* Of course, you realise I was not editor at the time or even a member of the editorial board.

YUKHOV: But you became one.

ANYA: Yes. I was honoured to be offered such an important and responsible position on a party journal.

YUKHOV: If you had been an editor in nineteen twenty-eight, would you have published Bukharin's essay?

ANYA: *(pausing)* No.

YUKHOV: Really.

ANYA: I have always been convinced of the need for rapid industrialisation. I have never considered the matter even debatable.

YUKHOV: Ahunh. That's interesting. So. It has always been your conviction that rapid industrialisation was of the essence?

ANYA: Pretty well, yes.

YUKHOV: You were a delegate to your first Party Congress in 1923.

ANYA: I was. The Twelfth.

YUKHOV: How did you vote on the Trotsky opposition programme in that year?

ANYA: Against.

YUKHOV: Against ?

ANYA: Against.

Yukhov flicks through the file.

YUKHOV: *(very deliberately)* It says here ... you abstained.

ANYA: *(equally deliberately)* Then it is wrong.

Another pause.

YUKHOV: Wasn't a part of the Twenty-three opposition programme to do with the rate of industrialisation?

ANYA: *(uncertainly)* Yes ... I think it was.

YUKHOV: They were in favour, were they not, of speeding up the rate of industrialisation? Mmm?

ANYA: Yes, I believe they were.

YUKHOV: Then, how come you voted against their programme?

ANYA: Because I believed then that Lenin's New Economic Policy of gradualism was what the country needed.

YUKHOV: Go on.

ANYA: Well. Just that. In nineteen twenty-three our economy simply had to develop, as Lenin himself never tired of saying, on state capitalist lines. Ours was a workers' and peasants' revolution. If that alliance had been allowed to fail, if we were casually to increase, for example, workers' wages at the expense of the peasant, we should soon have found ourselves facing economic, social and political disaster.

Pause. Plays his trump.

YUKHOV: Which is roughly what Bukharin was saying, is it not, in nineteen twenty-eight? In your journal?

ANYA: Yes it was. But by nineteen twenty-eight we had our base. We were ready for our launch, our first five-year plan.

YUKHOV: *(jotting something down)* You must have heard Trotsky speak many times, in those days.

ANYA: Yes. *(An attempt at humour.)* We all did. He was hardly noted for his reticence.

YUKHOV: What?

ANYA: Yes, I heard him.

YUKHOV: Did you meet him?

ANYA: No.

YUKHOV: What opinion did you form of him?

ANYA: *(pause)* I thought he was too clever. A dangerous and unreliable man.

YUKHOV: Did you ever meet any of his cronies? Who were they, Rakovski, Smilga, Radek, Tomsky, you know the people I mean?

ANYA: No, I never did. *(Pause)* Not Tomsky, by the way. He was part of the right opposition.

YUKHOV: (ignoring her) Now, I find that very interesting, *(Flicking file forward, as though to see how long this particular report is, then returning to the page he's on)* I have here on file a copy of an article you wrote under the title 'The True Nature of the Bolshevik Party', in which you quote Trotsky quite extensively. How do you explain that?

Long, odd pause. She fiddles for another cigarette.

ANYA: Don't you know, Comrade Yukhov?

YUKHOV: What ?

ANYA: I simply wondered whether you might not already know the answer to that question.

YUKHOV: Confine yourself to the facts. Your … reflections are of no importance.

ANYA: All right. It was an article in *Pravda,* actually. Though it began life as an address to the All-Moscow League of Youth Conference, summer nineteen twenty-five.

YUKHOV: Go on.

Pause.

ANYA: The quotation in question is as follows: *(Searching for the words)*
'Comrades, none of us wishes or is able to be right against his party. The party in
the last analysis is *always* right, because the party is the sole historical instrument
given to the proletariat for the solution of its basic problems. I know that one
cannot be right against the party. It is only possible to be right with the party and
through the party, for history has not created other ways for the realisation of
what is right.' Trotsky said that, in plenary session, at Thirteenth Party Congress
in nineteen twenty-four. And I copied it down and memorised it. Because I
believe it to be true, whether the party now wishes to use me or not, I believe it
to be true. *(Pause)* If I remember alright, a Gennadi Yukhov, aged about thirteen,
chaired my session and had tea with me afterwards. And talked.

Long silence. Yukhov looks down at the file several times, then back at Anya,

ANYA: *(soft, but emotional, a simple statement of her truth)* I never belonged to an
opposition, left or right. How could I, when I never had a shadow of a doubt
that the party line was correct?

YUKHOV: *(very low)* Was that you?

ANYA: Yes.

YUKHOV: *(looking at her)* Yes, of course.

Silence. Slightly uncomfortable.

YUKHOV: You've changed.

ANYA: So have you. You wear long trousers now.

YUKHOV: Your hair's … darker.

ANYA: Yes. It was summer. It bleaches on top, that's all.

*Silence. This mood informs the remainder of the play, though in gradually
diminishing measure,*

YUKHOV: *(undermined: tentative: gentled by this embarrassment)* You are … you
are quoted as saying – *(he reads from the file)* – 'I knew the Trotskyist *Volsky*
very well and visited his home often.'

ANYA: That's not true,

YUKHOV: You did not know Volsky?

ANYA: Yes, of course I knew Volsky. We were on the same party committee
together. All twenty-eight party members on that committee *knew* him …

YUKHOV: Then what is your objection to the quotation?

ANYA: I did not say I knew the *Trotskyist* Volsky.

YUKHOV: But he has been charged and found guilty of Trotskyist conspiracy
against the state.

ANYA: That may be. All I am saying is, I never knew him as a Trotskyist.

YUKHOV: It will be argued that you displayed a considerable lack of vigilance, Comrade Pakhanova.

ANYA: And I will argue that it's a lack I share with the whole of that district committee.

YUKHOV: Comrade Pakhanova, I think I should warn you that you would be advised to forget that line of defence tomorrow. It is sufficient –

ANYA: Tomorrow? You mean I am to come back *tomorrow?* There was nothing on the card about tomorrow.

YUKHOV: Comrade, you should realise, things are very serious for you here.

ANYA: I don't believe I can manage tomorrow. I have my family to take care of.

YUKHOV: I'm afraid there is little to be done about that, Comrade. There is very little to be done about anything, once charges have been laid and ... (due legal processes set in motion).

ANYA: *(with sharpening alarm, merging into mild hysteria)* Charges. What charges?

YUKHOV: Comrade Pakhanova ... (I have been trying to tell you ...).

ANYA: What charges? I know nothing about charges.

YUKHOV: I'm trying to tell you, Comrade ...

ANYA: You said nothing about charges. There was nothing ... (on the card about charges ...).

YUKHOV: *(fist)* Will you *listen* to me!

She is dead silent; trembles a little. He is embarrassed again, worried by the silence and her terror. Gently, but wanting the business ended.

Comrade, I have here a warrant for your arrest. It was issued last week, over the signature of Comrade Yezhov. The charges include 'political shortsightedness', 'lack of vigilance' and 'compromised with dubious elements'. *(Pause)* A more detailed specification of the charges will be drawn up as a result of this interview. Please read it. *(Pause)* Please read it!

She cannot bring herself to read it, shakes her head from side to side. Subsides.

ANYA: *(small; dead)* What will happen to my children?

YUKHOV: I don't know.

ANYA: What will happen to my children? I have three small children. What will happen to them?

YUKHOV: I'm sorry. You mustn't ask me. My brief does not extend to the welfare of your children.

Pause.

ANYA: Will I be allowed to see them?

YUKHOV: That may well depend upon whether you are willing to sign … a form of confession.

ANYA: I have nothing to confess.

Pause

YUKHOV: You knew the Trotskyist Volsky socially.

ANYA: *(dull; weary, rather hopeless)* I knew *Volsky* socially.

YUKHOV: But since Volsky is a convicted Trotskyist traitor, objectively, therefore, you knew the Trotskyist Volsky.

ANYA: Comrade Yukhov, please don't play these silly games with me. You will only waste your time and the people's money.

YUKHOV: *(doggedly)* Please answer … I asked you whether you agree that, objectively, you knew the Trotskyist Volsky.

ANYA: *(starting low, but building, some small fight left there)* There is no power in the world that can give you the right *to tell me what I know.* The I is *me,* comrade. Me. *I know* means all those things I have seen and smelt and tasted and touched and held, all those people I've talked to and waited for, married, slept with, given birth to; all those ideals I have fought for and believed in. *(Pause. Strong now.)* And *I* am the *only* subject of *know.* You cannot *tell* me I knew the Trotskyist Volsky. I knew Volsky the father of two teenage daughters. I knew committeeman Volsky. I knew Volsky the husband of fat-faced Katya with the red hair and bad teeth. *That* Volsky I knew. No other. No other.

Long pause.

YUKHOV: *(jotting a note)* No matter. In time you will come to realise that for most purposes there is very little difference between 'subjective' and 'objective'. Tomorrow you will meet Principal Investigator Baumann. If I could offer you one word of advice, try to drop your superior intellectual tone with him. He is, if it is possible, even less interested in … philosophical speculation … than I am.

ANYA: *(very low, broken, reflective)* What has happened to you? You used not to be so … inert. I can remember you, you know, that July day. You were so alive. You wanted to know everything. You asked me so many questions over tea I could hardly keep pace with you … (And) you told me about your father, how he had scrimped and saved to buy you books for your studies. And how ambitious you were then! To serve … the revolution. What has happened? What has happened to us?

YUKHOV: *(Intercom. It's impossible, but he tries to say it so that she does not hear him.)* Warder please. Cellars, yes. *(To her)* That's all for the moment. *(Tidying files.)* There'll be more tomorrow. Colonel Baumann is a busy man, as you can imagine. Some sort of confession would have been a great help, but … Through that door. There'll be someone waiting.

ANYA: This is a *soviet institution*. You cannot treat people this way in a soviet institution.

YUKHOV: Enemies … are no longer people.

ANYA: *(standing, moving, turning)* What about my children? I have three small children.

YUKHOV: They will be attended to. (*Pause*) Our children are our future.

ANYA: I'm innocent. You know that don't you. I'm innocent.

YUKHOV: Are you?

She leaves. He stretches. Drains his mug. Returns files to cabinet.

Poskrebyshev now. Then lunch.

END

THE PARTY

I wrote *The Party* in 1972, a first fast incomplete draft in Europe while researching a screenplay on the life of Strindberg, and a second revised and completed draft some months later. It was first produced by John Dexter at the National Theatre in 1973 and given a second completely new NT touring production by David Hare the following year. Both productions, compelling in their different ways, played to large and voluble audiences in London and around the country, together with a third major production of extraordinary clarity and great passion by Howard Davies and David Edgar at the RSC in the 1980s. All failed to persuade reviewers – though with important exceptions – that it was a piece worth doing. Some thirty years on, with a dozen or so files of correspondence from students, teachers and literary critics from around the world about the play, I have little doubt that it was.

The Party was first performed in Great Britain at the National Theatre, London, on 20 December 1973. The cast was as follows:

Angie Shawcross   Doran Godwin

Joe Shawcross   Ronald Pickup

Eddie Shawcross   John Shrapnel

Milanka   Sarah Atkinson

Malcolm Sloman   Frank Finlay

Susie Plaistow   Anna Carteret

Kate Stead   Rachel Davies

'Grease' Ball   Desmond McNamara

Richard Maine   Nicholas Clay

Jeremy Hayes   Gawn Grainger

Kara Massingham   Gillian Barge

Louis Preece   Ram John Holder

Andrew Ford   Denis Quilley

John Tagg   Laurence Olivier

Directed by   John Dexter
Designed by   John Napier

The Party

PROLOGUE

Black stage. Track of very bad theatre orchestra playing 'The Internationale' in spry waltz-time. Fade up huge, stage-high pic of Karl Marx; mix to pic of Lenin; mix to pic of Trotsky (last days in Mexico). Take pic down to black. Single roving spot in centre. Music up, cymbally. Joe dressed as an ancient Groucho Marx on – moustache, cigar, tails, bent back, fish eyes. He carries a clipboard of papers and a trail-mic, which he places in the mic-stand that squirts up from the boards. He looks at the darkness behind him.

GROUCHO: Good evening. (*to audience, but ignoring them*) So what happened to the happy guy with the whiskers.

Trotsky pic up.

Come on, come on, you think I don't know Abie the Fishpedlar when I see him? Give me the guy with the nests in his face.

Pic of Karl Marx reappears.

Poppa. So what's tickling you, pa – apart from the flora on the face, that is? (*to audience*) Which reminds me, did you ever hear the one about the 150,000 supporters of De Gaulle who marched through the streets of Paris on 30 June 1968 shouting 'France aux français!' and 'Cohn-Bendit à Dachau!'? You what? Oh, you were there. Well, well, well. Why don't I keep my big trap in my pocket? That way I could smile while I counted my money. But to our story, as they say. Captain Hugo C. Hackenbush, at your service. Explorer, adventurer, natural scientist, *bon viveur, homme moyen sensuel* bordering on the priapic and pretty nearly totally irrelevant to the rest of this play. But to our story. And talking of talkies I've been asked to put you in the picture with a few choice epigraphs. Sit down, madam. Your turn will come, I promise you. (*riffling papers on the board*) I have here a miscellaneous collection of choice quotations that I understand – nay, am authoritatively assured – has a more than glancing relevance to what follows. (*He looks at the giant Marx.*) Pity you can't be here to do it yourself, hunh. Eh? You old … boulevardier, you. Hummm. (*turning page, reading*) 'The bourgeoisie …' Wake up, madam, I'm talking about you. Give her a nudge, will you, sir? Thank you so much. May your back never buckle under the strain. 'The bourgeoisie cannot exist without constantly revolutionizing the instruments of production, and thereby the relations of production, and with them the whole relations of society. Constant revolutionizing of production, uninterrupted disturbance of all social conditions, everlasting uncertainty and agitation distinguish the bourgeois epoch from all earlier ones. All fixed fast, frozen relations, with their train of ancient and venerable prejudices and opinions, are swept away, all newly formed ones become antiquated before they can ossify. All that is solid melts into air, all that is holy is profaned, a man is at last compelled to face with sober senses his real condition of life and his relations with his kind.' Nobody's writing like that any more, believe me. (*to pic*) O.K.?

Pic of Lenin appears.

Ouch. Or as they have it in Russia – Ilyich! (*turning pages*) Steady as she goes! (*Deep breath*) 'Revolutionary phrase-making is a disease from which revolutionary parties suffer at times when the course of revolutionary events is marked by big, rapid zigzags. By revolutionary phrase-making we mean the repetition of revolutionary slogans irrespective of objective circumstances at a given turn in events, in the given state of affairs obtaining at the time. When people are seized by the itch of revolutionary phrase-making, the mere sight of this disease causes intolerable suffering.' (*He begins scratching his elbow.*) No, madam, that's a flea. I'm just a petty-bourgeois funny man with quasi-anarchic tendencies; it says here.

Pic reverts to Marx.

And talking of money – and if we weren't, by God we should have been – is he back? They do hug the stage these boys, don't they – talking yet again of money, see how this grabs you? Or indeed where. (*clipboard again; cough, sniff*) 'Money ...' My, how straight you're sitting now. Me too, folks. 'Money, since it has the property of purchasing everything, of appropriating objects to itself, is therefore the object par excellence. The universal character of this property corresponds to the omnipotence of money, which is regarded as an omnipotent essence. Money is the pander between need and object, between human life and the means of existence. But that which mediates my life, mediates also the existence of other men for me. It is for me the other person ...'

Another spot up, side of stage. In the spot, the actor playing Tagg appears, dressed as Olivier playing Timon.

OLIVIER: Gold? Yellow, glittering, precious gold? No, gods,
        I am no idle votarist: you roots, you clear heavens!
        Thus much of this will make black white; foul fair;
        wrong right; base noble; old young; coward valiant
        ... Why, this
        Will lug your priests and servants from your sides;
        Pluck stout men's pillows from below their heads:
        This yellow slave
        Will knit and break religions; bless th'accurst,
        Make the hoar leprosy adored; place thieves
        And give them title, knee and approbation,
        With senators on the bench; this is it
        That makes the wappen'd widow wed again;
        She whom the spittal house and ulcerous sores
        Would cast the gorge at, this embalms and spices
        To the April day again. Come, damned earth,
        Thou common whore of mankind, that putt'st odds
        Amongst the rout of nations, I will make thee
        Do thy right nature.

'O' light fades. 'G' light up.

GROUCHO: There's nobody speaking like that anymore, believe me. 'The power to confuse and invert all human and natural qualities, to bring about fraternization of incompatibles, the *divine power* of money, resides in its *essence* as the alienated and exteriorized species-life of men. It is the alienated *power of humanity.*' (*big breath*) Yeah, well. If I had the choice between you and a bedful of money, madam, you'd have trouble making second.

Pic of Trotsky asserts itself. He turns round.

All right, Abie, your turn will come, as the albatross said to the gannet.

Trotsky pic fades. Only black now.

Well, don't say I didn't tell you. If you see anything that looks like a ten-dollar bill – for instance, a hundred-dollar bill – don't hesitate to bring it round back, will you? You'll know it's mine because it'll have …

Pic of hundred-dollar bill.

Well there you go. (*muttering, leaving*) I really must do something about these *pockets*. How a man's supposed to keep a quiet mouth in there I'll never know, slipping down around your ankles, getting trodden underfoot.

Black.
Caption: 'Je Suis Marxiste, Tendance Groucho'.
Black.
Caption: 'Nous Sommes Tous Juifs Allemands'.
Black.
Caption: 'Violez Votre Alma Mater'.
Black.
Burst of sound; film of Paris students marching,
demonstrating.
Black.
Left screen: BERLEIT across a picture of the factory.
Letters leave the left screen one by one to form the word LIBERTÉ;
and reform on the right, over a pic of a clenched fist.
Chords of Archie Shepp's intro to 'Blasé' (Actuel 18) underneath.
Black again. Spot up on **Joe Shawcross** *and* **Angie** *in*
bedroom set.
Music up. A sort of abstracted fuck-ballet, the figures distinct
in the spot, the room barely there as yet. The fuck is bad.
Joe is frozen: Angie goes down with her lips. He kneels for a
while, inert, takes it; then imperceptibly draws away from her.
Music down; lights up. The bedroom.

ACT ONE

10 May 1968. Early evening.

Bedroom at the Shawcross house, SW7, somewhere. Big, white, sunny, rather cool. Hockneys and Botys. 7 ft. bed. Door to adjoining dressing-room. Door to landing.

Joe clicks off the record player, walks into the dressing-room. Angie half lies, half kneels on the bed, watching him; then stands, pulls on a pair of knickers and tights, sits smoking a cigarette, staring at nothing, deep in her own vacancy.

Silence. Gradually, the faintest sounds of retching from the dressing-room area. She smokes on, hardly aware of it. Finally.

ANGIE: You all right? (*Silence.*) You all right? (*No answer.*)

She looks round at the door, doesn't move. Joe appears. He wears a sweat shirt, underpants, sailing shoes.

JOE: What?

ANGIE: I said: Are you all right.

JOE: (*looking around rather aimlessly*) What time are you going out?

ANGIE: Nineish. (*looking at watch, standing*) Christ.

JOE: Will you be late back?

ANGIE: Possibly. I'm not sure.

JOE: I can't find my jeans.

ANGIE: In the basket. They stink.

JOE: (*into dressing-room*) Do they? (*back in hopping into them*) Does Milanka know you're …

ANGIE: Ahunh.

He sits down, drained, on the other side of the bed, back to Angie, begins to put on canvas shoes.

Are you all right?

JOE: Yes. I'm fine.

ANGIE: You look terrible.

JOE: I'm fine. Jesus Christ.

Silence. Each busy, separate.

ANGIE: How was your thing?

JOE: What time is it?

ANGIE: Ten to. (*She waits.*)

JOE: What?

ANGIE: Frau Elise?

JOE: Fine.

ANGIE: Good. (*lipstick*) And how is it?

JOE: (*getting up, zipping trousers, fastening belt*) Addictive. I talk, she listens. What more could a man ask of a woman? (*sings, absently*) 'Freudians are forever ...' We reached my father today. She told me to tell her the most significant fact I knew about him. So I said: 'My father takes less home in a week than I'm paying for this session.'

He looks at Angie. She continues making up.

And she said: 'No. Tell me something about your father.'

Charlie, *aged three or four, calls 'Mummy' several times. Angie gets up, looks round for her clothes.*

ANGIE: (*with undemonstrative resignation*) All right.

She walks into dressing-room. Joe stretches out, head propped on the bed. Charlie calls 'Mummy' once more, goes quiet. Joe smokes, vacantly.

(*off*) Try and get rid of Sloman, will you.

JOE: He's all right. He's lying down somewhere.

ANGIE: (*off*) This will be four nights running and he's pissed the bed every night.

JOE: I'll have a word with him.

ANGIE: (*off, half irony*) What will you say?

JOE: I'll say: Don't piss the bed so often, Malc.

ANGIE: (*in, short stunning dress, boots in hand*) Ha. Ha. You want to try getting it out sometime. (*Pause.*) Is he doing something for you?

JOE: Mmmm. A ninety. 'Play of the Month.' November.

ANGIE: Will he sober up in time?

JOE: Don't worry about Malc.

ANGIE: I'll try not to. If he wrote like he drank, he'd really be something.

JOE: He's something already. Drink helps him believe otherwise.

ANGIE: (*not understanding*) What?

JOE: Nothing.

She persists silently.

He ... can't bear the thought of himself as ... successful ... in a society he longs to destroy.

Long silence.

ANGIE: I see. (*Pause.*) Is that why he drinks?

JOE: I don't know. (*He begins rubbing the webs of his right foot through his socks.*)

ANGIE: (*inspecting herself in the wall mirror; casually*) Is that what's wrong with you, Joe?

JOE: No. It's athlete's foot actually.

She stares hard at him.

Tinea pedis.

Silence.

Don't be simple, Angie.

ANGIE: Can't you answer simple questions?

JOE: (*up*) No.

ANGIE: I meant: Is it getting ... better?

JOE: No. But as Harold Wilson might put it, it's getting worse more slowly. We have it in hand.

ANGIE: Do you want to talk?

JOE: I thought you were going out.

ANGIE: I am but ...

JOE: Well then. Go. I'm surviving.

ANGIE: Tell me ...

JOE: Don't go on about it, eh.

He walks into the dressing-room. She hunts for a pair of cotton gloves in a chest of drawers.

ANGIE: (*calling*) If I don't see your brother before he leaves ... say good-bye for me, won't you.

JOE: (*in, struggling into another tee-shirt*) Yeah.

ANGIE: Will he get the job?

JOE: I don't know. I hope not.

ANGIE: Oh? He seemed to think it was worth having.

JOE: There's nothing for our kid down here.

ANGIE: Have you told him that?

JOE: No.

ANGIE: He wouldn't thank you. What have you got on?

JOE: I've got a meeting. Just a few people.

ANGIE: Here?

JOE: Mmmmmmmmmm.

ANGIE: Anyone I know?

JOE: No, I don't think so.

ANGIE: Is *he* coming?

JOE: Who?

ANGIE: John whatsisname. You know.

JOE: You make him sound like Moloch. 'Is *he* coming?' Jesus.

ANGIE: Is he?

JOE: Yes.

ANGIE: He gives me the creeps.

JOE: You've only met him once.

ANGIE: Once was all I needed.

JOE: I thought he was very civil.

ANGIE: Yes. Civil. Like a hangman's civil.

JOE: Don't be so … bourgeois.

ANGIE: (*displaying herself*) What do you suggest I be? Proletarian?

He looks at her in silence.

When are we going to talk?

JOE: I don't know. Not now, eh.

ANGIE: No. Not now. Of course. (*She's ready to leave. Gives herself a final look in the long mirror.*) I'll call in and see Charlie on the way out. Shall I tell him you'll be coming?

JOE: Sure. Take care. (*He blows her a toy kiss.*)

ANGIE: Don't make plans for tomorrow night. We're going to the Aldwych with the Carters.

JOE: All right.

ANGIE: I want you, Joe.

She leaves abruptly. He sits for a moment, looking at the door, then crosses to the record player, places a record on the turntable, selects a track with care, returns to the bed, slowly kneels on it to face the wall-length mirror, takes out his penis, fists it, begins to beckon it to life. Fade in Archie Shepp/Jeanne Lee: 'Blasé'. Room lights down. Joe and his reflection remain lit.

Blasé
Ain't you darlin
You
Who shot your sperm into me
But never set me free
This ain't a hate thing
It's a love thing
If lovers ever really love that way
The way they say.
I give you a lump of sugar
You fill my womb till it runs
All of Ethiopia awaits you
My prodigal son.

A burst of mute film from the preparations for the night of the barricades. Pics, fast, like identiscan:

Cohn-Bendit.
Alain Geismar.
Jacques Sauvageot.
Yves Niaudet.
Jean Labib.
Alain Krivine.
Henri Weber.
Caption: 'Nous Sommes un Groupuscule.'
Take out Joe light. Black.
Caption: 'L'anarchie c'est moi.'
Black.

SCENE TWO

Music: 'Street Fighting Man' (Stones). Slow single spots light first a wall picture of Lenin, then, after some moments, a balancing shot of Trotsky (Army). They're joined by a fun pop print, sexual in content and blatant in feel. The images hold, disembodied, without context. A sudden surge of intense white light drowns the stage, washing out not only these images but the set as well. A gradual correction establishes the Shawcross living-room.

Same evening, moments later. Late light filters through the french windows. There is a suggestion of covered patio and lawn beyond.

The room is mainly white walls and black leather. The furniture is expensive, tasteful and tentative: Chesterfield, two big chairs, stools, rugs, huge floor cushions, white carpets, extensive Bang and Olufsen hi-fi, early colour TV (like a Wurlitzer), ½ in. VTR and monitor; mirror, paintings, prints, decorative plants and fronds, shelves of hardbacks, two shelves of LPs. There are a dozen or so slung or standing spots to light the room. The impression is of purpose narrowly triumphing over comfort; of rich ease scored by persisting puritan principle.

*A warm Friday evening, after a hot friendly day. The windows are open wide. The TV screen to the room is on; a news bulletin (9 o'clock) is almost at an end. We listen to it in the empty set for some moments, before **Eddie Shawcross** enters from the hall. He's about medium height, stocky, dark, balding slightly; uncomfortable in this room, this house. The unaccustomed dark suit, collar and tie don't help. He watches the set for some little while, then has a wander. Touches things tentatively, not caring to leave marks.*

NEWSREADER: ... In all, more than 150,000 people will have visited Danish Fortnight when it closes at the end of this week. In the local borough elections, Conservative Central Office is now claiming 571 gains to 13 losses. The gains include 16 London boroughs and 25 key towns, many of them thought to be impregnable Labour strongholds until now. Our political correspondent, Hardiman Scott, reports:

SCOTT: A black day for Labour. A swingeing defeat at the hands of the Tories in the local elections, coupled with an unprecedented personal attack on Mr Wilson by the editor of the *Daily Mirror*, will give Transport House much food for thought over the summer months. Continued silence from prominent Labour leaders – not least, Mr Wilson himself – has given rise to some speculation on the possibility of radical changes in policy, harnessed to a thorough-going Cabinet reshuffle. But it should be remembered that this defeat was expected by the Labour camp and that, paradoxically, the fact that it wasn't even more substantial may be read by the Prime Minister and by his colleagues as a qualified endorsement of government policies to date.

Eddie grins a little, turns away to perch on a stool and study his Evening Standard.

NEWSREADER: The new 50 penny piece was announced today. It has, as you can see, a seven-sided design and will replace the 10 shilling note by February 1971, when the conversion to decimal coinage is expected to be completed.

Joe in.

JOE: Hi, kid.

EDDIE: Hi.

Joe watches the set.

NEWSREADER: Finally, back to Paris and those students, reports are still reaching us of a massive build-up in the Left Bank area of Paris. Some 15,000 demonstrators have already begun their anti-government march, and informed sources claim double or even treble that number will be in action before midnight. Student leader Daniel Cohn-Bendit has called for the immediate withdrawal of French police from the Latin Quarter and the Sorbonne, which the students regard as their 'rightful home'. According to our Paris correspondent, it will be a miracle if large-scale clashes can be averted in the hours of darkness later tonight. (*Pause for the smile.*)

Joe winks at Eddie, who smiles back at him.

That's all from the newsroom. Late news at 10.45. And now a look at the weather.

JOE: Are you watching?

EDDIE: No.

Joe switches it off.

JOE: So, how'd it go?

EDDIE: (*head in racing results*) Bloody Europeana let us down for a tenner at Beverley. I don't know why I back that N. MacIntosh, I don't.

JOE: What about the job?

EDDIE: Yeah. They said I could have it. Foreman cutter.

JOE: Yeah? How do you feel about that?

EDDIE: All right. They showed me the bandknives. Honest, they looked like someat out of a ship's engine. Hundred dozen at a time they cut. It's not a cutter they want, it's a Chief Engineer.

Milanka, *the au pair, in, carrying a guinea pig. She's Czech, the first fruits of the Cernik accession: eighteen, between high school and university; tall; hefty but lithe, wears a blue and white tracksuit with a Czech national badge across the back.*

MILANKA: I put Novotny back, Mr Shawcross.

JOE: Yeah, that's fine, Milanka.

She crosses to the french windows, goes out on to the terrace. The pig squeals, high and grating.

EDDIE: Big girl.

JOE: Yes.

MILANKA: (*off*) All right, Novotny. All you do is squealing. You had good time, remember.

JOE: So. Do you take it or what?

EDDIE: I might. I'll have to talk to her first. She won't like it down here.

JOE: Will you?

EDDIE: I dunno. It'll be better than rowing third oar on a slave ship. Marginally.

They grin at their old joke. Milanka in.

MILANKA: Novotny is to bed. He said good night to Charlie.

JOE: That's nice. And I read him a story.

MILANKA: Good. Now I sing him asleep with my Czech song.

JOE: He'll like that.

MILANKA: Tonight I have training. (*Pause.*) I spoke with Mrs Shawcross. (*Pause.*) She said I should speak with you.

JOE: (*uneasy, fast*) Yes, sure, all right, Milanka, that's fine.

MILANKA: Thank you. I'm not late. Tomorrow I sing for you. 'Ej od Buchlova' perhaps.

JOE: Thanks.

She goes. Joe grins at Eddie.

EDDIE: I wouldn't mind a song meself. Don't you get tempted, our kid?

JOE: I don't have time.

Pause.

EDDIE: I thought I might go out. It's too late to go back.

JOE: Yeah. Have a night on the town, eh. Are you all right for …? (*Hand at back pocket.*)

EDDIE: I'm fine. They coughed up. Expenses.

Milanka back in, duffel bag over shoulder.

MILANKA: Some men brought food on wooden trays. In kitchen.

JOE: Good. Thanks.

MILANKA: And … the man with the beard is lost. Mister …

JOE: How do you mean, lost?

MILANKA: He was here in house. Now no longer.

JOE: Maybe he's just … gone. All right, I'll see to it, you get off.

She leaves, smiling.

EDDIE: Is that that … Malc?

JOE: Yes.

EDDIE: Is he still here?

JOE: There seems some doubt about it. He was an hour ago. I saw him.

EDDIE: He's all right him, inne?

JOE: Yeah. Good bloke.

EDDIE: Can't half shift some stuff. He's from up our way, inne?

JOE: Salford. Used to play for United Colts.

EDDIE: Gerrout. Him?

JOE: S'right. Left-back

EDDIE: Christ. I bet they were bloody terrible. What'd's'e do?

JOE: He's a writer.

EDDIE: Oh.

Silence.

Me mam said when're you coming down to see 'em.

JOE: I'll come up in the summer, tell her. August, p'raps.

EDDIE: She thought you might manage Wakes.

JOE: When's that?

EDDIE: *Wakes.*

JOE: Yes. No, I don't think so. I'm going to France. To see some films …

EDDIE: I'll tell her August then.

Silence.

You don't fancy a night out, do you?

JOE: (*uneasyish*) No … I'm babysitting. I've got some people coming round anyway.

EDDIE: (*tentative*) Have you thought any more about the 300 quid?

JOE: (*uneasier still*) Shit. No I haven't. I meant to mention it to Angie before she went out. Never mind, I'll have a word with her before you leave.

EDDIE: I should've set up on me own years ago really. All I need's a coupla rooms, coupla machines, a buttonholer and a bandknife, piece of cake. I'll show you the shop I've got in mind. Market Street. It's a blinder. I could do all me own stuff.

Phone rings. Joe looks at it, leaves it down.

EDDIE: I'll push then.

JOE: Stay if you want.

EDDIE: No. I fancy going out. See you later on?

JOE: Yeah. Sure. Got your key? (*Eddie nods.*) Go easy.

They exchange grins.

EDDIE: Oh yeah. (*He leaves.*)

JOE: (*to phone*) Hello? John. Uhuuh. Of course. What time is it now? *(checking watch)* No, that'll be fine. Well, we'll manage. Nobody yet, but it's early. Fine. It'll be on the latch. See you then.

A loud groaning bellow from the region of the floor cushions by the wall.

Sorry, I missed that.

Another groan. The cushions move, rise. Joe watches.

Got it. I'll expect you then. Take care.

Phone down. The cushions erupt like lava and **Sloman** *appears, on his knees. He is in some disarray. He is jacketless; his shirt is open to the waist; his shoes are tied neatly around his neck. He is pushing forty, gross, bearded, puffy with booze, yet powerful still. His eyes are closed. He moans, as though crying. Opens his eyes. Sees Joe.*

SLOMAN: Joe.

JOE: Hello, Malc.

SLOMAN: I'll have to stop this, Joe.

JOE: So you keep saying.

Sloman stands slowly, crosses to the drinks alcove.

SLOMAN: (*examining bottles, smelling glasses*) I've forgot what I were on.

He holds a bottle up to Joe, who shakes head.

No? (*Pours large Scotch.*) How was your meeting?

JOE: It hasn't happened yet.

SLOMAN: Really?

(*He almost retches at the first sip of the Scotch.*)

Oh. (*Pause.*)

JOE: What're you going to do, Malc?

SLOMAN: I've decided to dedicate the remainder of my life to subtlety, sexuality, ambivalence and malice. Anything Pinter can't quite say, I can't quite say better, as it were. How do you mean?

JOE: I mean, are you staying for the meeting?

SLOMAN: That too. Yes.

JOE: Fine. (*He begins redistributing cushions, rearranging chairs etc. for the meeting. It takes a little time and continues through the chat that follows. He ends by adjusting the ceiling and wall spots by means of a dimmer control switch by the doorway.*) The *News* rang again. Twice.

SLOMAN: Lovely people.

JOE: Why don't you tell them?

SLOMAN: I've told 'em. They can stick their best play award up their managing editor's capacious and much-lipped rectum. Why should I tell 'em anything? (*finger on nose*) Tell 'em nowt. Have a drink.

JOE: (*busy*) No. Not just yet.

Sloman pours himself another, kills the bottle, holds it to his cheek, mock-lovingly.

SLOMAN: Poor bugger. You're empty, son. They'll stop pestering you now, you see. (*He returns to the centre of the room, shoes and socks still round his neck.*) How's things, flower?

JOE: (*smiling*) Fine.

SLOMAN: (*acute*) Are they? (*Pause.*) Still with the Kraut?

Joe nods.

I've finished with her. I reckon two years is long enough with any analyst. The minute they start getting interested – I mean, *actually interested* in your life and that – it's time to flit, find yourself another cold sod with fish eyes and a new line in polyvinyl platitudes. The minute I walk out of that room I want to be forgotten. Zam. Door slams. 'Who? Malcolm Who? No, I don't think so.' Know what I mean? I can't be doing with the idea of actually forming the object of somebody's ... conjectures and ... musings, later on. It's undignified.

JOE: I find her pretty professional.

SLOMAN: Yeah? The last time I went, she smiled as I walked in and said: 'Take a seat won't you, Mr Sloman,' without looking at the file once. I don't have to take that sort of thing from an analyst. I'd have her struck off if I had my way. Failure to expunge all memory of client the moment he clears field of vision. She's probably a liberal. Probably can't help it.

Joe begins adjusting the lighting. Sloman falls silent, watches him, absorbed.

I think you want to take down ... er ...(*pointing*) six, is it? ... about two points. And four could go up a point or two: what've you got four at?

JOE: (*grinning*) Piss off.

SLOMAN: Bloody hell. This TV lark's going to your head, old son. I remember you when you were nobbut a scruffy little actor touting for walk-ons at the Court.

JOE: Aye. And I remember you when you used to write the Bedsit Cookery Column in the *Mirror*, so don't start that game.

SLOMAN: Ah. A thousand ways to make New Zealand lamb taste like meat. Halcyon days!

JOE: (*surveying the room*) Right. I'll have a drink. (*He crosses, pours himself a small red wine.*) Will you have another, Malc?

SLOMAN: It's dead. I can't find another.

Joe stoops, opens cupboard, surveys stack of bottles.

JOE: I've no blended. Could you drink a malt?

SLOMAN: I suppose I'll have to, if you've nowt else.

Joe pours him a long malt, hands it to him.

JOE: Cheers, Malc.

SLOMAN: Cheers, flower.

He drinks, pulls a face, shudders a little, sits opposite him. Silence.

Liked your kid.

JOE: Yeah, he's all right.

SLOMAN: We had a few pints in The Anchor, last night was it, yeah I think it was last night.

JOE: He said.

SLOMAN: He was going for a job or someat. How did he go on?

JOE: They've offered, I think.

SLOMAN: Good.

JOE: He's started getting ambitious.

SLOMAN: How d'you mean?

JOE: He wants to set up on his own.

SLOMAN: Uhunh.

JOE: Wants me to stake him.

SLOMAN: Mmmm? And will you?

JOE: I don't know.

SLOMAN: Is it a lot?

JOE: No. It's nothing. Couple of hundred.

SLOMAN: So what's the problem?

JOE: There's no problem. It just makes one feel ... uneasy.

SLOMAN: Yeah? Why?

JOE: It seems illogical to use my surpluses to help set up a capitalist enterprise, that's all.

SLOMAN: A what?

JOE: That's what it'll be, Malc. Our kid being the boss doesn't make it different or special. There'll be people working for him and he'll be making a profit on their labour, just as in any other capitalist enterprise. I ask myself: If this were someone else – not my brother – asking me to help him set up a shirt factory, what would I say? No, wouldn't I? And that fast too.

SLOMAN: So why the unease now, mmm? If it's that clearcut, say no and have done with it.

Pause. Joe looks away.

Unless there's something else.

Silence.

P'raps you need a brother ... down there ... with the workers, eh?

JOE: It's not that.

SLOMAN: No? Perhaps not.

Silence.

JOE: (*checking watch*) Do you want to talk about the ninety?

SLOMAN: (*reclining, eyes closed*) Jesus Christ, Joe, I sometimes wonder if there exists a background you couldn't adapt to. It's a play, Joe. Somehow or other, when it's written, it will be squeezed and tugged and shunted and fattened and primped until it finally slurps and slithers into the ninety minute ... hole ... your masters have graciously reserved for it. (*Pause.*) It's a play, Joe.

Pause.

JOE: Do you want to talk about the play then?

SLOMAN: No. (*He gets up, crosses to the cabinet; he's fairly sodden.*) How's the wife, as they say.

JOE: She's fine. She's out.

SLOMAN: Tell me something. (*Pours with exaggerated care.*) Why do your wives always hate me so. (*He smiles sweetly in Joe's direction, takes a testing sip from the glass he's just filled with Glenmorangie.*)

JOE: Do they?

SLOMAN: Kara was the same. Reviled the ground I trod on.

JOE: Your taste for melodrama is virtually bottomless, Mr Sloman. Neither Angie nor Kara hate you. They simply find you mildly detestable. Nothing singular in that: it's a finding they share with just about the whole of your social network.

SLOMAN: Ah, well, that's er obviously a matter of nuance, Mr Shawcross. The ... detestation with which most of those I know greet and treat me you very properly characterize as mild; whereas what I sense emanates from your erstwhile wife and her enviably beautiful successor is of such virulence and extent that not even my deep sentimental attachment to your good self can serve to persuade me from my original and persistent contention; namely, that both the bitches fucking well hate me. When did we learn to talk like puffs, Joe? Cheers.

JOE: You sneer more than you used to.

SLOMAN: I know. I lack love.

Joe leaves the room, headed for the kitchen. Sloman stands, has a little sodden wander barefooted round the room. He reaches the door Joe has gone through.

What're you doing?

JOE: Fetching the food.

SLOMAN: What food?

Joe appears with a trolley laden with chicken pieces, cole slaw, french rolls, etc.

JOE: The food. (*He places the trolley carefully by the drinks cabinet, looks around the room.*)

SLOMAN: You don't need a wife, Joe. You need a husband.

Joe ignores him, breaks open a 200 pack of Senior Service.

Who've you got coming then?

JOE: Hard to say. Ford, do you know Andrew Ford? *Review*? He said he'd be here.

SLOMAN: Not the Gower Street Terror, Flash Ford, the New Left's answer to Joseph Stalin!

JOE: Ford's OK. I've asked him to have something ready, in case we need it. General background, that kind of thing …

SLOMAN: Oh. Terrific. Who else?

JOE: Somebody from Agitprop. Ball, I think he's called. Doing good stuff in the factories.

SLOMAN: Women. What about women?

JOE: Kara. My erstwhile etc.

SLOMAN: Oh Jesus. Women I said. I think you've forgotten what they are! Kara's not a woman, she's a political position. (*Pause.*) And like I said, she hates the sight of me. (*He grins.*) It's a cunt, innit!

JOE: I asked a couple of girls from I.S.

SLOMAN: Ah. Thank God for I.S. Who else?

JOE: Jeremy Hayes.

SLOMAN: Oh Christ. Worse and worse. Listen, it's bad enough I have to see my agent on business. You're not serious.

JOE: Why not? He's starting a weekly paper soon. He's raised the bread, Malc. You know? While others sit and sneer at the playboy literary agent with a penchant for left-wing politics, he's raised two and a half grand and the paper is going to happen.

SLOMAN: Well, Joe, old flower, when you've seen a copy or two, mebbe you'll have cause to change your opinion. What's he going to call it? *The Opportunist?* Who else?

JOE: John Tagg.

Silence. Sloman puts his glass down.

SLOMAN: John Tagg?

JOE: That's right.

SLOMAN: You always had a touch of the marriage feast at Cana in you, Joe. S'what makes you a good producer, I suppose. How come?

JOE: Simple. He asked me to call the meeting.

SLOMAN: Asked you. Why you? I don't get the connection.

JOE: I met one or two of his people at the union branch. They seemed to talk a lot of sense.

SLOMAN: They do, they do.

JOE: So, I er … went down to Battersea and met … Tagg and one or two others. And er … he said he was keen to get some sort of dialogue going on the left. So I offered my place for a meeting.

SLOMAN: Nice of you. (*Pause.*) Is that what he said: Dialogue?

JOE: Ahuuh.

SLOMAN: A dialogue with the Trots. That should be worth trying to stay sober for.

JOE: Perhaps I should've told you earlier then.

SLOMAN: Don't worry about me, old son. I'll make out.

The doorbell rings twice.

Ah. Ladies first, I trust.

JOE: (*at doorway*) Are you er …?

He points to his neck and chest. Sloman blinks at his shoes, the socks half hanging from them.

SLOMAN: I lose 'em else, Joe. Yeah sure.

Joe leaves. Sloman stands unsteadily, tries to undo the knot at the back of his neck; can't. **Susie** *and* **Kate** *in (the two I.S. people) early twenties, attractive in an earnest sort of way.*

SUSIE: Hello. I'm Susie Plaistow.

SLOMAN: (*blinking, smiling a broad silly smile*) Welcome Susie. You look like an International Socialist to me.

SUSIE: That's right, how did you know.

SLOMAN: *(tapping it)* The nose knows, Susie. Trust it always. Malcolm Sloman.

KATE: '24 Hours'.

SLOMAN: *(looking at watch, frowning)* What?

SUSIE: '24 Hours' is on in three minutes. We want to see what's happening in Paris.

SLOMAN: That's no problem. *(He switches the set on.)* Come round here then where it's warm.

KATE: *(crossing)* Kate Stead. How do you do.

She shakes his hand firmly. Sloman has his hand shaken. They stand in front of him staring at the box. It's amateur boxing. Sloman peers from Susie to Kate and back again, over their shoulders. It's a thorough inspection.

KATE: It's late.

SUSIE: Mmmmm.

SLOMAN: *(tentatively)* On your own, are you then, Susie?

*The door opens and **Louis Preece**, black, big, American, mid twenties, enters, followed by **Richard Maine**, younger, I.S., into student politics at LSE.*

SUSIE: S'all right, you've missed nothing, it hasn't started yet.

MAINE: Fat lot you care. Why can't you park your own car?

SUSIE: *(to Sloman)* Sorry, what did you say?

SLOMAN: *(sad)* Nothing. I didn't say a thing, love.

KATE: Shh. It's on.

*'24 Hours' music. Louis turns the sound up. Sloman picks up his drink, walks slowly out through the french windows unobserved, shoes still around his neck. Joe ushers in **'Grease' Ball,** a burly north London anarchist working in street theatre.*

JOE: Make yourself at home, Grease. I'll do the introductions when that ends.

GREASE: Ta.

Grease sniffs round the room, pecks a smile or two at the watching others as he catches an eye, settles finally in front of the set.

JOE: There's food on the trolley, if anyone's interested. Booze over there. Give a shout if you want anything else. I'm expecting others … so … p'raps we should watch this for a bit anyway.

Mostly he's ignored. Louis gives him a bland wink but no smile and returns to the screen. Close but not vital attention at this stage, as Robert McKenzie gives a studio background to the present discontent. Suddenly they move by satellite to Paris itself and the scene of the student demonstration. Louis turns up the volume, the atmosphere becomes immediately more charged and sparky. Fade lights;

bring up the bulletin they're watching on the wall screen behind them. The grand march to the Sorbonne has begun. Torches flare, there is much banter, humour and resolution. Caped police and CRS line routes and hold strategic points along it. A rather breathless English commentary tries to account for what we see.

Fade everything to black.

Fade up again. TV, wall screen pic, followed by room lights. People still stand or sit, rather stunned and excited. On the screen, Harry Carpenter is sunnily welcoming us back to the ringside at the Albert Hall, where England are matched with Poland.

LOUIS: Right on! Doesn't that blow your mind though? Jesus Christ, I need a j. *(He fiddles in his pocket for grass and papers.)*

SUSIE: *(crossing to switch set off)* What're we doing here, for Christ's sake! It's started, man.

Animated chat develops among those who know each other. Wall pic disappears. Room back to full light. Others have arrived during the programme: **Kara Massingham,** *early thirties, attractively mannish, in light blue suede trousers and matching suede tasselled waistcoat, and* **Jeremy Hayes,** *late thirties, suave, attractive, a trace of south London still there beneath the Kensington charm.*

GREASE: *(at the food trolley)* All right if I help myself, is it?

JOE: Sure thing. Please do. Drink over there. *(generally)* Listen. P'raps it'd be better if we said who we were as and when. I'm Joe Shawcross.

For the next several minutes people settle in, grab food, help each other to drink etc.

LOUIS: *(licking paper delicately)* Louis Preece. I'm with Kate. Hi.

MAINE: Richard Maine. LSE.

JOE: Hello.

SUSIE: Is that all right?

JOE: Of course. This is er ... Ed, is it?

GREASE: *(chicken in each fist)* Someat like that. Grease'll do. Howdy.

JOE: Grease is in street theatre. Erm. Kara Massingham ... works for the *Guardian.*

Kara smiles.

And Jeremy Hayes.

HAYES: Hi.

JOE: *(to Kara)* Did you see Malcolm Sloman anywhere?

KARA: What, here? No.

SUSIE: *(pointing to window)* Through there.

Doorbell rings.

JOE: (*turning to Kara*) Watch out for him if he comes back. (*He swivels an imaginary glass.*)

KARA: No! Really?

Joe gets the door. Louis hands the joint to Susie.

KATE: (*mock-northern, at the splendid room*) Not short of a bob or two, are we!

LOUIS: Don't be small town, chickie. Some of my best friends are rich Liberals.

KATE: I bet.

SUSIE: Stop bitching, for Christ's sake.

MAINE: (*serious, taking joint*) That's right. Where should he live, a hovel?

GREASE: Why not? That's where most of us live.

MAINE: Speak for yourself.

GREASE: (*mildly*) I do, brother.

LOUIS: (*to Kate*) Hey, hey, hey, hey. Time enough for squabbles after the revolution. It's a nice pad. OK. Finish.

*Hayes and Kara look at each other frowningly. They feel themselves no longer this juvenile. Joe in with **Andrew Ford**, around thirty, tallish, blond, pale skinned, rather beautiful in the face. He's a lecturer in sociology; sharp, articulate, arrogant beneath the slight charm.*

SUSIE: Hello. How are you?

FORD: (*cool*) Fine. How're you?

SUSIE: OK.

JOE: Erm … Andrew Ford, LSE, etc., etc. Erm … well, I guess you'll find who everybody else is by closing time. Food (*pointing*), booze (*looking round*). Right. I suppose I ought to try and set things rolling.

People settle down a little. Ford helps himself to food and drink. Sloman in from terrace. He carries an empty Scotch bottle. He taps on the window.

SLOMAN: (*boy's voice*) Excuse me, is this where they're going to have the revolution?

JOE: Come on, Malc …

SLOMAN: (*in*) Hello, Susie. How you doing, chick? Oh, and beautiful Kara, up to her delectable *directoires* in theory. What a lovely surprise. It must be Ex-Wives' Night. I hope to Christ mine don't show.

KARA: (*to Susie*) It's all right. He has to rattle his balls from time to time, to make sure they're still there.

SLOMAN: (*to Susie*) Inspection's in an hour, love, if you're interested. Actually I'm looking for a small drink of thingie, you know. (*seeing Hayes*) Something for you, Jeremy? Small hemlock, maybe?

HAYES: I'm fine, Malcolm.

SLOMAN: Good. That good. (*He wanders over to the drinks, where Ford stands.*) Hello, Flash, how's it been then? Still sorting Cuba out are we?

FORD: (*cool*) Hello, Sloman.

SLOMAN: (*over shoulder, to Joe*) Where's Tagg, then, Shawkie? He'd be late for his own insurrection would that one.

JOE: Get your drink and sit down, Malc.

SLOMAN: Aye aye, sir. (*He carries a bottle over towards the windows, lies flat on the floor, the bottle on his chest. Muttering*) God help you, that's all. All of you.

FORD: Did he say Tagg?

JOE: Yes, I was trying to explain.

SLOMAN: (*muttering*) I bet.

JOE: This is one of a series of small, private meetings that the Revolutionary Socialist Party's organizing, both here in London and er … throughout the country generally. Now, I'm not a member of the Party, but I'm convinced that what the left in Britain needs now more than ever is a united and coherent focus for its efforts. But above all, we need theory. Not necessarily the RSP's but a genuine socialist analysis of our situation that will give us a rational basis for political action beyond the single-issue activities that have kept us fragmented and … impotent … in the past.

KARA: But why Tagg?

LOUIS: Who's Tagg, for Christ's sake?

SLOMAN: Who's Mighty Joe Young!

JOE: John Tagg is the National Organiser of the RSP and an executive member of the reconstituted Fourth International. Why Tagg? Why not? At least he's clear about what he wants. He has an organization. And above all he wants to talk. He wants a dialogue.

KARA: He's after money. I know Tagg.

JOE: (*calmly*) Put it to him. He'll be here directly.

GREASE: You mean we gotta sit around waiting for him?

JOE: No, no. Not at all. You got something to say, you say it.

GREASE: I mean, it's just bleeding pointless sitting here getting pissed, I can do that at home.

FORD: What does he aim to do when he does come?

JOE: I don't know. Talk, I suppose.

SLOMAN: (*from floor*) You bet.

KARA: He won't do much listening, that's for sure. P'raps he'll organize a séance. The last meeting of his I went to he called up the ghost of Lev Davidovitch from a bound copy of the Transitional Programme. It was amazing.

FORD: Tagg's all right. He can be handled.

SLOMAN: (*muttering but clear enough*) Cream bun, I've seen him eat bigger fellers than you with a pint of Guinness and a pickle on a plate. You'd do better sticking to your (*lies down again*) Late Night Line-Up.

KATE: (*bored*) Meantime …

SLOMAN: How about a sing song?

FORD: Who was it said personality is the gonorrhoea of the left? Would anybody mind if we talked politics? Mmmm? I don't mind kicking off, if there are no objections.

Silence of assent.

OK.

He looks at the students; he's assured, confident, pleased to be in charge; already rejecting the notes in his briefcase.

Joe asked me to make a few notes on general background theory, but it's pretty obvious where the body of our interest lies. So I suggest we put the notes away. (*He puts the case down and gets started.*)

The door opens and **Tagg** *walks in. He's short, stocky, very powerful, about sixty, Scots, from Glasgow. He wears an old-fashioned double-breasted suit, tie slack at open-collared neck; neck bursting to be free. His face is cragged, expressionless. He carries a small flat pigskin document case in his righthand.*

TAGG: (*mildly*) Good evening. Sorry I'm late.

Silence. Even Sloman sits up, relishing the moment.

JOE: John. Good to see you. Come in, come in. We were just getting underway. Eats and drinks over there, let me get you something.

TAGG: (*advancing into room*) No, I'm fine thanks. Why don't you just carry on and I'll sit and listen for a while?

JOE: Do you want me to introduce you …?

TAGG: No no. (*to room*) My name's John Tagg, for what it's worth. That'll do for now.

JOE: Fine. Andrew?

Ford deliberates for a moment, not sure whether to cede the floor at once; or perhaps unconsciously modifying his presentation now that Tagg's arrived.

FORD: Well. It seems there are a number of options open to us. Quite frankly, I'm more interested in talking about France – or Paris, to be more precise – than about general Marxist theory. On the other hand, perhaps it would do no harm to try and tease out some basic agreement on ... well, terminology, for example.

SLOMAN: (*muttering, on back*) Oh yeah, I think we should tease that out. Definitely.

FORD: (*to Tagg*) What do you think?

TAGG: (*simply*) I leave it to you.

FORD: I mean, I'm perfectly happy to hand over to you right now, if you'd prefer it.

TAGG: No no. You go ahead

GREASE: I don't wanna talk about terminology. Jesus Christ, what is this!

JOE: Well, what's the general feeling then? Mmmmm?

KATE: Let him speak.

LOUIS: (*rolling joint*) Right on.

MAINE: Right.

JOE: Kara? Jeremy?

They nod.

SUSIE: Come on, come on. There's twenty thousand people contesting state power in Paris and we can't even decide what to talk about! (*to Ford*) Say something eh!

FORD: Right. (*Brief-case back in hand and opened. Seminar voice developing – as he pushes at once into his favourite game of political theory.*) Let me try to offer a relatively unexceptional account of the basic Marxian analysis; and then suggest a few (*glance at Tagg*) ... revisions of my own. (*Pause.*) It's in *Economic and Philosophical Manuscripts*, written in 1844, that we receive our first authoritative definitions. Communism, says the young Marx, is the positive abolition of private property, of human self-alienation and thus the real appropriation of human nature, through and for man. It is therefore the return of man himself as a *social*, that is, really human being, a complete and conscious return which assimilates all the wealth of previous development. He elaborates the point later on thus: Communism is the *definitive* resolution of the antagonism between man and nature, and between man and man. It is the true solution of the conflict between existence and essence, between objectification and self-affirmation, between freedom and necessity, between individual and species. It is the solution of the riddle of History and knows itself to be this solution. Now I think we have there a crucial locus, both moral and scientific, for almost everything we say and do as socialists now. We have, there, at once a vision of future societies in which the social, that's to say, fully *human* aspects of mankind will flourish; and in addition, some indication of its historical inevitability. As Marx has it: 'Communism as a complete naturalism is humanism, and as a complete humanism is naturalism.' The task Marx and the nineteenth-century Marxists set themselves was to chart, precisely and empirically, the way in which these future societies would form or be formed. Part of that ... description concerned itself with the nature of social classes; in particular, with the three major classes in post-feudal society: bourgeoisie, peasantry, proletariat. The precondition for the domination of society in general by a single class is, according to Marx, that that class should identify itself with the society, and will be felt and recognized as the general representative of that society. Its aims and interests must genuinely be the aims and interests of society itself, of which it becomes, in Marx's phrase, the 'social head and heart'. But even that's not enough. For one class to represent the whole of society, another class must concentrate in itself all the evils of society and embody and represent a general obstacle and limitation. In his words: 'For one class to be the liberating class *par excellence*, it is essential that another class should be openly the oppressing class.' But notice: it is never enough that these competing classes should merely co-exist at a particular historical conjunction. Classes that wish to become liberating classes must possess, as it were, self-consciousness sufficient to enable them to organize their victory. Logic, insight, courage and clarity – these are the social qualities that would-be liberating classes must possess if they are to realize their full historical potential. I dwell on this part of the model, because it represents a most interesting duality or conjunction, between material inevitability on the one hand, and human agency on the other. A thumbnail sketch of Marxist praxis in the nineteenth century would show, I think, an increasing and debilitating emphasis on inevitability and a critical undermining of the role of agency. Hence the Second International, with its over-mechanistic view of what constituted the 'proper' historical-material conditions for a genuine proletarian revolution; and, in particular, a slavish adherence to the Marxian tenet that a proletarian revolution was impossible in societies that had not first undergone a bourgeois revolution. It was the unique and deeply original contribution of Lenin – a poor Marxist, in the academic sense of the term – that he redressed this balance; that he reintroduced human will and agency to the Marxist discourse. Stressing organization, ruthless discipline and the central role of the party, he pretty nearly single-handedly forced through a working-class revolution in what was, by any standards, a materially underdeveloped, still largely feudal society. In other words, he showed that it was possible to tear down the inflexible historical model and fashion history, to some extent at least, in the image of his own Bolshevik party. (*Pause.*) Of course, what I'm suggesting here is that ... 'revisionism' has a thoroughly ... revolutionary ... antecedence: the late Marx revised the early Marx, Engels revised the late Marx, Lenin revised the lot of them. (*Pause.*) Well, a few modest revisions of my own ... It seems to me that, from Lenin on, the older model has grown increasingly more irrelevant, for a number of reasons. I mean, one look at France or Britain today is enough to make the point, I think. The world we now inhabit and hope to act upon is a vastly different one from that on which Marx made his largely empirical calculations and observations. The Russian revolution is a fact. Its development – in a single country, with all the distortions that have inevitably occurred as a result – is a fact. The post-Second World War Soviet camp in Europe, modelled on those precise deformations of Russian socialism, is a fact. Equally, the nature of capitalism – particularly its deep technical and bureaucratic self-transformations and adaptations – national to multinational via multicorporative – is an empirical fact that in a sense leaves the classical nineteenth-century Marxian analysis behind. So that we must increasingly come to regard the history of twentieth-century Europe as a history of vacuums: no German revolution; no French revolution; no Italian revolution; no British revolution. Instead, the gradual absorption, the slow assimilation of European proletariats into the institutions of the reformed and superadaptive bourgeois state. And if we accept the model so far we cannot avoid taking some account of the what? – hegemonic mechanisms – through which that … inhibition of revolutionary potential was achieved. Because one of the first things those states have sought to do is to mediate, to obscure, to mystify their own class nature, by securing unto themselves a vastly more powerful and pervasive system of propaganda; by which I mean, of course, educational institutions, art forms, newspapers, television, and all the many large- and small-scale means of communication existing in contemporary post-industrial societies. In 1968, European proletariats can no longer be said to be a subversive force inside capitalism, because European proletariats no longer feel themselves faced by a European bourgeoisie that concentrates in itself, to return to Marx; 'All the evils of society, embodying and representing a general obstacle and limitation.'

He pauses, enjoying himself more than he dare show. In his proper element. Varieties of reaction: Tagg impassive. Finally.

SLOMAN: You don't say.

FORD: (*ignoring him*) So, we need a new model, perhaps a new concept. The Marxian notion of a revolution carried by the majority of the exploited masses, culminating in the seizure of power and in the setting up of a proletarian dictatorship which initiates socialization, is overtaken by historical development. I would even argue that Marx himself would now see that that analysis pertains to a stage of capitalist productivity and organization which has been overtaken; it does not project the higher stage of capitalist productivity self-evidently achieved in the last half-century, including the productivity of destruction and the terrifying concentration of the instruments of annihilation and of indoctrination in the hands of the state or its class representatives. Nor does that analysis take account of the machinery of what Marcuse calls the 'repressive tolerance' of neocapitalist societies, of which, if I may say so, we are all living, breathing examples. The very fact of our being tolerated tends to render us impotent. (*Pause. Another pan round the listening group*) The element so far omitted, of course, is what has been termed the Third World. China, Cuba, Vietnam: these are the new centres of the world revolutionary struggle. The national liberation movements in the colonial enclave are probably the sole and certainly the principal revolutionary forces at work in the world today. The capitalist heartland is no longer London, or Paris, or Turin: it is Saigon, it is Angola, it is Mozambique. The 'weak link' in the capitalist chain is now at the periphery, and it is there, if anywhere, that the chain will be induced to snap. We move from centre to epicentre, which becomes the new centre. Our function, in the old centres, is to assist, however we may, the final victory of these anti-capitalist, revolutionary movements. Whether we are blacks in Detroit or white proletarians in Manchester, that is our sole remaining revolutionary purpose and duty. And, a last note of direct application here, I think, we must not seek to impose upon these movements the theoretical and organizational patterns elaborated for and applied to the strategy of metropolitan areas; such as city-based leaderships, centralized party control, and all the dead wood of European practice. (*Pause. To Joe*) I'll stop there, if that's all right.

JOE: Sure, sure. Thanks very much.

FORD: (*coolly*) I don't want to steal anybody else's thunder.

An awkward silence develops. The students look at each other, pulling faces.

JOE: Well …

GREASE: It's just books. What's the point, I mean!

HAYES: I found it useful. But I thought you could've found a spot for students as a sub-class in your model. Bearing in mind what's been happening in Europe and America, I mean. You know, I think the Rudi Dutschke shooting and what's happening in Paris really do need some serious analysis.

LOUIS: Students! How about blacks, for Christ's sake! Holy Jesus!! Forty-six American cities under black siege this year and we haven't even started the summer yet. That's where the future lies, man. That's the only revolution that's gonna matter, believe it.

Some expostulation, counter-argument etc.

FORD: Blacks and students, sure. Nobody's denying their importance. All I've tried to do is give a general theoretical framework into which they can fit …

KARA: And women?

SLOMAN: (*sitting up*) Where, where?

FORD: Yes, but which women? Are they all equally oppressed? All potentially revolutionary?

MAINE: (*pompous*) I missed any telling reference to social democracy and its relation to capitalist structures.

Silence greets this. He grows uneasy.

I think … a socialist analysis should … have something to say about … the Wilson government … and its record.

Sloman gets up and walks to the drinks cabinet, saying 'Ehhhhhh' as he goes.

GREASE: It doesn't matter, any of it. It's not bloody relevant. None of it answers the question: What are we going to do? I've been to extra-mural classes ... That's why I'm here now.

SLOMAN: (*pouring drinks*) Why don't we form an International Brigade to keep the Spanish off Gibraltar!

FORD: (*to Joe*) Oh Jesus, is he going to go on all night with this puerile patter?

JOE: (*low*) No, it's all right, he'll ... er ... settle down.

The lack of direction is showing. Still Tagg sits tight, a hard and impassive Buddha. A few glance towards him, frustrated, a trifle angry at the fragmented nature of the meeting so far. Sloman ambles back to around centre, stops, chicken leg in one hand, Scotch in other, stares very deliberately at Ford.

SLOMAN: (*swaying very slightly*) I've heard better warm-ups at a funeral. (*He sniffs, drinks, tries to think. To Tagg*) How about it, John? Are you going to tell us about how, if the earth hadn't been created flat, man would have had to flatten it? I like that one. I think it's your best one, I do.

Silence. Sloman's smile hardens the offence.

TAGG: (*mild but deliberate*) Sloman. I'm not here to talk salon rubbish with a drunk. Is that all right?

JOE: Why don't you go out for a bit, Malc?

SLOMAN: (*bullish*) I don't want to go out!

KARA: Well, shut up, will you. You're a bloody nuisance!

SLOMAN: (*to Joe*) See! See! Don't tell me nothing. The bitch hates me!

HAYES: Rubbish, Malcolm. We all love you dearly.

SLOMAN: Oh yes. And you've twenty grand in the bank to prove it, agent.

TAGG: (*to Joe principally*) Did you agree a form?

JOE: I'm sorry?

TAGG: A form. For the meeting.

JOE: Erm, well no, not really, no. Do you have something in mind?

GREASE: What's wrong with just talking?

TAGG: Free for all is free for nobody. I'm not interested in conversation. I'm here for discussion. Structured. With a shape and an end.

GREASE: You want us to number from the left or something?

TAGG: No. But we could have a chair.

GREASE: What do we want a chair for? Jesus Christ. There's ten of us, man. Suddenly we need a bureaucracy.

JOE: Well, I don't know. What does anybody think?

HAYES: Doesn't bother me either way. If it makes Mr Tagg feel happier, we'll have a chair

KARA: The hell we will. He's right. Talk at will.

LOUIS: Jesus, elections! We haven't even got a platform!

KATE: That's right. (*She takes Louis's joint.*)

JOE: Andrew?

FORD: I've no objections to a chair. I don't even object to an elected executive that meets in the garden to draw up an agenda. I simply object to the tactic.

JOE: What does that mean?

FORD: It's all boringly familiar, Joe. Do we have a form, let's get ourselves organized. I've heard it all before. What's important is to stifle spontaneity. (*ironic*) By all means, let's have a chair.

Silence.

TAGG: (*mildly*) All right. No chair. It doesn't matter.

SLOMAN: (*by window now*) You should take that back, playboy.

TAGG: Why don't you go somewhere else, Sloman?

SLOMAN: (*raging suddenly*) Because I don't fucking well WANT to Tagg. Don't come your God the Father bit with me, right?

JOE: Easy, Malc.

SLOMAN: (*blowing*) FUCK OFF. I don't need your ...protection you creeping get. Just get off my back.

He lurches, kicks a bottle and some glasses over, clutches at a chair as he loses balance, drags it down to the floor with him, struggles to get up again, turns another chair over. People clear a circle for his mad sprawl. He stands at last, a bottle in his hand.

JOE: (*through this*) Malc, for Christ's sake take it EASY will you, man, will you?

SLOMAN: Fuck off. (*swallowing, puffing, searching for control*) What do you lot know, eh. Any of you? Preening. Preening. On the scene. It doesn't hurt, does it? Any of it. (*at the main group*) Does it!!

He swings round suddenly to hurl his bottle through a window. Glass cascades on to the floor. Joe closes.

JOE: Come on, Malc, let's have you. Come on.

Joe goes to put his arms round Sloman, is hurled backwards by a tremendous thrash of arms and shoulders.

SLOMAN: Get off me. Just get off. Just get your hands off me. I'm not a bloody plaything. (*He blinks and scowls, drunk, dangerous, in pain.*) I just want to say something. You see, if you could understand it, we could ... get somewhere. If you could feel it, I mean. (*quoting, searching for the words*) 'As long as I breathe I shall fight for the future, that ... radiant future, in which man, strong and beautiful, will become master of the drifting stream of his own history ...

He stands a little dazed and hypnotized, not sure where he is or why. One or two Jesuses from Kate and Kara. Everyone still apprehensive. Tagg gets up slowly and walks towards Sloman.

TAGG: (*Gently*) 'I can see the bright green ... strip of grass beneath the wall and the clear blue sky above the wall, and sunlight everywhere. Life ... is beautiful. Let the future generations cleanse it ... of all evil ... oppression, and violence, and enjoy it to the full.'

Sloman is quiet and close to tears. The tears are only half self-pitying, he is truly moved by the words and the delivery.

Have a sleep.

SLOMAN: You're ... old, John.

TAGG: Have a sleep.

Sloman looks around the room, at the broken window, then lurches out into the garden. The guinea pig sets up a whining squeal as he bangs against the cage.

SLOMAN: (*off*) Go thou! I'll fetch some flax and whites of egg, to apply to his bleeding face.

FORD: (*scathing*) What a wreck!

The pig's squeals get louder. Charlie begins to cry upstairs. Milanka in from training, bag on shoulder.

MILANKA: I'll see to him. *(She leaves.)*

Muttering and staring, Tagg looks round the room, as the squeals tail off and Charlie's crying is muted by Milanka's indistinct soothings.

TAGG: (*finally*) Will we make a start?

Black.

Black stage. 'The Red Flag', in French, vibrant, full-lunged; it fades. Lights up front left; a segment of terrace, hint of long, controlled lawn and gardens. A swing, a kid's bike, a climbing frame, canvas chairs, plants in tubs, the pig hutch knocked askew on its supporting brick stacks, the wall of the house. Joe carries a bulky flash-light with a flashing red top, scores the lawn area (out front, that is) with it. He stops to right the hutch, strokes the wires gently with his finger, returns to his search eventually. Upstairs, Milanka has been singing 'Ej Od Buchlova' to Charlie.

JOE: Malc. Malc. Come on in.

The singing stops. An upstairs window opens

MILANKA: (*from window, soft, into the darkness*) He is quiet.

JOE: (*whispering*) Fine. Thanks.

MILANKA: I make coffee?

JOE: Thanks. Big pot.

MILANKA: How is Novotny?

JOE: Indestructible.

MILANKA: I make the coffee.

She withdraws. Joe turns into the garden again.

JOE: Malc.

A crashing sound somewhere in the dark. The pig shrieks once.

MALC: It's Joe. Come on in.

No answer. Joe stands for a long time staring out, immobile, inert. He is without energy or direction. Kara appears behind him; watches him for several moments without speaking. She shivers a little in the cool night air.

KARA: (*finally*) Leave him. He'll be all right.

JOE: He's there somewhere. (*Pause.*) He's hurt.

KARA: He's just drunk.

Pause. Kara lights a Gauloise.

JOE: What's happening …?

KARA: Someone's cleaning up the mess.

JOE: Yeah?

They both laugh, though tentatively.

KARA: And then Tagg brings down the tablets.

Pause.

JOE: You with Hayes?

KARA: Sort of.

JOE: Uhunh. What about Margaret?

KARA: He's left her. There was nothing there.

JOE: Oh.

KARA: Is that all right?

JOE: Sorry. (*Pause.*) So, what're you doing with yourself?

KARA: Oh, surviving, as they say. Jeremy's trying to get this paper out.

JOE: I heard about it. Sounds good. Are you involved?

KARA: Yes. Sort of. We've formed a collective to run it. Seven of us.

JOE: Do you have a line?

KARA: Several. About seven.

JOE: Sounds familiar.

Pause.

KARA: How about you?

JOE: Yeah I'm fine.

KARA: Angie?

JOE: Yes. She's fine too. She's out.

KARA: I noticed. (*Pause.*) Do you want to talk?

JOE: No. I'm fine. Really.

KARA: Why don't you give me a call at the office, we'll have a drink sometime.

JOE: I will. D'be nice.

KARA: You've stopped talking, haven't you?

JOE: Howd'you mean?

KARA: You don't say anything. I watched you in there. You have … no opinions. You have no … energy.

JOE: They also serve who only keep their lips buttoned.

KARA: Don't go under, Joe.

JOE: D'you remember the Fields Season at the NFT? (*He flicks an imaginary cigar, perfect Fields voice.*) 'Never drink water. Fish make love in it.' (*own voice*) I just stopped drinking water.

Silence.

KARA: Drink water.

JOE: I'm sick of … opinions.

KARA: Oh yes?

JOE: No, it's … tones of voice I'm sick of. (*He points at the house.*) We do this like we do everything else. It's a game. It's an intellectual pursuit. Or something worse. It's part of being … bourgeois. Peel the onion: find the nuance beneath the hint, the insight in the discrimination, the complexity below the conceit. I'm sick of metaphors. They induce only inertia. (*Pause.*) We've got upper second souls. Do you know?

KARA: Mmmm. Well, at least you're drinking water again.

JOE: (*smiling*) Sipping.

KARA: We fucked out here once. Do you remember?

JOE: Yes.

KARA: It was good then.

JOE: Was it?

KARA: Only from here. (*She turns to go in. Turns back.*) What's your connection with Tagg?

JOE: Why?

KARA: I think he's poisonous. Don't let him bite you.

JOE: No. He doesn't play our sort of game, that's all.

KARA: Come on, Joe. You're not falling for all that sentimental working-man crap, are you. (*Pause.*) Think of your father. Eh?

JOE: Is it likely? I never fell for anything in my life. Perhaps that's why I'm such a sodding shambles.

KARA: He'll leach you dry. I'm telling you. I know Tagg. And he's irrelevant. You can drive a coach-and-four through his analysis. He's a brutal shite underneath with a fist where his mind used to be. Now I'm telling you.

Silence.

JOE: (*very quiet*) Yeah.

KARA: You coming in?

JOE: Sure. In a minute.

She wavers, finally leaves. Joe stands looking out into the garden, sweeps the darkness once, twice, with the torch, switches to red alarm signal, places the torch on the ground, walks slowly in. It flashes throughout the remainder of the Scene.

Living-room lights up, as Joe re-enters. Kara has rejoined Hayes. People sit or lie. Lights lower than before, no longer quite natural. Tagg roughly centred, marginally better lit, perches on a stool, not at home in this room. The mess has cleared. Milanka carries out the last of the glass in a dustpan.

TAGG: (*to Joe*) OK?

JOE: (*shutting french windows*) Yes, of course.

TAGG: I'll erm ... take issue with our comrade's er ... analysis and model presently. I'd like to start by explaining why I'm here. It's very simple really. I'm National Organizer and Executive Council Member of the RSP, which is the British branch of the reconstituted Fourth International, and bases itself on the *Transitional Programme* drawn up by Trotsky some years before his death. I spend most of my time with workers – dockers, miners, engineers, car-

workers, bricklayers, seamen. And as I'll try to explain later, a revolutionary
party or faction that fails to establish itself in the working class, to base itself
upon it, can lay no claim whatsoever to serious attention. (*Pause.*) But a
revolutionary Marxist who has lived in Europe, America, or almost anywhere
else, for that matter, during the last three or four years, would have to be blind
and deaf not to have noticed a considerable ... revolutionary potential, shall we
call it? growing among sections of the population whose relation to the
working class is either nonexistent, or extremely tenuous, or positively
antagonistic. I'm thinking of such categories as students, blacks, intellectuals,
social deviants of one sort or another, women, and so on. And so we've decided
to begin a general campaign of political education – including self-education, I
should add – that might result in a broader and more experienced base for all
our efforts. (*Pause.*) It's not a sudden accession of humility, I should point out.
It's not a drive for membership. It's not a fundraising effort. It's not a search
for ideological compromise and political blandness. If our analysis is correct,
we're entering a new phase in the revolutionary struggle against the forces and
the structures of capitalism. The disaffection is widespread: in London, in Paris,
in Berlin, in the American cities; wherever you care to look, bourgeois
institutions are under sustained and often violent attack. New forces are rising
up to throw themselves into the fray. The question is: How may they be
brought to help the revolution? Or are they simply doomed forever to be
merely 'protests' that the 'repressive tolerance' of 'late capitalist' societies will
absorb and render impotent? (*Pause.*) We shall need some theory, to answer
questions like those. But I suspect the theory will not be entirely in accord with
that which we have heard expounded by our comrade here tonight. (*Pause.*)
There's something profoundly saddening about that analysis. And, if I might be
permitted a small digression, it seems to reflect a basic sadness and pessimism
in you yourselves. You're intellectuals. You're frustrated by the ineffectual
character of your opposition to the things you loathe. Your main weapon is the
word. Your protest is verbal – it has to be: it wears itself out by repetition and
leads you nowhere. Somehow you sense – and properly so – that for a protest
to be effective, it must be rooted in the realities of social life, in the productive
processes of a nation or a society. In 1919 London dockers went on strike and
refused to load munitions for the White armies fighting against the Russian
revolution. In 1944 dockers in Amsterdam refused to help the Nazis transport
Jews to concentration camps. What can *you* do? You can't strike and refuse to
handle American cargoes until they get out of Vietnam. You're outside the
productive process. You have only the word. And you cannot make it become
the deed. And because the people who have the power seem uneager to use it,
you develop this ... cynicism ...this contempt. You say: The working class has
been assimilated, corrupted, demoralized. You point to his car and his house
and his pension scheme and his respectability, and you write him off. You build
a whole theory around it and you fill it with grandiloquent phrases like
'epicentres' and 'neocolonialism'. But basically what you do is you find some
scapegoat for your own frustration and misery and then you start backing the
field: blacks, students, homosexuals, terrorist groupings, Mao, Che Guevara,

anybody, just so long as they represent some repressed minority still capable of anger and the need for self-assertion. (*Pause.*) Well. Which workers have you spoken with recently? And for how long? How do you know they're not as frustrated as you are? Especially the young ones, who take the cars and the crumbs from the table for granted? If they don't satisfy *you*, why should they satisfy the people who actually create the wealth in the first place? You start from the presumption that only you are intelligent and sensitive enough to see how bad capitalist society is. Do you really think the young man who spends his whole life in monotonous and dehumanizing work doesn't see it too? And in a way more deeply, more woundingly? (*Pause.*) Suddenly you lose contact – not with ideas, not with abstractions, concepts, because they're after all your stock-in-trade. You lose contact with the moral tap-roots of socialism. In an objective sense, you actually stop believing in a revolutionary perspective, in the possibility of a socialist society and the creation of socialist man. You see the difficulties, you see the complexities and contradictions, and you settle for those as a sort of game you can play with each other. Finally, you learn to enjoy your pain; to need it, so that you have nothing to offer your bourgeois peers but a sort of moral exhaustion. You can't build socialism on fatigue, comrades. Shelley dreamed of man 'sceptreless, free, uncircumscribed, equal, classless, tribeless and nationless, exempt from all worship and awe'. Trotsky foresaw the ordinary socialist man on a par with an Aristotle, a Goethe, a Marx, with still new peaks rising above those heights. Have you any image at all to offer? The question embarrasses you. You've contracted the disease you're trying to cure. (*Pause.*) I called this a digression, but in a way it describes very accurately the difficulty I experience when I try to deal with our comrade's ... analysis. Comrade Sloman was right, under it all. Theory isn't abstract; it isn't words on a page; it isn't ... aesthetically pleasing patterns of ideas and evidence. Theory is concrete. It's distilled practice. Above all, theory is felt, in the veins, in the muscles, in the sweat on your forehead. In that sense, it's moral ... and binding. It's the essential connective imperative between past and future. (*Pause.*) Now when I look for any of this in our comrade's account, I can't find it; it isn't there. It's simply part of an elaborate game he enjoys playing and plays well.

FORD: (*angry but cool*) Do I get a chance to answer this?

TAGG: I hope you will. But let me finish first. (*Pause.*) I don't propose a catalogue of counter-assertions to refute the major points made, because I think we can use our time more profitably doing something else. And my text for tonight is really the role of the party in the formulation of revolutionary theory and the building of the socialist revolution. But I'll need to offer a vastly different political conspectus before I can do that. (*Pause.*) Comrade Ford describes the history of the twentieth century as a history of vacuums. That's to say, no proletarian revolutions in the heartland of world capitalism; initially Europe, increasingly, thereafter, America. Well, I felt he ran just a little fast through the actual events, you know. I mean, Germany 1919-20; Italy in the same period; Hungary; Bulgaria? Spain in '36. France in the same year, the year of the great

General Strike, five million workers raising the question of state power. Greece in '44. The absence of revolution is not final evidence of the elimination of revolutionary potential. But how does he account for this loss of revolutionary direction in Europe? Via Marcuse, we learn that the proletariats of advanced societies have been 'absorbed' into the value systems of the capitalist states, that they are now junior partners in capitalism with a stake in its future and the deepest resistance to anything that would upset the *status quo* of collective bargaining in a property-owning democracy. And this, in itself, is the final refutation of Marx's contention that capitalist societies were class societies whose inherent tensions and contradictions necessarily result in their supercession by social ownership of the already socialized productive forces of those same societies. All right, let's grant, descriptively, at least, an extraordinary low level of revolutionary militancy in metropolitan proletariats. What we have to decide, on the evidence, within the theory, is how this has come about and how it can be changed. Unless, of course, we slip the question altogether, by arguing that the revolutionary moment has gone floating off somewhere else and now rests with the peasant of Asia or Africa or South America, who presumably now must face not only the combined weight of imperialist expansion, massing behind the most sophisticated technology of destruction yet devised by man, but also the active opposition of bourgeoisified proletariats eager to defend their share of the cake against all comers, however oppressed and miserable they may be. (*Pause.*) What's missing is any genuine grasp of the dialectic, of the relationship between the class struggle *inside* the capitalist state and the extruded version of it being waged outwith. The fact is: the two are inextricably linked. There will be no victory in one without victory in both. But it must be the victory of the metropolitan proletariats that will herald the end of imperialist oppression. It is genuinely inconceivable that it could happen the other way round – think of it, think of it. Of course, the colonial struggle will go on, but does anyone really believe that America and Britain and France and Germany – mature capitalist states, at their level of technological development, with their economic resources and degree of destructive potential – will allow significant reversals to occur in their economic expansion without doing something about it? It's unthinkable. (*Pause.*) So we must answer the questions: How is it that metropolitan proletariats lack revolutionary potential; and how might this be changed? Because if we don't answer them, we might as well take up chess or billiards, because there will be no way in which we can effect the transition we've been talking about and trying to work towards. (*Pause.*) The European and American proletariats appear to have settled for the *status quo*, in my opinion, because they have been consistently and systematically betrayed by their leaders; and particularly by the Communist parties of the various European countries. A simple historical fact that finds no place in Comrade Ford's analysis: Stalinism. Socialism in one country meant the damping down of revolutionary ardour everywhere, even where the flame of revolution was breaking through every crevice of capitalist society. By 1933 the German Communist party, the strongest in Europe outside Russia, had delivered the

German working classes to Hitler on a plate. The French General Strike of
1936, which was undoubtedly based on a spontaneous proletarian desire to
contest state power, i.e. a genuine revolutionary situation, was cynically reined
back by the Stalinist hacks who led the PCF and turned quite deliberately into
a struggle for wage increases. Wage increases! At Stalin's behest. The working
class throughout Western Europe is even now, in most places, the prisoner of
those miserable, anti-revolutionary leaderships, where they are not the dupes of
the forces of social democracy. (*Pause.*) If we are to change all this, if we are
to put proletarian revolution back on the agenda of European history, we are
going to have to replace those defunct and corrupt leaderships with vital and
revolutionary ones. (*Pause.*) But those leaderships will emerge not as loose
coalitions or spontaneous coalescings, but as a result of patient organization
and disciplined effort. That's to say, those leaderships will develop from new
revolutionary *parties* which in turn will base themselves in and on the class
they seek to lead. There is only one slogan worth mouthing at this particular
historical conjunction. It is: 'Build the Revolutionary Party'. There is no other
slogan that can possibly take precedence.

*He stops, mops his wet face and neck. Nobody speaks. Buttocks are shifted, feet
wriggle, a match flares and sputters.*

FORD: (*finally*) Finished?

TAGG: Almost. (*Pause.*) The party means discipline. It means self-scrutiny,
criticism, responsibility, it means a great many things that run counter to the
traditions and values of Western bourgeois intellectuals. It means being bound
in and by a common purpose. But above all, it means deliberately severing
yourself from the prior claims on your time and moral commitment of personal
relationships, career, advancement, reputation and prestige. And from my
limited acquaintance with the intellectual stratum in Britain, I'd say that was
the greatest hurdle of all to cross. Imagine a life without the approval of your
peers. Imagine a life without *success*. The intellectual's problem is not vision,
it's commitment. You enjoy biting the hand that feeds you, but you'll never
bite it off. So those brave and foolish youths in Paris now will hold their heads
out for the baton and shout their crazy slogans for the night. But it won't stop
them from graduating and taking up their positions in the centres of ruling
class power and privilege later on.

Milanka in, with coffee etc, on trolley.

MILANKA: Some coffee?

Some release of tension. Buzz, hum.

TAGG: Why not?

*On the fade, the film screen bursts into life, CRS and students bloodily locked
around the Sorbonne, the volume massively up, the red alarm light still flashes on
the terrace.*

Blackout.

ACT TWO

Living-room. 2 a.m., Saturday, 11 May.

The meeting has broken. Louis, Maine and Kate have already left. Hayes is on the terrace looking for Sloman. Grease, crash-helmet on knee, leathers half buttoned, is listening to a record on expensive cans. Susie sits on a Chesterfield, thumbing quickly through a vast mound of papers and journals accreted over the week. Tagg is at the telephone, his back very much to the room, holding.

JOE: *(to Susie)* Any luck?

SUSIE: No. I thought it was the *Telegraph*, but there's no sign of it.

JOE: Never mind. There's a cuttings service provided. I'll get it sometime. Probably round about the third repeat.

SUSIE: Anyway, it implied the Drama Department was in the hands of communists and troublemakers and was clearly bent on subverting the democratic process and leading the country to the dogs.

JOE: Yeah? Things are looking up. I wish I knew who they were. I spend some lonely days in the East Tower, I can tell you.

TAGG: *(to phone)* Hello. Hello.

Ford, car keys in hand. Sound of lavatory flushing down the hall.

FORD: *(to Susie)* OK?

SUSIE: Sure.

FORD: Are you still at Wandsworth?

SUSIE: Yes.

FORD: OK. *(to Joe)* Thanks, Joe. Nice evening. I'm not sure what we achieved, but still …

JOE: Thanks for coming, Andrew. As long as you didn't find it a complete waste of time.

FORD: No, no. You know me. As the man said, words are our stock-in-trade …

A silence. Grease uncans, the record over.

JOE: Well. Good luck with the Cuba book.

FORD: Oh Jesus, don't remind me. There'll have been a counter-revolution before they've even got it in galleys. Thanks anyway.

GREASE: *(joining them)* It's all right. Lead guitar a bit flashy, but it's … funky. I like it. *(looking round)* Right then. Back to the pit.

FORD: Are you all right?

GREASE: *(helmet up)* Yeah. There's 120 ccs of concentrated Lambretta waiting out there for me. With the right conditions prevailing I could be in Camden by noon.

TAGG: (*on phone*) Hello. Hello. (*turning*) I think this thing's gone dead, Joe.

JOE: With you in a tick, John.

Tagg turns his back again, pushes rest up and down.

FORD: Right. We'll go. (*to Susie*) OK?

SUSIE: (*to Joe*) Thank you for the ... I enjoyed it. It was different anyway.

JOE: (*takes her hand*) Good-bye.   .

FORD: Bye.

They leave.

GREASE: Keep at it then.

JOE: Mmm. And you. Let me know what you're doing ... We might be able to put something on the box.

GREASE: That'll be the day. (*to Tagg's back*) Good-bye.

TAGG: (*turning slowly*) Aye.

Grease leaves. Joe crosses to the phone, takes it from Tagg, listens.

JOE: Hello. Hello. Oh hello. (*He listens, finally*) She's trying the number now. She's been waiting for lines. (*He hands the receiver back to Tagg.*) It takes a while.

He leaves Tagg again, mooches a moment, switches off the player. Hayes in from the garden, nearly ready for off.

HAYES: No sign of him. If it weren't Malcolm I'd begin to show signs of concern. He does happen to constitute a substantial part of my daily bread, you know. (*looking round*) Kara?

JOE: She's er ... looking at my kid. She won't be long.

Hayes nods, wanders over to the bookshelves.

TAGG: (*phone*) What? Oh Christ. Well will you keep trying? Ahuuh. 589 6129. That's it. Ta. (*He bangs the phone down.*) No answer. She's trying again.

HAYES: (*ironic*) Maybe the Paris exchange has fallen. De Gaulle too. They've probably already set up a provisional government under the leadership of an eleven-year-old grammar-school boy. (*turning*) Funnier things have happened. Not many though.

TAGG: (*to Joe*) Any sign of Sloman?

Joe shakes his head. Tagg crosses to the windows, peers out into the darkness.

HAYES: He'll be all right.

TAGG: (*deliberately*) Will he? How do you know?

HAYES: I'm his agent. I have to know these things.

TAGG: Do you know why he's always drunk?

HAYES: I said I was his agent. Not his wife.

TAGG: That must make him feel good.

Phone rings sharply. Tagg crosses at once to answer. Hayes pulls a mock injured face at Joe, sits down on the Chesterfield.

Hello. Hello. Yeah, hello. Thank Christ, I've been holding for hours. What? No, it's all right, I'm with Shawcross, Joe Shawcross? Aye. Go on then.

He listens for a long time. We never lose this call through what follows, though Tagg says very little for the rest of it, beyond reacting, prodding, asking for description, qualification and expansion.

HAYES: He has his own sort of charm, doesn't he?

JOE: We've got charm, Jeremy. Look at us.

Kara in from hallway. Hayes stands, ready to go.

HAYES: OK?

KARA: Why don't you get the car?

Pause.

HAYES: *(finally)* All right. Cheers, *(ironic)* Nice party.

JOE: Yeah.

HAYES: Any word on the Godard deal?

JOE: No. Frank's there now. He'll ring tomorrow. *(Looks at watch.)* Today.

HAYES: When are you going to Cannes, by the way?

JOE: I don't know. Saturday, I think. I don't think Julie's booked it yet.

HAYES: Tell her to give Biddy a ring, we'll go together.

JOE: Fine.

HAYES: Say goodnight to our … friend, won't you. And if you do manage to find Malcolm, pour him into a cab and send him home before he does any actual damage.

JOE: Will do. See you.

Hayes looks at Kara: leaves. Kara comes into the room.

KARA: Do you have a cigarette?

JOE: There's some around somewhere.

Kara searches mantelpiece, finds an open pack, lights one. She then turns to look at Joe. Tagg's call grows momentarily distinct, in the silence.

TAGG: Who did? Mandel! Mandel did! (*hard laugh*) Who else! (*Pause.*) So they marched back ... ahunh ... No. No ... they were perfectly right, I'd say ... Ahunh. (*He begins listening again, making the odd note on a pad in front of him.*)

KARA: He's lovely. (*Joe looks at her.*) Charlie.

JOE: Oh. Yes, he's a nice enough little bugger. He's got fallen arches. Like me. And he pees the bed.

KARA: Like Malcolm.

JOE: What?

KARA: Nothing. You always said you didn't want kids. They'd get in the way, you said.

JOE: Yes. (*Pause. Smiles.*) Embourgeoisement. Build the Family.

KARA: I don't know how you can sustain ... that amount of self-loathing, Joe.

JOE: (*ironic*) I know. It's quite a struggle, I can tell you.

KARA: Christ. (*Pause.*) You're ... terrified aren't you?

JOE: A bit. Mostly I'm numb. That's fairly terrifying.

She gets up, stubs the cigarette.

KARA: I'd better go. (*She crosses, kisses him softly on the cheek. Indicating Tagg*) Watch this one. He's the one who's playing games. He'll suck you dry if you give him half a chance. Listen. You've got a talent ... and a life to lead. So lead it. (*Pause.*) Make the revolution there where you are. Not in somebody else's head.

JOE: Sure thing.

KARA: I wish I'd been better for you.

JOE: *(softly)* Get stuffed.

KARA: Take it easy.

She looks hard at Tagg's back: leaves. Joe follows, when she's gone, as far as the doorway, as though to watch her.

Tagg finishes the call, looks around the room, crosses to the windows, still pondering the conversation he's just had. He draws a few deep lungfuls of air.

Joe plays with the lights, tries different combinations, using the dimmer, finally settles for the cluster of spots that pool the two leather armchairs, and leave the rest of the room dark. He sits down, gaunt and tired, in one.

TAGG: (*at window*) Frank.

JOE: Frank.

TAGG: In the thick, by the din.

JOE: Frank *Hetherley?*

TAGG: That's right.

JOE: I don't understand. He's supposed to be doing a deal with Godard for me. For ITV.

TAGG: He said he'd speak to you in the morning.

Silence.

JOE: Is Frank ... with you?

TAGG: Mmmm.

JOE: I didn't know. (*Pause.*) So what's happening?

TAGG: The riot police have attacked the students. The students are ... defending themselves.

JOE: With what?

TAGG: Barricades.

A long silence. Tagg crosses, sits opposite Joe.

The police are using gas and detonator caps. He could hardly speak, he was so hoarse. (*Pause.*) The students are tearing up the pavements and setting fire to cars.

Silence again.

JOE: Christ.

TAGG: We have a section there. (*Pause.*) The question is: Who will control the movement. As of now, it appears to be leaderless. (*Pause.*) But the opportunists are already thicker than maggots in a bone yard. Mandel for example. Mandel?

Joe nods.

Apparently Mandel had his car burned. The story is he stood on a barricade to watch it, shouting, 'Ah! Comme c'est beau! C'est la Revolution!' (*Pause. No irony*) A revisionist to the end.

JOE: Is Frank involved? I mean, is he actually fighting ... with your section?

TAGG: (*quietly, simply*) Our section is not fighting.

Pause.

JOE: Not?

TAGG: Not. (*Pause.*) A revolutionary faction cannot afford to be romantic. Because of the *folie de grandeur* of a handful of petty bourgeois anarchists who're making the running, hundreds upon hundreds of brave young men and women are having their bodies mangled right now by the armed might of the bourgeois state. It is true that without insurrection there is no revolution. But unless there is a party with the correct line to organize and lead it, insurrection is simply another term for suicide. (*Pause.*) How often must it be said before the truth is clearly seen? Revolution is not a speculative gamble, a flutter devised by casino playboys. Revolution is the implacable conjunction of objective material forces and human organization, discipline, courage and will. (*Pause.*) Our section walked away from the barricades before the major confrontations occurred. In my view, they took the correct decision. Because such a confrontation could only result in defeat, even rout. It lacks revolutionary perspective, and those who promoted it ... Mandel and his cronies ... are, in the objective sense, enemies of the working-class revolution in France.

Long silence. Tagg closes his eyes, appears to sleep. Joe is frozen, unable to comprehend what he has just heard.

JOE: Is that how you see it ending then?

TAGG: How else can it end? When the workers replace the students, and when the revolutionary party leads the workers, we will have a revolution. (*Pause.*) What ... terrifies me now is that the working class may well declare its solidarity with the students against the brutalities they have witnessed.

JOE: But ... isn't that what's wanted?

TAGG: (*banging chair arm suddenly*) No! Anything but! Who do you think will lead the workers, if they do decide to involve themselves? Us? It'll be the CP, through the CGT. So that, however it begins, whatever the spirit and resolution the workers evince, slowly the movement will be bled dry of genuine revolutionary content, until Waldeck-Rochet and his Stalinist henchmen can do a secret deal with De Gaulle and get the workers off the streets and back to their benches. Can't you see it? It's a nightmare. It'll be a massive defeat for the revolutionary spirit. It will make our task more difficult.

Silence.

JOE: I'm sorry the meeting ... wasn't better.

TAGG: It's a start. (*Pause. Tagg sinks into himself.*)

JOE: Don't you have ... doubts?

TAGG: Doubts?

JOE: I've been trying to figure out what makes you different. It's not your analysis. It's not your style either. I think it's ... there's no ... scepticism in you. I can find no trace of what my psychology tutor used to call 'the civilized worm' in you, gently insisting on the possibility of error. (*Pause.*) Perhaps it's just that you have no way of being wrong.

TAGG: (*softly*) Do you have a way of being right?

JOE: No. I don't.

TAGG: I'm not afraid of being wrong. As long as I'm right just once. That's all it'll take.

Silence.

(*smiling briefly*) I'm proletarian. I killed the worm before it turned. (*He takes in the room, piece by piece, then back to Joe.*) Mebbe you should've done the same.

JOE: Me? I'm just a … producer. I don't actually do anything? I just … set up the shows.

Silence again.

TAGG: I met Trotsky, you know. Just the once. In a pension in southern France. '36. '36 I think it was. He was trying to set up the Fourth International to counter the obscenities of Stalin's Third. There were about fifty of us, from all over: France, Italy, Switzerland, Belgium, Holland, Germany, Sweden, Denmark … Poland … Australia … America. And me, from Glasgow. Just thirty. (*Pause.*) He spoke mainly in French. I barely understood a word. But I watched him. Watched him. His big head. His eyes behind the spectacles. (*Pause.*) Authentic. This voice, speaking a language I didna comprehend, was the sole remaining authentic voice of the Russian revolution. While just about everything else was being expunged by Stalin or just … papered over by the Wilsons of their day … this one burning intelligence sat there refusing to be quenched, to be put out. (*Long pause.*) It's helped, that. Of course, it's no substitute for analysis and argument, for theory. But it helps a wee bit when the nights start getting longer. (*Pause.*) He said one thing I did understand. He said: 'We only die when we fail to take root in others.'

Silence for a long time

I'm trying to take root, Joe. (*Pause.*) I'll be dead by the end of the year. (*Pause.*) I have this tumour. (*He holds his stomach.*) They've been trying to treat it for a while now, you know. But it's … spread just the same. I was there tonight. That's why I was late.

JOE: I'm sorry.

TAGG: (*completely naturally*) Ach, it's nothing. It's just such a bloody waste. I was banking on ten more good years to build the party.

JOE: Are there … dependants?

TAGG: No. (*He stands up suddenly, a hard, stern lump.*) We'll meet again, eh?

JOE: (*standing too*) Yes.

Tagg holds his hand out. Joe takes it.

Let me call a cab.

TAGG: Not at all. It's only a couple of miles. The walk'll do me good.

He leaves, Joe in his wake to the front door. Joe in again, crosses to windows, draws curtains, returns to chair, checks time on watch, settles back as though to sleep.

Fade.

Black. Lutoslawski's Funeral Music.

Screen. Mute film. Dawn in Paris. Cars smoulder, barricades burn, char. Police poke in and out, like carrion. Silent, still. Fade slowly.

Fade up on scene as before. Dawn or just before. Joe asleep across two chairs. Sound of dawn chorus starting up.

A fumbling at the french window. Sloman in, draws curtains half back, to half light the room. He is grey, dirty, dishevelled. His shoes are, as before, in a neat knot round his neck.

Joe stirs as the light halves the darkness. Sloman watches him until he subsides, then moves towards the drinks shelves, stands a long time looking, finally selects a can of beer, punctures it, takes a big, rinsing mouthful, swallows, closes eyes, rubs the cool can across his forehead. He looks round the room, leaves for the kitchen, returns a moment later, carrying an open can of frankfurters. He tries one experimentally; another; is marginally impressed.

Joe wakens without moving. Stares at Sloman.

SLOMAN: Fancy one?

JOE: No. What are they?

SLOMAN: *(reads from the can, in perfect Hitler rally style)* Neu! Jedes Wurstchen dieser Dose ist mit einer besonderen Folie umgeben. Alle guten Eigenschaften, die man an feinen Wurstchen Schatzt, bleiben durch diese Folie volt erhalten – sie sind daher immer kostlick frisch, besonders zart im Biss und noch feiner im Geschmack. (*Pause.*) Frankfurters.

Joe turns back to his litter.

What's the matter, frightened to wake?

JOE: *(sitting up slowly)* As you to sleep, happen.

SLOMAN: Happen. What time is it?

JOE: *(checking)* Five o'clock.

SLOMAN: Is it? Listen them bloody birds. Aren't they incredible. They have an order, you know, for starting up. Finches, lapwings, first; larks; sparrows, last. Lazy little buggers. *(Pause.)* I was reading somewhere, it takes two hours, north to south, right down the country. So the finches here probably get their alarm call every morning from the sparrows of … Bedfordshire or somewhere.

JOE: Christ. It's five o'clock, Malc.

SLOMAN: That's what I'm telling you.

JOE: Have you thought of going home?

SLOMAN: Not recently. (*He removes the mound of journals etc. from the settee, lies down on it, takes a drink from the can of beer, fishes out another cold frankfurter.*) Which home did you have in mind anyway? The thin bitch in Salford with the kids packed in around her like forwards wheeling for the line? Or Sally Svelte from SW7 with the manicured mind and a We Never Closed sign in neon at the top of her legs? Home. Home. 'He that diggeth a pit shall fall into it.' Ecclesiastes.

Joe gets up, ignoring him: shivers a little.

Go on.

JOE: (*thinking*) 'Pride goeth before destruction, and an haughty spirit before a fall.' Proverbs.

SLOMAN: Good. Yes, Erm. 'They were as fed horses in the morning; everyone neighed after his neighbour's wife.' Jeremiah?

JOE: 'Saying peace, peace, when there is no peace.' Yes.

SLOMAN: 'Is there no balm in Gilead; is there no physician there?'

JOE: 'Write the vision, and make it plain upon tables, that he may run that readeth it.'

SLOMAN: Habukkuk! (*They both laugh.*) Cunt! 'His head and his hairs were white like wool, as white as snow; and his eyes were something … as the flame of fire.'

JOE: 'His voice as the sound of many waters.'

SLOMAN: 'I am he that liveth and was dead.'

JOE: 'Be then faithful unto death, and I will give thee a crown of life.'

SLOMAN: 'But he shall rule thee with a rod of iron.'

JOE: 'And because thou art lukewarm, and neither cold nor hot, I will spue thee out of my mouth.'

SLOMAN: 'And behold, a pale horse, and his name that sat on him was Death.' (*Long silence. Sloman finishes his can, swills a little of it over head and face, rubs it around.*) The Revelation of St. John. Apt enough for five o'clock of a Sat'day morning. (*Pause.*) There's nowt'll replace the formative intellectual matrices of a really well-run Sunday school. By Christ.

Joe crosses to the french windows, draws the remaining curtain, and begins to examine the glass still remaining in the broken pane. He goes into the kitchen, returns with a mallet, chisel, gloves, etc. He examines the job carefully, kneeling to get a better look.

JOE: Pass me a couple of those, will you. *(He points to the mound of papers on the floor by Sloman's hand.)*

SLOMAN: *(rummaging)* Financial Times? New Statesman? How big a job is it?

JOE: Just pass 'em, will you.

Sloman chucks two Times *towards the window. Joe spreads them by the foot of the window to catch any glass falling inwards, puts on the gloves, begins tapping glass carefully with mallet. Sloman evinces pretty nearly total disinterest, his attention, such as it is, now stuck on the pile of papers. He riffles through it, sampling for dates from top to bottom.*

SLOMAN: Jesus God, that's a week's worth!

JOE: What?

SLOMAN: You're so bloody *earnest*, Joe. I mean look at that lot. *The Economist*. *The Daily Telegraph*! *The Listener*? I mean, it's harmful.

Joe goes on with his job. Sloman begins to work his way down the pile.

(*A voice for each paper or item.*) 'Dockers Once More Support Powell on Issue of Immigration. Clashes with students averted.' (*on*) 'The centrepiece of the Cecil Beaton exhibition of theatre designs is a scale model of his principal sets for *My Fair Lady*, which he …' (*He studies the page more closely, blinks, coughs, picks up another paper.*) 'The *Sunday Telegraph* is pleased to announce that as from this Sunday its Drama Critic will be the distinguished playwright Frank Marcus.' (*Pause.*) 'It is understood from reliable sources that Mr. Marcus is considering an appeal.' (*on. New paper*) 'Russian Troop Movements on Czech-Polish Border Seen As Hint of Pressure on Dubcek and Svoboda.' 'Professor Herbert Marcuse, the eminent Marxist philosopher and father of the so-called New Left, arrived in Paris late this evening for the centenary celebrations of the death of Karl Marx arranged by … UNESCO?'

He looks at Joe, who works on.

(*new paper*) 'Welwyn Garden City – the drug-tormented town in Hertfordshire where, I can disclose today, at least three teenagers in every hundred are using the killer drug heroin.' (*He throws* The People *down, picks up another.*) '"France: Stable, Prosperous and Infuriating" by Patrick Brogan.' Ha. (*He flings* The Times *away and picks up another.*) 'In a survey conducted last month, in Bucharest, 2.5 per cent of the sample identified General de Gaulle as the First Secretary of the French Communist Party.' (*Pause.*) 'President de Gaulle leaves for his state visit of Romania later this week. In a statement issued by an aide last night, it was learnt that the French Communist Party would be led, in his absence, by M. Waldeck-Rochet (107) of 13 Tuileries Gardens, Paris 8.' (*Pause.*) 'It is understood from reliable sources that M. Waldeck-Rochet is considering an appeal.'

JOE: (*almost finished*) What are you on about?

SLOMAN: (*copy of* Evening Standard) Hang on. 'If there are no deaths tonight, I'll turn in my badge,' said a French police officer this afternoon. What?

Joe wraps the glass fragments in the newspaper, carries them out on to the terrace, picks up the pieces on the other side, dumps them carefully, returns. Sloman sits up.

JOE: What about the play?

SLOMAN: What about it?

JOE: When do you reckon you might have something for me to look at?

SLOMAN: What is it now?

JOE: (*looking at watch*) The 11th of May.

SLOMAN: I don't know.

JOE: It doesn't matter. I just thought you might be able to give me some idea.

SLOMAN: How does Monday sound?

JOE: What?

SLOMAN: Monday. About six in the evening?

JOE: Come on Malc, what?

SLOMAN: I could put in a hard day tomorrow.

JOE: Malc, we're talking about a ninety-minute play.

SLOMAN: You're right. Tuesday then.

Joe turns away, unwilling to be drawn further.

(*quietly*) It's a sort of … presumption you have that you're different, Joe. That's all. Nothing else. And you're not. There is nothing … objectively … to distinguish you from all the rest … Shaun and Gerry and Cedric and … Irene … mmm? You occupy the same relationship to the means of production as every other … producer in that golden hutch at Would Not Lane you call the Centre. Socialist? A socialist producer? What's that? It's irrelevant.

JOE: You're preaching, Malc. (*Pause.*) Fake it if you like.

SLOMAN: Wrong. I'm not asking your permission, I'm telling you, Joe, you have no right to expect anything other than a fake. Any more than the rest have. The pimps. The gold lamé boys. The shredders. The suckers-in. The apologies for the system. The machine's maintenance men.

JOE: Jesus, not *now*, Malc. It's five o'clock.

SLOMAN: Sure. Sure.

Silence.

JOE: So what are you going to do?

SLOMAN: Fuck knows.

JOE: Great. (*Pause.*) Look, I need a good piece. Right? Don't piss on me, Malc.

SLOMAN: It doesn't make any *difference*.

JOE: Malc…

SLOMAN: It *doesn't*. The only thing you're allowed to put in to the system is that which can be assimilated and absorbed by it. Joe, this is a society that has 'matured' on descriptions of its inequity and injustice. Poverty is one of its best favoured *spectacles*. Bad housing, class-divisive schools, plight of the sick and the aged, the alienating indignities of work, the fatuous vacuities of 'leisure' – Jesus God, man, we can't get enough of it. It's what makes us so 'humane', seeing all that, week in, week out. We've had centuries of it, man. I give you Wordsworth. Half a dozen years after the Revolution in France that …

implosive moment not yet completed, not yet in the past – our English Willie
was arguing for the unhampered ubiquity of beggars … beggars, Joe … as a
way of increasing the yield of virtue in society as a whole:

'While from door to door
This old man creeps, the villagers in him
Behold a record which together binds
Past deeds and offices of charity
Else unremembered, and so keeps alive
The kindly mood in hearts which lapse of years
And that half-wisdom half experience gives
Make slow to feel, and by sure steps resign
To selfishness and cold oblivious cares.
Among the farms and solitary huts,
Hamlets and thinly scattered villages
Where'er the aged Beggar takes his rounds,
The mild necessity of use compels
To acts of love; and habit does the work
Of reason; yet prepares that after joy
Which reason cherishes. And thus the soul,
By that sweet taste of pleasure unpursued,
Doth find herself insensibly disposed
To virtue and true goodness.'

Wednesday Plays? It's the Liberal heartland, Joe. Every half-grown, second rate,
soft-bowelled pupa in grub street is in there fighting with you. It's the
consensus. It's the condition of our time. Impetigo. Pink. Itchy. Mildly catching.

*Joe picks up some dead glasses, cans, etc., walks with them towards the kitchen,
talking as he does so.*

JOE: I know all this, Malc. (*Pause.*) I'd just sooner do a play by you than … you
know. You know? (*His voice lifted from outside.*)

SLOMAN: (*lifting too*) Yeah, I'd sooner play chess than draughts. So what?

Joe back in for more pots.

JOE: (*quietly, gathering*) I just once … want to say yes to something.

SLOMAN: Yeah. It'll pass.

JOE: Yes. (*He continues his cleaning, leaves the room with another handful calling
as he does so.*) Did you ever go to Chick's? Chick Hibbert's? Openshaw Palais?

SLOMAN: Oh aye. Couple of times. Birrofa dump.

JOE: (*off*) Mmm. I went every week, with our kid. Fighting. Fucking. Trying to. I had
my first woman there. Met her there anyway. Beryl. In the back of a mate's
Bedford, him in the front with his. And we kissed for a bit, and touched, and then
I took it out and pushed it between her legs and held it there and waited … silent
… it was there, you know … all but there. All it needed was a yes. And I could

hear a voice in my head saying: If I were thee I'd say no. And then she rolled on her back, up and out went her thighs and I sank, a foot, a yard, a mile into her yes. (*He's back in the doorway.*) It seemed – seems still – an act of absolute courage.

SLOMAN: Or absolute folly.

Silence. Joe collects more glasses etc., leaves for the kitchen. Sloman takes his shoes from round his neck, begins to put them on. Sounds of dishwasher distantly starting up. Angie in. Quiet, tired. Stands inside the doorway, leaning against wall. Sloman is down with his shoelaces.

(*Calling, abstractedly*) I knew a Beryl once. From Wythenshawe. She had huge calves. Her dad was a rozzer.

No sound from the kitchen. Sloman looks up, sees Angie. Normal voice, to her.

She showed a lot of courage.

ANGIE: Did she?

SLOMAN: Yes. I decorated her personally. Several times.

ANGIE: Where's Joe?

SLOMAN: Kitchen. Mopping up.

ANGIE: Why don't you send over for some things? You could move in.

SLOMAN: (*straight*) No, no. I wouldn't want to come between you.

ANGIE: Stay with comedy, whatever you do.

Pause.

SLOMAN: Been slagging?

ANGIE: Don't you ever get tired?

SLOMAN: I can remember you when you weren't a bitch. You were nice then.

ANGIE: Oh yes. That was when there was still a chance I might be induced to become common property ... To each according to his need, wasn't it. Like dogs around a lamppost.

Sound of dishwasher closing down; odd clank of pots. Birds again.

SLOMAN: It's the new sexual imperialism. Technologically necessary. Corporate cunt. It has nothing to do with the Communist Manifesto. Ask Kara. She knows.

ANGIE: Kara?

SLOMAN: She was here. To the meeting.

ANGIE: (*turning, leaving*) Go home, will you. (*She's gone.*)

SLOMAN: (*standing*) 'I will show unto thee the judgement of the great whore that sitteth upon many waters.' (*He crosses to the drinks shelves, punctures another can, takes an extravagant swig at it, is slightly sprayed by the contents. Joe in, two mugs of coffee, on a tray, and a large carrot. Taking his, draining can*) Ta. What's that?

JOE: For the pig.

SLOMAN: (*half turning to windows*) Oh yes. He's a fearsome bugger.

JOE: Yes. He nearly had you.

SLOMAN: Your wife's back. Upstairs.

JOE: Uhunh.

SLOMAN: She looked tired.

JOE: Yes?

SLOMAN: Mmm.

Long silence.

Joe I'm sorry about last night.

JOE: (*softly*) Get stuffed.

SLOMAN: The poor old sod.

JOE: Who?

SLOMAN: Tagg. Who do you think!

JOE: How do you mean?

SLOMAN: I don't know. He makes me want to cry. Every time I see him. (*Pause.*) He's a walking fetish. The 'Revolutionary Party' is a fetish. 'Build the "Revolutionary Party",' it's all he's ever said, over and over, all his bloody life. An absolute injunction. Timeless. No matter what the objective conditions, the other supervening historical processes, build the bleeding party.

JOE: While you get slewed out of your head … and I … wallow in my impotence.

SLOMAN: Maybe. I can't speak for you, old love, but sometimes I'm actually sober. You know? It doesn't matter where you meet Tagg, he'll be building the party. There's nothing else. There couldn't be. He'd have to tear it down and start again, if it ever did get built. (*deliberately*) Listen. I spent a year in that lot. Yes. On the rebound from the CP. And let me tell you, they make the Bolsheviks look like TOC-H. It's rigid. It doesn't bend for anything, least of all events. If reality doesn't come up to scratch, it's rejected, sent back down the line; expunged. (*Pause.*) The function of a party member is to carry out his orders, faithfully and without question. (*looking at wall pics*) 'Comrades, none of us wishes or is able to be right against his party. The party in the last analysis is always right, because the party is the sole historical instrument given to the proletariat for the solution of its basic problems. I know that one cannot be right against the party. It is only possible to be right with the party and through the party, for history has not created other ways for the realization of what is right.' (*Raises coffee mug*) Right, Lev Davidovitch? You didn't wait till '38 to snivel that out, did you? 1924, you coined that little gem. 13th Party Congress. He could've been Bukharin's scriptwriter.

Joe turns away. Sloman turns to look at him.

There won't be a revolution because John Tagg forms a tiny Bolshevik party in
South London. There'll be a revolution, and another, and another, because the
capacity for 'adjustment' and 'adaptation' within capitalism is not, contrary to
popular belief, infinite. And when *masses* of people, masses mind, decide to
take on the state and the ruling class, they won't wait for the word from the
'authentic voice of Trotsky' or anyone else. They'll be too busy 'practising the
revolution'. And the class will throw up its own leaders and its own structures
of leadership and responsibility. And they'll find the 'germ' from inside the
class, not from 'outwith'. Because the germ's there, the virus is there, and
however many generations of workers are pumped full of antibiotics or the pink
placebos of late capitalism, it will persist, the virus, under the skin, waiting. I
remember me dad. A model worker. A perfect working man. Chapel every
Sunday: blue serge suit, white shirt, tie. Shiny pointed shoes. Hair parted;
watered. Thirty-nine years for the same firm. Maintenance sparks. And when he
was fifty-five they gave him a fortnight's notice, declared him redundant. He
had a gold watch for long service, stuff like that. I remember him, he came
home the night they told him they were putting him down the road, and he sat
in his chair for about an hour and he didn't speak. Just looked into the fire. Then
he sniffed and spat. He said: 'I could kill the bastards.' I only ever heard him
swear once before. That was when me mam got her foot caught down a grid on
the front at Blackpool and an illuminated tram nearly cut her in half.

JOE: And meanwhile?

Sloman walking to the doorway, holds arms out. The front door bangs.

SLOMAN: Precisely. I think I'll go home. Joe. Beware the last revelation. 'I am
    Alpha and Omega, the beginning and the end, the first and the last.'

*He leaves. Some slight greeting and banter in the hall. Joe stands for a moment
longer, then takes the carrot out on to the terrace.*

*Eddie in. Tie off, jacket off shoulder. He's drawn, looks old. He looks around,
flops into a chair, draws a crumpled* Sun *from his jacket pocket, begins to check a
bet against a piece of paper he fumbles out of his wallet.*

Joe in.

EDDIE: Hello.

JOE: Hello, Ed. How was it?

EDDIE: Great. I had a good time.

JOE: (*looks at watch*) Musta bin.

EDDIE: What time is it?

JOE: S'nearly six.

EDDIE: Bloodyell. Eh, don't tell our Jean. She'd have a fit.

JOE: I bet.

Eddie back to the bet.

Fancy a coffee?

EDDIE: I wouldn't mind a tea.

Right.

He leaves. Eddie takes a pen out, begins making out a new bet.

JOE: (*off*) How many sugars?

EDDIE: Cup or a mug?

JOE: (*off*) Cup.

EDDIE: Three then.

Joe back in with cup on saucer.

Ta, kid. (*Drinks.*) By gum, that's welcome, it is an all. (*Becomes aware of Joe's stare.*) Owt up?

JOE: No. Just the way you said that. Me dad used to say it.

EDDIE: Did he? He liked his pot of tea, the old man. (*to paper*) Fancy a bet? Piggot's got five mounts at Leicester. He's flying back from France, so I reckon he's a good thing.

JOE: Do you ever win?

EDDIE: Win? Course I win. How'd you mean?

Pause.

JOE: Have you thought any more about the job?

EDDIE: No, not a lot. I'd take it, if there were just me. I suppose I could get used to watching Arsenal.

JOE: What would it ... mean to you?

EDDIE: Five quid a week, better hours, bit of free time.

JOE: Is that enough?

EDDIE: What's 'enough'? It'll do to be going on with. (*Pause.*) You don't want me to take it, do you?

JOE: I didn't say that Eddie ...

EDDIE: You don't. I can tell. (*Pause.*) Why not?

JOE: I ... don't know whether it's right for you ... down here.

EDDIE: How do you mean, down here? It's no different from Manchester, int this. There's factories and people work in 'em, there's houses and people live in 'em, there's dogtracks and racecourses and boozers and bingo halls, they have the same newspapers (*Sun*) and telly, that fat little get from Huddersfield tells *them* what to do just like us. It's just down the road. (*Pause.*) I don't know what you mean, down here. (*Pause.*) I wouldn't bother you.

JOE: Eddie.

EDDIE: I wouldn't. They said there might be a house in Islington if I wanted. I went to have a look last night. It's far enough.

JOE: Eddie, you're being ... daft.

EDDIE: Maybe. I just thought I'd say it. (*gently*) All right?

Joe nods. A silence.

Does that mean you've decided not to lend us the three hundred?

JOE: Is that what you want, your own place?

EDDIE: Yeah. Don't you?

JOE: All right. I'll send a cheque on Monday.

EDDIE: Do you mean that?

JOE: Yes, I mean it.

EDDIE: Thanks, (*Pause.*) I knew you would, our kid.

Silence.

I picked a bird up last night.

JOE: Did you?

EDDIE: Aye. She were all right too. (*Pause.*) Took me back to her flat and everything.

JOE: Great.

EDDIE: Yeah. She was all right. She wasn't a slag.

JOE: Not lost your touch then.

EDDIE: Aye. Don't let the hair fool you.

JOE: Are you still playing?

EDDIE: Nah. Sundays. British Legion.

JOE: Scrubbers.

EDDIE: It's a game. Gerra good thirst up for Sunday lunch. Wharrabout you?

JOE: No. Not kicked a ball in years.

EDDIE: (*getting up*) Ah, the loss to the game! (*Pause.*) Are they gonna win today?

JOE: Who?

EDDIE: City! They're at Newcastle. Need both points for t'league.

JOE: Yes?

EDDIE: They'll get 'em too! (*a touch inward, yet ironic*) I suppose I'd better get a new suit. Now I'm gonna be Mr Dynamic. (*turning back*) I can get a tube to Euston, can't I?

JOE: Change at Leicester Square.

EDDIE: I'll do that then.

JOE: Go easy.

EDDIE: Yea. And you. (*He stands in the doorway.*) Come and see ma. She's allus talking about you.

JOE: Yeah.

Pause.

EDDIE: It *was* a slag. Cost us four quid.

He leaves. Joe turns, surveys his room. Eyes objects, takes in spaces, between, around his objects. The guinea pig shrieks. Joe is rooted, frozen. Angie in, short bathrobe, naked underneath. Joe remains with his back to her.

ANGIE: Do you want anything?

JOE: No.

ANGIE: Come to bed, Joe.

JOE: Frank's ringing sometime.

ANGIE: Not at six o'clock.

JOE: (*turning*) He's going to say whether we become a company or not.

ANGIE: Is he back from Paris?

JOE: No, I don't think so. He'll call from there. If Godard will play.

Angie crosses to the window, inspects the neat gap.

ANGIE: Is it what you want?

JOE: (*numbly*) Is it what I want. I don't know how to answer that.

ANGIE: It seems the logical step.

He watches her. She continues to inspect the window.

Looks as if you had fun. (*She stands. Looks at him. Crosses to the door to the hall.*) Do you want to share my bath?

JOE: How's David?

ANGIE: (*deliberately*) I thought I'd take Charlie over to mother's this afternoon. She's talking of taking him to the Danish Fortnight at Earl's Court. I can't think why. I thought if I took your car and you took a cab over this evening, we could go straight on to the Aldwych from mother's and leave Charlie there. Or you could take a cab to the Aldwych if you prefer. (*Pause.*) You've remembered the Aldwych?

He nods.

Good. (*Long pause.*) David's fine. He sends his regards. Would you remind Milanka to clean the hutch? It's started to stink again.

She goes.

Joe stands; dead.

He crosses to the hi-fi. Brings up Jeanne Lee/Archie Shepp – 'Gilead'. She sings.

'There is a balm in Gilead
To make the wounded whole
There is a balm in Gilead
To heal the sin-sick soul.'

He goes out on to the terrace. Returns with the pig. He stands centre, pig in hand. Lights fade until he is in spot. As spot begins to fade, he appears, pig in hand, on the wall screen behind him.

END

COMEDIANS

Set in a Manchester working-class evening centre in the mid-1970s, the date of its writing, *Comedians* eschews political theory, professional ideologues and historically sourced discourse on political revolution – all the perceived hallmarks of my earlier pieces – in favour of a more or less unmediated address on a range of particular contemporary issues including class, gender, race and society in modern Britain. The luck the play had was not in its critical reception, divided as ever but on the whole supportive, nor in the response of theatre managements in London and elsewhere, but in its first founding production by Richard Eyre at Nottingham Playhouse. Good first productions (of which I have had my share) have never been easy to come by – not even back then in infinitely more propitious days – and are today grown rarer than the Norwegian fig. But great ones lie outside all laws of probability and distribution in any age. Such was Eyre's in the late winter of 1975 in Nottingham. The debt is immense and permanent.

Comedians was first performed in Great Britain at the Nottingham Playhouse on 20th February 1975. The cast was as follows:

Caretaker Richard Simpson

Gethin Price Jonathan Pryce

Phil Murray James Warrior

George McBrain Stephen Rea

Sammy Samuels Louis Raynes

Mick Connor Tom Wilkinson

Eddie Waters Jimmy Jewel

Ged Murray Dave Hill

Mr Patel Talat Hussain

Bert Challenor Ralph Nossek

Club Secretary John Joyce

Directed by Richard Eyre

Designed by John Gunter

Comedians

ACT ONE

A classroom in a secondary school in Manchester, about three miles east of the centre, on the way to Ashton-under-Lyne and the hills of east Lancashire. Built 1947 in the now disappearing but still familiar two-storey style, the school doubles as evening centre for the area, and will half-fill, as the evening progresses, with the followers of yoga, karate, cordon bleu cookery, 'O' level English, secretarial prelims, do-it-yourself, small investments and antique furniture. Adults will return to school and the school will do its sullen best to accommodate them.

This room, on the ground floor, is smallish, about a dozen chipped and fraying desks, two dozen chairs set out in rows facing the small dais on which stands the teacher's desk, with green blackboard unwiped from the day's last stand beyond. Two starkish lights, on the window side of the room, are on, flintily, lighting about a third of it. A clock (real: keeping real time for the evening) over the board says 7.27. Cupboards of haphazard heights and styles line the walls, above which the dogged maps, charts, tables, illustrations and notices warp, fray, tear, curl and droop their way to limbo. Windows on the left wall show the night dark and wet.

The **School Caretaker***, old, gnarled, tiny, is trying to sponge recent graffiti from the blackboard in the lit segment of the room. He has done away with the 'F' fairly successfully and now begins on the 'U'. C,K,O,F,F,N,O,B,H,O,L,E stretch out before him. He mutters 'Dirty bastards, filthy fuckers' as he sponges.*

Gethin Price *arrives, in wet raincoat, carrying a long canvas bag and a pint of hot water. He puts down bag and mug by a desk, removes coat and shirt, takes shaving tackle from the bag and sits, in his greying vest, to shave in the tiny mirror he has propped before him. Price wears a flat Lenin-like cloth or denim hat, which he leaves on.*

Corridor sounds, as people hurry for their classes. Price shaves with deft precision, surprisingly dainty-handed.

The Caretaker finishes, descends, catches sight of Price, almost falls the final step to the floor.

CARETAKER: Are you in here?

Price looks round, behind, about, with strange clown-like timing, the foam gleaming like a mask, brush poised.

PRICE: *(finally)* Yeah.

The Caretaker sniffs, looks for his clipboard and list of classes; scans it.

CARETAKER: I don't see it.

PRICE: Been here since January. (*Pause.*) Mr Waters …

CARETAKER: Waters. Oh, him. (*studying Price at his ablutions*) What is it, Gents' Hairdressing?

PRICE: Yeah. Some'at like that.

CARETAKER: I thought you practised on balloons. I saw it once in a film …

Caretaker stumps out, dragging his waste bag, pins **Phil Murray** *to the door as they pass. Murray in. Stops in doorway as he sees Price's foaming white face.*

PHIL: *(sour, his dominant note)* Jesus, is it Christmas already.

Price shaves on, smiling briefly. Murray carries his two suitcases to a desk and deposits them tidily before sitting down. He's twenty-nine, small, dapper, an insurance agent in thick-fitting dark three-piece suit.

Christ, what a flap. God knows where that bloody idiot of a brother of mine's got to. *(He checks his watch against the clock.)* He's probably forgot, the stupid mare. Be having a game o'bones in the New Inn. *(across to Price)* Are you ready then?

Price grunts yes or no, it makes no matter.

I am. By God, I am. I've worked meself puce for tonight. I have. I have that. And if that dozy prick …

He leaves it hanging, minatory. **George McBrain** *in, straight from work. He's a docker, big, beefy, wears an old parka, jeans, boots, shock of black hair, extrovert Ulsterman in his late thirties.*

McBRAIN: *(arms wide in doorway)* De Da!

Nothing. He looks from Murray to Price.

Well, I found the stones; now all I've gotta do is find the classroom. *(advancing, bag in hand)* Are we all ready then? Tonight you will see … something! Overtime every night this week but am I worried? Not a bit of it. Because I have what it takes. And when you have it … *(He produces a can of Worthington 'E' from his bag on the desk.)* … by God you have it!

PHIL: *(to Price)* He sounds as if he's had it for a while too.

McBRAIN: Mock on, brother. I can forgive your jealousy.

PHIL: You get more like that Paisley every day, George –

McBRAIN: *(Paisley at once)* Mock not the reverend doctor, Mr Murray. There's not many left of us can walk on water.

Price finishes, replaces shaving tackle, begins to dress. How's it going then, Geth?

PRICE: OK.

He picks up the mug. Leaves the room. McBrain slowly follows him half-way, stops, looks at Phil.

McBRAIN: Feeling the strain, doubtless.

PHIL: *(trying a shiny pair of black pointed shoes on)* Teacher's pet? He's just a moody bugger.

McBRAIN: Where's your kid, then? And where's the bloody rest of 'em? Look at the time …

PHIL: Don't ask me about our kid. It's bad enough I have to work with him. I was picking him up on Market Street wasn't I, seven o'clock. I was there. Parked on a double yellow line wasn't I? If he'd been there, there'd've been two of us.

Sammy Samuels *and* **Mick Connor** *in. Samuels, forty-one, fat, Manchester Jewish, cigar, heavy finely cut black overcoat, homburg, white silk scarf, black attaché case, first in.*

McBRAIN: *(Stan Laurel voice))* Hi, Olly.

SAMUELS: *(evenly)* Piss off.

He crosses to a desk, carefully removes hat, coat (which he shakes), scarf, and adjusts his shirt cuffs so that the diamond cufflinks do their work below the sleeve of his good wool suit. Connor stands in the doorway, rain dripping from his donkey jacket, beneath which we glimpse hired evening dress and crumpled buttonhole.

McBRAIN: Oh, Christ.

CONNOR: Almost, my son. Try again.

McBRAIN: You're drowned. What've you come in your gear for?

CONNOR: Laid off again. Thought I'd get it done with. Bloody weather. No pigging buses.

PHIL: You'll look like a dog's dinner.

McBRAIN: *(an explosion)* The Kennomeat Kid. Ha! That's good that! I like that! *(Frank Carson voice)* It's the way I tell 'em.

The groans of the others increase his glee.

SAMUELS: *(strong Manchester accent, occasional Jewish nasality)* These pipes are hot, Mick. Get over here and dry out.

Connor crosses to the pipes. We see 'Wimpey' on the PVC patch on the back of the jacket as he removes it.

(seeing the suit jacket) Hey, that's not a bad fit. Where'd you gerrit, Woolworth's?

CONNOR: S'matter of fact belonged to a feller I know passed on.

SAMUELS: Not surprised wearing a suit like that.

CONNOR: What's wrong with the suit? It's a bit wet .

SAMUELS: S'hard to put your finger on.

McBRAIN: … as the actress said to the bishop…

Groan.

SAMUELS: *(studiously contemptuous of the interruption)* It's the sort of suit you walk into a tailor's in and ask for the cheapest suit in the shop and he says you're wearing it.

Groan.

Don't groan, you scum, learn.

CONNOR: *(studying the suit)* S'been a good suit.

SAMUELS: It was doomed the moment it left the animal. Believe me, I know about these things.

PHIL: Christ, he's doing half his bloody act ...

SAMUELS: Don't worry about me, old son. Plenty more where that came from.

McBRAIN: Right. Why should Ken Dodd worry about some obscure Manchester Jew nicking his lines? Ha!

Samuels smiles, a little frost around the teeth, at McBrain.

SAMUELS: Why indeed. Why indeed.

CONNOR: *(aware of that faint crackle)* Sure it's a detail. A detail it is.

McBRAIN: *(in Waters' exact voice, assuming his manner)* Ah, but detail, friend, is all. Think on now.

Eddie Waters *in, quick, purposeful, behind Samuels' back.*

SAMUELS: Where *is* His Grace, by the way ... ?

WATERS: He's here.

There's a small but discernible reaction in the others, a regression to childhood responses.

(Already within reach of his desk) Sorry it's late. I had to check the equipment down at the club. No piano.

'Bloody hells' of concern.

It's all right, they've had one sent down from Edge Lane. *(Pause.)* Right, let's get cracking, we haven't got all night. *(He's deposited his gear around the desk, papers, books, a stop watch, other materials and equipment.)* Get the tables sorted and settle down while I take a leak ...

He's on his way to the door. The others break and begin drawing the desks and chairs into roughly parallel sides of a hollow square. In the doorway he meets Price, returning. Price has removed his hat to reveal an almost wholly shaven skull, the hair dense and metallic on the scalp.

(stopping, staring) Mr Price. *(over shoulder, very dry)* Less noise if you would, gentlemen. There may be people trying to sleep in other classrooms. *(Back to Price now, staring at head.)* All ... ready?

PRICE: Yeah. Just about, Mr Waters.

WATERS: *(the head incomprehensible yet unmentionable)* Still finishing on the song ...?

PRICE: I'm not doing a song.

WATERS: How d'you mean? How're you gonna get off?

PRICE: *(evasive, stubborn)* I've er … I've bin working on some'at else.

WATERS: *(some faint concern)* Since when?

PRICE: Oh, last week. I dint like the act. I found some'at in the book you lent us.

WATERS: Yes, but you've not changed the basic … I mean a week …

PRICE: *(breaking deliberately into the room)* It'll be all right, Mr Waters.

He takes a desk end with Phil. Waters watches him, leaves.

McBRAIN: *(to Price)* Hey.

Price looks at him over his shoulder.

Love the hairdo.

PRICE: *(evenly)* Nice, innit.

SAMUELS: Reminds me of a girl I used to know. *(reflective)* I've known some funny women.

McBRAIN: Reminds me of the wife. After the operation.

CONNOR: She's had it as well has she?

McBRAIN: Ey, eh …

They square up to each other in mock battle stances.

PHIL: Are you shifting these desks or what?

McBRAIN: I heard the Church had granted the Pope a special dispensation … to become a nun.

Beat.

CONNOR: That's right. Only on Fridays though.

They grin, begin humping a desk.

PHIL: Look at the bloody time. I'll cut his legs off.

SAMUELS: And he'll still be bigger than you.

Price has taken a tiny violin and large bow from his bag, begins to tune it quietly.

McBRAIN: *(miming M.C. in the cleared central area between the desks)* Ladies and gentlemen, welcome to the Factory Street Copacabana, where a feast of comedy talent on tonight's bill includes Mr Sammy Samuels, the Golda Meir of Gagland, hot from his recent sizzling successes in the Gaza Hilton, not forgetting, of course, the Telly Savalas of Comedy, author of the highly acclaimed *The Naked Jape,* Mr Gethin – what the *hell's* that thing?

PRICE: *(as to a child, slowly)* This? It's a … very, very small … violin. Vi. O. Lin. Try it. Vio. Lin.

McBRAIN: Vio. Nil. Vay. Lone. Velo. Line. No. Velo. No ...

PRICE: Vio. Lin. Keep practising. It'll come.

MacBrain stands blinking, trying to say the word.

SAMUELS: Hey. Vic Oliver. You're never Jewish.

PRICE: *(perfect Manchester Jewish)* You wanna make some kind of a bet, Moses?

McBRAIN: *(elated)* Violin! Got it! Vaseline, shit!

Waters back in. They sit down at their desks with a muffled clatter and scrape.

WATERS: Right, let's see who's here ... Jack Thomas is out. Tonsillitis.

McBRAIN: Tough. Poor old Jack.

WATERS: What about your brother, Mr Murray?

PHIL: *(nervous)* He'll be here, Mr Waters. He's probably been held up somewhere.

SAMUELS: Likely he got a bit behind with his milk-round.

CONNOR: I've heard tell it's more than behind these milkmen are after getting.
    Sure my wife's the only woman in the street ours hasn't parked his float in.

Beat.

CONNOR: ⎫
McBRAIN: ⎬ The stuck-up bitch!
SAMUELS: ⎭

Laughter.

WATERS: *(dry)* Oh, we're working tonight, gentlemen. How can they say Music
    Hall is dead when jokes like that survive ... down the ages? Right, settle down,
    we'll make a start. *(looking at clock)* Now, we're down at Grey Mare Lane at
    eight thirty-five or so for a nine o'clock start. That gives us till about twenty-
    five past. And remember we come back here as soon as it's finished, just to
    round things off and er ... listen to the verdict. Which brings me to the man
    they're sending. *(taking opened envelope from inside pocket, taking letter out)*
    His name's ... Bert Challenor ... some of you may have heard of him ... he
    worked Number Ones a fair while way back, before he took up ... talent-
    spotting. He'll be here back side of eight, so you'll get a chance to weigh him
    up before the off. *(Pause. Scanning them)* I don't want to say much about him.
    He's an agents' man. Which means he has power. I'd better say this, though:
    I've never rated him. And he doesn't reckon much to me either.

CONNOR: Sounds a nice chap.

WATERS: Now I'm not saying any of this is going to count against you. But we ...
    have our differences. I'd hoped for someone else, to tell the truth.

Puzzled looks, faint consternation.

SAMUELS: How do you mean, differences?

WATERS: I don't wanna spend all night on it … I never joined his … Comedy Artists and Managers Federation, for a kick-off. They took it bad, for some reason. I didn't like what they stood for. I've been a union man all my life, it wasn't that … They wanted the market … They wanted to control entry into the game. I told 'em no comedian *(odd, particular emphasis)* worth his salt could ever 'federate' with a manager. *(Pause, sniff.)* And as far as I'm concerned no comedian ever did …

PRICE: *(very distinctly)* You think he'd … fail us … just for that, Mr Waters, do you?

WATERS: That's not what I said …

McBRAIN: Nobody'll fail me. I'm unfailable.

CONNOR: Hark at the Pope, now.

PRICE: *(piercing, within the control)* Well, what then?

WATERS: Well, put baldly, if I've done a job with you lot, he'll see it, and he won't like it. That's all.

They look at each other, a trifle more concerned.

McBRAIN: *(reassuring)* What does it matter, a comic's a comic.

SAMUELS: Not in Rabbi Challenor's book he ain't.

WATERS: *(deliberate)* Not in Eddie Waters' book either.

Silence. Some sniffs.

I probably overstate the problem. You're all good enough … now … to force his hand, without playing down …

McBRAIN: Crème de la crème.

SAMUELS: A little clotted here and there perhaps.

McBRAIN: More there than here, Isaac.

PRICE: Why don't we start?

Others repeat 'Why don't we start? Why don't we start?' rather crazily to each other, begin to discuss it.

CONNOR: What an excellent suggestion, give that man a balaclava for his pains.

WATERS: All right. In the time remaining I thought we might just run through a few exercises to get the blood running …

Ged Murray *half backs into the room, soaked through. He's large, gentle, direct, open, very far from stupid. Pale, with bad teeth and balding. He wears a milkman's brown coat and hat. He continues, a line at a time, as he makes his way into the room, greets people with winks or smiles, finds his chair, adjusts it, sits down, apparently wholly unaware of the interruption of process he represents. A brilliant comic performance, in other words.*

GED: *(taking coat off, shaking it, adjusting himself)* Sorry I'm late. It's bloody pissing down out there. I fell asleep on the settee watching *Crossroads.* So I had to nip down t'depot and borrow a float to get here. And t'bloody battery were flat. Got stuck on the Old Road. Walked the last sodding mile. Evening, Mr Waters. *(He hits his seat next to brother Phil.)* Evening, all. (A *big friendly grin.)*

ALL: *(in chorus)* Good evening, Mr Woodentop.

Waters waits, a little impatient, for quiet.

PHIL: *(hoarse, hostile)* I waited ten minutes on a double yellow line ...

GED: *(easily)* Don't worry, I'm here now.

PHIL: Couldn't you have put some'at else on?

GED: What's wrong with this?

PHIL: What you watching *Crossroads* for?

GED: It helps me sleep.

WATERS: (*taps the desk with a piece of chalk.*) If you've nearly finished ...

GED: Sorry, Mr Waters.

PHIL: *(suppressed mutter)* So you bloody should be ...

CONNOR: How's the wife then, Ged?

GED: *(simply)* All right.

WATERS: Bloody hell, what is this? We'll do sewing if you like ...

Some laughter. Ged indicates his apology facially.

Right, let's get you warm. *(Points to McBrain, immediately to his right.)* Character. Stupid.

McBRAIN: *(fast, in character)* Excuse me, miss, where do I put this thing? *(Long pause.)* Oh ...

WATERS: *(to Samuels, next)* Ancient.

SAMUELS: *(fast, in character)* Course I remember Moses. Little feller ... *(musing)* ... bad teeth, oy that breath ...

WATERS: *(to Connor, on end)* Silly.

CONNOR: Erm ... *(furtive)* I'll take a pound of the sausages. With the leaves left on.

Waters snorts, sustaining the speeded rhythms of the exercise.

WATERS: *(to Price, end of left desk)* Feminine.

PRICE: *(fast, perfect)* Four quid, dearie.

Waters thrown a little, perhaps by the unexpected harshness.

WATERS: Try another.

PRICE: *(same voice)* … All I said was, all I *said was* …four quid doesn't cover sheets … Just take your shoes off, is that a lot to ask?

WATERS: *(to Ged, next)* Posh.

GED: *(almost own voice, a strange modification, after thought)* Could you get me some clean bread for this dip, miss … ?

WATERS: Nice. *(to Phil)* Absent-minded.

PHIL: *(bad Robb Wilton)* Al never forget –

CONNOR: *(distinct whisper)* Whatsisname.

PHIL: Whatsisname. Look, piss off will you, Mick … ?

WATERS: OK. Coming. It's speed … and it's detail. It's the detail inside the speed that makes the difference. A bit sluggish. We'll send it the other way. *(to Phil:)* Willy.

PHIL: Willy Nilly.

GED: Willy Won'ty.

PRICE: Willy Nocomebackagain.

CONNOR: Willy Ell.

SAMUELS: *(pulling face)* God Villy …

McBRAIN: *(same face)* Willy Nands.

WATERS: God. *(to McBrain)* Sammy.

McBRAIN: Sammy … ?

WATERS: Yes, yes …

McBRAIN: *(desperate)* Sammy Circle.

WATERS: *(urgent)* Right, come on.

SAMUELS: *(very Yiddish)* 'Sammyterwidyu?

CONNOR: *(Italian)* 'Sa me you wanta see? Why dincha say so?

PRICE: Sammykazi. *(Pause.)* The Suicidal Shithouse.

GED: *(singing)* Sammy, Sammy, you aren't half jammy

PHIL: Sammy Professional.

McBRAIN: Did someone call? I thought I heard my name.

WATERS: Not bad. Let's stretch it a bit. *(stopwatch, tape-recorder)* Let's see if you can handle a cough. Off you go.

They enter the half circle to play the coughing tape-recorder.

McBRAIN: *(fluent)* By, she's coughing well tonight. What've you been doing to her, eh? Dirty thing, you.

SAMUELS: There's an old Indian remedy for coughing in women, you know. Full of spices and herbs and other Asian comestibles. Do you like that? Grub. It's a sort of curry linctus ...

Groans all round.

They say it's very good ...

PRICE: *(perfectly acted)* Do you realize, we're all sharing the same air with that man. Just listen to him. *(Waits.)* Every time he does that there's a million infectious droplets joins the pool. He's emptying his lungs over everyone here. Go on, empty away, son, we don't mind ...

CONNOR: I tell you what, why don't you come up here and cough and we'll all sit down there and laugh at you ...

McBRAIN: Mek a change for *your* act, Mick.

GED: I think she's trying to tell me something.

PHIL: Yeah, you're rubbish.

GED: Oh you speak the language do you? That's nice.

PHIL: Yes, I learnt it at school.

GED: Oh they dint teach us out like that. They taught us spittin'. And peein' up walls ...

PHIL: Ay well, that's the secondary modern system for you init. S'just a bad system.

McBRAIN: Cough and the world coughs with you. Fart and you stand alone.

WATERS: *(tough)* All right ...

Price is already climbing up on to his desk.

PRICE: There was a young lady called Pratt ...

McBRAIN: Yes, yes ...

PRICE: Who would hang from the light by her hat ...

CONNOR: No, no.

PRICE: With a frightening cough ...

SAMUELS: Yes.

PRICE: She would jerk herself off

McBRAIN: Ah ...

PRICE: *(vicious but quiet)* By sinking her teeth in her twat.

ALL: Olé!

Waters stares at him. The others laugh, puzzled yet amused.

CARETAKER: *(from doorway)* Smoking is not allowed on these premises. Thank you. *(He turns again.)* Or standing on desks. Or anything else like that.

He leaves with dignity. Price gets down, white, impassive, avoiding Waters' eyes, which follow him, close and tense as he resumes his seat.

WATERS: *(quiet, still)* Is somebody trying to tell me something? *(Pause.)* Mmm?

No answer. Price twangs a tiny violin string, once, twice, three times. Slight sense of discomfiture as they try to locate his meaning.

The traitor distrusts truth.

They look at him.

The traitor distrusts truth. Tongue twisters. Shall we twist tongues, gentlemen?

They take it up in turn.

(he calls) Faster.

The phrase gradually loses its shape and meaning in the struggle for facility. Waters sends it down McBrain's line first, then Phil Murray's, so that we end on Price.

PRICE: *(effortlessly, at speed)* The traitor distrusts truth. The traitor distrusts truth. The traitor distrusts truth. The traitor distrusts truth. The traitor distrusts truth. The traitor distrusts truth. The traitor distrusts truth ... *(Long pause. Very levelly, measuredly, at Waters)* The traitor distrusts truth.

WATERS: *(finally, mild, matter-of-fact)* I've never liked the Irish, you know. Dr Johnson said they were a very truthful race, they never spoke well of each other, but then how could they have?

They look around, faintly puzzled, amused.

Big, thick, stupid heads, large cabbage ears, hairy nostrils, daft eyes, fat, flapping hands, stinking of soil and Guinness. The niggers of Europe. Huge, uncontrollable wangers, spawning their degenerate kind wherever they're allowed to settle. I'd stop them settling here if I had my way. Send 'em back to the primordial bog they came from. Potato heads.

Pause. McBrain clenches and unclenches his fists on the desk, watches them carefully.

CONNOR: *(slowly)* Would that be Southern Irish or Northern Irish, Mr Waters:?

WATERS: *(mildly on)* Or Jews, for that matter.

SAMUELS: What you staring at me for?

Uneasy laughter, dying fast.

WATERS: *(still very matter-of-fact)* They have this *greasy* quality, do Jews. Stick to their own. Grafters. Fixers. Money. Always money. Say Jew, say gold. Moneylenders, pawn-brokers, usurers. They have the nose for it, you might say. Hitler put it more bluntly: 'If we do not take steps to maintain the purity of blood, the Jew will destroy civilization by poisoning us all.' The effluent of history. Scarcely human. Grubs.

SAMUELS: *(unfunnily)* He must've met the wife's family.

WATERS: Negroes. Cripples. Defectives. The mad. Women. *(turning deliberately to Murray's row)* Workers. Dirty. Unschooled. Shifty. Grabbing all they can get. Putting coal in the bath. Chips with everything. Chips and beer. Trade Unions dedicated to maximizing wages and minimizing work. Strikes for the idle. Their greed. And their bottomless stupidity. Like children, unfit to look after themselves. Breeding like rabbits, sex-mad. And their mean vicious womenfolk, driving them on. Animals, to be fed slops and fastened up at night. *(Long pause.)* The traitor destroys the truth.

Silence. Coughing. Shuffling of feet.

PRICE: Gone very dark in here all of a sudden.

McBRAIN: Fancy a hand of crib?

Silence again. Waters looks down at his desk. They exchange inquiring looks across his space.

GED: *(finally)* I don't get that. *(Pause.)* Were it some kind of a joke, Mr Waters?

WATERS: Not exactly a joke, Mr Murray.

GED: I mean. There's good and bad in everyone.

WATERS: Is there now?

CONNOR: Didn't you say so yourself?

WATERS: Did I?

SAMUELS: You're always saying it. 'A comedian draws pictures of the world. The closer you look, the better you'll draw.'

In the silence that follows, a penny begins to drop.

PRICE: *(laconic, drawn out)* Lesson Three: 'Stereotypes'.

Some faint embarrassment, the sense, however obscure, of having let Waters down.

SAMUELS: You were having us on. That's a relief. I was beginning to get worried.

Some relaxation, smiles, off the hook.

WATERS: *(driving home)* If I've told you once I've told you a thousand times. We work *through* laughter, not *for* it. If all you're about is raising a laugh, OK, get on with it, good luck to you, but don't waste my time. There's plenty others as'll tek your money and do the necessary. Not Eddie Waters.

McBRAIN: *(conciliatory, apologetic)* So, a few crappy jokes, Mr Waters …

WATERS: It's not the jokes. It's not the jokes. It's what lies behind 'em. It's the attitude. A real comedian – that's a daring man. He *dares* to see what his listeners shy away from, fear to express. And what he sees is a sort of truth, about people, about their situation, about what hurts or terrifies them, about what's hard, above all, about what they *want*. A joke releases the tension, says the unsayable, any joke pretty well. But a true joke, a comedian's joke, has to do more than release tension, it has to *liberate* the will and the desire, it has to *change the situation*. *(Pause.)* There's very little won't take a joke. But when a joke bases itself upon a distortion – *(at Price, deliberately)* – a 'stereotype' perhaps – and gives the lie to the truth so as to win a laugh and stay in favour, we've moved away from a comic art and into the world of 'entertainment' and slick success. *(Pause.)* You're better than that, damn you. And even if you're not, you should bloody well want to be.

CONNOR: I want to be famous. I want to be rich and famous. What's wrong with that, Mr Waters?

WATERS: More than you want to be good?

McBRAIN: What's wrong with being all three?

WATERS: Nothing. So long as you're good *first*. Because you'll never be good later.

PRICE: *(suddenly)* Was it my limerick?

WATERS: I don't want to personalize this discussion …

PRICE: Oh, I see. You think talking to the six of us makes it impersonal, do you …?

PHIL: Oh, come on, Pricey, don't argue .

PRICE: Why not? He's accusing us … me … of doing some'at … immoral, I want to know what he means, it's pretty important to me …

SAMUELS: Look, we don't want a scene …

PRICE: Who wants a scene? I put a simple question. I'm just looking for a 'truth' . Was it my limerick he took objection to? *(Pause.)* Because if it was, I'd like to know what his objections are, that's all.

SAMUELS: Well just don't push your luck, OK?

GED: *(gentle but firm)* It's not up to you, Sammy.

WATERS: All right. Let's hear it again, Mr Price.

PRICE: What?

WATERS: Will you recite it for us?

PRICE: What for?

WATERS: Give us a chance to look it over, see what we're dealing with.

PRICE: It was it then, was it?

WATERS: *You* think it was.

SAMUELS: Let's hear it then.

PHIL: Yeah, let's hear it.

Pause. Price bites his lip, sullen, moody. Waters waits.

PRICE: *(slowly)* All right.
>   There was a young lady called Pratt
>   Who would hang from the light by her hat
>   With a frightening cough
>   She would jerk herself off
>   By sinking her teeth in her twat.

Silence.

WATERS: It's clever. Is it your own?

PRICE: You could say that.

WATERS: How do you mean?

PRICE: I made it up. Just then.

WATERS: It's very clever.

GED: *(marvelling)* You never made it up, did you?

PRICE: Look, Mr Waters, I don't want compliments, just say what you don't like and we can get on …

WATERS: What do you think it says?

PRICE: I don't know. You tell me. I felt like saying it.

WATERS: *(crossing to board, chalking up key words one beneath another, fast monotone)* Pratt. Pratt says twat. Lady, twat. Twat, bad word, unsayable. I've said it, will say it, might say it, *hat,* fooled you, build the suspense, cough, cough, jerked herself off, women masturbate, naughty, must say it now, dadadadadadada *twat. There!*

PRICE: So?

WATERS: It's a joke that hates women, Gethin.

PRICE: How come?

McBRAIN: Ha ha. *(He shuts up quickly.)*

WATERS: It's a joke that hates women *and* sex. Do I go on?

PRICE: *(cool)* Why not?

WATERS: In the Middle Ages men called the woman's sexual organ the devil's mark. According to Freud, men still see them as shark's mouths, in dreams. When you walk into that arena with a joke, you've gotta know why you're there.

PRICE: Maybe I'm just frightened.

WATERS: Maybe. But who do you blame, with your joke? Your lady 'jerks' herself off. Is she a man?

PRICE: It rhymes with cough.

WATERS: *Off* rhymes with cough. What do you *think* of your lady?

PRICE: Not a lot.

WATERS: Acrobatic but nasty? Sex-starved? Sex-mad? A nympho? Sexually insatiable?

McBRAIN: Can I say something?

WATERS: By all means.

McBRAIN: I mean, I do take your point and that, but doesn't his rhyme do just what you said you wanted? If fellers fear women and sex and that the way you say … doesn't that wee rhyme kind of … liberate the fear, sort of?

WATERS: I don't think it does. I think it recognizes it and *traps* it. Leaves it exactly where it is. Doesn't help it on. Doesn't do anything to *change* it. *(to everyone)* Look, this is probably the last chance I'll get, and I want to state it as simply as I can.·

The door opens and an **Asian** *enters, soaked and gleaming, small, slim, dark, delicate, a large muslin-wrapped something under his arm. He stops, smiles, shyly wavers. They turn to look at him. He leaves, closing the door behind him. Waters crosses to the door after a moment, looks out down the corridor.*

SAMUELS: *(sotto voce)* If that's Challenor, we're all done for.

PHIL: All blacked up for the evening.

Waters returns to his desk.

WATERS: A joke that feeds on ignorance starves its audience. We have the choice. We can say something or we can say nothing. Not everything true is funny, and not everything funny is true. Most comics feed prejudice and fear and blinkered vision, but the best ones, the best ones … illuminate them, make them clearer to see, easier to deal with. We've got to make people laugh till they cry. Cry. Till they find their pain and their beauty. Comedy is medicine. Not coloured sweeties to rot their teeth with.

The Asian reappears in the doorway.

Can I help you?

ASIAN: Please, Learning to Read?

WATERS: No …

ASIAN: Please.

He puts down his parcel, fishes a leaflet from his sodden overcoat, hands it to Waters: Waters studies it, turns it over to read the other side.

Learning to Read.

WATERS: *(reading)* 'Reading to Learn'.

ASIAN: No. Learning to Read.

WATERS: No, it says Reading to Learn. *(He shows him.)* Reading. To. Learn.

The Asian is perplexed.

It says it's a class in literary appreciation for intending students of the Open University. BBC. I'm no wiser than you, really ...

ASIAN: A man gave it to me in the library

WATERS: Aye, well he probably had a sense of humour.

ASIAN: Perhaps somewhere else ... ?

WATERS: *(glancing at clock)* Look. I'll take you up to the Principal, he'll sort you out ... *(He leads him towards door.)* I won't be a minute. Try and sort the order out while I'm away, will you, George. Look at you, you're soaked, man, how far've you come ... ?

They leave.

SAMUELS: *(standing, lighting cigarette)* What a fuck up *this* is! *(at Price)* Why don't you keep your bloody trap shut, eh?

McBRAIN: Come on, Sammy.

SAMUELS: Fuck off. I want to think about me act, not arse the night away on ... philosophy! Especially after he tells us we've got a bent adjudicator.

PHIL: Me too.

CONNOR: I thought you said you couldn't care less whether you did well or not tonight.

SAMUELS: *(terse)* Well I do.

CONNOR: With having your own club and that up Moston way.

GED: Yeah. You said you could always employ yourself.

SAMUELS: Listen, cretin, do you wanna know something, I wouldn't be seen dead working a club like mine, I want the tops, I want TV, I want the Palladium. You can work my club, I'll book you as soon as you're ready, you're just what they need. As for that little git ...

Points at Price, turns away angrily. Price moves, with some menace, towards him. McBrain gently interposes himself.

McBRAIN: There was this poacher, see. And he shoots this deer. Big 'un. Hatstands in its head an' that. And he puts it over his back – like that – and he's hunking it off when this gamekeeper catches him and says, Hey, you're poaching, and your man says, How do you mean? and he says, You've got a deer on your back, and he looks over his shoulder and he says, Get off.

They laugh, more at the telling than the tale. Price gets up, steps onto the rostrum, becoming, in the moment, uncannily, the seventy-year-old Waters.

PRICE: Now, Mr McBrain, you must see that that joke is totally supportive of all forms of blood sports. Besides which it undoubtedly hints at the dark secret of animal buggery or, at the very least, the stealthy buggering of men by beasts of the field and forest. A *comedian,* George, would have carried all this out into the open where we could all see it ... *(He looks for it.)* ... so that we'd all come to realize what should've been obvious from the start, or the Middle Ages, whichever you prefer: namely, deep down, all any of us want is fucking up the arse by antlered beasties. *(Pause.)* It's a joke that hates *deer,* George.

McBrain, Connor and Phil Murray laugh. Samuels scowls a bit in his corner.

GED: *(serious)* That's not so funny.

PRICE: *(sombre)* No. I suppose it isn't.

McBRAIN: Why've you got it in for him then?

CONNOR: Yeah, what's that about? His favourite an' all. I thought you rated him.

PRICE: I don't want telling what to think. That's all. I don't want telling what to feel.

SAMUELS: You'd've felt my bleeding boot up your hole if you'd talked that way to me. Look at the fucking time ...

PRICE: *(quiet, with great, inquiring grace)* I didn't know you was Irish, Sammy ...

Samuels laughs, a little slow splutter in spite of himself.

SAMUELS: You're a slippy fucker. Do you know that?

PRICE: *(rolling eyes)* Yes, baas. I know that, baas. Yessuh baas. Whup ma hahd an cawl me kinky.

McBRAIN: Answer the question. Why're you so bent on riling the old man? *He's* no different.

PRICE: So maybe I am. *(He strokes his cropped head, an unconscious gesture.)*

CONNOR: Yeah. Maybe it's more than your hairs you've been losing.

Price turns away, smiling.

I'll tell you some'at. He's a good old man. And he's a comic to his toenails. He doesn't *need* to do this for peanuts, you know, every Friday night, *here,* on two quid an hour or whatever it is. He could take a room in a pub and charge a fortune and he'd get it too. So that he can teach pricks like us he does it. *(Pause.)* And if I get out of the building game and earn a living doing what I want to do more than anything else, always have done, I'll have him to thank and no one else. *(deliberately)* And that goes for everyone here, whether they know it or not.

GED: It goes for me.

McBRAIN: Yeah.

PHIL: All right, he's a genius, what is this, Gala Night at the City Varieties?

GED: *We* knew less than nowt.

PHIL: Speak for yourself. I'd done clubs

GED: Two. Ardwick and Oldham. One of 'em withheld your money. The other called you a taxi to drive you off to safety.

PHIL: Like the bloody wild west, both of 'em. There was nothing wrong with *me*. My troubles started when I took you on, believe me.

GED: *(quiet, toughly serious)* When are you gonna face it: you're not funny. You're a straight. You can't work on your own. *(Pause.)* But I can.

PHIL: Try it.

GED: Maybe I will.

McBRAIN: Frying tonight, by God! Jees, listen to 'em go. All of 'em. Those poor bloody guinea pigs of an audience at this club'll know the meaning of tears tonight, by Christ, won't they just. Come on, let's get the order decided, who wants to go first? Sammy? How about you?

SAMUELS: No thanks.

McBRAIN: Anyone? *(Nobody.)* OK. *(Takes pack of cards from his pocket, cuts it twice.)* Lowest loses, aces high. *(He deals five cards in sequence to correspond to the five turns. They peer at the cards.)*

CONNOR: Shit!

McBRAIN: You Mick! Tough.

CONNOR: Ah well. At least they'll be awake.

SAMUELS: You'll no doubt manage to do something about it though …

McBRAIN: Second, Sammy?

SAMUELS: All right.

McBRAIN: Ged? Phil?

GED: OK.

McBRAIN: *(looking at Price)* How do you feel about last?

PRICE: All the same to me.

McBRAIN: Right. Top of the bill, kidda. Will they be waiting for you! Now, who wants music? *(They show. McBrain writes it down.)* Gethin, you have music don't you?

PRICE: No.

McBRAIN: I thought you got off with that song. What was it …?

PRICE: No, I've changed it. No music.

SAMUELS: You're a cool sod, I'll give you that. The bleeding nerve of it, working up an act for three months and then altering it half an hour before he goes on. You'll come a right cropper one day, you will. I can feel it in me water.

PRICE: *(deliberately)* Well, piss over somebody else for a change, Sammy.

McBRAIN: Hey, hey, hey, any more of that and you'll go in the book ... *(He brandishes a book in his right hand, a referee.)*

Waters in, followed by the Asian. Waters carries a tray with eight teas in plastic cups, spoons, sugar.

WATERS: I got the teas in.

They move towards the tray.

Gentlemen, this is Mr Patel.

GED: Hello, Mr Patel.

A few more grunts of acknowledgement.

McBRAIN: Hey, if you've got any good jokes, I'll have a word with you before you go ...

Patel smiles innocently.

WATERS: Mr Patel is going to stay with us a little while, I've promised him a lift into town on the way down to the Club. He's, erm ... he's been sent on a wild goose chase ... and the monsoon is still with us, as you'll no doubt have observed for yourselves. Sit there if you would, Mr Patel, by the pipes. Take your coat off if you like.

PATEL: *(sitting)* Thank you no, sir. I'm very comfortable, please ...

Waters resumes the desk, picks up McBrain's list.

McBRAIN: That's the order.

WATERS: Fine. And the asterisks are music, yes?

McBRAIN: Ahunh.

WATERS: *(at clock)* Right. I don't want anything from your acts from now on, all right. Just let them lie and get yourselves limber. OK. Close your eyes. Come on, close your eyes.

They close their eyes, frowning or amused.

Now think. Think about yourselves. What you've been, what you've done, what you are, what you want. All right? Keep thinking. Now, take one incident, anything, any little thing, that means something to you, maybe something that embarrasses you or haunts you or still makes you frightened, something you still can't deal with maybe, all right? Now think about it. It may be some'at very gentle, very tender, some'at you said, some'at you did, wanted to do ... All right. Open up.

They blink at each other.

GED: Bloody hellfire, I were just gettin' into that.

WATERS: Let's hear it then, Mr Murray.

GED: *(and others).* What?

WATERS: I want you to tell it. Any way you like, in your own time. *(Pause.)* But make it funny.

GED: Jesus wept!

SAMUELS: He'd been watching your act.

GED: I were thinking about wife.

McBRAIN: Haha. Very good, very good. It's the way he tells 'em you know.

WATERS: *(softly)* You're next, George. *(to Ged)* So tell us about it. Be funny. Try.

GED: She went in hospital, have the nipper. Ancoats. 'Bout two in the morning. He musta laid there best part of a year, all snug like, planning it. I rang up from Beswick depot next morning about half-five. Nothing. Seven, nothing. Half-nine. Half-ten. I musta bin nervous, I found mesel smoking me own fags. I went to our mother's dinnertime, for company I suppose. *(difficult now)* Me dad'd been off work for a while, Clayton Aniline ... he'd had a sorta breakdown ... *(He touches his head.)* ... gone a bit queer in the head ...

PHIL: Bloody hell, what you talkin' about that for ... ?

GED: Anyroad, I rang again and they said she'd had it so I got a bus and went down. *(Pause.)* When I got to the ward, I couldn't go in.

CONNOR: The door was locked.

GED: I suddenly thought, what if it runs in the family.

McBRAIN: Like crabs, you mean.

GED: I thought, what if there's some'at wrong with it.

Silence now, the story rivets.

She were holding it in her arm. I saw it ten beds away. Black hair. Red face. Little fists banging away on wife's face. *(Pause.)* He were bloody perfect. He were bloody perfect.

He looks around, unembarrassed, largely unaware of his effect. Some coughs, stirrings, sniffs.

PHIL: *(mutter)* What you talkin' about that for?

GED: *(simply)* I were thinkin' about it.

PHIL: You were thinking about it. Jesus wept.

McBRAIN: I'm not following that, Mr Waters. No thanks.

PRICE: I went nutty once.

SAMUELS: *(queer)* Well, you do surprise me, Gethin.

WATERS: Is that what you were thinking about?

PRICE: Sort of.

WATERS: Go on.

PRICE: I thumped a teacher.

CONNOR: Oh the hard bastard of a thing you are.

PRICE: *(simply)* Not really. Were a woman. She called us a guttersnipe. In music. I clocked her one. It seemed the only thing I could do. She went white. Whiter than me even. Then she cried. Little tears. They sent me to a psychologist. Thirteen. Me I mean, *he* were a bit older. Though not much. We developed a sort of tolerant hatred of each other. He kept insisting on treating me as an equal, you know. Patronizing me. The last time I saw him he gave me this long piece and he said, 'You see, Gethin, basically all any of us want is to be loved.' And I said, 'If you know so much, how come you wear a Crown Topper?' *(Pause.)* That's when I decided I'd be a comedian. *(He sniffs, twangs the violin string.)*

GED: That's about as funny as mine.

PHIL: Yeah, laugh a minute.

WATERS: It's hard isn't it. Not exactly queuing up to go, are we, gentlemen? *(He scans McBrain's row, then stares at Phil Murray.)* Why *is* that, do you think? It wouldn't have been *all* waste, Mr Murray, if your child had been born defective, would it? I mean, it would at least have afforded us a worthy subject for the comic's wit. *(Pause.)* Do we fear … other people … so much that we must mark *their* pain with laughter, our own with tears? People deserve respect because they are people, not because they are known to us. Hate your audience and you'll end up hating yourself. All right. We'll stop that there … *(Looks at clock: about 8.20.)* Any final queries about your spots? George? Sammy?

Both give negatives. Mick?

CONNOR: *(fiddling)* Y'aven't a dickie have you, this keeps fallin' off …

WATERS: I'll have a look at it in the van going down. Gethin?

Price shakes his head.

Sure?

Price nods.

What about you two?

PHIL: We're fine, Mr Waters.

WATERS: *(to everyone)* I want to wish you luck. You worked hard, you've sweated, you've been honester than most. I'll be pulling for you all tonight. And you'll *know* if you're good. You'll not need tellin'.

Challenor *knocks, enters on the knock. He's maybe five years younger than Waters, rather waxen, discreetly dressed, with a homburg, and umbrella, which he shakes. His self-regard is almost a mannerism, though he retains a residual lithe charm.*

CHALLENOR: Evening, Eddie. I'll never understand why they don't run boats to Manchester.

WATERS: We're waiting on London to give the word. Hello, Bert.

CHALLENOR: Spry as ever. Eddie Waters, the Lancashire Lad.

WATERS: Relax. You'll see forty, don't you fret.

CHALLENOR: I thought you'd have taken the bungalow at Southport by now, Eddie.

WATERS: Nay. I'm a Manchester man. I'd miss the rain.

The relaxed yet glinting spat ends

CHALLENOR: These your lads, then?

WATERS: Aye. Mr Challenor of the C.A.M.F., Phil and Ged Murray, Gethin Price, Mick Connor, Sammy Samuels, George McBrain.

CHALLENOR: How do you do. *(He's looking in Patel's direction, inquiringly.)*

WATERS: He's not part of the class.

CHALLENOR: No? There's one or two about, you know. Midland clubs. Awful lot of people, of course …

WATERS: Is there anything you want to say before we get down there?

CHALLENOR: *(checking watch)* I wouldn't mind a word or two, Eddie. Is it far?

WATERS: No. No. Ten minutes.

The Caretaker comes in. He carries a shattered lectern.

CARETAKER: *(to Waters)* I told the Principal you were looking for him. *(He points in Patel's direction)* He's back now. He had to go down to the other centre in Beswick. *(He makes a drinking sign with his right hand.)*

WATERS: Thank you, I think we can manage now …

CARETAKER: I told him you were looking. He's in his office. Waiting.

WATERS: It's very good of you.

CARETAKER: *(looking at lectern)* They've gone bloody *mad* down there, that Karate lot. *(He leaves.)*

Challenor looks at Waters.

CHALLENOR: Don't mind me, Eddie.

Waters doesn't want to leave, can't show it.

WATERS: We'll go and see the Principal, Mr Patel, just to make sure you're in the wrong place.

Patel crosses behind him to the door.

(to class) I'll be back ...

They leave. Challenor mounts the dais carefully, stands at the tall, sloping desk, places his black attaché case on the ledge.

CHALLENOR: Going to give me a good show then?

McBRAIN: That we are. Crème de la crème. You'll laugh tonight, Mr Challenor, that you will.

CHALLENOR: That's good news, brother. It's been a particularly unfunny day.

SAMUELS: Your worries are over, Mr Challenor, mark my words. Five of the finest comedy acts west of Royton. I'm *very* funny.

CHALLENOR: I'll watch out for you.

SAMUELS: Trap three. It'll guide in.

PHIL: I saw you at the Hulme Hippodrome just after the war, about 1951. Frank Randle top of the bill. Bert Challenor, the Cockney Character.

CHALLENOR: Right. Played Number Ones for twenty years, right through to the end. History to you lot ...

PRICE: Did you really play with Frank Randle?

CHALLENOR: I did.

PRICE: What were he like? Were he one of the best?

CHALLENOR: Best of his kind, I suppose.

PRICE: How do you mean, of his kind?

CHALLENOR: He was *local,* wasn't he? South of Birmingham he was nothing. A whole set of 'em – Sandy Powell, Albert Modley, Jimmy James. George was the giant. Took the country. George was the great one. He's the one to study, if you're keen to get on.

PRICE: Formby?

CHALLENOR: Ahunh.

CONNOR: Didn't Mr Waters work with your man before the war?

CHALLENOR: Eddie did a lot of things before the war.

SAMUELS: Was he good?

Pause.

CHALLENOR: He were brilliant.

SAMUELS: Yeah? What happened then?

CHALLENOR: *(quietly)* He didn't … want enough. *(Pause.)* I don't know. He just stayed up here …

Pause.

PRICE: Have you seen Randle's films? I've seen 'em all. He's untouchable. *(He gets up suddenly, assumes an uncanny Frank Randle stance and gait.)* 'I'm as full of vim as a butcher's dog – I'm as lively as a cricket. Baaa, I'll sup it if it keeps me up all neet. I'll take anybody on of my age and weight, dead or alive, and I'll run 'em, walk 'em, jump 'em, fight 'em, aye, and I'll play 'em dominoes. Baaa, I've supped some stuff toneet. Listen, ony t'other day I went to a funeral, I were stood at graveside, a chap looked at me, he said, How old are you? I said eighty-two, he said I'm eighty-four. I said, I don't think it's much use thee going home at all.'

The group laugh. Challenor smiles thinly, undazzled.

CHALLENOR: Try it in Bermondsey, sonny. Try it in Birmingham even.

PHIL: Pay him no heed, Mr Challenor.

SAMUELS: He argues like other people breathe.

CHALLENOR: Well. Nice meeting you. Good luck for tonight. *(He dwells, enjoying the attention.)* A couple of … hints. Don't try to be deep. Keep it simple. I'm not looking for philosophers, I'm looking for comics. I'm looking for someone who sees what the people want and knows how to give it them. It's the people pay the bills, remember, yours, mine … Mr Waters'. We're servants, that's all. They demand, we supply. Any good comedian can lead an audience by the nose. But only in the direction they're going. And that direction is, quite simply … escape. We're not missionaries, we're suppliers of laughter. I'd like you to remember that. See you down there. Oh. A text for tonight. Perhaps we can't all be Max Bygraves. But we can try.

He takes his leave. Silence. McBrain opens another two cans of 'E', hands one to Connor. Samuels lights a panatella. They sit looking at each other, scanning for concern or alarm.

SAMUELS: *(disgust staining his voice)* Oh, that's marvellous. That's … marvellous.

PHIL: *(backing his chair to the floor savagely as he stands)* What the fuck are we gonna do?

SAMUELS: We're gonna get the bum's rush, that's what we're gonna do.

McBRAIN: Not at all. What're you on about?

SAMUELS: Look, you heard him, Seamus …

McBRAIN: *(thinking, already doubtful)* He had to say that. He's an old enemy of the Boss's, what else could he say?

PHIL: Sod that, what're we gonna *do?*

GED: What's that supposed to mean? We're gonna do our act.

PHIL: He'll murder us. You've got to be joking.

McBRAIN: That's very nearly funny.

GED: *(to Phil, standing heavily)* Look, what are you talking about?

PRICE: *(piercing through the din)* He means – do you not? – how can you change your act at this short notice to suit Challenor. Isn't that what you mean?

He takes in the whole group in the silence that follows the question. People sniff, shuffle, look at others.

SAMUELS: *(finally)* It's not such a tragedy. I can paste some'at together. Fortunately, I've managed to keep my distance …

CONNOR: Challenor'll get the act I came with. He don't bother me.

SAMUELS: OK, so be the funniest hod-carrier at Wimpey's.

CONNOR: *(steely)* I don't carry a hod, Sammy.

GED: We've got an act …

PHIL: We've got several acts. What about the one we used Christmas?

GED: What? You heard what Mr Waters thought of that …

PHIL: Look, Ged, I mean, look, fuck Mr Waters, I don't intend to spend the rest of my days on the pigging knocker collecting club money. Now I don't. All right?

GED: *(implacable)* I don't care what you do or don't do tomorrow. Tonight, we do the act.

PHIL: Do we.

GED: We do.

PHIL: You're stupid.

GED: *(dangerous, very swift)* No, Phil. Leave it.

Price watches them all from a distance, limbering up.

SAMUELS: What about you, George?

McBRAIN: I'll think of something. Well known you know for my flexibility. In any case *(Frank Carson voice)* it's the way I tell 'em.

PHIL: *(splenetic)* If you hate those bloody docks as much as you claim, you'll know what to do all right.

SAMUELS: Somebody shoulda told Challenor they *do* run boats to Manchester. So that pricks like you can unload 'em.

McBRAIN: *(simply)* I know what to do. Trust Georgey.

Pause. Samuels turns to Price.

SAMUELS: Whorrabout you then?

Price is doing left-leg squats on the dais. Stops carefully. Swivels gracefully round.

PRICE: *(innocent)* Me?

SAMUELS: *You,* you slippy sod.

PRICE: *(distinctly)* The traitor distrusts truth. The traitor distorts truth. The traitor destroys truth.

SAMUELS: You're dafter than you think, you know.

PRICE: *(inward)* I drive a van all day for British Rail. And if Challenor were on fire I wouldn't piss him out. Max Bygraves! *(The venom muscles his throat.)*

McBRAIN: *(quietly)* Maybe you won't have to?

Price's raised eyebrows ask the question.

You've changed your act already, haven't you. Who's a clever boy then?

SAMUELS: *(sourly marvelling)* Slippy.

Silence. Ged frowns concern. Connor watches. McBrain chuckles. Samuels clicks his teeth. Phil Murray flops back in his chair. Price stands a moment longer, then moves for his gear, gathers it, turns, begins to leave.

PRICE: See you at the show, darlings ... *(He's gone, out on amazing tiptoe, like a dancer in a minefield.)*

SAMUELS: *(following slowly to door)* Waters musta mentioned Challenor, told him last week, after the lesson. They allus have a drink together in the Mare ...

CONNOR: *(far from content)* Forget it, for Christ's sake. Who cares about bloody Challenor ...

He gathers his things roughly, angrily: leaves. The others begin to gather their belongings. Waters back in. He carries six buttonholes in plastic bags. Looks at depleted company.

WATERS: Ah, the others have gone on, have they ... I brought one of these each for you ... Here ... *(He hands four out, pockets the remainder.)* Don't start boozing after your turn. I've promised the Principal we'll be out by ten at the latest. All set then? Let's get the van ...

They troop out one after the other, Waters standing in the doorway to see them through. He gives a final cursory look around the room and leaves, closing door behind him.

Sounds of footsteps, muffled talking. After a moment, car and van doors being opened and closed, engines starting up.

The door opens and the Caretaker peeps in, sees the room vacated, advances. He carries a smashed chair, the frame in the right hand, a leg in the left.

After a moment he sights Patel's muslin-covered package. Stops, scans. Signs of slight but rising apprehension. He reaches gingerly towards it with the chair leg. Touches. Prods more vigorously, yet still cringing from it, as though half-expecting an explosion. Nothing. He drops the chair leg, opens the neck of the bag, peers in, sniffs, sniffs again, sniffs several times, his face crinkling with disgust. Stands. Picks up his chair. Leaves, switching off all lights behind him.

ACT TWO

A small club stage. A club **Pianist** *has arrived during the interval and is just completing a medley of old favourites. The* **Concert Secretary** *arrives at his table at the side of the stage, calling, 'Yes, yes, all right Teddy. I'll see to it after the draw,' to someone off-stage and at the same time showing Challenor (Scotch in hand) to his own table stage right.*

CONCERT SECRETARY: *(dry, tolerably sour, in charge; but real,* not *caricature)* Right. As announced in last week's club bulletin, there will now be a brief interval in the bingo …

Groans, calls of 'No' etc.

a *brief* interval in the bingo, to listen to some new comics setting their feet on the first rung of the ladder of fame. Now this'll last half an hour at the most and I'd like you to show these lads the traditional courtesy of the club – and then we'll get straight back to the bingo as soon as it's all over. Now … these are all lads who've been coached by that favourite comic of yesteryear, the Lancashire Lad himself, Mr Eddie Waters. Take a bow, Eddie.

Waters appears and makes his way to an empty table on the other side of the stage, ignoring the Concert Secretary's urgings to say a few words, and sits down with his pint, stage left.

So I think we're in for a treat. *(checking tatty notes)* First off, then, a young man from Ireland, now domiciled in Moss Side, your welcome please for … Mick … Connor.

Connor appears from the wings in hired evening dress and black pumps, a white carnation and black dickie. The Pianist covers his entrance with 'If you're Irish, come into the parlour'.

CONNOR: *(very Irish)* I told him not to say anything about me bein' Irish. I wanted to creep up on yez, like.

The Concert Secretary shushes the audience authoritatively. Connor angles his head in the Concert Secretary's direction.

I'm talkin' as quiet as I can. *(to audience)* Good evening. Sorry about de bingo. *(Takes mic. from stand, begins a slow, easy walk that will take him down from the club stage and find him sitting on the theatre stage below.)* Wuz yez ever foreigners, any of yez? I don't mean the odd fortnight in Brighton now, I mean

like always. Jeez, it's a funny thing ... First day in Manchester I go lookin' for
rooms. Your woman answers the door, a neat little thing wi' gouty eyes. I says,
Do you have any low terms for Irishmen here? She says, Yes. Piss off. Mind
you that was before the blacks came to help us out, shoulder some of the white
man's burden. Troublemakers. I never knew we wuz troublemakers till I got to
England. You don't you know. I mean, what are you lot, eh, do you know? You
don't have to find out, do you? Just people. You'd have to go to India or ...
Africa ... or Ireland to find out. Mmm? They'd tell yer right enough. Well,
stick around, maybe we'll come to you. You know, even the Catholic Church is
different here. I went to Mass at the Holy Name, like a bloody opera. Back
home in Wexford it's more like a market. The priest charges ten per cent
commission on all transactions. And confessions ... Jesus ... In England you
can hear the candles melt, so you can ... Your Irish priest is either half deaf or
half stewed. Speak up my son, there's nothing to be ashamed of ... so you've
gotta burst your lungs off to get absolution, safact. (*bellow*) Bless me, Father,
for I have sinned, it is six years since my last confession ... I have missed
Mass seven hundred and twenty three times ... I have fornicated ... (*own
voice*) Then you can hear a pin drop. I tell yer, we'd sit there by the confession
box every Sunday night ... all the young buckos ... It was a great way for
picking up girls for the ceilidh. (*acting it*) Hey, dissun's a goer ... ten times
widat Heaney feller from Ballamadurphy ... Hey, wait while you hear where
he put his finger ... (*He laughs.*) None of that here, mind. Your English priest
enjoys it too much . Oh yes. (*English priest's voice, dripping with retracted
interest, low and breathy, close to mic*) Yes, I see, my son, and you put it
where? (*Self, very low, hesitant but intense*) I put it ... down her mouth, Father.
(*Priest, slight but controlled increase in excitement*) Did you now? Erm ... and
why did you do that, my son? (*Self*) She 'ad dis ... bone stuck, Father ... Or
there's the other sort, the feller that's gonna end up Bishop's secretary, he's
very bored (*Bored posh priest, testy*) All right, so you've been wearing your
sister's clothes *again*, don't you ever do anything else? ... Don't you fancy
your mother's? ... I mean, you're in here every week with the same story,
there's no plot, there's no development, look, it might excite you, there's
absolutely nothing in it for me. Your penance is five Our Fathers and five Hail
Marys ... and the next time you're tempted to get into a frock just ... count to
ten ... and ask God to make you a little more inventive. (*Pause.*) Reminds me
of the old spinster lady back home confesses fornication and the priest asks her
for details ... cause he's interested like ... and so he can get a good sight of her
through the grille, so she tells him about this wonderful night of love she spent
with a tinker, and the priest says, Mary McGuire, that's the most shameful
thing you're after telling me and you a respected spinster of seventy-three. And
she says (*old maid's girlish voice*) As a matter of fact, Father, I was thirty when
it happened. I just like talking about it. (*Pause.*) I married an English Catholic
girl you know. She's sitting on the bed, on our honeymoon, and I see her take
out these little yellow, tablety things, I says, What's that? She says, The pill,
why, can't you take it in Ireland? And I says, Oh, I can take it all right, it's the
women that aren't allowed. I says, How come you're on the pill? She says, Our

church says we must search our own individual consciences for the truth and then act accordingly. *(Self)* Did you ever hear of such a thing? Back home in Ireland them's what we call Protestants. 'Course we had other ways. Oh yes, we were very inventive. An uncle of mine practised coitus interruptus all his life – till he got it right. I had lots of cousins in Wexford ... God ... *(Long reflective pause.)* He was a sad man, though. So listen anyway. Don't believe all you hear, you know what I mean. Speak well of the living. Especially within earshot. And the next time you meet an Irishman, count to ten ... and ask God to make you a little bit more inventive. And don't keep slapping him on the back. One day he'll stick a pack of dynamite up his jacket and blow your bloody arm off. If he didn't do it already. Like the IRA man who knocks at the gates of Heaven and St Peter says, Who're you? And your man says, I'm from the IRA. St. Peter says, Oh no, you can't come in here, and your man says, I don't wanna come in, I'm giving yez all three minutes to get out. Goodnight. God bless.

Pianist plays through Connor's applause and exit.

CONCERT SECRETARY: *(mic.)* A Manchester man now, from Middleton, a warm welcome please for ... *(reading)* ... Mr Sammy Samuels.

Sammy walks on. He wears a fine-fitting white jacket, red carnation, black bow, red satin handkerchief, diamond cufflinks.

SAMUELS: A message for any nymphomaniacs in the audience ... Hello. Sit down, lady, we'll have no rushing the stage. 1929 I were born. Year of the Great Crash. The sound of me father's jaw dropping. He took one look at me and said, I'm not that Jewish. Nobody's that Jewish. So, anyway, in the divorce court the judge awards me mother twenty pounds a month maintenance. And me father says, Judge, dat's very generous of you and to tell you de truth, ven business gets better I'll mebbe also help out a little. Anyway, me mother's bringing us all up like and me sister comes home from college and she says, I'm afraid I can't continue with me studies, momma, Vy? says momma. She couldn't say why. Vy. Always vy. Vy? she says. My sister says, I'm sort of ... pregnant, momma. That did it. A chair, a seltzer, oi, oi ... finally she says, So who's de fadder? I send you to college, I'm simple people. You got education, I don't know de proper vay to be introduced but you don't even know to ask mit whom am I having de pleasure?! Something's running down my leg; I hope it's sweat. She was some woman, momma. Bank manager rings up, he says, Mrs Samuels, you have an overdraft of fifty pounds. Is dat so? she says. So vot vos de balance last month? He looks, he says: You had a credit of twenty-two pounds. All right, says momma, and did I ring you? *(He looks at the stone-faced Challenor, wipes his hands on the handkerchief.)* OK, forget the Jews. Everybody else did. Here, there was this poacher, see. Poacher? And he catches this deer. And he slings it over his shoulder and he's humping it through the forest and a gamekeeper catches him and he says, Hey you, you're poaching. And the guy says, How do you mean? And the gamekeeper says, You've got a deer on your back. And the guy goes . . *(Looks over his shoulder*

and screams.) Heard about the Irish lamp post? Pissed on a dog. Hear about the
Irish cargo ship carrying yoyos? Sank forty-four times. The Irish waterpolo
team. Drowned twelve horses. This secretary runs into the boss's office and
says, Can I use your dictaphone? He says, No, use your finger like everyone
else! There's this West Indian tries to get a labouring job on a building site.
Foreman says, No chance, I know you lot. I give one of you a job, you turn up
the next day with a gang of your friends. He begs and pleads and finally he gets
the job. Next day he turns up with a pigmy. *(indicating)* Pigmy. Down there.
The foreman said, What did I tell you, no friends! He says, That's not my
friend, that's my lunch. What do you think of this Women's Lib, then? Burnt
your bras have you? Did you sir, how interesting. I burnt the wife's. She went
bloody mad, she was still in it. I'm in a pub downtown and this liberated
woman person collars me, she says, You're a brutal, loud-mouthed, sadistic,
irrational, sexist, male chauvinist pig. I said, I suppose a quick screw is out of
the question? ... So later in bed, I'm giving her one and she says, You're
marvellous, you're marvellous. No one has ever made love to me like that
before. But, I'm sort of kinky. Would you mind biting my ears while you're
doing it? Sure. On the lobes, gentle like. *(He mimes the delicate lobe bites, quite
slowly.)* Now, she says, can you kiss my bust, real quick. *(He repeats lobes
slowly, then adds rapid bust kisses.)* Now, she says, can you put your hands
round the back here and pull the cheeks ... Certainly. *(He starts the mime at the
top, adding the buttock-tugging, returns to the lobes again.)* She says, You've
slipped out! I said, No bloody wonder, I've forgotten what I was doing! I was at
the bar there earlier and I thought I'd take a leak while it was slack. A big black
bugger rushes in. Aaaah, he says. Just made it! I took a look, I said, There's no
chance of making one in white for me is there? I'd like to thank the pianist.
(fast) Thanks. Actually he's a brilliant pianist, this man. He has a lovely touch.
Actually, he got that touch off Liberace. *(to pianist)* Am I right? And that other
thing you got off Liberace ... has it cleared up? OK, take care of yourselves,
and if any of you ladies are accosted on your way out by a dark, handsome
fellow in a white jacket and a red carnation, just remember, it's for your own
good. I leave you with this thought: impotence is just nature's way of saying,
Forget it. But remember ... Maestro – *(to Pianist. Sings, 'When You're Smiling.'
Bows, takes applause, leaves with mic., returns mic. to Concert Secretary, exits.)*

CONCERT SECRETARY:*(slowly returning mic. to stand)* Two lads now from Blackley ...
  a double act ... Phil and Ged Murray ... who call themselves ... *(checking
  scrap of paper, nose wrinkling)* ... Night and Day.

*Pianist plays 'Night and Day' to cover the entrance. Phil Murray, in black dinner
jacket and bow tie, pulls on a huge wicker basket, gestures to the deeply reluctant
Concert Secretary to help him lift it onto the club stage. When he's got it set, he
takes from it a small girl dummy, shy, long blonde hair, party dress.*

PHIL: *(a good 'best' voice)* Good evening ladies and gentlemen. Say good evening,
  Sophie.

DOLL: *(eyelashes demure)* Good evening.

PHIL: Are you ready to sing your song then, Sophie?

GED: *(strangulated, from box: minimal but effective dummy voice)* Hey.

PHIL: *(ignoring him)* What's it going to be then, Sophie?

GED: *(louder)* Hey, I'm talking to you.

PHIL: *(side of mouth)* Shut up. Sophie?

GED: Listen, I'm not lying here all bloody night. Have you got that stupid stick-doll in 'ere?

PHIL: Be quiet.

GED: Y'have, 'aven't you? Y'ave. You mighta lain 'im down.

PHIL: Excuse me, Sophie … *(He opens the trunk, places the doll on Ged's stomach, closes it again.)* Ladies and gentlemen, we were going to start with a song …

GED: *(to the girl doll in the trunk, voice warm and sexy)* Hello, love. *(Carries on flirting and laughing – as though being tickled.)* Hey, what you doing down there, hey, what you doing …

Phil abandons his attempts to entertain the audience, begins to get Ged out of the trunk. It's a painful floppy process. They flounder to the tall stool by the mic. Their patter throughout is serious, desperate.

PHIL: *(fixing him on his thigh)* Right, now sit there and sit still.

Ged's dressed and made up as a ventriloquist's dummy, in Manchester City supporter's colours, sky blue and white scarf, woollen hat, rattle, rosette. His blue and white half football boots are tied to his ankles, i.e. not on his feet. He slips off Phil's knee, is dragged back, all in one movement. Perches finally.

Can't you stay up?

GED: Longer than you can, if your wife's to be believed.

PHIL: That's enough.

GED: *(from side of mouth)* Face front and keep smiling. Smile, you fool. They might go away.

PHIL: Where have you been then?

GED: Evening. Nice out, sir, I might get mine out in a minute. *(to Phil)* That didn't go over too well. You were moving your lips, you dummy.

PHIL: I said, where have you been?

GED: *(deliberately posh)* Where have I been? Where have I been? I've been to the football match, haven't I, you daft pillock, where do you think I've been? Manchester City. *(Waves rattle, own voice.)* My dad were a City fan. *(rattle)* My dad said if he came home and found Colin Bell in bed with the old lady he'd brew him a cup of tea. *(The joke dies. Ged waits for Phil to throw the next line at him)* He said, if he came home and found Colin Bell in bed with me mother he'd brew him a cup of tea …

PHIL: *(suddenly diverting from the act; no warning)* Look, if you're so funny, why don't you tell us all a joke?

GED: *(turning his head to look at his brother and blinking a question)* What?

PHIL: *(uneasy at once, but insistent)* Tell us the one about the Pakistani up on a rape charge.

GED: *(half out of the act, trying to think, looking in Waters' direction, as if for help)* What you talking about?

PHIL: *(faintly desperate)* Tell the joke.

Ged turns his head slowly, stares at the audience, stands, very slowly, puts his hands on Phil's shoulders, removes him from the stool, takes his place, draws his brother mercilessly down on to his thigh, repositions the mic. stand.

GED: *(in character)* You tell it.

Phil blinks, thinks.

PHIL: *(terrified, struggling for confidence)* There's this Pakistani, see, up on a rape charge. So the coppers decide they'll have an identity parade. And they get eight or nine other Pakkies and they put this one at the front and explain what they're doing. Then they bring the girl in and the Pakistani shouts *(Pakistani voice)* She is the one, Officer. No doubt about it ...

Ged and Phil stare whitely out at the audience. Neither knows where to go next. Ged gets up, repeats the procedure in reverse until he's back on Phil's knee.

GED: *(finally)* How about the song?

PHIL: Why not?

GED: A song entitled 'If I had it all to do over again, I'd do it all over you'. How'd you like being the dummy?

PHIL: *(a nightmare: wholly dependent on Ged now)* Not a lot.

GED: No. It's not funny, is it?

PHIL: How d'you mean?

GED: Shall I tell you some'at. There's two fellers like and they're both crippled. One hasn't moved his hands for twenty years and the other's in a wheelchair paralysed from the neck down. And they go to Lourdes for a miracle cure. And they get to Lourdes and the priest calls for the one with the hands and he goes down and the priest immerses his hands in the water and he says, In nomine domine homine womine, like they do you know and suddenly the feeling comes back to his hands and he can use them again. He says, It's a miracle. For twenty years I haven't been able to use my hands, and he helps to push his dear old friend in the wheelchair into the water up to his neck and the priest says, In nomine homine womine and they pull him out and there's four new tyres on the chair.

PHIL: Maybe we should sing the song?

GED: Have a look at your watch.

Phil looks.

What's it say?

PHIL: Time for a song.

GED: *(back in the act's groove at last)* I'm not going back in that box after.

PHIL: Sing the song.

GED: All right, but I'm warning you, you *walk* me off, sod your hernia, I'm not going back in there with her and that cricket stump ...

PHIL: Maestro, please.

BOTH: *(sing)*   He's my brother
                Our kid
                Don't want another
                Our kid
                He watches over me
                When things get tough
                He pulls the strings
                That wipe the tears away on my cuff
                He's my brother
                Our kid
                And there's no other
                Our kid
                He is my friend, my mate and my mucker
                He is my brother
                Our kid.

They take bows like automatons, Ged striding off first, Phil following whitely, lugging the basket. Pianist covers.

CONCERT SECRETARY: Another Irishman now –

Ged and Phil explode into violent recriminations in the wings. The Concert Secretary looks frowningly behind him.

– from Belfast, this one – good job we kept them apart – hands together, please, for ... George ... McBrain.

McBrain on, carrying a hand-mic, the mania glands sweating freely. He wears a fine maroon evening jacket, horn-rimmed glasses on nose end, frills at chest and cuffs of royal blue shirt.

McBRAIN: In the garden of Eden lay Adam
                Complacently stroking his madam
                And loud was his mirth
                For he knew that on earth
                There were only two – and he had 'em.

I had a hundred jokes standing back there, now I can't remember a one of 'em. *(He looks at the audience: stares.)* Never mind, I'm good to look at. There's this coloured feller on his way to work. (*Stops.*) Don't you think that's funny? There's this very honest Jew. No favourites here. There's this very brilliant Irishman. From Dublin. I tried to get the wife to come. It gets harder, I dunnit though. I don't say she's jealous but she's the only woman I know. If music be the food of love, how about a bite of your maracas? I was in bed with the wife last Thursday. The wife lay there, very quiet, smoking her pipe. I leaned across and I said, Do you fancy anything, heart? And she said, Yes, I fancy an African about six-foot-three with a big fat ... cheque book. *(to audience)* Don't get ahead of yourselves! Naughty! I said, Yeah? And what do you reckon he'd make of that great fat idle bum of yours? And she said, what makes you think we'd be talking about you? Doesn't say a lot, my wife. Talks all the time but doesn't say a lot. I took her to the zoo. Belle Vue, to see the orang-utan. Enormous. Great painted whatsits, like rump-steak. *(Bunching hands, stomps a bit, pulls a face.)* Like Willie Whitelaw having a shower. She falls right over the wire, as sure as I'm standing here, she trips clean over the wire and lands on her back with her legs parted, her skirt up and her drawers flapping in the wind. I couldn't look, it was horrible. The big feller kinda sniffs and ambles towards her, and ... he ends up poised above her like that, and the wife whispers, *(breathless terror)* George, what shall I do? What shall I do? And I said, *(whisper)* Tell *him* you've got a headache ... Had a look at the alligators. Just floating handbags really. She's been a goer in her time, I tell you. Fast? I met her at a dance in Belfast, I said, Excuse me. She grabbed me by the lapels and stuck her tongue half-way down me throat. I was only asking for a light. We had a whirlwind romance, I wined her and dined her every week for a fortnight, bean soup, pie and peas, whirlwind. Then I plucked up courage enough to say the words I never imagined myself saying in a million years: You're *What?* And she was. God, what a slut. I went to see her father ... out to the Maze prison ... him and his six lads all in there together ... I never saw a family like it. Ugly? Listen, they wore hoods before they joined the UVF, safact. The neighbours made 'em, protect the kids. First thing he says, You're not a mick, are you? Certainly not, says I. So why didn't you use something, says he. Use something? says I. Listen, the first time I met your daughter she was wearing a notice pinned to her chest saying, I am an epileptic and will die unless you lie on top of me, there wasn't time for anything like that. Seamus, big friend of mine from Cork *(ape gestures)* ... Oh no, that's the monkey ... *(Straightens into Frankenstein.)* Seamus, not very bright ... He got a pair of water-skis for Xmas, spent the next three months looking for a sloping lake. True. Joined the IRA ... Tried to blow up the Queen Elizabeth. Couldn't get his mouth round the funnel. But see my wife, God she's a slut though. Every time I go for a leak the sink is full of dishes. And the food, instant pollution. She gave us rabbit for a fortnight once, every meal. Rabbit pie, rabbit stew, rabbit rashers, rabbit pâté, rabbit trotters ... rabbit eggs ... After two weeks I was done in, I collapsed holding my stomach. She said, I'll send for the doctor. I said, Sod the doctor, see if you can borrow a ferret. But ... Let's face it, few of us are perfect. Not even the Irish. I was in Belfast the other week, there's a feller lying out on the pavement with a bullet hole in his forehead. There's an old lady walks by, she stops and looks down at yer man for a minute, then she crosses herself and she says, Well, thank God it missed his eye. You can't hate 'em can you. Listen, I've gotta go, I'm wife swapping tonight. I gorra bloke's greyhound last week, made a change. So listen, I'll see yer, all right?

He takes his bow, sweating, a bit concerned, stiff with tension now, not looking in Waters' direction. McBrain catches Waters' eye, in a bow: a still moment. McBrain breaks, disappears.

CONCERT SECRETARY: *(mic.)* Last, this evening, a young man from Clayton making his first appearance before an audience, I'm told … a warm hand for … Gethin Price.

Price emerges, carrying the tiny violin and bow. He wears bagging half-mast trousers, large sullen boots, a red hard wool jersey, studded and battered denim jacket, sleeves rolled to elbows, a red and white scarf tied on to an arm. His face has been subtly whitened to deaden and mask the face. He is half clown, half this year's version of bovver boy. The effect is calculatedly eerie, funny and chill. He takes out a deeply filthy handkerchief, spreads it carefully, expertly across his right shoulder, slowly tucks the tiny violin on his left, stands perfectly still, looks for the first time at the audience. Cocks the bow, stares at it intently, apparently sinking into process. Notices a very fine thread of gut hanging down. Shakes the bow. Shakes it again. The thread hangs on. He brings the bow finally to his mouth, tries to bite the thread off, his teeth are set on edge, he winces mutely, tries again, can't. He thinks. Tries, bending oddly on one leg, to trap the thread under his huge boot. Fails. Thinks. Takes out a lighter. Sets fire to the thread. Satisfaction. Makes as if to play. The cocked bow slowly begins to smoulder at the far end. He waves it about, horrified. The violin now begins to play unaided in his other hand a piece of intricate Bach. He's trapped for a moment between the two events; finally he places the spent bow on the stage, puts the violin under his boot, dimps it like a cigarette until it's thoroughly crushed.

PRICE: (*to himself, not admitting the audience's existence*) Wish I had a train. I feel like smashing a train up. On me own. I feel really strong. Wish I had a train. I could do with some exercise.

He does a complicated kata, with praying mantis footsweeps, a tan-fui, pa-kua dao, and other kung fu exercises. A spot suddenly illuminates larger than life-size dummies of a youngish man and woman carried on by a club-hand. Well dressed, beautiful people, a faint unselfconscious arrogance in their carriage. The man wears evening dress, gloves, etc., the girl, a simple, stunning white full-length dress and wrap. Her arm is looped in his. They stand, perhaps waiting for a cab to show after the theatre. Price has continued his exercises throughout this 'arrival'. Becomes aware of them gradually: rises slowly: stares. Turns to the audience, slowly smiles, evil and childlike. Sniffs. Ambles over. Stands by the man, measuring, walks round to stand by the girl. We sense him being ignored. He begins to inspect the girl minutely. Takes a cigarette from pocket.

Cigarette? *(Nothing. He offers it to the man.)* No? *(He pockets the cigarette, turns, calls 'Taxi!' sharply out front, shakes his head as it disappears. Moves round to the man's side again.)* Are you the interpreter, then? Been to the match, have we? Were you at t'top end wi' lads? Good, wannit? D'you see Macari? Eh? *(Silence.)* P'raps I'm not here. Don't you like me? You hardly know me. Let's go and have a pint, get to know each other. Here, don't you live in Salford? I swear I've seen you at the dog track. *(Nothing. He takes a cigarette out of the man's top pocket.)* Very kind of you. Ta. *(He lights the cigarette, blows the smoke in slow separate puffs across the man's face.)* Int this nice? I like a good chat. *(intimate, man-to-man)* Eh. I bet she's a goer, int she, sunshine? She's got a fair pair of knockers on her too. Has she been around? Does she ever go dancing at Belle Vue, Satdays? I think Eric Yates took her home one night. If it's her, she's a right goer, according to Eric. *(Pause.)* I don't know whether to thump you one or what. I suppose I could just give you a clout, just to let you know I exist. *(He blows smoke into the man's face.)* Is that hair dyed? Looks dyed. Are you a puff? Are you a pufter? *(Sniffs. Front, fast)* Taxi! *(Pause.)* That's not a taxi, lady, it's a hearse. *(Evilish grin)* You're getting confused, lady. Unless you were thinking of a quick fun funeral before retiring for the night. *(to man)* Say something Alice? She's calling hearses, he's talking to himself. *(He turns back to the man.)* You do speak, do you? I'm trying to talk to you. Say some'at. Tell us what kind of day you've had. Are you on the buses? Eh. Shall I make you laugh? This feller pays twenty pounds for this whore, right? Only she dunt fancy him and runs out of the room. He chases her, stark nekkid, down t' street. Cop stops him, says, Where's the fire, lad? Feller says, I've no idea, but if you see a nude bird running down street, fuck her, it's paid for. *(Pause. Nothing.)* You can laugh, you know, I don't mind you laughing. I'm talking to you … There's people'd call this envy, you know, it's not, it's hate. *(Now very fast)* Are you a bi-sexual or is that your sister? You'll never get a taxi here, they're all up at Piccadilly waiting for t' last train from London. Ask me how I know. I work there that's why. And don't interrupt when I'm talking, dint your mother ever tell you, it's rude? *(He does a kung fu thrust, missing the man's head by inches.)* Bruce Lee, do you like him? God, he is. You're a stuck-up bastard, aren't you? Give me a kiss, then, go on Alice, give us a kiss. I love you, give us a kiss. *(He halts his burble. Blinks. Pads round to stand at woman's side.)* Say something? *(In her ear)* Listen … I've got a British Rail delivery truck round the corner, ditch Alice and we'll do the town. *(He notices a folded copy of* The Times *in the man's hand. Passes behind the figures, pops his head between them.)* Crosswords? *(Thinks a moment.)* Election. Nine across. Big poll in China, question mark. *(Chinaman)* E-lection, *(Price looks from one to the other, laughs suddenly. He takes hold of their handles, begins to lift them up and down, to indicate their mirth.)* Election! Election! Big poll in China. Laugh you buggers, laugh! *(Price exhorts them to laugh, squeezing their bodies up and down and voicing their laughter for them. Then, very suddenly)* Here. *(He takes a flower out of his pocket, offers it to them.)* For the lady. No, no, I have a pin. *(Pause. He pins the flower – a marigold – with the greatest delicacy between the girl's breasts. Steps back to look at his work.)* No need for thanks. My pleasure entirely. Believe me.

Silence. Nothing. Then a dark red stain, gradually widening, begins to form behind the flower.

Aagh, aagh, aagh, aagh ...

The spot shrinks slowly on the dummies, centring finally on the red stain. Price's 'aaghs' become short barks of laughter. Innocence.

I wonder what happened. P'raps it pierced a vein.

Their light goes out altogether. We're left with his single chill image.

I made them laugh, though. *(depressed)* Who needs them? Hunh. Who needs them? We manage. *(chanting)* U-n-i-ted. Uni-ted. You won't keep us down there for long, don't worry. We're coming up there where we can gerrat yer *(Chants.)* Lou Macari, Lou Macari ... I shoulda smashed him one. They allus mek you feel sorry for 'em, out in the open. I suppose I shoulda just kicked him without looking at him. *(Pause. He looks after them. Calling)* National Unity? Up yours, sunshine. *(Pause. He picks up a tiny violin, i.e. another, switched, uncrushed, and a bow. Addresses it. Plays 'The Red Flag' – very simple and direct.)* Still, I made the buggers laugh ...

Price walks off. The Concert Secretary, probably shocked, embarrassed, not wishing to dwell. Lights fade. Waters stands, face gaunt, grey. Challenor tosses down a scotch, sheafs his notes, pockets pen.

CONCERT SECRETARY: That's the lot, ladies and gentlemen. You have your cards, I think. Charlie Shaw has 'em for them that hasn't, and we're starting right away, settle yourselves down, now. And it's eyes down for a full house ...

Lights fade gradually.

Always look after ... Number One.

Lights fade to black.

ACT THREE

Classroom. Time: 9.43. Empty.

McBrain, Samuels and Connor return slowly, to sit in their respective places, though an almost deliberate distance apart. Phil Murray in. They sit, glum, drained, separate.

Simple exhaustion underpins the low, tense, anxious, angry, baffled mood of the four. No eye contacts. People sit or fiddle. Samuels sits in his coat, ready for away. Connor is again pretty wet. McBrain has changed back to his parka and jeans, his bag on the desk in front of him.

Price, off, suddenly starts up with 'There's no business like show business ...'

PHIL: Listen to that stupid cunt.

SAMUELS: There'll be no pigging business for *him*, that's for a certainty. Did you ever see owt like it? He's bloody puddled.

Price in, dressed as in Act One: smells the mood of the others; dwells for a moment in the doorway.

McBRAIN: Did you see that Challenor feller? He smiled twice all evening, and both times it was at some'at the sodding Concert Secretary said.

CONNOR: (*low*) I don't reckon it was much fun for Mr Waters either.

PHIL: (*checking door with a look*) Look, sod Mr Waters. He's not handing jobs out, is he, Seamus?

CONNOR: (*dangerous, suddenly, very deliberately*) My name's Mick.

Silence.

McBRAIN: Take it easy, Michael ...

CONNOR: (*ignoring him*) Mick.

PHIL: All right. Mick.

Ged Murray has appeared wet through in the doorway, in time for the last exchange.

GED: (*finally*) Fish and chips. It's teeming down.

McBRAIN: About bloody time. Did you nip home to make 'em?

GED: (*giving them out*) Ha bloody ha. There was a queue a mile long. It's next t'British Legion, innit. (*He's with Samuels.*) They dint have any silver hake. I got you a pie.

SAMUELS: A pie? What d'you get a pie for?

GED: (*handing it to him*) I thought you might be hungry.

SAMUELS: (*opening package*) A pie? I don't eat pies.

Ged moves back towards his seat, taking in Price with a wave on the way back.

GED: (*to Price*) Hey, that was great, Geth ...

Price winks.

McBRAIN: They're stone bloody cold.

GED: (*on way*) It's a long bloody way.

SAMUELS: (*staring at the pie he's broken*) It's a bloody *pork* pie!

GED: Is it? Don't you like pork?

SAMUELS: God almighty, I ask for silver hake, he brings us a pork pie ...

PRICE: (*about dressed, approaching: Revivalist voice*) Holy pig. Here, give us it here.

He takes the pie, carries it over to the desks.

Ged moves to Price's chair very deliberately, passing his own on the way, sits facing out, his back to his brother: Phil stares at Ged with hostility. Price notes the change in seating, takes up the centre position between them, stands for a moment, leaning on the chairback, regards the other five very carefully for a moment without speaking.

Dearly beloved, we are gathered here in the sight of Mammon to mourn the passing of several very promising careers in the comedic arts. For those who live on … the words of the great and holy musical *The Song of Norway* will be of special comfort: De cuntibus minibus tuum, rectum anus mirabilis est. Which loosely translated means: It's easy to be a bit of a cunt, you've got to work to become a shithouse. Here endeth lesson one. *(He blesses them gravely, sits down.)*

Silence.

SAMUELS: *(finally, ugly)* You got anyone … special in mind, Charlie?

Price gets up swiftly, crosses to the dais, picks up a chair leg left by the Caretaker, holds it in two hands a foot or so from his forehead, breathes very deeply three or four times, then smashes it cleanly with his forehead. He carries the two ends to Samuels, puts them carefully on his desk.

PRICE: You're gonna crucify the man, do the job properly.

He turns, walks away, resumes his seat. Samuels grasps the two ends, McBrain takes them from him with gentle power, carries them to the wastepaper basket.

McBRAIN: There was this feller, see …

CONNOR: *(fraying)* No more jokes, George. All right?

McBrain deposits the ends, returns to his seat. Silence. Ged finishes his chips, wipes his hands on the paper.

GED: *(casual, innocent, knowing)* You'll be all right, George. You knew what to do all right.

McBRAIN: *(a freak of anger at the vent)* So when do I get the thirty pieces of silver? *(He bangs the desk with his fist, a harsh, half-self-punishing gesture.)* I don't want inquests, I want work.

SAMUELS: Right! Who the fuck does he *(Price)* think he is anyway! *(to Price)* What about your … performance then, Coco the bloody clown? It was bloody embarrassing …

GED: It were different.

SAMUELS: Different? It was putrid. Different from bloody comedy, that's for sure.

CONNOR: Look, for Jesus Christ's sake, it's over, will you forget it …

GED: Hey, *you* were good, Mick, what I could hear of it. You got most of 'em in too, dint you.

CONNOR: Yeah. I went down like a fart at a funeral.

PHIL: What a bleeding audience. Thick as pig shit.

PRICE: A bad lover blames his tool.

SAMUELS: So why didn't the great Lancashire Lad do a warm-up then, eh? He sent you out cold, and I had to follow you.

GED: Oh, *you* found your feet all right, Sammy ...

SAMUELS: What does that mean then?

The Caretaker comes in, a large battery lamp in his hand.

CARETAKER: You lot still here? I'm waiting to lock up you know. I've got a home to go to. Somebody left that thing . (*He points to the muslin sack.*) ... Meat.

He leaves, turning into Waters.

WATERS: We won't be long now ...

CARETAKER: I hope not. I'm not on overtime you know ...

He leaves. Waters stands a moment in the doorway looking into the room. They stare, some of them half-turning, at him. He's white, drained, tired and old. He walks, less spryly, to the desk. Sits down. Stares at the desk top. Silence. Some looks round the room.

GED: (*holding them up*) There's a packet of chips if you want them, Mr Waters.

Waters looks at him, makes no answer. Challenor in, shaking his coat.

CHALLENOR: Sorry, gentlemen. Several calls of nature on the way. You won't have reached your prostates yet, but you will. Mind if I use the desk, Eddie?

Waters relinquishes the desk, goes to lean by the windows, an onlooker. Challenor places his case down, opens it, removes notes and forms, flicks through them, sniffs. Looks at Price covertly once or twice. Gathers.

Right, there's not much time, so I'll get cracking. Interesting evening. Lot of promise. I'll take you one by one so we don't get mixed up. Mick Connor.

CONNOR: Yeah.

CHALLENOR: Aye. You've not done a lot, have you?

CONNOR: No, I've done nothing. Concerts, works do's.

CHALLENOR: I quite liked it. One or two quite nice jokes, quite nicely told. (*studying notes*) Bit old-fashioned. I thought, you know, following a single topic through your act. It mighta worked even so, if you'd taken something more up the audience's street. I mean, you might find being an Irishman in England fascinating, there's no reason we should, is there? (*Pause.*) Had a sort of ... earnestness about it I didn't much take to. You know, as if you were giving a sermon. One thing you've gotta learn, people don't learn, they don't want to, and if they did, they won't look to the likes of us to teach 'em. You've got to be very good indeed to patronize your audience, I can tell you. *(Pause.)* The sex was crude. I've nothing against it, but it requires taste, if you see what I mean, I've never heard a good joke yet about coitus interruptus. Still, you had your moments. Some promise there. *(Turns Connor's sheet on to its face.)* Sammy Samuels?

SAMUELS: Himself.

CHALLENOR: I thought you'd never get started. First thing you want to do is ditch the first half of your act.

SAMUELS: Yeah, it's stuff I've been shedding, you know.

CHALLENOR: S'too Jewish. What's a Jew nowadays eh? Who wants to know I mean.

SAMUELS: Yeah, I can see that.

CHALLENOR: Same mistake as the Irishman. *(Looks at notes.)* Fortunately, you pulled out of it and got very good. It was a different act, the wife, blacks, Irish, women, you spread it around, you can score, keep it tight they'll fall asleep on you. *(Pause.)* Liked the Women's Lib bits. *(Pause.)* You need an ending, you were just sticking one after another till you'd done. No climax. People want a climax.

SAMUELS: Yeah, I er … got off the rails a bit actually …

CHALLENOR: Stay on 'em. Phil and Ged Murray.

PHIL: Here.

CHALLENOR: Aye well, what went wrong there?

Phil and Ged look at each other briefly.

There was a distinct smell of cock-up on the air about half-way through. *(reading notes)* I've got a note about a Pakistani on a rape charge … Aye, that's it. What happened then?

Phil looks at Ged. Finally.

GED: *(very quietly)* We got lost.

CHALLENOR: What, was it new material or something?

GED: Yeah. Something like that.

CHALLENOR: Well it was horrible. The cardinal sin for any performer is embarrassing the audience. You had 'em doing up their shoelaces and picking up old beer mats. *(Pause.)* I don't know. It's a nice idea, but you need the material, my God, if you're gonna carry it off.

GED: We missed a lot out, after we got lost.

CHALLENOR: *(interest faded)* I'm sure you did. I'm sure you did. Liked the song, nice sentiment. Quite catchy really … *(He slashes his pencil across their page of notes, turns over.)* George McBrain.

McBrain shows.

Cracking opening. Bang, No messing. Liked it. Lot of sex but well handled, if
you see what I mean. Near the knuckle but not half-way up the armpit. A
question of taste. Knowing when to draw back. Even with yobbos like that lot
down there. *(Pause.)* Quite subtle but not too subtle. 'Tell *him* you've gotta
headache ...' 'Floating handbags' ... Yes, yes ... Good character, I believed it,
it was all of a piece. Confident, a bit aggressive, like that. Like the joke about
the thick Seamus. *(to Connor)* See, that's what I mean, don't push your own
particular prejudice, you're there on *their* terms, not your own. *(Notes again)*
Good ending. *(Nodding in Samuels' direction)* See, it was downbeat, but it was
firm. You know, diminuendo. Well thought out ...

*There's a long pause now, as he stares at Price's notes. People make sweating
faces on their own chances. Waters leans, half sits, against the window, staring
nowhere, withdrawn, remote. Price leans almost horizontally back in his chair,
staring at the ceiling. He remains like this throughout most of the following.*

(Finally) Gethin Price. *(Another pause.)* Mmmmmmm. Mmmmmmmm.

*Looks across at Price finally, no nonsense, man to man ... Price is about to
levitate. Challenor looks in Waters' direction, seeking guidance. Waters purses his
lips, looks out of the window.*

Not a lot to say about your piece, Price. You have a certain talent maybe as a
mime, something like that. What you did tonight just ... won't do. Music hall
maybe, but there *is* no music hall ... You wanna be a comedian, you'd better
start somewhere else, there's no way you'll get started with what you've got.
Not viable. You've got to speak to the audience, for God's sake. *(Pause.
Studying notes)* Personally, I found the content of your act ... how shall I put
it? ... repulsive.

He stares on at his notes. Price slowly resumes an upright position in the chair.

And aggressively unfunny. *(He looks at Price, practisedly kindly.)* If you want to
get on, lad, you'd better sort a few problems out first. Get some distance, see
what I mean. Don't give us your hang-ups straight. Too hot to handle. *(Closes
note-file decisively.)* Four golden rules. For all of you, though some more than
others. One. All audiences are thick, collectively, but it's a bad comedian who
lets 'em know it. Two. Two laughs are better than one. Always. Three. You don't
have to love the people, but the people *have* to love you. Four. Sell yourself. If
you're giving it away, it won't be worth having. *(Pause.)* All right, I coulda left
this till I got back south, but I'm not that sorta person. At the moment, on
tonight, I'm interested in just two of you ... you *(McBrain)* and you *(Samuels)*.
I've got forms here *(Holds them up)* ... enrolment. When these've been received,
there'll be an agent to look after your business and develop your career. Don't
give your jobs up just now, mind. There'll be time enough for that when you're
getting the bookings. *(He gives forms to McBrain and Samuels.)* For the rest of
you, I'll see you again. Drop me a line, I'm approachable. Just as long as you've
learnt your lessons from tonight, that is. It's not the talent's lacking, it's
application of a few basic rules of professional life. *(Turns to Waters.)* Thanks,
Eddie. Nice evening. Some good lads. Few wild notions mebbe but ...

Waters walks towards him, takes the proffered hand.

I'm down at the Midland. How about a drink?

WATERS: Still full of shit, Bert. Fuller than a large intestine.

CHALLENOR: How's that, Eddie?

WATERS: You wouldn't know a comedian from a barrowload of crap.

CHALLENOR: *(light, unruffled)* Meaning you disagree. Oh. Send in a report.

WATERS: I don't belong, remember?

CHALLENOR: What do you expect? A hundred per cent?

WATERS: They were nobbled, Bert. They're great lads.

CHALLENOR: Your opinion. Don't be ungracious.

WATERS: Yeah. Enjoy the Midland.

CHALLENOR: *(smiling evenly)* Always do, Eddie. *Like* the best.

He picks up his briefcase, leaves with what dignity he can salvage. A deep, uneasy silence. Price tosses and catches the pork pie, rhythmically, like a juggler.

PRICE: *(without venom)* There goes nothing. A man who doesn't rate Frank Randle, what does *he* know?

WATERS: *(deliberately)* He knows enough, Mr Price. He knows where the door marked In is.

PRICE: Yeah, but you know where it leads? *(Looking at McBrain and Samuels)* It leads to a room with a notice on the wall and the notice says 'Kindly ensure that you leave this room as you found it'. A shitheap.

McBRAIN: No need to be bitter, Geth. You'll make out …

Price laughs, hard, unpleasant, remote.

PRICE: *(perfect Ulster)* Thanks, George. S'very good of you. Just you remember now – stand you your ground.

McBrain stands up, a little uncertainly. Picks up the bag.

McBRAIN: A comic's a comic. Ain't that right though. *(Sniff. Pause.)* Thanks, Mr Waters. It's been a great great pleasure. I'll never forget what you've done for me …

WATERS: *(with effort)* Yes. Enjoy yourself, George. I'll watch out for you.

McBRAIN: We'll have a drink sometime.

WATERS: Yes.

McBRAIN: Look after yourself. *(Turning)* And you lot. Scrubbers. *(Going.)*

SAMUELS: *(standing)* Hang on, George. I'll give you a lift, we can stop off at the club for a drink.

McBRAIN: No good, Sammy. I'm late as it is. The wife's not bin too good lately ...
I'd best get off.

SAMUELS: She'll not begrudge you a celebration pint, surely to God?

McBRAIN: *(steel suddenly)* She begrudges me nothing, Sammy.

Small silence. He leaves, kiln-fired, hard inside the compromise.

SAMUELS: How about you, Phil? *(Phil shakes his head whitely.)*

Well ... Cheers, Mr Waters. A pleasure to know you *(Offers hand.)*

WATERS: *(taking it)* Aye.

SAMUELS: Hard work, by Christ. Lost me script completely tonight. Don't know
how I kept going ...

WATERS: No.

SAMUELS: Couldn'ta done it without you, Mr Waters, that's for a certainty.

*He treks the lonely walk to the door. Leaves. Everyone stands, preparing to go.
Phil Murray suddenly stands, lifts his bag, slams it down on the desk.*

PHIL: *(to Ged, smouldering)* You coming?

GED: *(turning slowly)* No. I'll catch a bus.

PHIL: It's pissing down.

GED: Yeah well ... I need the air.

PHIL: *(vicious)* Suit yourself. *(He turns to leave. Turns back again.)* Are you going
up the Infirmary Sunday?

GED: Yeah. Why?

PHIL: *(pulls a quid out of his back pocket, hands it to Ged)* Give him this will
you? Some fags or some'at. Tell him I'll ... try and make it week after.

Ged takes the note. Phil leaves.

CONNOR: *(approaching Waters' desk)* Sorry if we let you down.

WATERS: Not you, son. Not in a million years. Stay that way. Because that way is a
good way.

He holds his hand out. Connor takes it.

I'm ... sorry.

CONNOR: *(soft)* Get stuffed. *(He winks at Price and Ged Murray, leaves briskly,
stops suddenly in the doorway.)* Shit! I never told me copper joke! I've been
working on it all week ... *(He bangs his temple with his palm several times.)*
Dummy, dummy. *(He's gone.)*

GED: Anyone fancy a pint? I fancy a pint. Or seven. Better get me skates on. *(He
crosses to Waters.)* Will there be ... will you be doing this again another time,
Mr Waters?

WATERS: Yes, I've a few lads lined up starting May …

GED: I'd like to come back, if you'd have me.

WATERS: No no. You need to *do* it now, Ged. You *have* it, lad. Believe that.

GED: Mebbe, mebbe not. I wanna go solo, see. *(Exchanges look with Price.)* That cock-up … it weren't nerves, it weren't … technique … it were deliberate. *(pointing at* door) Him. He wanted to put some'at in for Challenor. I wouldn't have it, *(Grins, sniffs.)* I thought I were going reet well up to then. Felt good too.

WATERS: Remember it, how it feels when it's good. It's important. *(Holds hand out.)* Good-night. I'll see you soon.

GED: *(embarrassed)* Oh, I nearly forgot. Erm. *(Takes small package from pocket.)* We … er … we clubbed together some of us and bought you this. *(He hands him the package, smiles, leaves.)*

In the corridor we hear the Caretaker quizzing Ged.

CARETAKER: *(off)* It's not a bloody all-night session is it? Because if it is I'm on the bloody phone t'Union right away …

Waters unwraps the package. It's a pipe. Waters studies it.

PRICE: No one … clubbed together.

WATERS: *(gravely)* That's all right. I don't smoke either.

Waters begins to pack his things, put on his overcoat, etc. Price watches him, fascinated.

I don't know what to say, Gethin. It's late. Maybe you shouldn't ask. It's been a funny night all round. *(He waves towards the door. Pause.)* And you. You've always been a bit wild, it's why I liked you, reminded me of me at twenty-five. Tonight … *(He leaves it, fastens his bag.)* I don't know …

PRICE: Did you like what I did? I'm asking.

WATERS: Like? *(Pause.)* It was terrifying.

PRICE: You know what they did, don't you?

WATERS: Oh yes.

PRICE: Do you blame 'em?

WATERS: *(emphatic)* No. We make our own beds.

PRICE: *(angry suddenly)* I didn't sell you out, Eddie.

Waters frowns, turns slowly, straightening, to face Price.

WATERS: Is that what you think I think?

PRICE: Samuels, McBrain, they're nothing. They'll just float through the system like turds on the Irwell, they sold out because they've nothing worth holding on to. You can't blame them for doing it any more than you can praise Connor and Ged Murray for not. They stayed put because they've nowhere else to go …

WATERS: Listen, don't go on, we'll talk again ...

PRICE: I just wanted it to be *me* talking out there. I didn't want to do something *we'd* worked on. You know.

WATERS: *(lifting very suddenly, disturbed)* Look, I *saw* it, you don't have to tell me what I already know ...

PRICE: I want you to see the *difference* ...

WATERS: *(shouting)* ... I *see* the difference. God Almighty, I see it, I see it, I just ... don't understand it.

PRICE: *(shouting)* Well then why don't you listen to what I'm *saying*, Eddie?

Silence. Waters looks at the clock.

WATERS: All right.

Pause.

PRICE: *(quiet)* I can't paint your pictures. *(Points to eyes.)* These see.

WATERS: It's not only what you see, it's what you feel when you see it.

PRICE: What *I* feel. *I* feel.

WATERS: No compassion, no truth. You threw it all out, Gethin. Love, care, concern, call it what you like, you junked it over the side.

PRICE: I didn't junk it. It was never there ...

WATERS: What're you talking about ...?

PRICE: ... you're avoiding the question, Eddie.

WATERS: I don't know what to say ...

PRICE: ... Was I good or was I crap ...?

WATERS: *(loud, compelled)* ...You were *brilliant!*

Pause. Price blinks. Waters glowers at the new terrain.

PRICE: *(slowly)* But you ... didn't like it.

Waters shakes his head

PRICE: *(soft, slow)* Why not?

WATERS: *(eventually)* It was ugly. It was drowning in hate. You can't change today into tomorrow on that basis. You forget a thing called ... the truth.

PRICE: The truth. Can I say ... look, I wanna say something. What do you know about the *truth,* Mr Waters? You think the truth is *beautiful?* You've forgotten what it's *like.* You knew it when you started off, Oldham Empire, People's Music Hall, Colne Hippodrome, Bolton Grand, New Brighton Palace, Ardwick Empire, Ardwick Hippodrome, the Met, the Star in Ancoats ... the Lancashire

Lad – you knew it then all right. Nobody hit harder than Eddie Waters, that's what they say. Because you were still in touch with what made you … hunger, diphtheria, filth, unemployment, penny clubs, means tests, bed bugs, head lice … Was all *that* truth beautiful?

Pause. Waters stares at him, blinded.

Truth was a fist you hit with. Now it's like … now it's like cowflop, a day old, hard until it's underfoot and then it's … green, soft. Shitten. *(Pause.)* Nothing's changed, Mr Waters, is what I'm saying. When I stand upright – like tonight at that club – I bang my head on the ceiling. Just like you fifty years ago. We're still caged, exploited, prodded and pulled at, milked, fattened, slaughtered, cut up, fed out. We still don't belong to ourselves. Nothing's changed. You've just forgotten, that's all.

Waters gathers his things about him, using the process.

And you … stopped laughing, didn't you? Not even a warm-up tonight. You had nothing to say to those people down there tonight, did you?

Waters turns slowly to face him.

In three months or more, you never said a single funny thing. *(Pause.)* Challenor reckons you could have been great … he said you just stopped wanting it.

Waters sits down heavily at the desk, the pain hurting now.

Maybe you lost your hate, Mr Waters.

WATERS: *(fierce)* What are you, twenty-six, twenty-five?

PRICE: What?

WATERS: Before you were born, I was touring with E.N.S.A., the war had just ended, a year, maybe more. We were in Germany, B.A.O.R., fooling about till we got our blighty bonds. Somebody … somebody said there was a guided tour of a bit of East Germany on offer, I got a ticket. I saw Dresden. Dresden? Twenty-five miles of rubble. Freddie Tarleton was with us, good comic, he said it reminded him of Ancoats … Then they took us to a place called Weimar, where Bach had a house. Saw his work room, his desk, piano, books. These perfect rooms, all over the house, the sun on the windows … Down the road, four miles maybe, we pulled up at this camp. There was a party of schoolkids getting down off a truck ahead of us. And we followed 'em in. 'To each his own' over the gate. They'd cleaned it up, it was like a museum, each room with its separate, special collection. In one of 'em … the showers … there was a box of cyanide pellets on a table. 'Ciankali' the label said, just that. A block away, the incinerators, with a big proud maker's label moulded on its middle, someone in Hamburg … And then this extraordinary thing. *(Longish pause.)* In this hell-place, a special block, 'Der Straf-bloc', 'Punishment Block'. It took a minute to register, I almost laughed, it seemed so ludicrous. Then I saw it. It was a world like any other. It was the logic of our world … extended …

(pulling out of the deep involvement phase of the story) We crossed back into West Germany the same night. Freddie was doing a concert in Bielefeld. *(Long pause.)* And he ... quite normally, he's going along, getting the laughs, he tells this joke about a Jew ... I don't remember what it was ... I don't remember what it was ... people laughed, not inordinately, just ... easily ... And I sat there. And I didn't laugh. *(He stands suddenly. Looks hard at Price.)* That exercise we do ... thinking of something deep, personal, serious ... then being funny about it ... That's where it came from. *(Long pause.)* And I discovered ... there were no jokes left. Every joke was a little pellet, a ... final solution. We're the only animal that laughs. The only one. You know when you see the chimpanzees on the PG Tips things snickering, do you know what that is? Fear. They're signalling their terror. We've got to do some'at about it, Gethin.

PRICE: Did you learn to love the Nazis then ... *(He says it with soft z, as in Churchill.)*

WATERS: ... I'm not saying *that* ...

PRICE: ... That's what I'm *hearing* ...

WATERS: ... It's not as simple ...

PRICE: ... It's simple to me ...

WATERS: ... It wasn't only repulsive ...

PRICE: What else was it then ...?

WATERS: *(wrenched from him, finally)* I got an erection in that ... place! An erection! Gethin. Something ... *(He touches his stomach.)* ... loved it, too.

Silence. Price turns away from Waters, takes two precise paces towards the back of the room, turns back again.

We've gotta get deeper than hate. Hate's no help.

PRICE: A German joke is no laughing matter.

WATERS: See it.

Price turns away again, prods the muslin sack with his boot.

PRICE: I found it in the book you lent me. The idea for the act.

WATERS: It was Grock. I worked with him once.

PRICE: It was Grock. Thing I liked was his ... hardness. Not like Chaplin, all coy and covered in kids. This book said he weren't even funny. He was just very truthful, everything he did. *(He fiddles in his pocket, takes out some paper, etc. Finds the piece of paper he's looking for, opens it.)* I found this in another book. I brought it to show you. Some say the world will end in fire. Some say in ice. From what I've tasted of desire I hold with those who favour fire, but if I had to perish twice, I think I know enough of hate to say that for destruction ice is also great and would suffice. *(He folds the paper, puts it back in his pocket, moves to desk, picks up his bag, rather casually.)* It was all ice out there tonight. I lived it. I felt … expressed. *(Pause. Lifting suddenly)* The Jews still stayed in line, even when they *knew,* Eddie! What's *that* about? *(He swings his bag off the desk, ready for off.)* I stand in no line. I refuse my consent.

Pause. Waters fastens his coat collar.

WATERS: *(very quiet)* What do you do now then?

PRICE: I go back. I wait. I'm ready.

WATERS: Driving, you mean?

PRICE: Driving. It doesn't matter.

WATERS: Wait for what?

PRICE: Wait for it to happen.

WATERS: *(very low)* Do you want help?

PRICE: No, I'm OK. Watch out for me.

WATERS: How's Margaret?

PRICE: *(plain)* She left. Took the kiddie. Gone to her sister's in Bolton.

WATERS: *(finally)* I'm sorry.

PRICE: It's nothing. I cope. *(Pause.)* What do you do then? Carry on with this?

WATERS: I don't know.

PRICE: You should. You do it well.

They stay a moment longer, perhaps pondering a handshake. Price turns, leaves.

Waters sits on at the desk, his back half-turned to the door.

After a moment, Patel arrives, knocks on the open door. Waters stands without turning.

WATERS: *(as though to Caretaker)* All right, I'm on my way…

PATEL: Please, I left this parcel …

WATERS: *(turning, standing)* So you did. Not been your night, has it. Me too.

Patel smiles, humps the sack under his arm.

WATERS: What's in there, anyway?

PATEL: Some beef. A big piece. I work at abattoir.

WATERS: Y'eat beef do you then?

PATEL: No, no, I'm Hindu. Beef, cow is sacred. This is for a friend.

WATERS: Oh. *(Pause.)* Don't you mind … handling it?

PATEL: At first. Not now. *(He puts the sack down, stares around the desk.)* All your funny men have gone home?

WATERS: Yeah. All the funny men have gone home.

PATEL: You like to hear a joke from my country?

WATERS: *(frowning)* Try me.

PATEL: *(laughing, excited)* It's very funny, it's very, very funny. A man has many children, wife, in the South. His crop fail, he have nothing, the skin shrivel on his children's ribs, his wife's milk dries. They lie outside the house starving. All around them, the sacred cows, ten, twenty, more, eating grass. One day he take sharp knife, mm? He creep up on a big white cow, just as he lift knife the cow see him and the cow say, Hey, aren't you knowing you not permitted to kill me? And the man say, What do you know, a talking horse.

Patel laughs a lot. Waters suddenly begins to laugh too. Patel lifts the sack again.

WATERS: What do you know, a talking horse. That's Jewish. It is. Come on, I'll give you a lift. Listen, I'm starting another class in May, why don't you join it? You might enjoy it ...

They leave the room. Waters snicks off the lights, one pair, two. The room is lit by corridor lighting only now. We hear shouted goodnights, the clanking of keys, the banging of a pair of doors. A torch light flashes into the room through the corridor window and the Caretaker arrives for a final check. He flashes the light round the room, teacher's desk, desks, dais, blackboard. The beam picks out the scrawled radiograph of Price's limerick: Pratt (Twat), etc.

CARETAKER: *(finally, with considerable sourness)* The dirty buggers.

He crosses, fishes out a rag, begins to wipe it away.

END

THE CHERRY ORCHARD

*An English version
of Chekhov's play*

*From a translation by
Helen Rappaport*

This version of *The Cherry Orchard* was written in two distinct stages. In the first, I commissioned a new, very literal translation from the Russian, discussed the language and metaphoric life of the play with the translator, tried to map out for myself the specific literary and theatrical problems I would need to solve, and tackled the first act, as a sort of test run. After two months on other work, I entered the second phase, in which I revised parts of the first act before writing the remaining three.

The literary problems were several and oppressive. Chekhov's major status as playwright, his 'poetic sensibility', 'delicate realism' and the rest, seemed for a time major obstacles, inhibiting mediations, in the process of relating freshly and directly to the text itself; and it's impossible to overstress the role played by Helen Rappaport, who made the initial translation, in helping me to distinguish wood from trees in the first phase of the project. But it was the specific nature of Richard Eyre's commission – to prepare a version of the play for *performance* – that proved to be decisive in giving this version its shape, its tone and its texture. For it was not, finally, the *literary* tradition that my version of the play was intended to act upon, but the theatrical. For half a century now, in England as elsewhere, Chekhov has been the almost exclusive property of theatrical class sectaries for whom the plays have been plangent and sorrowing evocations of an 'ordered' past no longer with 'us', its passing greatly to be mourned. For theatre-goers, if not for all literary critics (cf. Raymond Williams' penetrating essay in *Drama from Ibsen to Brecht*), Chekhov's tough, bright-eyed complexity was dulced into swallowable sacs of sentimental morality. (The definitive Chekhov movie, in this reading, would have had to be called 'It's a Sad Sad Sad Sad Sad World'.) Translation followed translation, *that* idiom became 'our' idiom, that class 'our' class, until the play's specific historicity and precise sociological imagination had been bleached of all meanings beyond those required to convey the necessary 'natural' sense that the fine will always be undermined by the crude and that the 'human condition' can for all essential purposes be equated with 'the plight of the middle classes'.

I'm speaking here of a dominant mode of translation, performance and production, not of course of all Chekhov work done in this country in this time; but it has been a dominance so oppressive as to distance, especially from the early sixties on, the larger part of a whole generation of theatre writers and workers for whom Chekhov had come to seem, in his content as much as his form, inalienably bound up with the fine regretful weeping of the privileged fallen on hard times. The optimistic among them turned to Brecht, the nihilistic to Beckett, but always at some level as a rejection of Chekhov as a possible comrade in the search for perspectives on the world they live in. And yet who would blame them for failing to see his potency, given the nature of the gelding in the arena.

I can't explain how I never came to see Chekhov in this way. From the age of fifteen, when I had my first exposure to his work via radio, I have always looked *straight through* the productions to the counter-meanings and counter-intentions screaming out to be realised. To come to cases, *The Cherry Orchard* has always seemed to me to be dealing not only with the subjective pain of property-loss but also and more importantly with its objective *necessity*. To present it as the first is to celebrate a pessimism; as to see it as both is to redress an important political balance potent in the text Chekhov wrote but in *practice* almost wholly ignored. Readers will judge for themselves whether the version I've written speaks to them more pertinently about the world they live in than other versions they've encountered; but they would have had to *see* it, in a production as truthful as Richard Eyre's at Nottingham, to feel that relevance bite into the flesh, since plays, unlike theses, require more of us than careful reflection and analysis: they demand to be *experienced*, on both sides of the text, with actors and audience both listening and making, which is arguably now the only truly *social* validity theatre can lay claim to in a television age.

Those familiar with the play in other versions (and productions) have claimed, though on the whole with considerable sympathy, that my version has shifted the focus of the play and re-ordered its inherent balances; so that, for example, Mme Ranevsky's pivotal role has been reduced, while Trofimov's – and to some extent Lopakhin's – have been strengthened. There isn't space here to argue this fully, but the *simple* facts are that (a) I *edited out* next to nothing, save for patronymics (though I debated hard about the often unplayably expository structure of Act One); (b) I *added* fewer than fifty words of dialogue to a play that has approximately 21,000; (c) not a single line or action was transposed to another part of the play. If Ranevsky seems less 'important' in my version, and Trofimov and Lopakhin (and the ideological tension between them) more central to an understanding of the play's meanings, let it be Chekhov who answers for it, not me.

Less gentle critics, I should add, have hinted that I found what I was looking for rather than what was there; that I substituted, for an elegy, a cheerful and cheering march. My answer might well be 'Don't make me laugh' save for the possibility that, given *their* view of Chekhov, I might well be accused of stealing their line. For to dare to see his world as both subjectively painful and objectively comic is somehow, for them, to fail to sound the right note or to play 'The Last Post' as punk rock. It's to these last, 'high priests of the sacred art' as Trepleff calls them in *The Seagull*, that I'd like to dedicate this new version of their favourite play, in the hope that by reading it they'll come to question one of the central tenets of their faith; namely, that Anton Chekhov, that lively class heretic, can continue to be considered one of the faithful.

Trevor Griffiths, September 1977

A Note on Trofimov

Given the severity of the official censorship and the cravenness of theatres, Chekhov was very limited in what he could say about Trofimov's work at the University and his political activities. His own notes refer to the suppression of Trofimov, as a character, and as a set of meanings and statements. I had to imagine what those meanings and statements were, which Chekhov felt he had been denied the possibility of making. As a student in 1903, Trofimov could not have been unaware of what was happening in the political underground. *Iskra* groups were being formed throughout this period, all over Russia. In 1901, Lenin's *What is to be Done?* was published in Germany; and from 1902, the book would have been available and circulating in Russia. A new language was in the air: a new way of perceiving and accounting for the conditions of social reality and the possibilities of change. And that new language represents a huge break with the past. I was seeking to embrace that language, not comprehensively, but in oblique, tangential ways. It seemed to me not improper to give Trofimov a *hint*, at least, of a different kind of language from the traditional nineteenth-century bourgeois-liberal language that student intellectuals would have deployed.

Trevor Griffiths, from an interview with David Allen in
Chekhov on the British Stage, *Cambridge University Press, 1993*

This version of Anton Chekhov's *The Cherry Orchard* was first performed at the Nottingham Playhouse on 10th March 1977, with the following cast:

Mme Ranevsky (Liuba): landowner Bridget Turner

Gayev (Leon) Ralph Nossek

Simeonov-Pischik (Boris) Brian Glover

Lopakhin (Alexander) Dave Hill

Anya Lynsey Baxter

Varya Annie Hayes

Charlotte Susan Porrett

Epikhodov (Simon) Antony Sher

Dunyasha Helen Brammer

Firs (Nicholas) John Barrett

Yasha Malcom Storry

Other servants

Frank Robinson
Walter Lindley
Julian Webber

Trofimov (Peter) Mick Ford

Stationmaster John C. Williams

Guests

Jo Scott-Matthews
Peggy Pedley
Walter Lindley
Eric Parker

Stranger David Beames

Charlotte's dog Craiglyn Cavalcade

Directed by Richard Eyre

Set designed by John Gunter

Lighting by Rory Dempster

The Cherry Orchard

ACT ONE

Black.

A slow gathering of light reveals a single cherry tree in flower. The image steadies; holds. A long way away, the sound of a steel cable groaning under stress.

Closer, though still distant, a train whistles its approach.

Silence.

Fade to black.

Black.

TAPE *(*LOPAKHIN'S VOICE): «Пришёл по́езд, сла́ва Бо́гу. Кото́рый час?»

Early dawn light reveals the old nursery, several doors leading from it, one to Anya's room. May. Frost. Shut windows. **Lopakhin**, *late thirties, strong-shouldered, bearded, in suit, white shirt, light calf-skin boots, sprawls uneasily in a winged chair, an open book across his chest, sleeping fitfully. The sound of the train's whistle wakes him.* **Dunyasha** *comes in, carrying a lit candle, as Lopakhin fumbles for his watch.*

LOPAKHIN: That's the train. At last. What's the time?

DUNYASHA: Two nearly. (*Blows out candle.*) It's day.

LOPAKHIN: (*Checking watch.*) Only two hours behind time, this one. Mmm. (*Stands, yawns, stretches.*) God, look at me. Come here on purpose to meet them all at the station and ptt ... wake up to find I've been asleep ... This won't do at all, Lopakhin.

He watches Dunyasha, who's rather pointlessly dusting the furniture, her mind elsewhere.

Why didn't you waken me?

DUNYASHA: (*Listening for something.*) I thought you'd gone ... Oh, it's them, they're coming.

LOPAKHIN: (*Listening briefly, tries to straighten trouser creases.*) No, no ... They have to get the luggage, find the tickets, be greeted by the stationmaster ...

He sits down again, to polish his boots with a handkerchief, his back to Dunyasha, who has crossed, excited, to the window.

Five years she's been away, I wonder what she looks like. (*Chuckles*) She's a good woman, easy-going, no side.

The dogs begin to bark in the yard, Dunyasha leaves unnoticed to tend them.

I remember when I was a lad, fifteen mebbe, my father ran that little grocer's in the village, he punched me in the face with his fist – (*shows his fist*) – and my nose were bleeding, we'd come up to this place for something, I can't remember what, he was drunk, I remember that ... (*Stops polishing shoes, stares ahead of him.*) ... and *she* said, thin little, young little thing that she was, she said, 'No need for tears, little peasant. It'll heal before your wedding day.' And she washed the blood from my face, here, in the nursery.

He stands, inspects his boots and trousers.

And here I am, a rich man, in white waistcoat and yellow boots, but the son of a peasant still, with my pig's snout in the teacup ...

Dunyasha comes back in, with a shawl on, again unnoticed, returns to window. Lopakhin laughs, turns.

This book put me to sleep, couldn't understand a word.

DUNYASHA: Those dogs have howled all night. They know who's coming home ...

Lopakhin sniffs, not understanding, frowns.

LOPAKHIN: Dogs? What's wrong with you, Dunyasha. You're all ...

DUNYASHA: Look at my hands. I think I'm going to faint.

LOPAKHIN: (*Gently*) Here, come here. (*Takes her hands gently; amused.*) Look at you. (*Fingers her shawl.*) You dress like a lady, do your hair like one too. You're much too refined, Dunyasha. We have to remember what we are, mm?

She blinks at him, calmer. **Epikhodov** *comes in, boots squeaking, looking for someone, a bunch of flowers in his hands. Sees Dunyasha, half-presents them to her, sees Lopakhin, drops them. Picks them up.*

EPIKHODOV: The gardener sent them. He says they're for the dining-room. Here.

He hands them to Dunyasha, tender-brusque.

LOPAKHIN: I'll have some cider while you're about it.

DUNYASHA: Very good, sir.

She leaves.

EPIKHODOV: (*Pacing a little, squeaking.*) It's a morning, er ... it's a *frosty* morning. Three degrees. Er, below. (*Waving awkwardly at the window.*) And yet the cherry trees are all ... in bloom. I do not approbate this climate of ours. I do not. Unco-operative and untimely, that's what it is. Another thing, Alexander Lopakhin, by way of footnote – (*he stares at his feet*) – let me tell you I bought these boots the day before yesterday but they travel – I assure you – beyond the bounds of possibility. (*They squeak very slightly, as he shifts weight.*) Would grease help, do you think? ...

LOPAKHIN: Go away. You bore me.

EPIKHODOV: Every day of my life I befall something dreadful. But no longer do I grumble. Now I even smile sometimes ...

Dunyasha has entered, handed Lopakhin the cider. His eyes follow her.

Well, I'll be off ... (*Falls disastrously over a chair.*) Aah, see. If you'll excuse my language, that's ... (*Long pause.*) ... the sort of thing ... I had in mind ... Beware the clam before the storm. At least in my opinion.

He squeaks off.

DUNYASHA: If you promise you'll keep a secret, Mr Lopakhin ...

Lopakhin nods.

... Epikhodov has asked me to marry him.

LOPAKHIN: Ah.

This slides effortlessly into a yawn; Dunyasha misses it.

DUNYASHA: I really can't make up my mind what to do. He's quiet really, but when he gets started, I mean you can't make head or tail of it. I mean it's very nice and ... I mean and even ... moving ... except I can't understand a word he says. I mean I quite like him. And he loves me to distraction, of course. Such a sad man. Every day something else befalls him, so everyone teases him and calls him ... (*Laughing*) ... 'Million Miseries' ...

LOPAKHIN: Sh. That's them. (*Listens. We hear nothing. He nods.*) Ahunh.

DUNYASHA: (*Galvanised and paralysed.*) They're here! They're here! What do I do? Look at my hands.

LOPAKHIN: Yes, they've arrived. Let's go and meet them at the door. I wonder if She'll even know me, after five years ...

DUNYASHA: I'll faint, this minute, I know I will.

She follows Lopakhin from the room. Sounds of carriages drawing up before the house. Doors. Sounds of people in farther rooms. **Firs** *crosses the room in the other direction at slow speed, leaning on a stick. He wears old-style livery and a top hat. He mutters to himself throughout, but unintelligibly. Voices getting nearer. One calls, 'No, we can go through here!'* **Mme Ranevsky** *comes in, followed by* **Anya**, **Charlotte**, *with a dog on a lead, all dressed in travelling clothes,* **Varya**, *in coat and headscarf,* **Gayev**, **Pischik**, *Lopakhin, Dunyasha with small bag and umbrella, and* **Servants** *carrying luggage. Anya pushes ahead to take the centre of the room.*

ANYA: You remember this room, Mother.

MME RANEVSKY: (*As though racking her brains.*) The er ... (*Changes suddenly, smiling.*) ... nursery.

VARYA: It's rather cold, I'm afraid. (*Rubbing the backs of her thin white hands.*) Your rooms – the white one and the blue one – are exactly as you left them, Mother.

MME RANEVSKY: (*Deep in the room now, her arm on Anya's shoulder.*) Look. The nursery. My dear and lovely room. I was a child here. And I'm a child again ... (*She kisses Gayev.*) Remember, brother? Mmm. And you haven't changed at all, Varya – (*kisses her*) – my little nun. (*Over Varya's shoulder.*) Dunyasha?

Dunyasha nods, curtseys, excited to be recognised.

GAYEV: Two hours late, that train. What a way to run things!

CHARLOTTE: (*To Pischik, who's stroking the dog's ears.*) It eats nuts.

PISCHIK: (*Withdrawing slightly.*) Imagine.

They all leave, except for Anya and Dunyasha. Dunyasha begins to remove Anya's coat and hat.

DUNYASHA: It's been a long wait ...

ANYA: I haven't slept for four nights ... It's so *cold*.

DUNYASHA: (*Rubbing Anya's hands.*) You left in winter, you come back in spring ... and it's not changed at all. My lovely ... (*Kisses her shyly.*) We're done with waiting, my lovely. Now, I've something to tell you that can't wait

ANYA: (*Tired, barely listening.*) I'm sure you have.

DUNYASHA: I've had a proposal.

ANYA: Really.

DUNYASHA: From Epikhodov. The clerk.

ANYA: (*Sitting down, exhausted.*) Dunyasha, Dunyasha. (*Fiddling with her hair.*) There's not a pin left.

DUNYASHA: I wish I knew what to do. He really is mad about me.

ANYA: (*Staring through door at her room.*) My room, windows ... Have l been away at all? Home. And the orchard ... the first place I'll go, tomorrow. But first I must sleep. I didn't sleep the whole journey. I've been so anxious ...

DUNYASHA: Mr Trofimov arrived two days ago.

ANYA: Peter!

DUNYASHA: He's putting up in the wash-house. He says he doesn't want to put on anybody. (*Looking at watch.*) I know he'd want me to wake him, but Miss Varya said I mustn't. (*Varya's tones.*) 'Don't you wake him,' she said.

Varya comes in, a bunch of keys at her waist.

VARYA: Dunyasha, coffee. Quickly, girl ... Mama is asking for coffee.

DUNYASHA: I'm going, I'm going. (*Leaves*)

VARYA: Well, thank God you're home. You're back home again.

Strokes Anya's temples, rhythming the endearments.

My most dear, most pure, most precious sister's back again.

ANYA: It's been ... (*awful*).

VARYA: (*Soothing Anya's forehead, eyelids.*) I know, I know.

ANYA: Passion Sunday I left. I thought I'd die of cold on the train. And Charlotte either gabbled or did card tricks all the way to Paris. I told you not to saddle me with her.

VARYA: You're seventeen, child. You couldn't have travelled alone.

ANYA: We arrive in Paris. It's snowing. My French is useless. Mother's living in a fifth-floor apartment and when I arrive she has some French people visiting her, some ladies, an old priest with a Bible in his hand, the room's dingy and full of cigarette smoke. (*Pause*) I just suddenly – I felt so sorry for her – I just suddenly took Mama's head in my hands and held on tight and couldn't let go. And Mama ... hugged me. Cried.

VARYA: Sh. That's enough.

ANYA: She'd sold the villa in the south before I arrived and she was still penniless. And I only just made it to Paris, so I wasn't much help. But it made no difference. We had dinner in the most expensive restaurants and she'd order the most expensive dishes and make the waiters rich men overnight with her tips. Charlotte was just as bad. It was appalling. (*Afterthought*) *And* Yasha. He's mother's valet now, you know; so he had to come back with us.

VARYA: (*Frosty*) Yes, I noticed him.

ANYA: (*Straightening.*) Well then. What about here? Have we paid the interest?

VARYA: With what?

ANYA: None of it?

VARYA: They're putting the estate up for auction in August.

ANYA: Dear Jesus!

Lopakhin puts his head round the door, clucks like a chicken, leaves.

VARYA: (*Startled, angered.*) Holy Mother of God, I could ...

She clenches her fists, staring at the doorway. Anya takes her fists, strokes them into hands again.

ANYA: What about Lopakhin? Has he asked you yet?

Varya shakes her head once, curt.

Why don't you have it out with him. Isn't he supposed to love you?

VARYA: There's nothing there. He's too busy with his ... business. He has no time for me. Barely notices I'm in the room. I can't take any more ... There's great talk about the impending wedding, him and me, I'm congratulated all the time, but in reality ... there's nothing, it's just ... a dream. (*She fingers a brooch on Anya's bosom.*) Where did you get that? What is it, a bee?

ANYA: Mama bought it. For the journey home. It cost a fortune!

She laughs suddenly, goes into her room. Her voice is gay now, almost carefree.

Guess what? In Paris, I went up in a balloon!

VARYA: (*Following as far as the door.*) And now you are home, precious one.

Dunyasha comes in with a coffee pot. Begins to make coffee.

DUNYASHA: (*Importantly.*) Coffee.

VARYA: (*At Anya's door, looking in.*) You know what I do as I go about my jobs around the house? I dream. I dream you were going to marry a rich man. I dream that I could then retreat from all this, to some remote convent somewhere, and leave it only to make pilgrimages to holy places, Kiev, Moscow, on and on. Such peace it would bring ...

ANYA: (*Listening.*) The birds. Listen. In the garden. What time is it?

VARYA: Past two. Time you were in bed, dear child. (*Going into Anya's room.*) It would bring such peace.

Yasha *comes in, with travelling rug and case. He stands for a moment, self-importantly surveying the scene. Dunyasha is filtering the coffee.*

YASHA: (*Affectedly refined air.*) Excuse me, Madame, is one permitted to pass this way ...?

DUNYASHA: (*Staring at him.*) My, haven't you changed though, Yasha. I barely recognised you.

YASHA: I'm sorry, I don't think I've had the ...

DUNYASHA: Dunyasha! When you went away I was this high. (*Shows him with her hand.*) Fyodor Kozeyodov's daughter. Don't you remember?

YASHA: (*Closing in, inspecting her.*) Hmmm. (*Sniffs*) Quite a ... cucumber!

Yasha checks the doors with a glance. Puts his hands under her arms and cups her breasts. She yelps, drops a saucer. Yasha evaporates.

VARYA: (*In the doorway, cross.*) What's going on?

DUNYASHA: (*Upset*) I dropped a saucer.

VARYA: (*Crosses herself*) Let's hope it bodes well. (*Pause. Dunyasha crosses herself*) Pick it up then.

ANYA: (*Re-entering*) We should warn Mama Peter Trofimov's here.

VARYA: He won't be wakened, it's all right. I've given orders.

ANYA: But *she* must know, Varya. Think what might happen if he were to walk in on her unannounced. Father dying. Grisha drowning in the river. Mother abandoning us, fleeing to Paris, all that grief, all that guilt flooding back ... Even now, six years later, she still won't believe she's forgiven ... whatever one tells her ...

Firs comes in. He wears a jacket over a white waistcoat. Advances laboriously on the coffee pot.

FIRS: The mistress will take her coffee here. (*Puts on white gloves*) Is it ready? (*Looks around the table. To Dunyasha, sharp.*) Hey! Cream!

DUNYASHA: Oh my God!

She hurries off excitedly.

FIRS: (*Fussing*) Witless wench! (*Muttering to himself*) They've arrived ...ahunh ... all the way from Paris ... the master used to go to Paris ... I remember that ... ahunh, yes he did ... In a coach (*Laughs suddenly.*)

VARYA: Who are you talking to, Firs?

FIRS: (*Mishearing*) Almost three, Ma'am. (*Happy*) The mistress is home, the long wait is over, now I can die. (*Begins to weep with happiness.*)

Enter Mme Ranevsky, Gayev, Pischik. Pischik wears a long Russian coat of fine cloth, wide trousers tucked into his boots. Gayev mimes billiard shots, very seriously.

MME RANEVSKY: (*Laughing a little.*) Let's see if I can remember how it goes now. Pot into the corner pocket, double off the cush –

GAYEV: Cut, sister, cut into the corner! (*Taken suddenly by the room.*) Ah ... We used to sleep in here as children, if I'm not ... And now, odd as it may seem, I'm fifty-one.

LOPAKHIN: (*Ironic*) Yes. Tempus fugit.

GAYEV: What?

LOPAKHIN: Time... (*lamely*) ... flies.

GAYEV: (*Glaring*) Stinks of patchouli in here.

ANYA: I'm for bed. (*Kissing Mme Ranevsky.*) Good night Maman.

MME RANEVSKY: (*Kissing her hands.*) Mmm. Sweet child. Aren't you glad to be home. I'm still a little dazed by it all.

ANYA: Uncle.

GAYEV: (*Kissing her cheek and hand.*) Bless you, just like your mother. You were just like her at her age, Liuba.

Anya shakes hands with Lopakhin and Pischik and leaves, shutting her door behind her.

MME RANEVSKY: She's worn out.

PISCHIK: The journey.

Pause. Silence. A sort of blankness settles. Firs mutters something nobody hears. Silence again.

VARYA: Well then, gentlemen. It's late. Time you were gone.

MME RANEVSKY: (*Laughing suddenly*) Varya, you haven't changed a bit.

Draws her to her, kisses her brow.

I'll just drink my coffee and then we'll all go.

Firs places a cushion under her feet.

Thank you, my dear.

She waits while Firs regains his feet, a tightrope performance but in the subtlest miniature.

I've grown used to it, you know. (*Shows cup.*) Coffee. Drink it all the time. (*To Firs, swaying still, but upright.*) Thank you, dear old man. (*She kisses him on the brow.*)

VARYA: I ought to check the luggage is all there. (*Leaves*)

MME RANEVSKY: Is this really me, sitting here like this? (*Excited*) Oh, I feel like... dancing, I feel like dancing! If it's a dream, don't waken me. Because ... I love this place. I love it so much I couldn't see it properly from the train. For tears. (*Pause*) Coffee. (*She drains the cup.*) Thank you, Firs, thank you, dear old man. It's good you still live.

FIRS: Not yesterday. Day before.

GAYEV: But deaf.

Firs mumbles his way to the coffee table.

LOPAKHIN: (*Checking watch.*) I have to catch a train to Kharkov in an hour. Pity. I wanted a good look at you. And a talk. (*Pause*) You're as magnificent as ever.

PISCHIK: And even more beautiful! *À la mode*, is it? I swear my heart's not stopped pounding like a race horse's since she arrived.

LOPAKHIN: (*Slight awkwardness.*) Your brother here, Leon, says I'm a boor, a kulak, but it doesn't hurt me. He's welcome to his opinion. All I ask is that you trust me as before, hold me in the same regard as before. My father was serf to yours and to his father, too. But you've done so much for me, you've helped me forget all that ... history ... and love you ... as my own sister. More, perhaps.

Mme Ranevsky stands, cup in hands, crosses to the table, where Firs laboriously pours another cup of coffee.

MME RANEVSKY: I can't sit still, forgive me. (*Paces room a little, touching things. Laughs suddenly.*) This happiness is insufferable. Laugh if you like, I know it's silly. (*She presses the bookcase with her cheek.*) My own bookcase. (*Strokes table.*) My own table. (*Kisses it.*)

GAYEV: Nurse died while you were away.

MME RANEVSKY: Yes, I know. May she rest in God's arms. They wrote me.

Crosses to her seat, coffee in hands.

GAYEV: Anastasi died too. Oh, and Peter ... erm ... the one with the squint ... handed in his notice. He's joined the police force.

Takes a box of sweets from his pocket, removes one, sucks it.

PISCHIK: My daughter ... Dashenka ... sends her ... regards.

LOPAKHIN: Mme Ranevsky is right, this is no time for gloom. Let me cheer you up with this. (*Checking watch.*) There isn't time for a full discussion – I can't miss my train – but here it is in essence. The cherry orchard is down to be sold by auction to pay off your debts. This much you know. Now, the date of the auction has been set for August the twenty-second. (*Mme Ranevsky puts down her cup suddenly.*) But you can go to your bed tonight and dream pleasant dreams, because there's a way out. Now listen. Your land is less than twenty miles from town and near the railway, right? If the orchard and the land by the river were to be parcelled up into plots and leased out for weekend cottages, you'd have a per annum yield of twenty-five or even thirty thousand. What about that!

GAYEV: Bloody nonsense. Absolute bloody … (*He internalises his thought suddenly.*)

MME RANEVSKY: I'm not sure I understand … what you're saying, Mr …

LOPAKHIN: How do I get the yield figure? Well, look, you can ask at least ten roubles per year per acre plot, and if you put it on the market right away there won't be a plot left by the autumn, take the word of a man who knows. In fact, dear lady, you are to be congratulated: you're comprehensively saved. It's a fine location; bathing to be had in the river. All you'll have to do is a bit of … cleaning and tidying. All those outbuildings and things will have to go, of course … and this place too, which is of only marginal value to anyone now. And the cherry orchard.

MME RANEVSKY: The cherry orchard what?

LOPAKHIN: Five men could clear it in … (*calculates*) … less than a week …

MME RANEVSKY: Cut it down? How … Forgive me, you appear not to understand … If there is one truly remarkable thing in this entire region it is my cherry orchard.

LOPAKHIN: Forgive me, Mme Ranevsky, but the only remarkable thing about your cherry orchard is its dimensions. It's very large. But there is nothing at all remarkable in producing a crop every other year which nobody actually wants.

GAYEV: This orchard has an entry to itself in the *Encyclopaedia Russkaya*.

LOPAKHIN: (*Deliberately, looking at his watch.*) All right. But unless there's some pretty clear thinking and some sensible decisions forthcoming, both it and the estate will come under the hammer on the twenty-second of August. (*Pause. Carefully.*) You will have to make up your minds. (*Pause*) But be assured: there is no other way out. None at all.

He's ready to go, but not able. Gayev is agitated, pacing a little, Pischik is half-asleep, Mme Ranevsky pale, ghostly. A bird sings, rather brightly, in the lightening orchard beyond the windows.

FIRS: Once upon a time they would dry the cherries, preserve them in jars, or turn them into jam, or sometimes even …

GAYEV: Shut up, please, Firs.

FIRS: ... and sometimes even send them dried, you see, in carts, to Moscow and Kharkov. People wanted them then. I can still smell them sometimes, soft and sweet, the dried cherries. They knew how to do it then ...

MME RANEVSKY: (*Softly*) And now?

FIRS: Forgotten now. No one remembers.

PISCHIK: How was the food in Paris then, eh? Did you eat frogs?

MME RANEVSKY: I ate crocodiles.

PISCHIK: (*Uncertainly*) Imagine.

LOPAKHIN: The recipe for drying cherries is no longer the point, Mme Ranevsky. Once there were just masters and serfs in these parts: now there are weekenders, holidaymakers. And twenty years from now there'll be masses of them, in summer cottages, round every town, even the smallest. As of now they just ... drink tea on their verandahs, but I see a day when these same people will take to planting out their little acre, growing things, and the orchards will ... live again, will be alive again with growing things ...

GAYEV: Bloody nonsense. Absolute bloody ...

Varya comes in, Yasha behind her.

VARYA: (*Crossing to bookcase, selecting key as she walks.*) I forgot the telegrams that came for you, Mama. (*Finding them.*) Here they are.

Gayev has followed Varya to the bookcase, placed his hands on its sides. Mme Ranevsky studies the telegrams briefly, then tears them up.

MME RANEVSKY: Paris. I've forgotten Paris.

GAYEV: Do you know how old this bookcase is, Liuba? The other day I was rummaging in this bottom drawer and noticed some figures burned in the wood. Eighteen hundred and three. A hundred years ago, mmm? Perhaps we should celebrate its centenary. True it's ... inanimate, a ... thing, yet it remains, a bookcase.

PISCHIK: (*Impressed*) A hundred years! Imagine!

GAYEV: Yes. That is truly something! (*He half embraces it, tender, gentle.*) My dear, honoured bookcase. I salute your life. For one hundred years you have borne witness to the noble ideals of goodness and of justice. For one hundred years your silent call to hard work has sounded in the ears of generations of this, our family, sustaining us in our moments of weakness, strengthening in us our belief in a better tomorrow, and implanting in us the moral idea of virtue and the moral ideal of social order.

Long pause.

LOPAKHIN: Yes ...

MME RANEVSKY: (*Dry but fond.*) Plus ça change, plus c'est la même chose avec toi, Leon.

GAYEV: (*A little embarrassed.*) In off into the corner. Cut into the middle.

LOPAKHIN: (*Watch in hand.*) I'll have to go.

YASHA: (*Carrying small box on tray.*) I think it's time for your pills.

PISCHIK: Tcha, pills. Never take pills, dear lady. Never did anybody any good. Never did anybody any harm, come to that. Here.

He takes the box, empties the pills into his palm, blows on them, scoops them into his mouth and swallows them with a glass of cider.

See!

MME RANEVSKY: (*Surprised, a little alarmed.*) You'll be ill!

PISCHIK: No no. One gulp. (*He mimes the action, pleased at the attention.*) Nothing.

LOPAKHIN: What guts the man must have.

Laughter.

FIRS: The honoured gentleman was here at Easter; ate half a bucket of pickled cucumbers. (*Mutters on unintelligibly.*)

MME RANEVSKY: What's he saying?

VARYA: He's muttered for three years. We barely notice it now.

YASHA: He's senile.

They look at him, frowning, rather hostile. Yasha takes a pace back, uncertainly, narrowly missing Charlotte, who's just entering behind him, on her way to bed. She's extremely thin, tightly laced, in a white dress with a lorgnette at the waist.

LOPAKHIN: Ah, forgive me, Charlotte, I haven't had the opportunity to say how do you do yet …

He reaches for her hand, to kiss it.

CHARLOTTE: (*Withdrawing her hand smartly.*) First the hand, elbow next, then the shoulder … Tututut.

LOPAKHIN: Some days it's barely worth getting out of bed! (*Laughter*) Show us a trick then, dear lady.

MME RANEVSKY: Excellent idea. Yes.

CHARLOTTE: Sorry. Too tired. (*Leaves*)

LOPAKHIN: Well, I'll be away for three weeks. (*Kissing Mme Ranevsky's hand.*) Good-bye, Madame. (*To Gayev.*) Time to go.

He shakes hands with Varya; then, inappropriately, with Firs and Yasha.

Good-bye.

He walks towards the door, then turns back.

I don't actually feel like going ... Think about the summer cottage scheme ... You've only to let me know ... I'm pretty sure I can raise fifty thousand or so to set things in motion. (*Pause*) Think hard, mm?

VARYA: (*Angry*) Go, will you. Go!

LOPAKHIN: I'm going, I'm going. (*Leaves*)

Gayev follows a few steps towards the door.

GAYEV: A perfect boor, that man! Oh, I do beg your pardon, Varya's going to marry him, he's Varya's intended, isn't he ...

VARYA: Thank you, Uncle.

MME RANEVSKY: No matter, Varya. I shall be more than happy. He's a good man.

PISCHIK: Fine man, admirable fellow, oh yes. My daughter Dashenka says it all the time. My daughter Dashenka says all sorts of things, as a matter of fact.

He nods off at once, snores once, wakes himself up.

While we're on the subject, dear lady, would you lend me two hundred and forty roubles ... the interest on my mortgage is due tomorrow.

VARYA: (*Alarmed*) We haven't got it! There isn't any!

MME RANEVSKY: I'm afraid that's true. I have nothing.

PISCHIK: Not to worry. (*Laughs*) Never say die, that's the thing. There are times when I think everything's gone, I'm done for. And then, hey presto, there's a railway line or something across my land and I get paid for it! Something will happen, you see; if not today, then tomorrow. I wouldn't be surprised if Dashenka won two hundred thousand roubles in the lottery. She's got a ticket, you know.

MME RANEVSKY: So much for coffee. Now I must sleep.

FIRS: (*Scolding a little, brushing Gayev's trousers.*) Ach, you've put on the wrong trousers again ... What am I to do with you!

Gayev stands like a statue, barely aware of Firs' fussing.

VARYA: (*Low*) Sh. Anya's sleeping. (*Opens window quietly.*) The sun's up. Can you feel it? Look, Mama, the trees. Aren't they wonderful ... You can smell them on the air. Can you hear the starlings?

Gayev detaches from the kneeling Firs, perhaps not noticing him at all, opens another window.

GAYEV: How white the orchard, Liuba. Do you remember ... on and on, the avenue of trees ... unending ... shining under the moon like a young maiden's ribbon, ironed and ready for the ball. Remember?

MME RANEVSKY: (*Taking the window between them.*) Childhood. And innocence. Oh. (*Long pause, in the hush of the house.*) My bed was … here … by the window; I could see the orchard from it. And out there at least, nothing has changed. My orchard gleams as white, as pure as ever, untouched by autumn's storms and winter's dead hand. Here you are again, and again, and again, young, innocent … your own self. Some god watches over you. No … past to weigh you down like a great stone …

GAYEV: Yes, and odd as it may sound, this same orchard is to be ...

MME RANEVSKY: Look! There's Mother … walking through that grove … in her white dress! It is her! See?

GAYEV: Where?

VARYA: (*On her knees, kissing the crucifix on her breast.*) God is with you, Mama.

MME RANEVSKY: There's no one. I imagined it. See, over there, on the right, by the path to the summer house, a little white tree, bent over somehow … looks like a woman.

Enter **Trofimov**, *very quietly. He's dressed in shabby student's uniform; he's rather bedraggled; wears thick-lensed glasses in wire frames.*

How white and wonderful the blossom against the blue sky …

TROFIMOV: Madame Ranevsky.

She turns quickly, startled, stifles a small shriek, stares, recognising him in some part of her mind but unable to acknowledge it.

I just wanted to pay my respects. I'll go. (*He bows formally.*) Forgive me, I was told to wait until the morning, but I still lack patience …

VARYA: (*To Mme Ranevsky.*) It's… Peter Trofimov.

TROFIMOV: Peter Trofimov, your son's tutor … Can I have changed so much?

Mme Ranevsky turns quickly back to the window, leaning fractionally on the frame. Gayev puts his hand on her shoulder, uncertain what to do.

GAYEV: Come, Liuba, come …

VARYA: I told you to wait until tomorrow, Peter …

MME RANEVSKY: (*In a plain, very normal voice, her back to the room.*) Grisha. Little Grisha.

VARYA: It was God's will, Mama.

TROFIMOV: I'm sorry. Please.

MME RANEVSKY: Was it? To drown a six-year-old child? For what? (*She turns into the room, controlled, steady. Holds her hands out, takes Trofimov's.*) Do you know why it happened, my friend? (*She hugs him to her bosom, he begins to greet her more emotionally.*)

Sh, sh. Anya's sleeping. We mustn't make a noise, mm? (*Standing him away from her.*) Well, Peter. You look terrible. You've grown old.

TROFIMOV: (*Laughing*) A peasant woman in the train called me a 'gentleman gone to seed'.

MME RANEVSKY: Then you were just a boy, a pretty young student, and now your hair is thin and you have glasses. What do you do now?

TROFIMOV: I'm still a student. If the authorities have their way, I suspect I'll always be one.

MME RANEVSKY: Well. Go to bed now. (*She detaches, kisses Gayev.*) You've grown old too, Leon. (*She kisses Varya, looks at her, says nothing.*)

Pischik begins to follow her out.

PISCHIK: Ah. Seems to be time for bed. Ooh, this gout. (*Hobbling*) I'll stay the night here, if that's ... And tomorrow morning, if you could let me have that er two hundred and forty roubles, I'd be of course ...

GAYEV: There's no shaking that one.

PISCHIK: ... most grateful, a mere two hundred and forty roubles, interest on the erm thingumajig ...

MME RANEVSKY: My dear, I have no money.

PISCHIK: Trifling sum. And of course you'd have it back in a, in erm ...

MME RANEVSKY: (*Decisively, from the doorway.*) All right then. Leon will give you the money. Give him the money, Leon.

GAYEV: Of course. I'll just stand here with my pockets open. (*He does so.*) Come on, help yourself.

MME RANEVSKY: What else can we do? He needs it. He'll pay it back.

Mme Ranevsky, Trofimov and Pischik leave, followed by Firs, losing ground all the time.

GAYEV: My sister still knows how to throw money away. Especially mine. (*Sniffing around, locating something. To Yasha.*) Go away. You smell of chickens.

YASHA: (*Moving behind him.*) And you, Mr Leon ... are just the same as ever.

GAYEV: What did he say? What did he say?

VARYA: (*To Yasha.*) Your mother's come from the village – she's been sitting in the servants' quarters since yesterday, waiting for you to give her an audience.

YASHA: (*Padding out.*) God should have called her long ago.

VARYA: (*Fierce, crossing herself*) Have you no shame!

YASHA: None at all. She could have come just as well tomorrow.

He leaves. Varya begins to clear odd things around the room. Gayev stands for a moment, inside himself, then sits on the sofa carefully, staring at the room as though trying to remember how he got there.

VARYA: Mama hasn't changed at all. If it was left to her, she'd give everything we have away.

GAYEV: Mmm. (*Pause*) Here's what I think: the greater the number of cures you can suggest for a sickness, the more certain you can be it's incurable. I've been rattling my brains a good deal and I've come up with a good many ways out, oh yes, lots and lots … so I'm pretty certain we've had it. Anyway, for instance: somebody could leave us some money, that'd be a good thing. Another fine thing would be if Anya were to wed an extremely rich man. And it couldn't hurt for one of us to go to Yaroslavl to try our luck with our old aunt, the countess. Who is, as we all know, exceedingly rich.

VARYA: (*Overwhelmed, hopeless.*) If only God would see our plight and help us!

GAYEV: (*A reflex, minimal.*) Don't whine, darling. Now aunt is exceedingly rich, but happens not to like us … First, because my sister decides to marry some lawyer fellow instead of a nobleman.

Anya appears in the doorway, in a white cotton nightgown, like the image of her mother that Liuba saw in the orchard. Gayev has his back to her.

… So, she marries beneath herself … And then she's behaved, erm … How can one put it … She's not exactly lived the life of a saint. I love her dearly, she's a good, kind … impulsive woman, but whatever allowances one cares to make, she has been a trifle what? wanton, mmm? loose, anyway. I mean, my God, it's there every time she moves an eyelash …

VARYA: (*Whispers*) Anya's in the doorway.

GAYEV: Ach … Something in my eye, an eyelash … Can't see at all. So … Thursday I was at District Council …

Anya comes into the room.

VARYA: You should be sleeping, Anya.

ANYA: I've tried. I can't.

GAYEV: (*Kissing Anya's face and hands.*) Dear, dear girl. Little little girl. (*Weeping*) Niece, angel, everything. Believe me. Please believe me.

ANYA: Of course I believe you, Uncle. Everyone loves and respects you … but you talk too much, Uncle, you should try to keep quiet. What made you say those things about my mother, your sister?

GAYEV: (*Covering his face with her hand.*) I know, I know, it was awful, it was awful of me. Oh my God, my God! And the speech I made to the bookcase … so foolish. It wasn't until I'd finished that I saw how … foolish I was being …

VARYA: It's true, your tongue wags, and there you are. Just keep it still, that's all.

ANYA: It'll make you happier.

GAYEV: I'll be quiet.

He kisses Anya's and Varya's hands.

(*Hands to lips. Silent.*) Nothing. (*He's about to leave.*) Oh, just one thing. I was talking with some friends at the District Council on Thursday and it does look as though it might be possible to raise a loan ... against promissory notes and so on ... to at least pay the bank the interest on the erm ... (*He subsides a moment.*)

VARYA: May the good Lord help us! (*She mutters a prayer, fearful.*)

GAYEV: I'm due there again Tuesday and I'll ... talk some more about it. Do stop whining, Varya. Then, erm, your mother's going to have a talk with Lopakhin: and he'll not refuse her. And when you've rested, you can go to Yaroslavl to see your great-aunt, the countess. And so we'll launch the attack on three fronts and click! it's in the pocket! We'll pay the interest. Sure of it. (*Sweet into mouth. Hand on breast. Sonorous.*) Upon my word of honour, upon anything you like, I swear this estate will not be sold. I hereby solemnly stake my happiness on it! I hereby solemnly give you my hand to it and you can call me a worthless liar if I allow it to come under the hammer. And I do swear all this, by everything I am.

ANYA: (*Calm now, happier.*) You're a good and clever uncle. (*Puts arm around him.*) I feel calmer now. Calm and happy.

Enter Firs.

FIRS: (*Reproaches him.*) Leon Gayev, to bed! Have you lost all fear of the Almighty One?

GAYEV: I'm coming, I'm coming. Off you trot, Firs, I can manage by myself, I can undress myself. (*Firs stands sternly by.*) Well ... children ... time for beddy-byebyes. Further details can wait until tomorrow, but now it's time you were in bed. (*Kisses each in turn*). Me, I'm an 'eighties man. Those days are out of fashion with most people now, but I've endured much in my life in upholding my beliefs. It's not an accident that I am loved by the peasants hereabouts. Because you have to know your peasant. You have to understand his ...

ANYA: Again, Uncle?

VARYA: Listen to it.

FIRS: (*Sternly*) Mr Gayev.

GAYEV: Sh! I'm coming! Of course! Go to bed! Off two cushes into the middle, tut, tut, chuc. Pot white, click, chuh.

He leaves. Firs totters after him.

ANYA: It's so ... at peace here. I don't want to go to Yaroslavl. I can't stand our great-aunt the countess. Still, I'm at peace here. (*To the doorway.*) Thank you, Uncle.

She sits down, very tired.

VARYA: I must go to bed. (*Pauses*) You know, a quite nasty thing happened while you were away. The old servants – Efimyushka, Polya, Evstignei, oh and Karp, yes – they started letting vagrants stay in the empty servants' quarters. I didn't say anything at first. Then I heard the gossip they were putting round; that I'd ordered them to be fed on mushy peas and nothing else, because I was mean, you see ... and I heard that all this started with Evstignei ... so I thought, right, we'll see about this ... so I sent for him ... (*She yawns, long and deep. Blinks her eyes.*) ... 'So, you silly old man, what's this you've been saying about me ... and stand still when I'm ...' (*Looks at Anya.*) Anya. (*Anya sleeps. Varya takes her gently by the arm.*) Come. Sleep in your bed.

She supports Anya tenderly towards her bedroom door. In the distance, a shepherd's pipe starts up. Trofimov comes in, sees Anya on Varya's arm.

VARYA: (*To Trofimov.*) Shhh,

ANYA: (*Half asleep.*) Hear the bells, Varya.

VARYA: Sh. Sh. Sh. Sh.

They go into Anya's room. Sun floods the nursery now.

TROFIMOV: Anya. Sun. Spring.

Tape: (*Trofimov's voice*): «Со́лнышко моё!! Весна́ моя!»

ACT TWO

Black.

Charlotte's voice on tape delivers first line in Russian «У меня нет настоя́щего па́спорта» *etc. Lights up, revealing a stage-wide cyc., dark blue. A guitar strums. A crow barks overhead, once, twice; is answered by another. More lights reveal Yasha (smoking a long thin cigar), and Dunyasha (powdering her face in a mirror), seated on a crude old country bench: Epikhodov standing, leg up on a tilted gravestone, playing a love song on a guitar; and Charlotte, in hunting clothes and cap, shortening the canvas sling on her rifle. They sit or stand, absorbed, separate, facing out. Behind them, set into the remnant of a wall, a traveller's shrine with a faded blue and gold icon of the Virgin Mary. It's twenty minutes to sunset. A full moon is already faintly silvering their skin.*

CHARLOTTE: (*To no one, deep in herself.*) I wonder how old I am. Without papers there's no way of telling. I still think of myself as young, when my father and mother played the fairs and I used to do the death dive into a tub of water. Then they died. A German lady took me in and taught me things. And I grew up. Became a governess. But I have no papers. I could be anybody, from anywhere. I don't even know if my parents were married.

She takes a large cucumber from a jacket pocket, eats it.

I know nothing. If I could talk to someone about it it would help, I know it would. (*Pause*) But there's no one.

EPIKHODOV: (*Sings*)   'I've put the world behind me.
                        The world of friend and foe ...'
Is it not a thing of beauty, the mandolin ...?

DUNYASHA: (*Powdering face.*) It's a guitar.

EPIKHODOV: To a man inflamed, it's a mandolin. (*Sings*)
                        If I had your hand to guide me
                        Then true love my soul would know.

YASHA: (*Sings*)   If I had your hand to guide me
                        I would kiss your little toe.

CHARLOTTE: *Ach, mein Gott,* they sing like goats, these people.

DUNYASHA: (*To Yasha.*) Admit it though. You're very fortunate to have been abroad.

YASHA: (*Yawning*) If you like. I agree with you. (*Relights his cigar.*)

EPIKHODOV: I agree too. Abroad they've been a century ahead for years.

YASHA: Took the words right out of my mouth.

Epikhodov takes a revolver from his waistband, stares at it for a moment, then places the barrel experimentally in his mouth. Removes it.

EPIKHODOV: I'm a man of some learning, you know. Oh yes, I've read a good many difficult books, I just can't seem to find my way forward. To be or not to be, really. I should draw your attention here to my habit of always carrying a revolver on my person.

He holds it up. They see it.

CHARLOTTE: Right, that's me. (*She slings the rifle over her shoulder.*) I'm off. Epikhodov, you're clearly a very clever man and I'd wager an extremely dangerous one. Women must be forming lines to fall in love with you. Ha! (*Moves off.*) Oh, the clever ones, the clever ones, I have no one I can talk to, I live alone, I don't know who I am or why I am.

She leaves. Yasha flicks his cigar, smiling lazily after her. Dunyasha waves the smoke out of her face. Epikhodov sits on the gravestone, untouched by Charlotte's irony.

EPIKHODOV: I will say this about that. In essence, and without wishing to burk the issues raised, by the way, I feel I should point out that life handles me ruthlessly, as a hurricane might treat a small boat, for instance. Now, in case you imagine I'm mistaken in the matter, explain to me if you can, to take one instance from many, why I should open my eyes this morning and find squatting on my breast a spider of terrifying dimensions ... (*He picks up a large stone.*) ... like this, mm? Or. Suppose I go to pour a glass of cider, why will the jug inevitably contain some monstrous thing inside it – a cockroach perhaps? Or worse. (*Pause*) Have you read, by chance, the English historian Buckle?

Pause. He crosses to stand behind Dunyasha, speaks in her ear.

May I beg a brief word of you …?

DUNYASHA: Go on.

EPIKHODOV: Could it be in private, do you think?

DUNYASHA: (*Discomfited.*) I suppose so. (*She shivers, rubs her upper arms.*) I shall need my cloak first though. It's by the wardrobe. It's growing quite cold out here …

EPIKHODOV: As you wish, Madame. (*Collects his guitar, begins to leave.*) I think I know now what I should do with my revolver.

(*Leaves*)

YASHA: (*Yawning. Finally.*) Treat this as a confidence, won't you, but that man is very stupid.

DUNYASHA: Please God he doesn't shoot himself. (*Checks her image in the mirror, angles it to take in Yasha.*) These days I'm nervy all the time, worrying. I've worked at the big house since I was a child, see. My hands are as fair as any lady's, I don't know how to live ordinarily any more. See. (*She holds her hands out.*) I've grown so soft and delicate that the least thing sets me off trembling … the least thing. (*Turns to face him.*) I mean, Yasha, if you play me false, I'll break into tiny pieces, I know I will …

YASHA: (*Kissing her hands.*) Sh, little cucumber. Sh. (*Calms her.*) A girl must know her station, of course. In my view, there's nothing less endearing than a girl who doesn't know how to behave well.

DUNYASHA: But I love you, Yasha. Terribly. You're so … cultured, you can talk about anything …

YASHA: (*Yawning*) Yes, I know. And yet, see it my way, child: a girl who loves is a girl who sins, isn't that so. (*Shifts, looks around, lounges back a little on the bench.*) Is there anything more luxurious than smoking a cigar outdoors. (*Listens*) Christ, there's someone coming … it's the gentry.

He lobs the cigar away at once, goes to stand up and fasten his jacket, is thwarted by Dunyasha, who has knelt between his legs and is now clinging to them, whispering, 'Your word, Yasha, your word.' Yasha swipes the cigar smoke away as best he can.

You'd best go on back. Quickly. (*Drawing her up.*) Here. (*He picks up a bottle of wine, pours some over her head.*) Look as if you've been swimming in the river or something. Not that way, that way … I don't want them thinking I've been making assignations

DUNYASHA: (*Coughing*) My head's reeling. I think it's your cigar. (*Leaves*)

Yasha crosses to the shrine, sits. Mme Ranevsky and Gayev are heard approaching for quite a while, then seen, arm in arm, cresting the bank. Mme Ranevsky sings a French love song (perhaps Bizet), Gayev tum-tums a rhythm out. Behind them comes Lopakhin, his jacket over his arm. We hear his opening line before we see him.

LOPAKHIN: I need a decision – time is not on your side. It's a simple enough question: will you agree to lease the land for weekend cottages or not? One word will do: yes or no.

They sway a little, still slightly fumed from luncheon wine.

MME RANEVSKY: Somebody's been smoking cigars. Filthy things.

She sits on the bench, ignoring Yasha.

GAYEV: See, Liuba, it's over there. (*She follows his finger, frowning.*) The railway, (*She nods.*) Very convenient. (*To Lopakhin.*) We've been to town for lunch …Yellow in the … middle, I think. (*He gestures the nomination.*) I think I'd like to go off and have a quick frame …

MME RANEVSKY: No hurry.

LOPAKHIN: Just one tiny word, mm?

GAYEV: What?

MME RANEVSKY: (*Rummaging in her purse.*) All gone. Yesterday it was full to here. My poor Varya skimps and saves and feeds the servants mushy peas and milk soup and here am I throwing it away on nothing … (*She drops the purse; her remaining gold coins scatter around her feet.*) See. Just look at me. (*She laughs suddenly, unamusedly.*)

YASHA: Allow me.

He kneels before her, begins gathering the coins from under the bench, brushing her feet and ankles with his hands.

MME RANEVSKY: Thank you, Yasha … (*Gayev sits by her, pats her hand.*) Oh why in God's name did I go out to lunch? That dismal restaurant of yours, Leon, with its ageing trio in the corner and the tablecloths smelling of the laundry. Need we drink so much? Or eat? Or talk? Today, Leon, you talked everyone to the point of physical extinction, and about what? Trivia. Irrelevancies. The seventies, for God's sake. The Decadents. And to whom? (*To Lopakhin.*) Fancy talking to waiters about poets!

LOPAKHIN: Quite.

Yasha begins to reach for a coin between Gayev's feet.

GAYEV: Yes, I'm quite beyond redemption, I can see that … (*To Yasha.*) What are you worming around at, eh?

YASHA: (*Half sotto, directed with care and precision.*) Trying not to laugh at you.

GAYEV: (*Stands dramatically.*) It's him or me, Liuba ...

MME RANEVSKY: (*Casual, dismissive, kicks Yasha on the hip.*) Out. Go. Allez-vous en.

YASHA: (*Standing, giving her the purse.*) At once, Madame. (*He bows low.*) Il faut!

He leaves slowly, clicking something in his hand, laughing a little, not quite discreetly, something in his manner suggesting a secret shared with Mme Ranevsky that will protect him.

Lopakhin watches him leave. He homes in deliberately on Ranevsky.

LOPAKHIN: So. Deriganov intends spending a fraction of his fortune on buying your estate. They say he'll attend the auction in person.

MME RANEVSKY: Who says so ?

LOPAKHIN: It's what they say in town.

GAYEV: There's money promised from Yaroslavl, our aunt, you know, but when and how much of it, ppp, nobody knows ...

LOPAKHIN: (*Ignores him.*) Will she send a hundred thousand, two hundred thousand, what do you think?

MME RANEVSKY: Well, let me see, if we're very lucky it could be as much as fifteen.

LOPAKHIN: Thousand. (*She nods, smiles.*) I'm trying not to give offence, but you two must be just about the most reckless and feckless people I've ever met. You're told in words of one syllable – you are about to lose your land – and it seems to make no impression.

MME RANEVSKY: (*Teasing, tipsy still.*) But what can we *do* about it? Have *you* an answer?

LOPAKHIN: (*Blowing a little, seeking and quickly finding his self-control.*) I give you the answer every single day, there is only one answer: the orchard and the land down to the river must be leased out for summer cottages. And it must be done now, the auction's almost upon us. Do you understand? (*He looks from one to the other. Mme Ranevsky has removed a shoe to stroke the arch of her foot. Gayev chalks his cue with languid precision.*) When you make *that* decision, you'll get the credit you need and you'll be saved.

MME RANEVSKY: Summer cottages, weekenders – it's all so 'bourgeois'.

GAYEV: Absolutely.

LOPAKHIN: You know something, you people would make a saint lose his temper, or burst into tears or something. (*Looks at Gayev.*) And you, you're driving me mad, you old woman you.

GAYEV: Old what did he say?

LOPAKHIN: (*Shouts*) Woman. Old woman!

He prepares to leave, grim, disturbed, and somehow resolute.

MME RANEVSKY: (*Standing*) Don't go. Please. Dear man. Please. Perhaps. We can
think of something ... together.

LOPAKHIN: I doubt it.

MME RANEVSKY: Please. (*Lopakhin walks in looping circles, charmed into
indirection yet trying to stay firm.*) I beg of you. It's always so much cheerier
when you're with us. (*Pause. She watches him carefully.*)

I'm terrified something will happen – the house fall down around us, or worse.

GAYEV: Double into the middle there, spot into the top ...

LOPAKHIN: How do you mean?

MME RANEVSKY: We have committed many sins.

LOPAKHIN: You?

GAYEV: Sins? Oh yes. (*Puts a sweet in his mouth.*) They say I've sucked a fortune
away in sweeties. (*He laughs*)

MME RANEVSKY: (*Taking Lopakhin's fixed gaze.*) Yes. A great many. I've thrown
money away all my life, like someone mad, and I chose a husband whose
only talent lay in the creation of debts. Oh and drinking – he was a fairly
active drunkard – died eventually of a surfeit of champagne. And what do I do?
I fall in love with his double. And while we're having our affair, I receive
my first punishment, like a bullet here, here ... (*She places a hand on her
breast, the brittleness falling away in the silence.*) ... my first born drowns,
here, in the river. (*Pause*) I went abroad, away for good, I swore I'd never
look at this river again, I shut my eyes to all responsibilities, grief makes one
cruel you know, and ran away. He followed me, this second brutal man,
fell ill in Menton and forced me to buy a house there and nurse him. For three
years I slaved over him, day and night, until he ... wore me out and my soul
withered. (*Pause*) A year ago I sold the house to pay off our debts and fled to
Paris. Where he robbed me, threw me over and took up with someone else. I
tried poisoning myself ... I couldn't bear the shame ... it was all so futile
suddenly. (*She's weeping, barely aware of it; wipes her face with the heel of
her hand.*) And just as suddenly, I longed to be in Russia again, home again,
with my little girl again. May the Lord have mercy on me and forgive me my
trespasses and let the punishment come to an end. (*She takes out a
handkerchief to wipe her face, draws out a telegram with it.*) This came today
from Paris ... He wants me back, asks my forgiveness ... (*She tears it up
slowly but without malice.*) Is that music I can hear ?

They listen. We hear nothing.

GAYEV: It's probably our famous Jewish orchestra. Remember? Three violins, flute, double bass?

MME RANEVSKY: Are they still going? We should have them to the house sometime and arrange a ball or something.

LOPAKHIN: (*Still listening.*) Don't hear it. (*Sings*)
        For a schilling the kraut
        Turns a bear inside out
        Until he can dance like a frog.

(*Laughs*) I saw an excellent piece at the theatre yesterday. Very very funny.

MME RANEVSKY: I'm sure it wasn't in the least funny. (*Pause*) I believe people like you would do better examining their own lives instead of going to the theatre to observe others'. Don't you sense how vapid your life is and how silly your attempts to explain it.

LOPAKHIN: I suppose it's true. Looked at rationally life is pretty meaningless. (*Pause*) Look at me and my father. He was a peasant, a clod, incapable of learning anything or of handing anything on to me by way of wisdom. The closest we ever got was when he'd come home drunk and thrash me with a stick. (*Pause*) So: am I any different? I'm scarcely less mindless than him, I've learned next to nothing, my handwriting's ... I write like a pig ... I'm ashamed to let it be seen.

Long pause. Lopakhin kicks at a stone bedded in the earth. Gayev stares at the moon, his face almost lost behind him.

MME RANEVSKY: (*Soft, gentle.*) You need a wife, old friend.

LOPAKHIN: Yes.

MME RANEVSKY: You should marry my Varya. She's a good girl.

LOPAKHIN: Yes.

MME RANEVSKY: (*Slow, distinct, simple.*) She comes from sturdy, common stock, works the clock round, and loves you. You've been fond of her for a long time, am I right?

LOPAKHIN: I wouldn't say no, I suppose. She's a good girl.

Pause. They're on the delicate brink of something.

GAYEV: I've been offered a position at the bank, six thousand a year, did I tell you?

MME RANEVSKY: (*The moment blown for her: angered into coldness and contempt.*) What, you? You just stay here ...

Firs mumbles his way over the knoll, an overcoat in his arms.

FIRS: Be so kind as to put this on, sir. You'll take a chill.

GAYEV: (*Snatches it from him, puts it on.*) You begin to annoy me, my man.

FIRS: Exactly. Off you go this morning and not a word to me.

(*Inspects him minutely.*)

MME RANEVSKY: You've grown old, Firs.

FIRS: What can I bring you, Madam?

LOPAKHIN: The mistress said you've grown old.

FIRS: It's all the years I've been alive, that's what it is. They were trying to marry *me* off before your father was born. (*Laughs*) And by the time we got our freedom, I was already principal valet. So I refused to take it, the freedom, and stayed with the master and the mistress ... (*Thinks, laughing a little still.*) I remember the celebrations when the freedom came. (*Thinks on.*) Everyone so happy and no one knowing what there was to be glad about.

LOPAKHIN: Ah, those good old days, when you could depend on things ... Getting flogged, for example.

FIRS: (*Deep in himself*) Precisely. The serfs belonged to their masters and the masters owned the serfs. Now it is all so messy and you can't make sense of any of it.

GAYEV: (*A bark.*) Firs!

Firs turns to look at him.

(*Distinctly*) Shut up. (*Pause*) Tomorrow I go to town. I'm told there's a certain general who's prepared to advance me a loan against my signature.

LOPAKHIN: I shouldn't bother. You couldn't raise the interest on the loan you'll need ...

MME RANEVSKY: He's daydreaming. There is no general.

Anya and Varya arrive, arm in arm.

GAYEV: Ah, the children.

ANYA: (*To Varya.*) There's mother.

Trofimov has followed them on, some paces behind.

MME RANEVSKY: Come, come my darlings. (*She kisses each in turn.*) I love you both very much. Here – (*she pats the bench*) – sit here beside me.

They join her on the bench.

LOPAKHIN: (*Sees Trofimov.*) Aha. The 'everlasting undergraduate' is never very far from the ladies.

TROFIMOV: So? What's that to you?

LOPAKHIN: Fifty next birthday and still no degree.

TROFIMOV: You have the wit of a polar bear, Lopakhin.

LOPAKHIN: Easy, boy, easy. Just joking.

TROFIMOV: So don't. All right?

LOPAKHIN: (*Laughs*) One question, then, and I'll leave you alone. (*Trofimov doesn't dissent.*) What do you think of me?

Small silence. The others watch.

TROFIMOV: (*Finally*) Well, I think of you this way, Alex: you're rich already and nothing will stop you getting richer; in the larger perspective, based upon the scientific laws of nature, I'd say you were 'necessary' in exactly the way that a wild animal that must eat its prey is necessary.

Laughter, though not too much from Lopakhin.

VARYA: You're better on astral bodies, Peter.

MME RANEVSKY: No, I want to go on with yesterday's subject.

TROFIMOV: What was that?

GAYEV: Pride, wasn't it?

TROFIMOV: We talked about many things and agreed on none of them. (*Settling himself.*) All right. You people talk about 'the proud man' as though the concept were in some way importantly mystical. It's possible you're right, for yourselves anyway. Yet if we choose to look at it in basic terms and avoid sophisticated complications, we *have* to ask: what has man to be proud *about*? When most men on earth are physically underdeveloped, intellectually retarded and emotionally profoundly miserable, what right have we to be proud? It's time we stopped praising our species and got down to work. There's nothing else.

GAYEV: Does it matter what we do? We all die in the end.

TROFIMOV: Do we? What does it mean: to die? Suppose man to have … a hundred senses and five of them – the five we know – are lost to us in death, while the rest live on …

MME RANEVSKY: What a clever thought, Peter.

LOPAKHIN: (*Ironic*) Brilliant, Peter.

TROFIMOV: Man *can* make progress, struggle for perfection. There *is* a discernible future in which we'll find solutions to the problems that confront us now; but we'll achieve it only through unremitting struggle, by working with all our strength to help those who are even now seeking the answers. Here, now, in Russia, very few are embarked on that course. The greater part of the intelligentsia seek nothing, do nothing and appear congenitally incapable of work of any kind. They bask in the term 'intelligentsia' and treat their servants like an inferior species and peasants like beasts of burden. Their scholarship is banal, their level of culture nil, their grasp of science non-existent and their feeling for art trivial and irrelevant. Of course, they can look as grave as anyone and talk about important matters and make metaphysical speculations

with the best, while all around them, right beneath their eyes, the workers eat
scraps of rancid meat and sleep on bare boards thirty or forty to a room.
Bedbugs, shit, leaking roofs, moral degradation. And then it becomes obvious
that all our 'philosophical' salon chat has only one purpose: namely, to distract
ourselves *and everyone else* in society from the real issues. What happened to
all those crèches we talked about so far into the night, year after year, those
libraries, those workers' housing schemes? You'll find them in novels; they
don't actually exist. What we have achieved is widespread misery, bourgeois
vulgarity and moral barbarism. (*Pause*) I fear those 'grave' faces we pull, these
'earnest' discussions we endlessly embark on. Fear them and despise them.
We'd do better to hold our tongues.

*Silence. Trofimov walks away towards the knoll, the anger still working. Lopakhin
follows him a few paces, looks back at the seated group.*

LOPAKHIN: (*Quietly*) I speak only for myself. I'm up before five every day and I
work from morning to night. I handle a good deal of money, my own and
others', so I get a chance to meet people and see what they're like. Only
through working can one appreciate how few honest and honourable people
there are. (*Pause, as he searches.*) There are nights I lie awake, trying to make
sense of it all; and I think ... God, you have given us endless forests, endless
fields, endless horizons ... why are we not giants, in such a place as this ... ?

MME RANEVSKY: Giants? (*Long pause.*) Giants are for fairy tales. In life they're
always terrifying.

Epikhodov crosses the skyline, strumming a sad tune.

MME RANEVSKY: Epikhodov ...

ANYA: Epikhodov ...

GAYEV: Exit the sun, my friends.

TROFIMOV: Exit the sun.

GAYEV: (*Quiet, as though reciting.*) Nature, so glorious, burning with undying
fires, so fair and yet so unfeeling, you, whom we call mother, fusing in your
core both life and death, making gifts of both indifferently ...

VARYA: Uncle!

ANYA: Not again, Uncle, please ...

TROFIMOV: (*Gently*) Try the red into the middle.

GAYEV: I'm quiet. (*Fingers to lips.*) Nothing.

*They sit or stand in silence, save for Firs' muttering. Suddenly a sound is heard,
far off, yet fractionally closer than before (Act I). The sound of a string snapping
and dying away.*

MME RANEVSKY: What was it?

LOPAKHIN: I don't know. It sounded like a cable snapping in a mineshaft a long way away.

GAYEV: Perhaps it was a bird. It could've been a heron.

TROFIMOV: Or an owl.

MME RANEVSKY: (*Trembles a little.*) Something ... unpleasant ...

Silence.

FIRS: It's happened before. Just before the misfortune. An owl hooted. (*Pause*) And the samovar coughed.

GAYEV: Before what misfortune?

FIRS: Before they set us free.

Silence.

MME RANEVSKY: (*Standing*) We should go, my friends. It's almost night. (*To Anya.*) You're crying ... what is it, my love? (*Draws Anya to her.*)

ANYA: Nothing. It's nothing.

TROFIMOV: We have company.

*A **man** appears, youngish, in a battered military hat and greatcoat. He weaves a little on his approach. The group defines itself against him.*

MAN: Would you know if there's a way through to the station from here?

GAYEV: There is indeed. That road there.

MAN: Greatly beholden ...(*Begins to cough, at first almost comically, but it uglily persists.*) Handsome weather ... handsome. (*Half shouts.*) Brothers, starving and suffering comrades, unite now by the river, let them hear your misery ... (*To Varya, very suddenly.*) Mamselle, a starving Russian asks you for thirty kopeks ...

Varya yelps, frightened, pulls away from him.

LOPAKHIN: (*Stepping forward, angry.*) You'd do better learning a few manners ...

The man gives no ground. Lopakhin advances no further.

MME RANEVSKY: You. (*The man looks at her.*) Here, take this.

She has her purse open, fiddles for a coin.

I have no silver ... here, here's a gold one.

The man takes it carefully, studies it and then the group.

MAN: (*Bows, ironically.*) Greatly beholden, I'm sure.

He leaves in a long, winding movement, laughing to himself. They watch him off; a small laugh spreading and growing among them when he's finally gone.

VARYA: (*Still trembling.*) I'm going back. Oh Mother, how could you, what am I to feed the servants with ... ?

MME RANEVSKY: (*The irony harshening, as the wine sours.*) There's nothing to be done with a fool like me, eh? I'll give you everything I have when we get back. Lopakhin: let me have some more money please.

LOPAKHIN: A pleasure.

MME RANEVSKY: Come along, it's time we went. (*They gather themselves around her to depart.*) Oh by the way, Varya, we've just been arranging your wedding! My warmest congratulations.

VARYA: (*Hurt, low voice.*) It's sad you find that so ... amusing, Mama ...

LOPAKHIN: Euphemia, get thee to a monastery.

GAYEV: See my hands ... itching for the cue.

LOPAKHIN: (*In Varya's ear.*) Euphemia, sprite, remember me in your horizons.

MME RANEVSKY: We must go. It's almost time for dinner ...

VARYA: What a dreadful man. My heart's still pounding.

They leave en bloc, with no particular haste. Lopakhin strides after them, calling after them as he goes, leaving Anya and Trofimov together.

LOPAKHIN: I trust nobody needs reminding that orchard and estate come under the auctioneer's hammer in two weeks' time ... Two weeks, friends. Try to think of it a little, while you dine ...

He leaves.

Anya has followed the group a little before turning back to Trofimov. She watches him as he crosses to the bench, sits on its back, his feet on the seat, staring out. She laughs. He looks at her briefly.

ANYA: It was good of our travelling friend to scare dear Varya. (*Pause*) It means we can be alone.

TROFIMOV: Varya's scared by most things. For days on end she's trailed us, scared we're going to suddenly fall in love. She can't get it into her narrow bourgeois head that we've no use for it, this 'falling in love'. (*He stands on the bench, strides in a little, an orator of sorts.*) We have one goal and one meaning for our lives: to throw off the shackles of the metaphysical and the second-hand and everything else that makes us unfree and unhappy. Forward, mes amis, meine Kameraden. We're on the march towards the brightest star in all history ... (*He stops, smiles a little at Anya's rapt, silvered face below him.*) ... the one over there, see it? (*She nods vigorously.*)
So forward! No faltering now.

He laughs, exhilarated. Anya claps her hands, part of his vast audience.

ANYA: Bravo, Monsieur! I love your words, I love them.

He gets down from the bench, approaches her, stares at her a long moment. She hesitates, perhaps not knowing what will happen.

Isn't it ... wonderful here ... today ... ?

TROFIMOV: (*Dry, still staring at her face.*) Yes. Perfect weather.

ANYA: You've done something to me, Peter. (*His face gestures the question.*) Something. (*She detaches, walks behind the bench, turns to look at him.*) Why do I … care less about the cherry orchard than I used to? I loved it once like a … like a person, family, there was nothing dearer in the world than our orchard.

TROFIMOV: Because. Our orchard is all of Russia. Mmm? This vast, amazing continent, think of all the fine places there are in it. (*Pause*) And think of something else, Anya: your father's father, and his father, and his, were owners of serfs. They owned human lives, Anya. From every tree in your orchard there are people hanging, they peer at you through the branches, you can hear their voices moaning in the leaves … Owning other human beings is what has destroyed your line – those who came before, those who live on – so that your mother, your uncle, you yourself still can't quite grasp that you're living and always have lived off the sweat and labour of someone else, off those same people you wouldn't allow across your back doorstep. Don't you see, Anya, we're still living two hundred years back somewhere, we haven't understood our own history. Instead, we gravely talk, bewail our boredom and drink ourselves stupid. (*Pause*) When we can expiate the past, redeem our history, we can put a match to it for good and begin living in the present. But we can redeem ourselves only by struggle, only by hard and attritional effort. It's this you must understand, little one.

ANYA: (*Low, intense.*) I shall leave that house – it has never been ours – I give you my word.

TROFIMOV: Throw the keys in the well and go, free as air.

ANYA: Free as air. Yes.

TROFIMOV: And here's my word, Anya. Being a student and still relatively young hasn't protected me from hard times. Come winter, I'm forced to scrounge for food, I fall ill and I'm never sure I'll see another spring. And life drives me before it as it does the really poor, the truly oppressed. And yet – you have my word for it, Anya – there is not a moment passes that my spirit does not teem with the marvellous possibilities of this species. There is … such joy to come, Anya: I can see it.

Silence.

ANYA: (*Finally*) See, Peter. The moon.

Epikhodov's guitar can be heard, slow, sad. The moon has risen. Varya calls, 'Anya. Anya,' *somewhere else.*

TROFIMOV: (*Softly*) Varya. Will she never stop!

ANYA: (*Gently*) It doesn't matter. Let's go to the river. It'll be good there.

TROFIMOV: Yes.

They leave. Varya calls on, on tape, in Russian: «Аня! Аня!»

ACT THREE

Black.

A double bass bows a slow, menacing rhythm; in time, a flute lays down a funereal melody; a violin eventually joins it with harmony.

Half lights up on the ballroom, seen through an arch and through thick, semi-transparent gauze drapes that constitute the dividing wall, on each side of it, between ballroom and drawing-room.

Five men and five women, variously masked, stand in a line facing out, men left, women right. Pischik's voice is heard on tape: 'Promenade à une paire.' The men select their partners, the remaining violins augment the funereal 'rond' and a slow circular promenade begins.

Pischik, one of the dancers, calls: 'Grand rond, balancez.' Ballroom and drawing-room lights to full; the dance picks up.

Pischik and Charlotte, the leading pair, draw the dance down the two steps beneath the chandeliered archway and into the drawing-room (where furniture has been relocated around a dancing circle in the centre). Trofimov and Ranevsky, Anya and the post office clerk, Varya and the stationmaster follow. As they clear the ballroom, we see the five-man Jewish band, bearded to a man, on the ballroom's far wall. Dunyasha and her partner bring up the rear. As Pischik leads the pairs back into the ballroom, Firs enters the drawing-room from the hall. He wears a tail coat and carries a tray of mineral water. Pischik calls, 'Les cavaliers à genoux et remerciez vos dames,' to signal the end of the rond; the men kneel and kiss the women's gloves. Firs places the tray on a table, begins his slow rattle off again. Pischik and Trofimov, pushing masks on to foreheads, come down into the drawing-room, as the others break into talking groups beyond.

PISCHIK: Too much blood, that's my trouble. Had a couple of strokes already, makes dancing hard for me, but you know what they say, if you run with the pack you've got to waggle your tail whether you've teeth left or not. Actually, I've got the strength of a horse. My dear departed father always claimed the Pischiks were direct descendants of the very horse the Emperor Caligula installed in the Roman Senate – father always loved a joke, God bless him. (*He sits on a deep chair.*) Trouble is, I've no money. And a hungry horse can only think of feed (*Settles a little, eyes closed, snores; snorts awake.*) Me too: only with me it's money …

TROFIMOV: (*Studying him; ironic.*) You know, Simon, there is something of the horse about you …

People are playing billiards in the billiard room to the right; Varya appears on the steps beneath the connecting arch.

TROFIMOV: (*Seeing her; teasing.*) Ah, it's Madame Lopakhin.

VARYA: (*Steely*) Ah, the gentleman gone to seed.

TROFIMOV: (*Bowing*) Gone to seed and proud of it, Ma'am.

VARYA: (*Leaving; bitter.*) Now we have an orchestra ... Pity nobody thought about paying for it ...

TROFIMOV: (*To Pischik.*) You know, if all the energy we directed towards 'finding the money' and 'paying for it' had been put to some other end, we could have ... re-made the universe by now.

PISCHIK: Do you know Nietzsche says – the philosopher, you know, great man, very famous, first-class intellect – he says ... somewhere ... one has the right to forge banknotes?

TROFIMOV: You've read Nietzsche then?

PISCHIK: No, not exactly. Dashenka told me... about it. But at the moment I'm in such a mess I might be forced to follow his advice, I can tell you. I've got to find three hundred and ten roubles for the day after tomorrow, and so far I've managed a mere hundred and thirty ... (*Pats his pocket, to indicate them; feels nothing.*) Oh my God, I've lost it, it's not there, I've lost the money. (*Hands feverish around other pockets.*) Sweet Jesus, where's the money ... (*Shout of relief, as he locates it.*) Aaah! It's here! Inside the lining! Look at me, I'm sweating. Oh.

Mme Ranevsky and Charlotte come in, Mme Ranevsky singing a rough, spry Caucasian dance tune (Legzinka).

MME RANEVSKY: What's keeping Leon? What's he doing in town anyway? (*To Dunyasha, mooning by.*) Tea for the musicians, Dunyasha. Tea.

TROFIMOV: It's possible the auction didn't even get off the ground.

MME RANEVSKY: It's all so ... inappropriate. Hiring musicians. Giving a ball. Ah well ...

She sits, rather heavily; tired; hums the legzinka a moment, but as fragments, slow tempo, lifelessly.

Charlotte still masked; top hat, checked trousers; gives Pischik a pack of cards.

CHARLOTTE: Here. Now think of a card.

PISCHIK: Done. (*Thinks*) I've thought.

CHARLOTTE: Right, shuffle. Sehr gut. Now ... hand it to me, sweet Pischik. Ein, zwei, drei. And ... look in your side pocket there ...

PISCHIK: (*Producing it.*) Well I'm damned, the eight of spades! Just imagine!

CHARLOTTE: (*Palming deck; to Trofimov.*) Top card, name it. Quick!

TROFIMOV: Erm ...Queen of Spades.

CHARLOTTE: (*Showing it, casual*) Parfait! (*To Pischik.*) And you. Go!

PISCHIK: Ace of Hearts.

CHARLOTTE: (*Showing it.*) Just so! (*Claps hands, cards disappear.*) Beautiful weather we're having. (*A mysterious feminine voice from under the floor boards*) 'Yes indeed, beautiful, Madame.' You're a very charming beau, you know. (*Voice*) 'And I have the highest regard for you, Madame.'

STATIONMASTER: (*Who's approached through the arch during the performance.*) Bravo, Madame ventriloquist!

PISCHIK: Never saw anything like it! Mamselle Charlotte, you're ravishing. I could eat you ...

CHARLOTTE: Really? You wouldn't know where to begin. 'A good enough man, but a lousy musician.'

TROFIMOV: Never mind, old horse.

CHARLOTTE: Attention, please. One more.

She whisks a knee rug from a chair. People filter down from the ballroom to watch.

This very fine rug for sale, what am I offered now, who'll start the bidding?

PISCHIK: Did you ever see anything like it!

CHARLOTTE: Ein, zwei, drei!

Whips the rug away, to reveal Anya standing behind it. Anya curtseys, runs to her mother, kisses her, retires to the ballroom to applause.

MME RANEVSKY: Bravo, bravo.

CHARLOTTE: One more. Ein, zwei, drei.

Varya appears, bows.

PISCHIK: She's done it again, the little devil!

CHARLOTTE: Fin! C'est tout!

She flings the rug over Pischik, curtseys, runs into the ballroom. Pischik gallomphs after her, struggling with the rug, lusting visibly.

PISCHIK: (*Leaving*) What about that then, eh? The little vixen, let me at her ...

People filter off, leaving Mme Ranevsky, Varya and Trofimov in the drawing-room. Mme Ranevsky looks at Varya, who shakes her head: no word.

MME RANEVSKY: Still no sign of Leon. I can't imagine what he's found to do in town that could keep him so long. Either the estate's been sold or it hasn't – why keep us in ignorance?

VARYA: Uncle will have bought it, I'm sure of it.

TROFIMOV: Oh, of course.

VARYA: (*Sparking a little at his sarcasm.*) Great aunt has authorised uncle to buy it in her name and transfer the debt. She's doing it for Anya. And I'm sure God would not have it otherwise – uncle will have bought it.

MME RANEVSKY: (*Cutting across the rhetoric.*) Our good great aunt in Yaroslavl has sent fifteen thousand roubles – not even enough to cover the interest, let alone purchase the estate, in her or anyone else's name … (*Covers face with hands. Uncovers it.*) It's my life they're handling down there. My life.

TROFIMOV: (*Whisper*) Madame Lopakhin.

VARYA: (*Angry whisper.*) Everlasting undergraduate. Who ever heard of being expelled *twice*!

MME RANEVSKY: Varya! Stop spitting, girl. So he teases you about Lopakhin, why should it matter? If you like Lopakhin, marry him and be done with it. He's a decent man, not without … interest. If you don't want to, don't. Nobody's forcing you, child.

VARYA: I know that, Mother. It's just not something I can … joke about. (*Pause*) He *is* a good man … and I do have … feelings for him …

MME RANEVSKY: So marry him. I don't understand what you're waiting for.

VARYA: Mother, I can't do it on my *own*, can I? For two years it's been in the air, everybody's talked about it. But he says nothing. Or jokes. And I can see why. He's busy … building, getting rich: there's no time for me. (*Pause*) If I had any money at all, a … hundred roubles would do, I'd leave it all, everything and everyone, I'd find a convent at the other end of the country …

TROFIMOV: Ah, and such peace you'd find there!

VARYA: Our undergraduate must have his wit, mustn't he. (*Soft, regret and pity staining the voice.*) You've grown so ... ugly, Peter. So old. (*Gathering; to Mme Ranevsky.*) I need to be *working*, Mother. I need to be doing things …

Yasha comes in, poorly suppressing a giggling fit.

YASHA: (*Affecting solemnity at last, as though announcing a guest.*) Epikhodov has broken a billiard cue.

He leaves.

VARYA: (*Huge frustration.*) Why is Epikhodov even *here*? And who gave him per*miss*ion to play billiards? I don't understand these … people …

She leaves.

MME RANEVSKY: (*Gently*) Don't tease her, Peter. She's unhappy enough as it is, without that.

TROFIMOV: (*Roaming a little.*) She's so officious, Liuba. She … interferes in everything. She's plagued Anya and me all summer long, looking to nip some hypothetical romance in the bud. (*Pause*) It's none of her business. (*Pause*) Besides which, it's bloody insulting; I'm above that sort of crass sentimentalism … we're both above it, as a matter of fact.

MME RANEVSKY: (*Standing*) Meaning I'm below it, I suppose.

(*He begins to protest her interpretation, she gestures him not to.*)

Where's Leon! All I want to know is: have I been sold or not? I suppose all ...
disasters are incomprehensible; I don't know what to think, I seem ... lost
somehow. I feel like screaming or something even more banal and stupid.
(*Turning to Trofimov.*) Help me. Say something. Please.

*She's distraught, under the effort of control. Trofimov takes her by the arm,
restores her to her chair, squats beside her.*

TROFIMOV: (*Distinctly*) Liuba. It doesn't matter. Sold or not sold, it has no
meaning now. That's all in the past; finished with long ago. The fields have
reclaimed the thin road you travelled. Be easy now. Eschew ... self-deceptions.
For perhaps the first time in your life, you're allowed to stare truth frankly in
the face.

MME RANEVSKY: Truth? What's that? Perhaps you can see it, your eyes are young.
I look and I see nothing. Such confidence you have, Peter – is there a problem
in the world you can't solve? But think about it: isn't it only that none of the
problems you solve has ever really touched you; hurt you. When you look so
... bravely to the future, isn't it only that you haven't had the experience to
make you fearful. You're braver, deeper, honester than any of us, but you lack
... generosity, you lack consideration. Just think a little more about *us*, Peter,
just a little, mm? I was born here, and my father, and his father before him. I
love it, this place, house, orchard; without them, there's no meaning to my life.
I'd sooner be sold with them than left without them.

She takes Trofimov's head in her hands, kisses him on the forehead.

It's where my son was drowned. Here. Give me *some* pity, dear, loving friend.

TROFIMOV: I sympathise deeply, you know that.

MME RANEVSKY: (*Pushing him away rather violently.*) Then why can't you say it
differently? Differently! (*She rips a handkerchief from her pocket; a telegram
falls to the floor.*) Do you have any idea how things like this ... drag one
down? Like millstones. (*Noisy laughter erupts in the ballroom.*) Listen to them
... They make noise and know nothing and every sound they make puts a drill
to my soul. Look, see me trembling ... but I can't go to my room. Because the
silence frightens me more. (*Pause. She holds her hand out for his, draws him
back to the chair.*) So don't judge me, Peter, you're like a son to me. Marry
Anya if you will, you have my blessing, only you must get down to your
studies and graduate. What do you actually do, eh? Nothing. Life drives you
along like the rest of us – (*stroking his hair now*) – isn't that odd, mm? N'est-
ce pas, cheri? (*Laughs*) And you'll just have to do something with this beard,
it's so piffling. What a funny boy you are.

TROFIMOV: (*Picking up the telegram; nettled.*) I have no wish to be a beau, Mme
Ranevsky.

MME RANEVSKY: It's from Paris. They come every day. That ... farouche man is ill again, he's 'up against it' again ... He wants me to forgive him and ... go back to Paris. And I think I should go and be with him for a time. Don't frown, Peter, what else can I do, darling, what else is there? He's on his own; sick; miserable; who'll look after him, keep him sane, wash his face and hands and give him his pills if I don't? I love him. (*Pause. She watches him.*) Without shame, without fear: *love* him. Isn't it obvious? He's like a great stone round my neck and it'll drag me to the bottom with him ... but it's a stone I love and can't live without. (*Trofimov goes to say something.*) Don't *judge* me, Peter, all right? Don't say anything. Don't talk at all.

TROFIMOV: (*Upset; angry at his overt emotion.*) By God, I will though, and you'll have to forgive my candour, but that ... man has ... robbed you, over and over ...

MME RANEVSKY: (*Covering her ears.*) ... That's enough. I'll hear no more of that talk ...

TROFIMOV: ... That man is a pig and everyone knows it save you. A scrounger, a grubby nothing ...

MME RANEVSKY: ... Peter, you're twenty-seven years of age, for God's sake *act* it ...

TROFIMOV: ... What's my age got to do with it?

MME RANEVSKY: ... Because you're not a *man*, that's why. (*Long pause. They stare at each other. Trofimov is white with anger and perhaps a little fear.*) A man ... should be capable of understanding ... love. A man ... needs it. Not to love *isn't* purity, it's weakness, it's fear, it's prudish, ridiculous and ... abnormal.

TROFIMOV: What are you saying?

MME RANEVSKY: 'I am above love.' You're not above it, Peter, you're just not up to it. Why else would you be without a mistress, at twenty-seven?

TROFIMOV: Are you really saying this? To me? (*Turns quickly towards the hall.*) Excuse me, will you ...

MME RANEVSKY: Peter ...

TROFIMOV: ... No no, I'd prefer not to hear the rest, if you don't mind.

MME RANEVSKY: Peter, wait ...

Trofimov leaves, returns almost at once.

(*Pleading, a little desperate.*) Peter, I was joking ... It was a *joke*, darling.

TROFIMOV: What a pity then our relationship could not have ended on a better one.

He goes out into the hall. Mme Ranevsky stands alone, facing in. We hear someone running quickly upstairs, then a crash as he falls. Anya and Varya shriek; then laughter.

MME RANEVSKY: What is it? What's happened?

Anya enters.

ANYA: Petya's fallen down the stairs. (*Leaves laughing.*)

MME RANEVSKY: So: he had the last laugh after all.

The Stationmaster appears in the centre of the ballroom, framed by the arch, and begins to clear his throat. Dancers gather. Presently the orchestra will return to their places. Mme Ranevsky stands alone in the drawing-room facing him. For a moment it seems he's addressing her.

STATIONMASTER: A recitation entitled *The Sinner* by Alexei Tolstoy. The eponymous heroine is one Nadezhda Varkova, a young lady of good family whom fateful circumstance and impulsive desires conspire to turn into a fallen woman of doubtful virtue. *The Sinner.*

> She stands alone in darkened room
> And softly calls his name;
> But no one hears ...

The orchestra strikes up a waltz. A dance begins. The Stationmaster hovers for a moment, then retires with such dignity as he can muster. Anya returns from the hall, drawing a slightly dishevelled Trofimov behind her. Varya brings up the rear.

MME RANEVSKY: Dear dear boy, forgive me, please. Say you will. (*He bows stiffly, kisses her offered hand.*) Come, we'll dance together ...

They move off into the ballroom, followed by Anya and Varya, who dance together.

Firs hobbles into the drawing-room and props his stick against the door. Yasha enters from the billiard room to watch the dancing; notices Firs.

YASHA: How are you, young whippersnapper?

FIRS: Not good. I've seen the day we had generals, admirals, barons dancing, now they send for post office clerks and stationmasters and even they have to be coaxed. I seem to have lost my strength somehow. The old master used to give us sealing wax for everything, whatever it was that ailed us. I've taken sealing wax every day for twenty years or more. I think it's that that's kept me going.

YASHA: Grandad ... you're a bore. (*Yawns*) You're ready for the knacker's yard.

FIRS: (*Deliberately*) Up yours, butterballs.

Trofimov and Mme Ranevsky dance from ballroom to drawing-room.

MME RANEVSKY: Merci, mon beau. Let me rest a moment. I'm tired. (*She sits.*)

Anya in, excited.

ANYA: A man in the kitchen says the orchard's been sold ...

MME RANEVSKY: To whom?

ANYA: He didn't say. He's gone now. (*To Trofimov.*) We should dance!

Anya and Trofimov whirl off into the ballroom. Mme Ranevsky sits very still.

YASHA: Kitchen gossip. Some old man passing the time of day.

FIRS: And Master Leon still not back. He's gone off in the thinnest of top-coats as though it were spring, if he's not careful he'll take a chill. Ach, these green young men!

MME RANEVSKY: I can't breathe. Yasha, find out who bought it.

YASHA: The old man left hours ago. (*He laughs suddenly.*)

MME RANEVSKY: You think it funny? It pleases you, all this, does it?

YASHA: It's that Epikhodov ... he's such a clown. Million miseries, they call him.

MME RANEVSKY: What about you, Firs. Where will you go, if the estate's sold?

FIRS: Where you order me, Ma'am.

MME RANEVSKY: Are you unwell? You should go to bed if you're ill.

FIRS: (*Smiles ironically.*) Oh yes. And who'll serve you all and keep things going? There's only me for the whole house ...

YASHA: Madame Liuba, may I ask a favour of you. Should you return to Paris, may I have the honour of going with you? It's quite impossible I should be asked to stay here. (*Dropping voice.*) I'm sure you take my meaning – the lack of culture, the low level of moral refinement ... the boredom ... the food ... and Firs here, stumbling around muttering his nonsense. I beg of you Ma'am: take me with you.

Pischik in, enjoying himself, panting a little.

PISCHIK: Beautiful lady, permit me one tiny waltz, you're irresistible. (*He waltzes her round the room.*) Now, sweetest Madam, could I interest you in a small loan? I find myself temporarily deficient of a trifling one hundred and eighty roubles ...

He waltzes her off into the ballroom.

YASHA: (*Ironic, to himself.*) Ah, what devotion!

In the ballroom Charlotte does cartwheels and forward and reverse handsprings, to cries of, 'Bravo, Charlotte.' Dunyasha, red-faced and swooning with excitement, cascades down the steps into the drawing-room. Firs clucks at her disapprovingly.

DUNYASHA: It's the young mistress, she ordered me to. And there are men galore and hardly any of us and my brain's whirling and my heart's pounding and pounding. (*She sees her red face in the mirror; quickly begins to powder it.*) That clerk, you know; the one from the post office, he whispered things in my ear that almost made me swoon. It's true.

FIRS: Like what ?

DUNYASHA: He said: You're like ... a flower.

YASHA: (*Leaving*) He's probably never seen one.

DUNYASHA: Like a flower ... I have this delicate nature, you see, a delicate phrase can make me quiver with pleasure ...

FIRS: Don't quiver too much, you'll break your stem.

Enter Epikhodov.

EPIKHODOV: At least look at me ... You turn away as though I were an earwig or something. This is no life!

DUNYASHA: You wanted something?

EPIKHODOV: All right, you may not be wrong. Naturally, if you insist on looking at things from your own point of view – if you'll pardon my putting it this way and with such forcefulness – it becomes clear at once that it's you who've brought me to this ... state. I know what my life is like, every day I befall some new misery. I've known it for so long I can even smile at it, once in a while. (*Pause*) But you did give me your word, Dunyasha, in spite of ...

DUNYASHA: ... Do you think we could discuss it later? I'd rather you left me in peace just now. I'm in something of a dream just now, you see. (*She plays with her fan.*)

EPIKHODOV: Every day sees a new horror engulf me and yet, forgive me for saying it, I simply smile at it all. (*Pause*) Sometimes I even laugh ...

Varya in from the ballroom, a relentless broom.

VARYA: (*To Epikhodov.*) Haven't you gone yet? There's not an ounce of respect in your whole body, is there. (*Seeing Dunyasha.*) Out ! (*Dunyasha runs off.*) First you wreck the billiard room, now you're lounging in the drawing-room like one of the guests.

EPIKHODOV: You have no right to reprimand me, let me make that quite clear here and now ...

VARYA: I am *not* reprimanding you, I'm merely telling you that you spend all your time wandering from one room to another and never lifting a finger, that's all. As a rule, clerks are expected to work – why else would one keep one?

EPIKHODOV: Whether I work, walk, stand, sit or play billiards, those who sit in judgement of me will need to be considerably older and more sapient than you, M'mselle ...

VARYA: How dare you speak to me that way. (*Wildly angry.*) You dare to suggest I don't know what I'm talking about? Get out! Go on, get out, now, at once, do you hear?

EPIKHODOV: Please, I beg you, if you could just mollify your language a little ...

VARYA: Out ! Out! Get out this instant! (*He backs away towards the door. She follows him, beside herself.*) You ... million miseries! I don't want to see you in here again, is that understood!

Epikhodov leaves. From behind the door we hear: 'A complaint will be filed in due course on this matter.'

VARYA: Are you going or aren't you? (*She grabs Firs' stick from behind the door, raises it above her head.*) All right, I'm ready for you. What's keeping you? In you come then ...

Lopakhin enters, a bottle of cognac sticking out from the pocket of his fur coat. She brings the stick down, he swerves to avoid it, it catches the side of his head and bounces off his shoulder. They stare at each other.

LOPAKHIN: (*Smiling, puzzled.*) Very kind of you.

VARYA: (*Breathless; far from recovered.*) I'm sorry.

LOPAKHIN: No no. I've had worse welcomes in my time. On the whole, one of the better ones.

VARYA: Please. You'll be thanking me next. (*She goes to leave, placing stick by door; turns back into the room.*) Did I hurt you?

LOPAKHIN: Not at all.

He touches the side of his head, lurches a little, grips the back of a chair to steady himself. Varya lets out the tiniest of shrieks. Lopakhin straightens, grinning broadly at her, pleased with himself. She smiles back, tentative, uncertain, liking and fearing it.

People swell into the ballroom. Lopakhin's name buzzes around the house.

Pischik leads the pack.

PISCHIK: He's here! The man himself. (*He hugs Lopakhin, kisses him heavily on the lips.*) Mmm. Just the slightest hint of cognac on the breath, my dear fellow. Never mind, we've been having fun here too ...

MME RANEVSKY: (*Appearing at last.*) What took you so long, Alex? Where's Leon?

LOPAKHIN: Leon's here. Came back with me ...

MME RANEVSKY: (*Very still; breathless.*) Well then? The auction, what happened? Tell me everything.

LOPAKHIN: (*Embarrassment masking elation.*) The auction finished at four. But we missed the train and had to wait till nine for the next one ... Shaa ... It's made me a little light in the head .

Gayev comes in, weeping steadily, snuffling, carrying parcels.

MME RANEVSKY: Leon. What happened ? ... For God's sake, will someone tell me and hurry up about it!

GAYEV: (*Waving a hand in her direction, handing parcel to Firs.*) Here, take these ... Now that's er ... anchovies and ... herrings in kirsch and er ... I haven't eaten a thing all day ... That's it ... What I've endured today ...

From the billiard room, distinctly, the click of balls and Yasha calling a break: 'Eighteen and seven make twenty-five.' *Gayev grows calm as he listens.*

  I'm tired. (*Pause. A deep vacancy has settled on him.*) Help me, Firs, will you
  ...

Gayev leaves through the ballroom, Firs in his wake.

PISCHIK: (*To Lopakhin.*) So tell us what happened at the auction, man.

Lopakhin says nothing, his hand on the neck of the bottle.

MME RANEVSKY: Is it sold ?

LOPAKHIN: (*Turning to face her.*) Yes?

MME RANEVSKY: To whom?

LOPAKHIN: (*Simply*) Me.

Mme Ranevsky steadies herself against a table, stunned. Varya very quietly removes the keys from her belt, throws them into the middle of the room and leaves.

Lopakhin wades through the others until he reaches the steps.

LOPAKHIN: If you'd be so kind, ladies and gentlemen. Thank you. Thank you. (*They part as though for a leper. He stands on the top step, looks down on the group. Mme Ranevsky has sat down on the chair at the table, her face white and still.*) I'm sorry, you'll have to excuse me, my head's still whirling from it all ... (*He begins to laugh, nervous, elated.*) All right then. We get to the auction, Deriganov's already in position. Right off he tops Mr Gayev's fifteen thousand with a straight bid of thirty on top of the arrears. So there it was. I took him on. Forty thousand. He bid forty-five. Fifty-five. He bid sixty. I'm bidding in tens, he's hitting me with fives. Fine. We reach ninety thousand roubles and he's out! Withdraws! I have it! It's mine. The cherry orchard is mine! (*He laughs out loud, takes the bottle from his pocket, sups deep.*) All right, tell me I'm drunk, crazy, imagining every last bit of it ...(*He breaks into a strange stamping peasant dance, his bright boots flashing in the bright room.*) ... but don't laugh too soon, friends ... Don't ever laugh at me again! (*Turns*) Musicians, where are you, let there be music then ... (*They're not to be seen. Their instruments lie about their chairs. The leader appears, stares at Lopakhin a moment, then retires.*) Where are you, Father, Grandfather, get up from your graves and see me now, the one you kicked and starved and sent around half-naked in the snow ... It's *me* ...the man himself ... and I've just bought this estate and you won't find a finer one anywhere in the world! I've bought the estate you were both serfs on, where you weren't even allowed inside the kitchen. Do you hear me? Eh? Ha! You think I'm imagining it, dreaming it ... oh these ignorant yearnings ... is that it ? (*He strides down into the drawing-room, collects the keys from the floor.*) She threw away the keys, to show her reign is ended ... (*The orchestra returns, begins tuning up.*) ... Hey, musicians, let's have some music, I want to hear you ... a legzinka for the people ... who have come to see how the dull and lowly Lopakhin will take his axe to the cherry orchard and send the trees whistling to the ground! And … summer cottages we'll build in their stead and our children's children's children will hear the distant music of a new life blossoming about them … Music! There must be music!

The orchestra begins the spry legzinka. The room empties around Lopakhin, who seems wholly unaware of it. Pischik remains; and Mme Ranevsky, whose head rests on her steepled hands. She makes no sound, no movement. Lopakhin sees her finally, focuses frowningly. Approaches her, at a loss now for the words.

LOPAKHIN: Why? Why? Why? (*Pause*) Why didn't you hear me? (*Pause*) There's no way back, friend. (*Pause. Moved by her stillness.*) Why do I have to be the cause of your pain? Why can't we somehow … rebuild these awkward, crumbling lives …?

PISCHIK: (*Softly, his arm in Lopakhin's.*) Ssh now. Let's leave her to her sadness … Come. (*Leads him gently to the ballroom.*)

Lopakhin snaps from his daze in the centre of the ballroom. Notices that the music has tailed away.

LOPAKHIN: What's this then? I said music. Play. If I *want* music, let there *be* music. (*They strike up again. Ironic.*) This is the new master speaking, the owner of the cherry orchard. (*He lumbers against a small table, knocks a lit candelabra to the floor. Pischik stamps it carefully out.*) Leave it! I can pay!

He leaves with Pischik.

Mme Ranevsky sits alone in the drawing-room. The musicians play some moments longer, watching the doorway rather nervously, stop finally, case their instruments and leave. Mme Ranevsky begins to weep now, very softly, undistractedly. Anya and Trofimov enter quickly. Anya kneels at her mother's feet. Trofimov stays inside the archway.

ANYA: Mother Mother Mother don't good gentle precious Mother I love you let me bless you here here don't don't cry please it's gone now it's sold all right but you're alive good and pure and whole with a life to live come come with me come we'll go away from here grow new things better finer than these and then you'll see how right all this has been and fulfilment will smile on your skin like evening sunlight and you'll breathe again Mother I promise I promise.

Mme Ranevsky has stopped weeping. Stares now into Anya's eyes. Trofimov shakes his head slowly, leaves.

TAPE: (*Anya's voice*): «Пойдём, милая! Пойдём!...»

Black.

ACT FOUR

Black.

Tape: (Yasha's voice): «Простóй нарóд порщáться пришёл.»

Lights up, harsh and bright on the bare white nursery. Nothing of furniture or decoration remains save for a huddle of pieces in a corner marked 'sale'. Trunks, bags and bundles mound about the door and the back wall.

Lopakhin stands in the middle of the room, staring at the door, which is open.

Yasha stands by the window, a tray of champagne and glasses in his hands. The glasses are full and flattening.

Odd voices – Varya's, Anya's – flit through the house.

Epikhodov drags a trunk in through the door, a piece of looped rope to tie it with in his hand. He places the loop round his neck to stand on the recalcitrant trunk to close it. Varya in briefly, ignores Lopakhin's wave at the tray, reads the room, stares pointedly at Epikhodov, leaves. Epikhodov frowns, half-attempts a mute explanation, gets down, goes out after her.

A cheer from outside. Gayev's voice grows out of it: 'Thank you, dear people, thank you.'

YASHA: It's the rural idiots come to say good-bye. If you want my opinion, it is that the common folk have big hearts but tiny brains.

Silence. Lopakhin stares on at the door, ignoring him. Mme Ranevsky enters, Gayev following. Mme Ranevsky is pale, on edge.

GAYEV: ... but not the whole purse, Liuba. You can't go on like that, it's too much ...

MME RANEVSKY: ... I couldn't help it, all right. (*Deliberately*) It couldn't be helped ...

She skirts him quickly, leaves. He follows her. Lopakhin has indicated the champagne but been ignored.

LOPAKHIN: (*Following to doorway.*) A glass of champagne? Won't you join me in one farewell glass? Dear friends, I beg of you ... I didn't think to bring any from town and I could find only one bottle at the station ... Still, we could have a glass together ... (*Returning from door.*) It seems I didn't need to buy any ... Fine. I'll abstain with you.

Yasha places the tray down carefully on a chair.

Have a glass yourself, Yasha.

YASHA: (*Toasting*) To those who journey, to those who wave them off. (*Drains glass.*) Not the real thing, I'm afraid. Pity, that.

LOPAKHIN: Eight roubles a bottle anyway. It's bloody cold in here today.

YASHA: No one bothered with stoves today. Not that it matters. Since we're going. (*He laughs.*)

LOPAKHIN: Something funny?

YASHA: Just happy.

LOPAKHIN: Look at it, October, and smooth as summer out here. Building weather. (*Checks watch, calls through open door.*) The train leaves in forty-six minutes precisely, ladies and gentlemen. (*Silence*) So we should leave in ... twenty minutes, I think. (*Silence*) Please ... hurry.

Trofimov enters, in an old battered overcoat, from outside.

TROFIMOV: You know, I think it's time we were off ... the carriage has arrived. God knows where my overshoes have got to – thin air. (*Calling through door.*) Anya, have you seen my overshoes? I can't find them anywhere.

LOPAKHIN: And I'm for Kharkov. I'll take the same train. I'll spend the winter there. I've spent too long sitting around here chattering, I need to be doing. I'm useless, if I'm not working; don't know what to do with my hands – (*flaps them, serious and comic*) – look at them – they just hang, like someone else's ...

TROFIMOV: Well, we'll be gone soon and you'll be able to get back to your valuable labours again ...

LOPAKHIN: (*Indicating glasses.*) Fancy a small one? (*Trofimov shakes his head.*) So, you're off to Moscow then.

TROFIMOV: Ahunh. I'll go as far as town with them. And tomorrow I go to Moscow.

LOPAKHIN: Mmm. No doubt the university's delaying the start of the session till you get there?

TROFIMOV: I can't see why it should concern you.

LOPAKHIN: How many years is it now you've been a student ...?

TROFIMOV: That the best you can do? You've worn it smooth, man. (*Resumes the hunt for his overshoes.*) By the way, it's unlikely we'll meet again; so let me give you a piece of advice by way of farewell: try not waving your arms about – it's a bad habit, arm-waving. And this talk about building summer cottages, all these visionary predictions that their tenants will one day become their owners, that's all a kind of ... arm-waving too.

(*Pause.*)

I say all this because ... when all's said that can be ... I like you. (*Pause*) You have the hands of a painter, slender and full of grace; and a gentle, generous soul ...

LOPAKHIN: (*Embracing him warmly.*) Good-bye, then, little dove. And thank you. (*Looks at him, close up.*) What about money, let me give you some for the journey.

TROFIMOV: What for? I've no need of it.

LOPAKHIN: You haven't a penny.

TROFIMOV: Yes I have. I just got some for a translation. (*Pats his pocket.*) It's here. (*Looks around the room.*) Overshoes are a different matter entirely ...

A pair of rubber overshoes fly across the room, flung from the doorway. Varya's voice follows them. 'Take the filthy things!'

TROFIMOV: Ah, such shy and gentle charms. Mmm. (*Picks up overshoes.*) These aren't mine!

LOPAKHIN: I put out a thousand acres of poppy last spring and I got in a clear forty thousand profit ... that's something to behold, I can tell you, a poppy field in bloom ... Anyway, the point is I made the forty thousand and you're welcome to a loan because I'm flush, you see ... (*Pause*) And there's no point being 'proud' about it. You're dealing with a peasant, son of a peasant ... just that ...

TROFIMOV: ... And you're dealing with the son of a chemist's assistant. Which means nothing either. (*Lopakhin goes for his wallet.*) Leave it, let it be ... You could offer me two hundred thousand and I still wouldn't want it. I'm free of all that. All the things you all cherish and crave after – rich and poor alike – are for me no more than ... flocculence ... shimmering on the air. And because I have the will and ... the pride ... (*he smiles*) ... I can go on without you, transcend you, if you like. Men are on the move, headed for the higher truths, the greater happiness, and I count myself an outrider for the expedition.

LOPAKHIN: Will you get there?

TROFIMOV: Oh yes. (*Pause*) Get there or show others the route.

An axe hits a tree, in the distance.

LOPAKHIN: (*Hand out.*) Take care, little dove. (*Handclasp.*) Time for us to go. (*Pause.*) Seems to me we're both pretty good at striking poses ... but life couldn't give a damn and carries on course regardless. When I've worked myself into the ground for days on end without rest, the pleasure it gives me half-persuades me I know why I'm alive. But Russia is overflowing with people who see no purpose at all to their existence. (*Pause*) But ... maybe that's not the point either. (*Pause*) They say Mr Gayev has taken the position in the bank – six thousand a year, they say. Won't hang on to it, shouldn't wonder; too ... idle ...

ANYA: (*From doorway.*) Mother says will you not let them cut down the orchard until we've gone

TROFIMOV: (*Leaving through hall.*) Tact, Lopakhin. Where's your tact?

LOPAKHIN: Of course, of course. My god, these workmen ...

Follows Trofimov

ANYA: Have they taken Firs to hospital?

YASHA: I left instructions for this morning. I'm sure he's gone.

ANYA: (*To Epikhodov, in doorway.*) Simon Epikhodov. Please make sure Firs has been taken to the hospital …

YASHA: Yegov was told to do it this morning. Why go on about it?

EPIKHODOV: In my definitive opinion, the ancient Firs is beyond medicine and should make ready to join his ancestors. For my part … I can but envy him.

He's placed a suitcase on a hatbox, squashing it flat. Stares at it, nodding several times. Turns to see Dunyasha in doorway, looking at Yasha, who's turned his back on her. Stares up at the heavens, gestures at the crushed hatbox, smiles resignedly at his 'fate', walks dolefully off.

YASHA: … Nine hundred and ninety-nine thousand nine hundred and ninety-nine …

VARYA: (*From the hall.*) Has Firs been taken to the hospital?

ANYA: Yes.

VARYA: Then why is the letter for the doctor still here?

ANYA: I don't know. I'll send someone after them with it …

She leaves.

Dunyasha has busied herself rather fussily with items of baggage. She now approaches Yasha.

DUNYASHA: Yasha. Please look at me. You're going, aren't you … you're deserting me, aren't you …

She tries to put her arms around his neck, but he detaches them with practised ease, a glass of champagne in his hand.

YASHA: No need for tears, girl. In under a week I'll be back home in Paris. Tomorrow we'll join the Pullman and Zzam, we'll shoot across Europe like a bullet. Isn't it incredible. (*He dedahs the Marseillaise.*) This is no place for me, there's no life here, nothing happens here. I'm full up to here of … backwardness and mediocrity. Up to here. (*Another glass disappears.*) For God's sake don't cry, girl. Behave yourself and you'll have no need of tears.

DUNYASHA: Write to me, won't you. From Paris. (*Begins to powder her face.*) You know how I've loved you, Yasha. I've been good to you, Yasha. You know how … soft I am …

YASHA: Shh, someone's coming.

He unlocks a suitcase swiftly, repositions it, begins to lock it again. Mme Ranevsky comes in, with Gayev and Charlotte.

GAYEV: We really ought to be going, Liuba, it's getting late … (*Stares at Yasha.*) Who's smelling of herring in here? …

MME RANEVSKY: …Ten minutes and then we shall leave. (*Surveys the room swiftly.*) Good-bye, house. Old Grandfather. Winter, spring … and you'll be gone too, they'll have pulled you down. (*Reflective, rather cool.*) And you've seen it all, old walls, haven't you? (*Kisses Anya, embraces her.*) Ah, *mon petit trésor*, how brilliantly you glow, you have ... diamonds in your eyes. You're happy, aren't you? Are you?

ANYA: Yes, Mama. It's like being born again.

GAYEV: Absolutely. Everything's as it should be now. How depressed we all were before the orchard went ... what we all endured. But now it's all done with ... irreversible ... everyone's calm and cheerful once again. I hold an office in a bank now, a financier you might say ... Red into the middle ... tla ... and you look so much better too, Liuba, all in all. No doubt about it.

MME RANEVSKY: (*Being helped into her coat and hat.*) Yes, I'm calmer, it's true. And sleeping again at night. Yasha, my things, it's time.

Yasha begins carrying her cases outside.

(*To Anya.*) We'll be together again very soon, my baby. I'll live in Paris for a little while on the money your great-aunt sent us to buy the estate – God bless Yaroslavl – but that won't last forever ...

ANYA: Come back soon. You will, won't you ... I'll work hard and pass all my exams and then I'll be ready to work for you. We'll devour whole libraries together, you and me, won't we ... (*kissing her hand*) ... on autumn evenings; we'll learn new things for this ... new life ...

MME RANEVSKY: I'll be back, golden one.

Charlotte begins crooning. Lopakhin enters.

GAYEV: Charlotte's happy, too. She's singing.

Charlotte picks up a bundle (Trofimov's overshoes wrapped in a cloth), holds it like a swaddled baby.

CHARLOTTE: Bye bye my baby.

The bundle cries twice.

Shh sweet little boy, there there ... (*Further cries.*) ... Yes, it's not fair is it, my darling. (*She drops the bundle without looking at it.*) I shall need a new post. I can't survive without one.

LOPAKHIN: I'll find you something, Charlotte. No need to worry yourself.

GAYEV: So, everyone's abandoning us ... Varya ... suddenly no one wants us any more.

CHARLOTTE: There's nowhere for me in town. I shall have to leave the area. (*Hums*) Ach, I don't really care.

Pischik enters, red, sweating, breathless.

LOPAKHIN: My god, it's the eighth wonder of the world!

PISCHIK: Oooph ... let me get my breath back ... I'm done for ... Dear friends, water, please ...

GAYEV: Water first, then a loan, I suppose. Forgive me, I have to go ... (*Leaves*)

PISCHIK: (*Mopping face and neck, seated on a box.*) Ah, dear lady, so long since I saw you ... (*Sees Lopakhin.*) And you ... glad to see you ... a man of the highest discernment ... Here, this is for you – (*hands money to Lopakhin*) – four hundred roubles. That leaves eight hundred and forty still outstanding ...

Dunyasha brings a glass of water, which he swigs straight off. She pours him another.

LOPAKHIN: (*Stares at the money.*) Am I dreaming this? Where did it come from?

PISCHIK: Please, a moment. (*Swigging*) That's better. Something quite extra-ordinary happened. Some English folk called at my place and discovered some sort of white ... clay on my land ... (*To Mme Ranevsky.*) And four hundred for you, my ... marvellous ... madam ... (*hands her money*) ... the rest later. (*Another glass of water, splashing drops down his neck.*) This fellow I was talking to just now on the train says that some great philosopher or other seriously urges people to jump off roofs. 'Jump off roofs,' he says, 'and your worries are over.' What about that then? More water, please ...

LOPAKHIN: These English ...

PISCHIK: Oh yes. I gave a twenty-four year lease on the land where the clay is. (*Standing, a bunch of currency notes in his fist.*) And now you'll kindly excuse me, I must trot along, got to see Znoikov ... and Kardamonov ... pay my debts, you know. (*Drains glass.*) Good health to all here ... Probably drop round Thursday ...

MME RANEVSKY: We're just about to move into town and tomorrow I'll be *en route* for France.

PISCHIK: Town? (*Long silence. He scans the room, the baggage, the coats.*) Oh yes. The furniture and erm. (*Long pause.*) Luggage. Yes, I see. No matter. (*He weeps very quietly, with no attempt to hide or dissemble it.*) Can't be helped. These ... English, men of the highest discernment, you know. Never mind. Everything you wish yourselves, and God go with you. Nothing lives without it dies. (*Kisses Mme Ranevsky's hand.*) So, when you hear they've put me under, remember the old horse and say, 'I used to know the creature – Pischik, he was called – God be with him!' Isn't this splendid weather? Yes ... (*He goes out, returns at once.*) Dashenka sends regards. (*Leaves*)

MME RANEVSKY: Now we can go. Two things bother me. Firs is sick ... (*Checks watch.*) Perhaps a couple of minutes longer ...

ANYA: Mother, Firs has been driven to the hospital. Yasha saw to it this morning.

MME RANEVSKY: ... And Varya. Rising early and working late is her life; without it she'll be like a fish in sand. She's grown so thin and wan and ... tearful. Poor Varya. (*Pause*) You do know, Alex, that I'd always dreamt of giving her to you ... And all the signs were that you would take her.

She gestures something to Anya, who takes Charlotte by the sleeve and leads her out of the room.

She loves you, you know … and I know you're not … unfond of her … I can't see at all why you both keep … so separate. It doesn't make sense.

Lopakhin stares at her for a long time, carefully suppressing, but at cost. what he most wants to say. Finally:

LOPAKHIN: No, I'm sure you're right. It is … very confusing. (*Pause*) If there's still the time, why not, we could settle it now and get it over with. Once you've … gone, I'll never do it.

MME RANEVSKY: Wonderful idea, it won't take a minute, let me call her …

LOPAKHIN: There's even champagne, to mark the occasion. (*Glances at glasses.*) Or there was. (*Yasha coughs discreetly.*) You could drink it by the bucket, couldn't you?

MME RANEVSKY: (*Excited now.*) It doesn't matter. We'll leave you alone. Yasha, *allez!* (*Yasha leaves quickly on the sharp command. Calling*) Varya, come here, will you … (*Varya calls something.*) … No, leave that and come in here. Quickly girl.

She goes out into the hall. Lopakhin looks at his watch, then carefully turns each glass upside down in turn, to check their dryness. Some whispering in the hall. Varya arrives finally, begins at once to check the luggage against a list in her hand. Silence. Then:

VARYA: That's odd, I just can't seem to (see it …).

LOPAKHIN: What's that?

VARYA: … I packed it this morning, where is it? …

Silence.

LOPAKHIN: Where do you go now, Varya?

VARYA: What? Oh, to the Rogulins. I said I'd go and look after things there. A sort of housekeeper, I suppose.

LOPAKHIN: That's er … that's Yashnyevo, isn't it?

VARYA: Mmmm.

LOPAKHIN: What's that, fifty miles? (*Long pause.*) So. It's all over, here.

VARYA: (*Searching again.*) … It's here somewhere … Unless I put it with the trunk ... (*To Lopakhin.*) Yes, that's right. There's nothing else now …

LOPAKHIN: And I'm away to Kharkov directly … I catch the next train. (*Rubs his finger on a glass edge.*) There's plenty to do there. I'll leave Epikhodov here … I've taken him on, you know.

VARYA: (*Disdain beneath the cool neutral tone.*) Have you.

LOPAKHIN: This time last year we'd had snow … Remember? Just look at that sun. (*Pause*) Still, it's cold enough. Frost on the grass there ...

VARYA: Is there? I haven't looked. (*Pause*) Our thermometer's broken, as it happens ...

Silence. They stare at each other briefly, then look away. Someone calls, 'Mr Lopakhin, Mr Lopakhin,' from outside the house.

LOPAKHIN: (*Nods slowly, calls.*) Yes. I'm here.

He leaves, quite quickly, but with no sense of scurry. Varya sits down very slowly on a bundle in the corner of the room. Stares out into space, seeing nothing, her hands on her breasts, the fingers almost touching the wooden cross between them.

Mme Ranevsky enters quietly, searches for her, sees her.

MME RANEVSKY: Well? (*Pause. Varya doesn't move.*) We have to go.

VARYA: (*Getting up.*) Yes, I know. (*Straightening her belt and hair.*) I should make the Rogulins this evening, if I don't miss the train ...

MME RANEVSKY: (*Calling through the doorway.*) Anya, put your things on.

Anya in, with Gayev and Charlotte, ready for off. Gayev wears a thick topcoat with a hood. Servants and Coachmen crowd the room. Epikhodov sputters around the luggage.

MME RANEVSKY: Good. (*Drily*) Let the journey commence!

ANYA: Ready, ready ...

GAYEV: My friends, dear, loving friends. Now, on the brink of departing this house forever, no one will insist that I keep silent ... For how can I not express to you all, as I bid you farewell, the emotions that swell up in my heart (and swamp me with their) ...

ANYA: Uncle!

VARYA: (*Quiet*) No, Uncle. Please.

GAYEV: (*At once.*) Double the red into the middle. (*Finger to lip.*) See, shh, nothing.

Enter Trofimov, then Lopakhin.

TROFIMOV: All aboard, ladies and gentlemen, time to go.

LOPAKHIN: Epikhodov – coat !

Movement begins. It lacks order, eddies and dribbles, here and there.

MME RANEVSKY: Give me one minute. One minute.

She stands in the centre of the room. Takes it in.

I feel as if I'm seeing this room, this house, for the first time. Those walls, this ceiling ... all new ... I'm suddenly filled with a terrible ... greed for them ...

GAYEV: (*Very clearly.*) I remember when I was six years old I sat at that window one Feast Day and watched my father striding off to church ...

MME RANEVSKY: (*Surveying floor, now cleared of luggage.*) Is that it then ?

LOPAKHIN: Yes. I think so. (*To Epikhodov.*) You're in charge while I'm gone, all right?

EPIKHODOV: (*Croaking*) It's in good hands, never fear.

LOPAKHIN: What're you whispering for?

EPIKHODOV: I drank some water a moment ago. I must've swallowed something.

YASHA: What a clown!

MME RANEVSKY: You'll leave it empty, then?

LOPAKHIN: Till the spring.

Varya pulls an umbrella from a bundle of clothes, appears menacing for a moment. Lopakhin feigns a tactical retreat.

VARYA: (*Very quiet, contained.*) There's no need for that ... You won't get hurt.

TROFIMOV: Let's go then. Into the carriage now or we miss the train.

VARYA: (*Seeing his overshoes in Charlotte's doll.*) Peter, your overshoes ...(*She picks them up, hands them to him.*) Look at them, they're falling apart ...

TROFIMOV: (*Putting them on.*) Last call for the carriage!

GAYEV: (*Suddenly distressed and disorientated.*) The train, the station ... spot into the middle, double the white into the bottom, click, chuck ...

MME RANEVSKY: We're going

LOPAKHIN: All out? No one left behind? (*Locks a door.*) I've stored some things in there, best to keep it locked. Right.

ANYA: (*Cheerful*) 'Bye, old house. 'Bye old life.

TROFIMOV: And a big ... hell ... o ... o – (*he throws the echo round the house*) – to tomorrow.

They leave together. Varya glances at the room and leaves. Yasha and Charlotte and her dog follow.

LOPAKHIN: (*To Gayev*) Till spring then. (*To Mme Ranevsky.*) Au ... revoir? ... Is that how you say it?

He leaves.

Gayev and Mme Ranevsky stand in the room alone. Gayev walks to her side, puts his hand in hers, as a child might. They stand very still, side by side, looking out. Sounds of hooves on gravel, snuffles, wheels rocking, from outside, some calling.

ANYA: (*Voice off, calling, happy.*) Mother! Trofimov (*Voice off, some echo.*) Hello ... o ... o ...

GAYEV: Sister ...

ANYA: (*Voice off, calling*) Mother!

TROFIMOV: (*Voice off, echoing it.*) Tomorrow ... ow ... ow ... ow ...

Mme Ranevsky blinks, stirs, drops Gayev's hand.

MME RANEVSKY: (*Calling*) Yes.

They leave.

The room is empty, save for a solitary chair on the back wall. Sound of doors being locked, carriages leaving.

Silence.

An axe hits a tree, once, twice, three times.

Slow, shuffling footsteps. Firs enters, in jacket, white waistcoat, as ever, but with slippers. He's ill. He crosses to the door, tries the handle.

FIRS: Locked. They've gone. (*There's a solitary chair left, it's back broken. Firs painfully drags it into the middle of the room, sits on it.*) They forgot me. Never mind. I'll sit here for a while. (*He picks up the cloth that covered Trofimov's overshoes, shivering a little, places it over his head and ears. The axe starts up again, closer.*) I don't imagine for one minute he's put his fur coat on ... No, no ... he'll be wearing the thin one ... (*He blows on his hands.*) ... If I don't see to it ... mmm? These green lads ... (*Mutters, unintelligibly, for a moment. The axe persists, closing in.*) ... It's gone ... it's gone ... as if I'd never lived it ... (*Looks at the floor.*) I might lie down in a minute. You've no strength left in you, have you ... you've nothing left, eh ... you've nothing ... (*He begins to rock backwards and forwards in the chair, slowly at first, but the arcs grow longer, the legs lifting front and back.*) You silly old nothing. Silly old nothing. Silly old nothing.

The axe pounds towards the house. Firs rocks on, muttering.

TAPE: (*Firs' voice*): «Недотёпа!» (*Over and over.*)

Cut, abruptly.

He topples to the floor, felled. The axe stops. A distant sound is heard. It's the sound of a snapping string.

Black

END

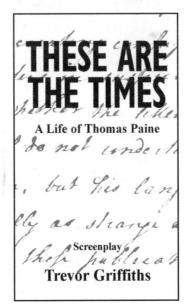